# The Evolution of Leadership

I0128667

The publication of this book was made possible, in part, by a generous grant from The Brown Foundation, Inc., of Houston, Texas.

**School for Advanced Research**
**Advanced Seminar Series**

James F. Brooks
*General Editor*

# The Evolution of Leadership

## Contributors

Jeanne E. Arnold
*Department of Anthropology, Cotsen Institute of Archaeology*
*University of California–Los Angeles*

Douglas W. Bird and Rebecca Bliege Bird
*Anthropological Sciences, Stanford University*

Brenda J. Bowser and John Q. Patton
*Department of Anthropology, California State University–Fullerton*

Jelmer W. Eerkens
*Department of Anthropology, University of California–Davis*

John Kantner
*Academic & Institutional Advancement, School for Advanced Research*

Chapurukha M. Kusimba and Sibel B. Kusimba
*Department of Anthropology, The Field Museum*

Timothy R. Pauketat
*Department of Anthropology, University of Illinois–Urbana-Champaign*

Charles Stanish
*Cotsen Institute of Archaeology, University of California–Los Angeles*

Kevin J. Vaughn
*Department of Sociology and Anthropology, Purdue University*

Polly Wiessner
*Department of Anthropology, University of Utah*

# The Evolution of Leadership

*Transitions in Decision Making from Small-Scale to Middle-Range Societies*

*Edited by Kevin J. Vaughn, Jelmer W. Eerkens, and John Kantner*

**SAR**
**PRESS**

**School for Advanced Research Press**

*Santa Fe*

**School for Advanced Research Press**
Post Office Box 2188
Santa Fe, New Mexico 87504-2188
www.sarpress.org

Managing Editor: Lisa Pacheco
Manuscript Editor: Margaret J. Goldstein
Designer and Production Manager: Cynthia Dyer
Proofreader: Kate Whelan
Indexer: Margaret Moore Booker

**Library of Congress Cataloging-in-Publication Data:**

The evolution of leadership : transitions in decision making from small-scale to middle-range
societies / edited by Kevin J. Vaughn, Jelmer W. Eerkens, and John Kantner.
    p. cm. – (Advanced seminar series)
 Includes bibliographical references and index.
 ISBN 978-1-934691-13-7 (alk. paper)
 1. Leadership–History. 2. Leadership–Cross cultural studies. I. Vaughn, Kevin J.
II. Eerkens, Jelmer W. III. Kantner, John, 1967-
 HM1261.E96 2009
 303.3'409–dc22
2009035661

Library of Congress Catalog Card Number 2009035661
International Standard Book Number 978-1-934691-13-7
First edition 2010.

Cover illustration: Oromo elected leaders, Addis Ababa, Ethiopia, 1927. Photograph by
Alfred M. Bailey (digital identifier CSZ56342). Courtesy the Field Museum.

# Contents

# Figures

# Tables

# Acknowledgments

The editors would like to thank the School for Advanced Research for generously supporting both this book and the advanced seminar upon which it is based. We wish to acknowledge our colleagues who contributed to this book, not only for their productive participation in the advanced seminar but also for writing such a valuable set of papers. Two anonymous reviewers provided helpful comments, for which we are grateful. Thanks too to former SAR Press co-director Catherine Cocks, current director Lynn Baca, and managing editor Lisa Pacheco, all of whom were instrumental in shepherding this project forward. We are also appreciative of Peg Goldstein's excellent copyediting skills. Thanks are due the University of Washington's Helen Riaboff Whiteley Center at Friday Harbor Laboratories, where the idea for the SAR advanced seminar was launched during a two-day workshop held by the co-editors.

# The Evolution of Leadership

# 1

## Introduction

### *The Evolution of Leadership*

**Jelmer W. Eerkens, Kevin J. Vaughn,**

**and John Kantner**

Leaders make decisions that have significant effects on the lives of others. They have the ability to influence events and impact the evolutionary trajectories of societies. Indeed, the "Great Man" theory suggests that these individuals essentially "make" history (Carlyle 1888). Leaders exist in all societies, ranging from smaller-scale heads of households to larger-scale elected governing bodies to dictators with vast coercive powers at their disposal. As typically conceived, "leaders" are individuals who have decision-making authority that extends beyond the household to include non-kin. Today all of us are familiar with and see (and feel) the influence of leaders. However, ethnographic research in the nineteenth and twentieth centuries showed that many small-scale societies lack permanent institutionalized leaders with extensive decision-making power. Hunters and gatherers are especially well represented among such groups, but some small-scale pastoralists and horticulturalists also fall into this category.

Given that leaders and leadership are so influential on human social behavior yet are variably represented among different societies in the past and present, generations of scholars have examined these social phenomena from a variety of humanistic and scientific perspectives. This book, the product of an advanced seminar at the School for Advanced Research

(SAR), brings together the perspectives of cultural anthropologists and archaeologists to explore why and how leadership emerges and variously becomes institutionalized among disparate small-scale and middle-range human societies. This introductory chapter examines the background for leadership studies in anthropology, proposes the value of approaches that consider leadership from multiple sociopolitical and temporal scales, and introduces the chapters in this volume.

## LEADERSHIP STUDIES IN ANTHROPOLOGY

Leadership has long been of interest in cultural and biological anthropology. A complete review of the literature is beyond the scope of this chapter; it has been summarized in other recent research (for example, Butler and Welch 2006; Feinman 1995, 2005; Hayden 2001; Spikins 2008). Beginning with early social theorists such as Weber, who explored different kinds of leaders throughout history (1968[1921]), cultural anthropologists have evaluated the topic of leadership in a variety of ways. Later theorists, such as Fried (1967), Sahlins (1963), and Service (1962; see also Barth 1959; Sahlins and Service 1960), wrote much about the evolution of social complexity, a higher-level notion but one in which leaders were an essential component in the transformation of societies from bands to tribes, chiefdoms, and states. More recently, Gramsci's (1971) theory of hegemony, as well as practice theory (Bourdieu 1977; Giddens 1979; Ortner 1984), forms the foundation of much anthropological inquiry, but these theories tend to emphasize unequal power relationships that already exist. They are less clear on how these inequities become established in the first place. Biosocial anthropologists consider the role of warriorship and coalition building in the maintenance of leaders in their positions of authority, whereas biological anthropologists study the effects of leadership on somatic and reproductive success (for example, Betzig 1986; Borgerhoff Mulder 1995; Chagnon 1990; Maschner and Patton 1996). Again, however, considerations of diachronic processes by which positions of leadership are established in the first place receive less attention.

Leadership in human societies also has been a persistent theme in archaeological studies from the mid-1900s (for example, Childe 1936) continuing through today (for example, Byrd 2005; Fitzhugh 2003; Kuijt and Goring-Morris 2002; Spikins 2008). The focus, however, often has been on higher-level social organizations, such as the characteristics of social hierarchy and ranked societies (for example, Earle 1991, 1997; Haas 1982). Many archaeologists also tend to emphasize synchronic structural explanations. The political economy and practice approaches (for example, Cobb 1996;

Earle 1997; Pauketat and Emerson 1999; Stein 1998), for example, evaluate the ways in which unequal status is maintained within a discrete time frame but do not focus on the emergence of the leadership required to attain this unequal status in the first place.

Even though archaeologists have emphasized synchronic and societal scales when discussing leadership, the role of individual leaders in this process has been recognized by many (for example, Adams 1966; Blanton et al. 1996; Carneiro 1970; Rathje 1971; Wittfogel 1957). Part of the long-standing interest in leaders and leadership surely relates to a goal of many early archaeologists, sometimes explicit and other times implicit, to better understand the history and development of Western civilizations. Powerful leaders are nearly ubiquitous in the ancient writings from these societies, and archaeological efforts were often aimed at verifying such texts rather than understanding the activities of non-elites. A second reason for the focus on leaders likely relates to the high visibility of archaeological remains that result from the organizational skills of leaders, such as pyramids, irrigation canals, and monuments. Such impressive works have captured the interest of the public and archaeological community, often at the expense of the common people of the past.

Yet, perhaps the most pertinent reason for the continued anthropological interest in leadership is the consistency with which leaders appear in human societies. In spite of very different environments, technologies, and culture histories, leaders in the past and present are identifiable in some form on almost every continent. As a result, scholars have sought to construct general models based on anthropological theory to explain their seemingly universal presence (for example, Brumfiel and Earle 1987; Feinman 1995; Flannery 1976; Hayden and Gargett 1990; Wenke 1981). Because leaders have developed in human societies so often, in different places and times and under different circumstances, there are ample opportunities to test such models against detailed case studies. Indeed, we believe that this scientific approach—the building of models, the extraction of testable hypotheses, and the repeated testing of these against the archaeological and anthropological record—contributes significantly to the continued interest in and vibrancy of research on the evolution of leadership.

Although many previous studies have discussed leaders and leadership as part of larger models of differentiation, the mechanisms by which individual leaders emerge are surprisingly undertheorized across the fields of anthropology. The origin of sociopolitical hierarchies has been well studied in archaeology (for example, Earle 1991), but the emergence of leaders, the key feature in distinguishing hierarchical societies from egalitarian ones, has not. The distinction here is critical and relates to the scale at which these issues are examined. Past studies have focused on the evolution of inequality or hierarchy at the level of the society and considered macroevolutionary processes over long time scales (for example, Ames 1981; Blanton et al. 1996; Haas 1982; Paynter 1989). Models that do focus on individual leaders usually assume, as a point of departure, that such leaders already exist. Rather than consider their genesis, these models focus on the maintenance and development of positions of power (for example, Earle 1997).

Special emphasis on the individual as an active agent of diachronic structural change brings such research in line with two major bodies of theory that have been actively developed in archaeological research over the past twenty years: practice theory and neo-Darwinian theory (for example, Ortner 1984; Shennan 2002; Wolf 2001). Both approaches focus on individuals and their role in change, though they also recognize that the collective behaviors of individuals add up to broader changes at the societal level. The time scales of such studies are generally shorter, or microevolutionary, in nature. Accordingly, the types of data required for these approaches are different, focusing on evidence for the actions of individual people as measured, for example, in discrete artifacts, burials, or households. In contrast, models examining macroevolutionary patterns often rely on, or are tested, using large-scale and aggregated data, such as those from regional site distributions. The collection of fine-scaled data useful for examining the behavior of individuals is standard in ethnographic studies. However, many archaeological excavations over the past thirty to forty years have also collected high-resolution data, making it possible to test sophisticated hypotheses regarding the evolution of leaders across different social and environmental contexts.

Newer approaches focusing on the evolution of leadership from the point of view of the individual do not contradict older ones, but they examine the question in new ways and at finer scales that can highlight aspects of leadership not previously visible. For example, where other studies tend to conflate notions of status and wealth with those of leadership, finer-scale and individual-based research has the potential to decouple these different variables and examine their interplay. Likewise, instead of examining the evolution of societies as a whole, in which all parts are assumed generally to change in concert, finer-scaled studies can distinguish change in certain segments of society—at least at the chronological resolution typically used—such as among leaders themselves or among their followers, or in the economic versus religious behavioral arenas.

## NEW PERSPECTIVES ON THE EVOLUTION OF LEADERSHIP

Small-scale and middle-range societies often have in place formal rules that effectively inhibit the development of leaders and emphasize cooperation over competition (Boehm 1993; Winterhalder 2001). Such social-leveling mechanisms include a broad range of behaviors that limit the influence individuals can gain over non-kin, such as self-deprecation, gossip, ridicule, physical punishment, and ostracism (see Fried 1967). These mechanisms are strongly enforced, and egalitarian notions often pervade many aspects of culture (for example, from food sharing to kinship structures to the spatial layout of communities), providing significant challenges to the development of inequitable decision-making power.

Recent cross-cultural behavioral experiments indicate that egalitarian convictions run deep (Henrich et al. 2006). Experimental games in which participants may observe the sharing and distribution of a resource show that some individuals will severely punish noncooperators and people who do not reciprocate, often at great cost to themselves. Such costs may greatly exceed the unreceived benefits to which the punishers feel they are entitled. Although the level of costly punishment varies (societies with higher rates of altruism punish more frequently), such behavior is observed in a range of societies across the world. Indeed, humans are keen at detecting individuals who violate sharing or cooperative norms. Cosmides (1989) has even proposed that the human brain has specialized modules devoted to detecting "cheaters" (see also Beaman 2002). All of this suggests a strong commitment to cooperation and sharing, as well as maintenance of these ideals across generations. If these ideals are hardwired (that is, maintained genetically), then overcoming them presents a strong challenge to aspiring leaders whose decision-making authority disenfranchises others not only of their autonomy but also often of their resources.

In contrast, many nonhuman primate societies, such as chimpanzees and gorillas, are characterized by influential leaders with broad decision-making powers (Boehm 1999). Whether human societies "lost" such leaders as they evolved during the Pleistocene and developed social institutions to repress the decision-making power of leaders, or whether leaders evolved among nonhuman primates only after their split from humans (perhaps several times independently), these issues are beyond the scope of the chapters in this volume. Most anthropologists agree (for example, Boehm 1999; Winterhalder 2001) that small-scale human societies of the late Pleistocene generally lacked formalized and permanent leaders with authority to make decisions about a broad range of activities (such as economics, religion, and politics).

Only during the early Holocene do we see the expression (or re-expression) of such leaders among human societies. How did these positions of leadership emerge? Given the strength of social-leveling mechanisms and the commitment that egalitarian societies make to enforcing them, it is unlikely that leaders could have simply asserted or forcibly taken their positions. Likewise, given the human propensity for detecting unequal distributions in resources, it is also unlikely that aspiring individuals could have cheated or duped others into accepting subservient positions. If becoming a leader were so simple, then such permanent positions would surely have evolved long before the early Holocene.

One view on the evolution of leadership suggests that there was a mutually—if perhaps unevenly—beneficial relationship between leaders and their subjects in the evolution of such positions. Around the globe, societies with leaders consistently recognize the qualities and importance of certain individuals as decision makers. These individuals possess certain valuable skills and abilities that promote their status as effective decision makers (for example, Boehm 1999:70–72, 106–108). Leaders also tend to work harder and longer than the average person in maintaining their positions, although they often enjoy certain material or other benefits as a result of their positions (for example, Arnold 2000a; Betzig 1986; Hayden 2001). Thus, for nonleaders, the organizing skills of leaders and the benefits that come from group-level coordination (for example, communal hunting, trading, socializing opportunities at organized social events, or increased efficiency in craft production) may justify some loss in equal distribution of resources and decision-making power. At the same time, in most societies, nonleaders often maintain the means to sanction and/or remove leaders who overextend or abuse their powers, by voting them out of office, using magic or witchcraft to rein them in, or even banishing or executing those with despotic predilections.

A slightly different approach to the evolution of leadership, though not necessarily oppositional to the first, suggests that the costs to aspiring leaders were sufficiently high during the Pleistocene that the development and formalization of such positions were not tenable. Some event or set of events, according to this view, conspired during the Holocene to change these dynamics such that leadership became an attractive alternative, despite the costs. What these events were has been the subject of much theorizing, but changes in population levels, changing climate, or some combination of these are common components (for example, Carneiro

1967; Richerson, Boyd, and Bettinger 2001; Wittfogel 1957). For example, increases in population densities may have lowered the social-leveling penalties incurred by noncooperators, such as gossip and ostracism, making the maintenance of egalitarian formations more difficult. Similarly, storage and mass harvesting of certain resources not available in the Pleistocene may have changed the costs and benefits of cooperation.

The specific strategies employed by aspiring leaders to overcome social-leveling mechanisms, particularly with regard to property, are of great importance (Earle 2000). Common property and common-pool resources are widespread among hunting and gathering societies and were presumably ubiquitous in Pleistocene societies (for example, Beckerman and Valentine 1996; Eerkens 1999; Hawkes 1992). How leaders were able to gain private control over property, labor, and other goods is a theme that seems to be at the core of the development of such positions. In recent research, related strategies are theorized to have included using ritual or religion to circumvent traditional rules (for example, Brown 2006; Hollimon 2004; Roscoe 2000a); increasing organizational oversight over the production of goods (for example, Vaughn 2006); controlling the transmission of information, particularly regarding the production of complex technologies (for example, Barth 1990; Peregrine 1991; Sinopoli 2003); gaining access to the labor of non-kin (for example, Arnold 1996b, 2000a); shifting focus to the extraction and production of previously unused resources, for which rules regarding ownership had not yet been established; and producing goods out of view from others, which may have included physical isolation or separation from a community.

## DIMENSIONS OF LEADERSHIP

So far in this introduction, the concept of leadership has been presented simply as decision-making authority beyond the household level, including the capacity to make decisions on behalf of non-kin. As the chapters in this book explore in more detail, leadership can be measured along different scales and dimensions. These are briefly explored below both to standardize terminology used in this book and to introduce the more elaborate considerations of leadership presented in each chapter.

First, leadership occurs at different temporal scales. Terminology related to temporal scale that is most often employed in the scholarly literature includes the distinction between transitory, permanent, and inherited leadership (for example, Hayden 2001; Redmond 1998b; Wills 2000). Transitory or temporary leaders, such as "bosses" whose leadership is limited to seasonal ceremonies, animal drives, or small-scale conflict, enjoy very situational decision-making authority. More permanent leaders include headmen, shamans, scribes, and kings who retain a level of authority for long periods, perhaps for life. Some forms of permanent leadership transcend a single human life span. These positions are inherited or passed along according to culturally defined rules (for example, father to son, mother to daughter, or uncle to maternal nephew). Although this leadership includes chiefly positions that are passed from one generation to the next, other kinds of leadership, such as shamanistic ability and authority over extrasocietal exchange relations, can also be inherited (for example, McAnany 2001; Wiessner and Tumu 1998). Of course, there are middle grounds between these conceptual categories. For example, the permanent position of king may normally be inherited from father to son, but occasionally an outsider can assume this position by force (for example, by homicide or military action).

Second, temporal scales of leadership can usefully be distinguished from structural forms of leadership. For example, religious authority may be permanently endowed in an individual, but the context in which decision making occurs may be situational, such as only during specific ceremonies. An especially important structural concept is institutionalization, which addresses the degree to which a leadership position is culturally encoded. Institutionalized leadership exists largely separately from the individuals who fill a particular position. The position of the classic hereditary chief, for example, is part of the sociopolitical structure, whereas a classic "Big Man" (Sahlins 1963) is not filling an institutionalized position but instead creates a position for him- or herself. This is of course not a simple dichotomy—the ability to achieve Big Man status depends to some degree on cultural institutions that allow the position to exist at all—but a consideration of the degree of leadership institutionalization is a useful way to examine the interaction between agentive political action and sociocultural structure.

Third, considerations of structure also include the degree to which societywide forms of leadership are heterarchically or hierarchically related to one another. Again, this dimension is not invariably tied to the temporal scale of leadership, and it is also not inseparable from the degree of institutionalization. Heterarchical positions of leadership—those related to one another horizontally rather than hierarchically—can be transitory or permanent, and they can be institutionalized or purely achieved (for example, Crumley 1987; Ehrenreich, Crumley, and Levy 1995; Frangipane 2007). Although anthropologists generally equate heterarchy with limited authority and transitory leaders, and consider hierarchy to be linked to permanent, institutionalized leaders it is useful to analytically separate each of these dimensions to understand more comprehensively the evolution of leadership (Kantner 2002; Paynter 1989).

Fourth, leadership also varies according to the arenas or domains in which it emerges or is most often exercised. Scholars tend to consider early leaders as maintaining authority over merged political, economic, and ritual domains, emphasizing the holistic and intertwined nature of small-scale societies (for example, Redmond 1998b:9; Spencer 1994). Many ethnographic examples, however, especially of egalitarian and transegalitarian societies, demonstrate that incipient forms of leadership are usually domain-specific, with the evolution of leadership often involving the cooperation of multiple emergent leaders who separately enjoy authority over secular, religious, diplomatic, or kinship arenas (for example, Hobart 1975). This process comprises more than just heterarchical formations reorganizing into hierarchical ones. Instead, a few heterarchically organized leaders can, through intrigue, manipulation, cooperation, and other mechanisms, combine their authority in ways that promote the emergence of hierarchical and centralized sociopolitical structures.

Fifth and finally, a related issue revolves around the types of goods that leaders control or make decisions about within these realms, whether it be information (or the distribution of information), labor, or actual material supplies (for example, McIntosh 1999a). The level of ownership of or decision-making power over these goods is also relevant—that is, whether they are privately controlled by individual leaders, controlled by a select group of individuals, or publicly controlled. In most cases, increasing decision-making power is directly correlated with increasing degrees of privatization of such goods. Equally important is the number of people over whom a leader holds decision-making power. Such power may vary by realm. For example, a leader may hold extensive decision-making power with respect to the production of material goods, by overseeing such activities on a regional level, but only slight influence with respect to religious activities—among only a few households, for example.

Clearly, some fields of anthropology are better suited to studying certain of these dimensions than others. Given the focus on material remains, archaeological studies are likely to focus on economic and technological decision-making power and on long-term, permanent, and institutionalized forms of leadership. Ethnographic studies are likely to focus on a broader range of realms, including those that are religious and narrative, but are less likely to inform on the degree of temporal permanence for such positions. A comprehensive assessment of leaders and leadership in human societies accordingly requires the marshaling of different perspectives and sources of data.

## THE SAR ADVANCED SEMINAR

Ten scholars who work with ethnographic and archaeological cases of leadership formation in small-scale and middle-range societies gathered at the School for Advanced Research in December 2006 to discuss the evolution of leadership. In many ways inspired and informed by the highly influential SAR advanced seminar book *Chiefdoms: Power, Economy, and Ideology* (Earle 1991), our goal was to examine leadership at a level more incipient than is typically understood for chiefly societies. Thus, this book can be considered something of a prequel to the 1991 volume.

Participants in the 2006 seminar were selected to represent a wide range of geographic areas, as well as for their differing theoretical perspectives and use of a variety of data sets, including ethnographic, historical, and archaeological sources. Each participant was asked to prepare in advance a working paper examining the evolution of leaders and leadership in his or her particular part of the world, with an emphasis on leadership emergence and processes of institutionalization.

Over the course of five days, lengthy discussions about each working paper developed, resulting in the identification and exploration of general themes regarding the evolution of leadership. Seminar participants were then asked to revise their initial papers in light of these discussions; the chapters in this book represent the end product of that process. Although complementary in their basic philosophy and content, the chapters comprise original and fresh examinations of leadership from a range of perspectives and regions.

We have organized the chapters into three conceptual sections: (1) "Roots of Decision-Making Inequity"; (2) "Pathways to Institutionalized Leadership"; and (3) "History, Process, and the Evolution of Leadership." Although there is overlap between all chapters in the volume, this organization reflects the focus of each contribution and how it relates to overarching issues concerning the development of leadership in small-scale and middle-range societies. The organization of the volume is not intended to imply a linear or single path in the development of leaders. Indeed, if there is one thing that all seminar participants agree upon, it is that there was never a simple, unilineal pathway to leadership in human history. The chapters in this volume reflect the diversity of ways in which leaders came into their positions.

The first group of chapters, by Bird and Bliege Bird, Bowser and

Patton, and Eerkens, focuses on incipient levels of impermanent leadership at smaller social scales. The chapters include ethnographic examples from the Martu of Australia's Western Desert, from the Ecuadorian Amazon, and from the Paiute of the American Great Basin. The chapters consider hunting magnanimity, ritual gerontocracies, alliance formation, and the development of private property in small-scale societies, as well as their relation to leadership formation. Not surprisingly, a common theme in the three chapters, because they focus on societies of a smaller scale, is that incipient leaders go to great lengths both to reinforce (in the case of the Martu) and to break down (in the case of the Owens Valley Paiute) an egalitarian ethos. These seem to be contradictory strategies, but aspiring leaders often pursue both at the same time. In all cases, as the chapters by Bird and Bliege Bird and Bowser and Patton especially show, emerging leaders cannot be analyzed separately from the kin-based networks and coalitions of which they are a part.

In chapter 2, "Competing to Be Leaderless: Food Sharing and Magnanimity among Martu Aborigines," for example, Bird and Bliege Bird argue that prestige among Martu male and female hunters (referred to as *mirtilya*) is based primarily on magnanimity, equity, and generosity. This situation has less to do with social strategies for "buffering risk" in a precarious environment, as some anthropologists have argued (for example, Gould 1982), and more to do with agentive construction of an individual's political reputation. The authors juxtapose the egalitarian nature of much of Martu life (especially with regard to private property and material resources such as food) with the strongly hierarchical nature of ritual life, illustrating how the former is a critical building block for the latter—positions in the powerful ritual gerontocracy are attained through a lifetime of hunting success and magnanimity.

In chapter 3, "Women's Leadership: Political Alliance, Economic Resources, and Reproductive Success in the Ecuadorian Amazon," Bowser and Patton use ethnographic and ethnoarchaeological data to reconstruct how coalition building contributes to the process of emergent leadership, especially among women in Conambo, a village in the Ecuadorian Amazon. Their chapter identifies the complementary strategies that men and women employ to attain mutually reinforcing positions of authority within the community.

Eerkens, in contrast, argues in chapter 4, "Privatization of Resources and the Evolution of Prehistoric Leadership Strategies," that the key element in the evolution of leadership is the development of private property and surplus, without which inequities in wealth and authority cannot develop. Using ethnographic examples from the Owens Valley Paiute as background, Eerkens demonstrates this argument with an archaeological example showing how households had become differentiated by AD 1400 and correlates this situation with the development of private property. The three chapters in this section provide rich ethnographic descriptions of incipient leadership and examples of what leadership might look like archaeologically.

Drawing from ethnographic, ethnohistoric, and archaeological data, the second group of chapters, by Stanish, Arnold, Vaughn, and Pauketat, focuses on specific elements for institutionalizing and legitimizing leadership. Although different theoretical perspectives provide each chapter with distinct points of departure, they all assume that the egalitarian ethos (critical in smaller-scale societies, such as those described in the first section of the book) has been broken down or disrupted in their case studies. Thus, the chapters do not focus on the *first* instances of leadership to have emerged in their respective regions and instead focus on the various pathways that can lead to increasingly institutionalized, and hence more permanent, forms of leadership. The chapters consider economies of scale, labor cooperation, ownership of property (both material and intellectual), costly technologies, materialized ideology, and the role of historical narratives in the construction of institutionalized leadership. Examples are derived from the Central Andes (Titicaca Basin and the South Coast of Peru), eastern North America, and the North American Pacific Coast, but the common theme running through the chapters is that to be institutionalized, leadership needs to be legitimated.

Stanish, for example, evaluates the role of cooperative labor in the development of leaders in chapter 5, "The Evolution of Managerial Elites in Intermediate Societies." Specifically, he argues that the emergence of rank from previously egalitarian social formations requires the establishment of labor organizations that can take advantage of economies of scale and that become reinforced by culturally encoded group ritual. To illustrate the model in detail, Stanish turns to the evolution of managerial elites in the Titicaca Basin beginning approximately 1400 BC.

In chapter 6, "The Role of Politically Charged Property in the Appearance of Institutionalized Leadership: A View from the North American Pacific Coast," Arnold focuses on the institutionalized, permanent leadership that develops in middle-range societies as a result of costly technologies (such as plank canoe production), ownership of resource collection areas (including raw material sources such as chert quarries), and the development of intellectual property (especially ritual knowledge).

Focusing on the South Coast of Peru, Vaughn similarly argues in chapter 7, "Emergent Leadership in Middle-Range Societies: An Example from Nasca, Peru," that institutionalized leadership emerged among the Nasca because of multiple factors. Leadership was based on feasting, reinforced in group ceremonies, and materialized in ideologically charged polychrome ceramics.

Pauketat argues in chapter 8, "Of Leaders and Legacies in Native North America," that critical to the discussion of the evolution of leadership is the fact that all leaders are legitimated by historical narratives. He argues that leadership "was a historical process of becoming" and suggests that leaders in native North American history were able to draw on historical narrative to attain and sustain their positions. With many examples derived primarily from historic sources, the chapter provides greater detail on how leaders in middle-range societies may legitimate their positions.

The final section, consisting of chapters by Wiessner, Kusimba and Kusimba, and Kantner, focuses on the historical and contingent nature of leadership development, with all three contributions drawing on processes outlined in the first two groups of chapters. The final section is diverse in terms of geographic region (Papua New Guinea, sub-Saharan and East Africa, and the American Southwest) and in scale of society (from a relatively small scale in the case of the Enga to a very large scale in the case of East African iron-producing societies).

Wiessner, using her own ethnographic and historic data from the Enga of Papua New Guinea, in chapter 9, "The Power of One? Big Men Revisited," argues that when considering the evolution of leadership, archaeologists generally make two problematic assumptions: first, that egalitarianism is somehow the "natural" order from which hierarchy evolved and, second, that "aggrandizers" (for example, Hayden 1995) in small-scale societies are capable of developing and maintaining complex economic and ritual systems. Instead, Wiessner argues, hierarchy is the "norm," and aggrandizers actually have to focus on cooperation and coalition building ("wealth in people"; see Guyer 1995) before leaders can influence the economic and ritual arenas of sociopolitical life. Her chapter provides a rich historical study of the emergence of leadership among the Enga.

In chapter 10, "Leadership in Middle-Range African Societies," Kusimba and Kusimba illustrate the various ways in which leadership emerged and was sustained in three East African societies: the Bukusu, the Swahili, and the Oromo. In one society, hereditary forms of leadership are lacking (the Bukusu); another is a hierarchical society with hereditary elites (the Swahili); and one has an elected representative government (the Oromo). Again, noting the historically contingent nature of the evolution

15

of leadership, this contribution provides an ethnographically rich study of these East African societies.

Kantner concludes the book with chapter 11, "Identifying the Pathways to Permanent Leadership." His chapter ties together many themes brought up in the seminar and the resulting papers while also providing a case study from the Puebloan Southwest. The themes that Kantner addresses include the skills and abilities of leaders, socioeconomic qualities of leadership (and whether there is a conflation in the archaeological literature between leadership per se and status and wealth), scales of leadership, and pathways to leadership.

## CONCLUDING THOUGHTS

A topic as broad as leadership in the past and present cannot be fully addressed in a single seminar or presented in just one edited volume. Recognizing this, we hope that this book adds to an interdisciplinary dialogue on the topic of how leaders emerge and how leadership becomes institutionalized. The week of conversations at the School for Advanced Research contributed to this topic in three ways. First, the seminar emphasized the variability in leadership strategies and how critical it is for anthropologists to accommodate this variability in both diachronic and synchronic models of leadership. The range of anthropological disciplines represented, including ethnography, ethnohistory, ethnoarchaeology, and archaeology, as well as the widespread geographic areas in which the participants work, including the Americas, Africa, Asia, and the Pacific Islands, demonstrated the importance of the culturally specific dimensions of leaders and leadership.

Second, the seminar revealed some of the general processes by which leaders take or obtain their positions and how such positions change and become institutionalized over time. The approaches to understanding this process were varied, drawing from a range of high-level theoretical frameworks, but the chapters in this book share several themes, including the ubiquity of decision-making inequity, the impact of reverse dominance hierarchies in small-scale settings, gendered differences in political action, the role of resource privatization, the beneficial labor organization that leadership provides, and the critical place of religion and historical narrative in the institutionalization of leadership positions. These themes are addressed in more detail throughout the volume and brought together in the concluding chapter by Kantner.

Third, although drawing from a diversity of anthropological fields,

almost all the chapters consider the material correlates of leadership, especially as manifested in the archaeological record. Unless they were written
on a permanent medium, such as a clay tablet, we cannot dig up ancient
decisions themselves. Instead, we are left with only the material results of
such decisions. The chapters consider how the archaeological record can
inform on whether those decisions were made by certain individuals on
behalf of others, were reached by group consensus, or were simply individual decisions with little or no repercussions for others. Because the leader
is an entity that archaeologists consider essential in all models of sociopolitical complexity, the results of this advanced seminar help archaeologists plan investigations that reveal evidence of such persons and their
behavior, and they link this evidence to specific models for the emergence
of leadership.

# PART I

*Roots of Decision-Making Inequity*

# 2

## Competing to Be Leaderless

### *Food Sharing and Magnanimity among Martu Aborigines*

**Douglas W. Bird and Rebecca Bliege Bird**

Conventional explanations of hereditary inequality and institutionalized forms of leadership have long focused on the nature of material production, especially agriculture, as the prime catalyst for their development (for example, Childe 1946). The model is a familiar one: enduring socioeconomic and political leadership evolves under conditions of sedentism and privileged control of key resources and agricultural surplus. This notion was overturned in part when Fried (1967) demonstrated that hunter-gatherer societies exhibit significant variability in hierarchy. A large body of literature now suggests that institutionalized leadership and centralized political formations were features of a number of hunter-gatherer societies, especially those of the Northwest Coast of North America (see Ames 1981; Arnold 1993, 1996a, 1996b, 2000a, chapter 6, this volume; Eerkens, chapter 4, this volume; Fitzhugh 2003; Hayden 1995, 2001; Keeley 1988; Keen 2006; Kelly 1995; Price and Feinman 1995; Sassaman 2004 for review). Moreover, as Wiessner (2002, chapter 9, this volume) and others (for example, Boehm 1999) demonstrate, hierarchy did not evolve from an ancestral state of hunter-gather egalitarian social relations—there is good reason to suspect that hierarchy is the slate upon which egalitarianism is written.

Nevertheless, as Keeley (1988) shows, many "complex" hunter-gatherers have (or had) much in common with many agricultural societies: they are marked by some reliance on defendable and stored resources, relatively low residential mobility, large settlements and dense populations, high levels of interpersonal competition and intergroup conflict, and the use of wealth, luxury goods, and moneylike currencies. Arnold (1996b, 2000a, chapter 6, this volume) argues convincingly that many of these features are coupled with the ability of some individuals to maintain inherited distinctions and enduring institutions that manage non-kin labor across multiple arenas of production and administer access to valued forms of property. Other contributors to this volume (especially Eerkens, Stanish, and Vaughn) also draw our attention to the way in which institutionalized leadership coevolves with privatization and novel opportunities for suprafamilial control over the production, distribution, and use rights of prestige goods and knowledge. Political power coalesces around leaders who can accumulate extrahousehold surplus, mobilize the labor to generate it, and direct its distribution. Where it is impossible to intensify production and renew the control of non-kin labor (such as when resources are unpredictable and asynchronously acquired and when their distribution is bound by kinship obligation), leadership is more situational and transitory, and social relationships are more egalitarian. In turn, production, storage, and labor are limited by the widespread sharing documented in many mobile foraging societies.

## EGALITARIANISM AND FOOD SHARING

A nexus of food sharing and egalitarianism is at the core of many influential scenarios of the evolution of human social arrangements (see Stanford and Bunn 2001 for background; Hill 1982; Isaac 1978; Kaplan et al. 2000; Lovejoy 1981; Washburn and DeVore 1961; Washburn and Lancaster 1968). Mobile hunter-gatherers are often characterized as having situational leadership and shallow hierarchies, and many scholars have suggested that their lack of enduring institutional authority is a product of a distinctly human reliance on cooperation, leveling, sanctioning, and reciprocal sharing in small groups living in unpredictable environments (for example, Boehm 1993, 1999; Fried 1967; Knauft 1991; Tooby and Cosmides 1992). When groups are small and individuals have a high probability of continued interaction, variance in the supply of resources can be reduced via a cooperative system of reciprocal sharing (Trivers 1971). This is especially the case with a heavy reliance on high-variance, difficult-to-store but nutrient-dense resources such as large game: reciprocal obligations ensure that a hunter and his family will be fed when his efforts fail (Kaplan and Hill 1985). Sharing, however, makes work a public good such

that if one person works more, others can free-ride off his or her production (Hawkes 1992, 1993). Resultant collective-action problems can reduce
the payoffs from investing in labor for defendable surplus and may account
for the cavalier attitude that many "immediate-return" mobile foragers
have toward accumulating property and storage (Sahlins 1972; Woodburn
1982). Under such conditions, enduring leadership is undercut by the
effect that sharing has in evening out resource distribution, and no individual or group can, with any permanency, capitalize on opportunities to
control non-kin labor and their production. The ability of an individual to
wield power over another's labor is thus swamped by constant social leveling ("reverse dominance hierarchies"; Boehm 1993) underwritten by the
prohibitive costs of accumulation (see Wiessner, chapter 9, this volume).

Food sharing is commonly thought to increase the reliability of key
resources: risk is pooled, and the arrangement is maintained by individuals
directing shares toward those they can count on to share in return. This
situation is analogous to what Sahlins (1972:191–196) calls balanced reciprocity. Conversely, when key resources are storable and predictable and
societies large and settled, the payoffs from risk-reduction sharing decrease.
Under such conditions, supply variance is better reduced by storing and
defending surplus. And the ability to defend predictable resources, including the labor of others, almost by definition creates conditions favorable for
intensifying production and the maintenance of enduring leadership—
favorable from the perspective of both the public (in terms of the public
goods leaders might be able to provide, such as defense) and those who
seek leadership to enhance their own prestige and political capital (see
Vaughn, chapter 7, this volume).

## THE AUSTRALIAN PARADOX

Aboriginal Australia has long presented special difficulties for catego-
rizing conditions that might maintain relationships that are mostly egalitarian versus those characterized by interpersonal domination and
hierarchical leadership. Although highly centralized and permanent
offices of inherited political and economic leadership are rare or absent in
classical Aboriginal societies, ethnographers and archaeologists have
described a broad continuum of politically and religiously constituted leadership and control of labor and production (see Keen 2004 and Ross 2006
for recent references). And although wealth differentials are mostly absent,
many Aboriginal societies exhibit aspects of asymmetrical structuring, with
positions of authority for ritual purposes, some management of others'
labor through bride-service and ceremonial commitments, and restricted

access to esoteric knowledge and totemic estates, along with formal jural rules and punitive procedures associated with their administration (for example, Meggitt 1962; Myers 1988; Peterson 1969; Strehlow 1970; Tonkinson 1988a). These are maintained despite low population densities, high residential mobility, a lack of food storage, and little in the way of differential access to material resources (see Hiatt 1996:78–99).

Keen (2004, 2006) has argued that throughout Australia, the lack of storable and defendable resources limited population pressures and constrained the contexts of institutionalized leadership. Keen's analysis suggests that social asymmetries are correlated with increased polygyny brought on by increases in resource density and predictability, which create denser human populations and conditions for intensifying production. These correlations, however, are not strong. Even in the arid center, where resources are especially unpredictable and material wealth differentials absent, contextualized gerontocracies, exhibiting substantial differences in access to ritual and reproductive power, are common (for example, Bern 1979; Peterson 1969; Strehlow 1970).

In this chapter, we explore an alternative means by which leadership emerges and is maintained. We do so in an attempt to build a set of interlinked hypotheses to account for both the egalitarian and hierarchical nature of Aboriginal society as a product of the same socio-ecological process. Our basic argument is that in many circumstances in Aboriginal Australia, authority in mundane contexts is expressed in ways that enforce egalitarianism: influence, renown, and power are often sustained by generously providing equal access to valued material resources (Myers 1986:265). This situation is especially salient in the magnanimity of food sharing. This notion—that disengaging with property is often a key to acquiring social prestige—has a long history in anthropology (for example, Firth 1936; Mauss 1924; Woodburn 1982). We develop this idea with analysis of food sharing among Martu Aborigines.

We begin with some general comments about leadership and subsistence strategies among contemporary Martu hunters of Australia's Western Desert. We then present an analysis of Martu hunting and meat sharing patterns, comparing the distribution of different kinds of resources characterized by predictable differences in acquisition variance. The analysis investigates whether Martu food sharing is designed to ensure against the risky nature of hunting in an unpredictable environment, which would in turn constrain the development of defendable wealth and enduring inequalities, or whether it is better conceived of as nonreciprocal public goods provisioning. We then discuss "egalitarian" sharing in light of recent developments in signaling theory from behavioral ecology, suggesting that certain aspects of Martu production and sharing are a product of competitive display and the ability of individuals to bear the costs of generosity.

## THE MARTU

*Martu* (also *Mardu* or *Mardujarra*) is a contemporary term used to identify a community of about one thousand Aborigines whose homelands comprise about 150,000 square kilometers in the northwest section of Australia's Western Desert. The term is now commonly used as self-reference by people from eight dialect-named units with estates in the deserts surrounding the Percival Lakes, the Rudall River, and Lake Disappointment. The literature with respect to Martu social organization and history is quite large. Tonkinson (1974, 1978, 1988a, 1988b, 1990, 1991, 2000, 2007a, 2007b) provides extensive details on Martu identity, religion, gender, politics, autonomy, and change. Veth and Walsh have analyzed aspects of Martu prehistory, subsistence, and mobility (Veth 1987, 1989, 1995, 2000; Veth and Walsh 1988; Walsh 1990). And recently Davenport, Johnson, and Yuwali (2005) have described the international events and social implications surrounding the interaction between Australian society and remote Martu bands. Here we will restrict our description and analysis to the social relations and subsistence strategies among Martu in three remote communities in the heart of the Western Desert: Parnngurr, Punmu, and Kunawarritji.

Interaction between Martu and Europeans remained very limited until after 1930, somewhat later than in the mining settlements in the Goldfields to the south. Particularly in the period between 1940 and 1967, Martu (initially those from Kartujarra, Putijarra, Kurajarra, and Pijakarli dialects) began a process of increasing involvement with the European frontier. In a slow migration from their home country, many Martu gravitated west and north, with permanent encampments eventually growing around European outposts at Jigalong, Nullagine, Marble Bar, and Balgo. Between 1955 and 1965, there remained a minimum of 164 Martu (mostly Manyjilyjarra and Warnman) in nine flexible composite bands, living completely autonomously outside Western influence and ranging throughout the McKay Range–Rudall River and Percival Lakes–northern Canning Stock Route regions (Peterson and Long 1986:116–121; Scelza and Bliege Bird 2008). As Davenport and colleagues (2005) detail, some of these bands were cleared from their homelands in preparation for joint British–Australian missile tests; others remained until 1966–1967, when they were brought in by government patrols or walked in to rejoin their families at Jigalong.

Members of these bands never planned to settle there permanently, and in the mid-1980s they reestablished occupation of the desert at three "outstation" communities: Parnngurr, Punmu, and Kunawarritji. In some respects, their lives have changed dramatically, but these Martu retain a distinct hunter-gatherer orientation, with strong commitments to the continuity of their foraging way of life, sustaining their Law, their ritual arts, their extensive kin obligations, and the expression of these on the desert landscape. The maintenance of these commitments provided the foundation for the 2002 native title settlement that formally recognized Martu as the customary owners of 136,000 square kilometers of their country.

### Leadership, Hierarchy, and Egalitarian Relationships

Western Desert Aborigines are commonly characterized as having broadly symmetrical, interpersonal material and social relationships in daily life (for example, Myers 1986; Tonkinson 1988a). This is most certainly the case for Martu we live with: they live up to their common refrain, "We are all bosses." There are no secular positions of leadership that provide authority for individuals to regularly renew or reinforce their control over the mundane labor of others. This independence extends to children, who are continually encouraged to assert their individual autonomy in daily decision making. As Myers (1986:252–255) and Martu describe it, authority lies in *holding* (*kanyirnimpa*) or nurturing the autonomy of others. There is shame (*kurnta*) in forceful command and overt assertiveness. In practical terms, this means anticipating asymmetries and giving to each individual on demand rather than *withholding* resources for the common good or future use (Folds 2001:48–60).

This situation seems to be in stark contrast to much of the religiously constituted leadership among Martu, which requires *withholding* access to valued resources. Although there is no council of elders or "rulers" as such, under the rubric of "the Law" (*Yulupirti*), Martu identify a number of interrelated arenas of steep hierarchy and strict deference, with a clear gerontocratic bias (Tonkinson 1988a). These include initiations and the festivities that surround them; funerals, with their ritually laden feasts and increasingly lavish distributions of material goods; formal jural rules and their administration; and, in the past, revenge expeditions.

Today the rights to *hold* the Law are acquired in adherence to years of rigorous ritual training and physical initiation. The *Jukurrpa* (Dreamtime) rituals and their associated paraphernalia are *withheld* from the public by elders with tremendous authority, and access to these obligates one to protect and uphold their power. The administration of the Law is carried out by all initiated men and women, but it is most powerfully held by the *ngurraru*, the caretaker of the Yulupirti and Jukurrpa for a given area or community. The ngurraru negotiates failure to uphold the Law (for example, homicide, unauthorized possession of sacred knowledge or objects, sorcery, incest, and irresponsibility leading to death or destruction of sacred property), which requires formal punitive procedures that involve violent public exhibitions of dominance, including spearing a transgressor's thigh, sharp boomerangs to shoulders, and clubs to the back and head. These punishments are arranged and carried out by the ngurraru in collaboration with supporters and political allies, with formidable displays of skillfully crafted weapons and regalia imbued with power from the Jukurrpa.

Likewise, contemporary mortuary activities, especially those surrounding "reburial" (*laka*) ceremonies, involve leaders who withhold valued resources for months or years at a time. The activities surrounding funeral procedures intensify production and control labor directed at accumulating tremendous stores of resources (especially blankets and purchased food) given out following ritualized acquisition and distribution of plains kangaroo. Below we argue that such control over labor and resources is actually sustained by the egalitarian nature of mundane subsistence and sharing, embodied in values displayed by renowned and magnanimous hunters referred to as *mirtilya*.

### Data Collection

We began working with Martu while they were compiling their native title claim in 2000. Since then, we have spent twenty-eight months across all seasons living in the communities. Data reported here (table 2.1) were collected during daily foraging trips out from the community or temporary residential camps. Foraging is defined as the total time spent searching for, pursuing, capturing, and processing wild food resources. During foraging trips, we recorded the identity of each participant in the foraging party (the group that leaves together), time they spent traveling to foraging locales, route taken, foraging location, and foraging bouts of all participants. Typically, a foraging party leaves together from the community. At an agreed-upon locale, they establish a temporary camp ("dinnertime camp"), where all will meet up again after foraging to cook, distribute, and eat the food acquired. During each trip, we recorded the time all participants spent foraging (time away from the dinnertime camp), the type of foraging each individual engaged in, and the counts and weights of all resources acquired. A "foraging bout" is thus the time per day each participant in a

TABLE 2.1

*Martu Foraging Activities*

| Foraging Activity | Primary Resource Type(s) | Secondary Resource type(s) | Primary Season* | Habitat+ | n (Bouts) |
|---|---|---|---|---|---|
| Parnaparnti hunting | Sand goanna: *Varanus gouldii* | Skink, python, cat, larvae, ridge tail goanna | All, peak May–October | S | 575 |
| Kipara hunting | Bustard: *Ardeotis australis* | Sand goanna | May–January | M, S | 260 |
| Kirti-kirti hunting | Euro: *Macropus robustus* | | All | R | 76 |
| Yalapara/ Marantu hunting | Perentie: *V. gigantius*, Yellow spotted goanna: *V. panoptes* | Sand goanna | November– April | W | 76 |
| Wamurla/ Jinjuwiri collecting | Fruit: *Solanum diversiflorum, S. central* | | Variable, usual peak April–May, October– November | S | 58 |
| Kanyjamarra/ Minyarra collecting | Root: *Vigna lanceolata*, Bulb: *Cyperus bulbosus* | | Variable, usual peak May–August | W | 43 |
| Cat hunting | Feral cat: *Felis silvestris* | Sand goanna, skink, python, larvae | All | S | 25 |
| Lunki collecting | Cossid larvae: *Endoxyla* spp. | | Variable | S, M, W | 33 |
| Wilyki collecting | Seeds: *Acacia aneura, Eragrostis eriopoda* | | Tree: October– December, Grass: April–June | S, M | 10 |
| Honey collecting | Honeybee: *Apis mellifera* | | Variable++ | W | 17 |
| Wama collecting | Nectar: *Hakea* spp. | *Grevillea eriostachya* | September+++ | S | 15 |
| Other | Emu, red kangaroo | Feral camel | - | - | 8 |

Sample covers 1,179 bouts on 196 foraging days in June–July 2000, June–August 2001, January–August 2002, March–September 2004, and August–November 2005.

*Availability of many resource types, especially plants, depends on highly variable rains. The Martu calendar is divided into three roughly equal seasons: Yalijarra (hot/wet) January–April; Wantajarra (cool/dry) May–August; Tulparra (hot/dry) September–December.

+S = Spinifex sandhills, M = Mulga woodland, R = Rocky range, W = Watercourse margin.

++Feral honey bees first established hives in the region in 2003. Since then, honey collecting has become a common activity.

+++Nectar from Hakea flowers is available only during a two- to four-week period in Tulparra. In a given patch, the flowers will produce nectar only for about a week.

COMPETING TO BE LEADERLESS

| Foraging Time/Bout (Min) | | Kcal/Bout | | Return Rate/Bout (Kcal/Hr) | | % Total Foraging Time | | % Total Foraged Kcal | |
|---|---|---|---|---|---|---|---|---|---|
| Mean | SD | Mean | SD | Mean | SD | Women | Men | Women | Men |
| 194 | 76 | 1,971 | 1,693 | 635 | 513 | 73.8 | 28.3 | 58.5 | 15.3 |
| 139 | 92 | 3,413 | 5765 | 1,800 | 4,767 | 4.6 | 41.5 | 9.2 | 51.5 |
| 203 | 90 | 3,292 | 5,023 | 967 | 2,763 | 1.5 | 18.9 | 0.6 | 17.7 |
| 162 | 81 | 2,075 | 2,373 | 704 | 941 | 6.2 | 6.3 | 5.6 | 4.9 |
| 76 | 38 | 3,044 | 2,031 | 2,757 | 1,797 | 3.2 | 0.7 | 10.1 | 1.3 |
| 81 | 54 | 548 | 441 | 416 | 237 | 2.8 | 0 | 1.6 | 0.1 |
| 213 | 59 | 3,103 | 3,617 | 913 | 1,185 | 3.4 | 1.6 | 2.8 | 2.4 |
| 74 | 26 | 632 | 379 | 515 | 253 | 2.2 | 0.1 | 1.5 | 0.04 |
| | | 2,968 | 3,608 | | | 1.5 | 0 | 4.2 | 0 |
| 65 | 57 | 5,461 | 4,739 | 5,378 | 3,081 | 0.2 | 1.2 | 2.1 | 4.6 |
| 45 | 25 | 6,355 | 4,881 | 8,482 | 3,350 | 0.4 | 0.3 | 4.0 | 2.2 |
| 188 | 101 | NA | – | NA | – | 0.1 | 1.0 | NA | NA |

**FIGURE 2.1**

*Nyalangka Taylor returns to a dinnertime camp after parnaparnti hunting. She carries sand goanna and perentie (*Varanus gouldii *and* V. gigantius*) to be cooked and shared with all the foragers who will congregate at the camp. Photo by R. Bliege Bird, 2005.*

party spent in a given type of foraging activity and the yield from that activity. We use Martu definitions of foraging activities, which correspond to mutually exclusive activity types associated with acquiring a particular suite of resources. Martu designate a given foraging activity by the term for its primary resource type and a directional suffix (for example, *parnaparnti* [sand goanna], plus *karti* [to]; see table 2.1). In addition to recording all foraging bouts during each foraging trip, we asked permission to follow at least one focal individual to record the various components of foraging: search time; time spent in different components of handling (pursuit, capture, transport, and processing) all resources; and counts, weights, and taxa of all resources captured. After foraging bouts, when the party reconvened at a dinnertime camp (figure 2.1), we recorded "distribution

**FIGURE 2.2**

*Waka Taylor, a well-known mirtilya (skilled and generous hunter), butchers a kirti-kirti (hill kangaroo;* Macropus robustus) *in preparation for sharing at a dinnertime camp. Such respected men are responsible for cooking, butchering, and distributing large game in a manner that ensures equality. Photo by D. Bird, 2005.*

sequences" of all resources. This record included the identity of acquirers, distributors, and recipients and the amount of resources involved in "primary transfers" from the acquirer to the distributor to consumers.

For game animals (figure 2.2), to convert whole weight to edible weight acquired and shared, we measured the proportion of refuse to whole weight in forty-six specimens of all types of small game and four bustards (*Ardeotis australis*). Proportional meat and marrow weights for each shared parcel of male or female hill kangaroo (*Macropus robustus*) were obtained from O'Connell and Marshall 1989:tables 3 and 4. Edible weights of all resources according to species and body part were then converted to kilocalories following Brand-Miller, Maggiore, and James 1993.

These records comprise three data sets used in the description and analysis below: 1,196 adult foraging bouts, 649 focal forager follows, and 251 primary distribution sequences following foraging bouts (155 sequences for two of the most important resource types are used here).

## CONTEMPORARY PATTERNS OF FORAGING AND SHARING

We have previously written about Martu subsistence strategies in relation to mosaic burning, seasonality, gender, and age (Bird and Bliege Bird 2004, 2005; Bird, Bliege Bird, and Codding 2009; Bird, Bliege Bird, and Parker 2004, 2005; Bliege Bird and Bird 2005, 2008; Bliege Bird et al. 2008; Bliege Bird, Codding, and Bird 2009). Below we focus on describing routine patterns of adult foraging and food sharing among Martu from Parnngurr, Punmu, and Kunawarritji.

Although the nutritional importance of foraging has declined somewhat with increased reliance on purchased foods, the social value of wild food has not (see also Povinelli 1992). Martu often say that amid the tensions at Jigalong, they returned to their homelands to care for the Law, protect their estates, and maintain their hunting and gathering priorities. Today foraging is the dominant daily activity in the communities. At least one party of men, women, and children hunt or collect wild plants every day, providing on average 1,000 calories per capita per day and about 80 percent of the meat calories (Bliege Bird, Codding, and Bird 2009).

As shown in table 2.1, Martu participate in a range of foraging activities and routinely hunt a wide array of prey, with a focus on goanna lizards (*Varanus gouldii*, *V. gigantius*, *V. panoptes*, and *V. acanthurus*), bustards (*Ardeotis australis*), feral cats, skinks (*Tiliqua scincoides*), snakes (especially *Aspidites* sp.), and hill kangaroo (*Macropus robustus*) (see Bird, Bliege Bird, and Codding 2009 for details). Collecting insects and their products is also important, especially cossid moth larvae (*Endoxyla* spp.), which are extracted from acacia roots and eucalyptus trees, and, recently, honey from feral European bees that have migrated into the area. During the period when Martu returned to establish the outstations, Walsh (1990) recorded 106 species of plant foods, the most important being acacia tree seeds, grass seeds (especially *Eragrostis eriopoda*), bush tomatoes (*Solanum centrale*, *S. diversiflorum*, and *S. gilessi*), nectar from *Hakea suberea* and *Grevillea eriostachya* flowers, and roots and bulbs (especially

*Vigna lanceolata* and *Cyperus bulbosus*). Martu reliance on seeds has declined, but they continue to harvest large amounts of *Solanum* fruit, *Hakea* nectar, *Vigna* roots, and *Cyperus* bulbs when in season.

### Foraging Activities and the Lack of Leadership

Typically, a foraging party leaves from the settlement or a temporary residential camp in late morning following household or community business. Vehicles are regularly used to access the general foraging locale, but on arrival much of the foraging is conducted on foot. Martu generally operate within a radius of about 30 to 40 kilometers from the settlement and 10 kilometers from a temporary camp. Foraging parties average 8.0±3.3 participants (2.3±1.1 men, 3.6±0.8 women, 2.1±1.4 children).[1]

A given foraging location is decided upon by consensus among the adults in the party, often involving much discussion about intricate ecological and social factors likely to impinge on the success of some foragers. Martu clearly recognize differences in foraging prowess, with the most skilled and generous men and women revered as mirtilya. But mirtilya are not hunt leaders: it is very rare to see other adults defer to mirtilya, or attempts by renowned hunters to impose their will on others. The style, especially among respected men and women, is one of modest suggestion, good humor, and consideration of all participants. It is not that open disagreements never occur, but any participant is free to offer an opinion, which is generally taken seriously by all. This process is remarkable given that men and women (and children!) often have conflicting foraging goals (Bliege Bird and Bird 2008).

Likewise, no person is responsible for organizing mundane foraging labor, and nearly anyone who wishes can participate in a given foraging party, the primary constraints being the number of operating vehicles and space (on one occasion, we recorded twenty-three people with gear in a Land Cruiser, but fifteen is not uncommon). As in all aspects of Martu life, kinship considerations are ever present in the style of interaction among members of a foraging party, and they are a common basis for redressing issues of participation ("I am your *kurndili* [father's sister]! Why didn't you pick me up when you went hunting yesterday!?"). But neither leadership nor kinship determine the overall composition of foraging parties. Daily composition is highly fluid and almost always consists of members of different households. As we discuss below, this fluidity has an important effect on food sharing patterns because primary distributions occur among members of a foraging party, not among or between households.

Upon arrival in the agreed-upon area, a temporary dinnertime camp is designated, and the party splits up, generally in groups of one or two. Depending on locale, season, goals, and expected returns, participants typically engage in one of a range of possible foraging activities (see table 2.1). No one directs anyone else with regard to foraging activities—even children are encouraged to make autonomous decisions about how they spend their time. The most important foraging activity, in terms of both time and calories across all bouts, is parnaparnti (sand goanna) hunting: it makes up 53 percent of all foraging time and contributes 34 percent of all calories acquired from foraged resources. Parnaparnti hunters operate on foot, often burning large patches of spinifex grass in the sand hills to aid their search and pursuit of a range of small game (Bird, Bliege Bird, and Codding 2009; Bird, Bliege Bird, and Parker 2005; Bliege Bird et al. 2008). This activity typically incorporates significant amounts of time tracking and chasing prey and extracting them from their burrows with specialized digging sticks. Women allocate most of their foraging time (74 percent) to this activity, although it tends to be more important during Wantajarra, the cool/dry season (see table 2.1; also see Bliege Bird and Bird 2008).

Sometimes men participate in parnaparnti hunting, but more of their foraging is focused on *kipara* (bustard) hunting or *kirti-kirti* (hill kangaroo) hunting (see table 2.1). Together, these animals make up more than 60 percent of the total foraging effort (42 and 19 percent, respectively), contributing 40 percent of all calories from foraged foods. Small-gauge rifles are commonly used during these hunts. Kipara hunters usually operate from a vehicle, using it to search large tracts of country and as a mobile blind that can approach close enough for a shot when the birds are sighted. Unlike kipara hunting, kirti-kirti hunting is conducted on foot in low-lying rocky ranges. This is typical encounter hunting, usually involving a search along the acacia band at the base of a range, with pursuits that incorporate extensive stalking and tracking punctuated by fast chases over rugged country (see Bird, Bliege Bird, and Codding 2009).

### Leadership in Food Distribution and Material Egalitarianism

On more than 90 percent of the trips we have recorded, after foraging, participants gathered at the designated dinnertime camp, cooked all the food, butchered and distributed portions, ate their fill, and then returned to the settlement well after dark. According to many Martu, this practice results from a lack of firewood around the settlements and facilitates quick distributions of meat, reducing potential conflicts surrounding sharing.

We have often heard Martu say that they share widely because they "are all one family." In that sense, food sharing at dinnertime camps is an expression of relatedness, but its outcome is not determined by rules of kinship (see Altman's description of Gunwinggu sharing, 1987:131–139). This is not to say that Martu sharing is free of conventions regarding control of distributions or concerns about kinship. Treatment of hill kangaroo (kirti-kirti) carcasses illustrates the point.

A successful kirti-kirti hunter, especially if he is young, is expected to make no claim to the carcass and usually plays no part in its cooking, butchery, or distribution. This is characteristic of a hunter's disengagement from property (Tonkinson 1988a:550; Woodburn 1982; see "Discussion" below). He usually drops his kill at the edge of the dinnertime camp without drawing attention to himself and plays no further role in handling the carcass. Proper cooking and butchery require strict attention to ritual procedures and are thus almost always conducted by a senior male mirtilya in a manner similar to that described for other desert Aboriginal groups (for example, Gould 1967, 1982; O'Connell and Marshall 1989). The cook (in ritual contexts, this is always a role filled by a person with powerful authority; see Tonkinson 1991:96–97) controls distributions following butchery, nominally along lines of kinship relative to the hunter. Along with the tail, the head and cervical vertebrae are often designated as the hunter's, although the tail is inevitably eaten by all at the dinnertime camp while the rest of the carcass cooks. On distribution, the hunter's father-in-law (often classificatory mother's brother, *kaka*) or mother-in-law (classificatory father's sister, *yumari*) can claim the rump (the cut with the most meat), an elder brother (*kurta*) or his wife (*nyupa*) can claim a forequarter, and a brother-in-law (*makurta*) or married elder sister (*jurtu*) can claim a rear leg. If these kin are not present, the cook-distributor can give the portion to any other adult at his discretion. However, *even if present, the appropriate kin often wave their rights to any special claim*, and shares are given based on immediate circumstances as evaluated by the cook-distributor. Each parcel is then consumed immediately or taken back to the recipient's household in the settlement for secondary distributions. These proceed without formality or convention: whoever is present and wants a share, especially children, can eat what they want without deference to kinship asymmetries.

We suspect that this process makes it difficult for people who are not present in the foraging party to make a strong case for perceived slights, even if they can make a particular claim based on kinship (that is, if you are not part of the foraging party, you cannot be assured of a share). The hunter modestly gave up his kill, the cook-distributor paid kind attention to the immediate needs of all present in the foraging party, and appropriate kin made no special claims for larger shares. The responsibility for perceived unfairness is thus diffused by magnanimous concern, and accusations of greediness (*malya*) usually can be leveled only at the *recipients* of shares, not the hunter or distributor. It is this attention to equality in distribution that Martu say best describes characteristics of the prestigious hunters referred to as mirtilya.

Sharing of small game and plant resources proceeds in a somewhat different fashion. The distribution of game following parnaparnti hunting provides a useful example. When foragers return to a dinnertime camp, they gather around one or two cooking hearths, depending on the size of the foraging party. Even though all goannas at a given hearth are cooked together (almost always by a senior woman), each hunter keeps track of her own game, and following cooking, the hunters often claim those that they acquired. Primary distributions follow. These involve hunters effectively pooling their catch among all members of a hearth group at the dinnertime camp. Goannas are passed back and forth from hunter to hunter and from those who have more to those who have less. If there is more than one hearth group at the dinnertime camp and significant asymmetries between hearths are obvious, sometimes participants demand "fairness," with secondary transfers between hearths. After these distributions, everyone eats his or her fill. Leftover portions are taken back to the recipients' households for further sharing with anyone present. No kinship rules guide these tiers of distribution, and as we show below, because longer parnaparnti hunting increases the harvest size, the evenness of sharing means that mirtilya (the renowned hunters), through their magnanimity, support those who work less.

## ANALYSIS

As we described in the introduction, a lack of institutionalized leadership in some foraging societies is thought to be the result of a lack of opportunities to control non-kin labor. This is especially the case in settings where coping with foraging risk is facilitated by reciprocal sharing rather than hoarding, making it difficult to amass wealth or maintain structured social asymmetries, privatization, and suprafamilial control over labor. This leads us to ask whether Martu share in order to ensure against risk (that is, future production uncertainties) and whether this reciprocity structures their lack of institutional hierarchy outside ritual contexts. Here we evaluate these questions relative to some specific predictions of a reciprocity hypothesis from behavioral ecology (for explicit parameters and assumptions, see Bliege Bird, Smith, and Bird 2001; Cashdan 1985; Kaplan and Hill 1985; Winterhalder 1986). If mundane egalitarianism and food sharing as described above for Martu are structured by risk-reduction reciprocity, then we would predict that, relative to the acquirer,

1. Resources acquired from foraging activities that are less risky (those with lower variance in return rates or lower failure rates) should be shared less frequently and more narrowly because under risk-reduction reciprocity, foragers share as insurance against uncertainty in acquisition. The best insurance against production uncertainty for low-risk activities is to work longer (Winterhalder 1986).

2. Distributions of resources should be biased toward recipients who have a higher probability of acquiring surplus. Hunters in a given foraging activity who consistently provide more food than others, and do so more efficiently, should keep more of the distribution or direct shares toward those who are on average less of a security risk (those who are more efficient across all foraging activities).

3. If sharing is designed as reciprocity more broadly defined—in that it serves to create and maintain social networks of cooperation and obligation for resources and services beyond food—then, when present, coresidents and affines should be favored in sharing distributions. All things being equal, coresidents and affines would be present to reciprocate most effectively with other currencies.

We evaluate these predictions with comparisons of parnaparnti (sand goanna) and kirti-kirti (hill kangaroo) hunting and distributions of the associated resources at dinnertime camps. These activities are illustrative given that their resources are two of the three most commonly shared and on every occasion that a hunter chose kirti-kirti hunting, he or she traded off the opportunity to hunt for parnaparnti. Doing so is a risky choice unless the hunter can be assured that he or she will be compensated with future shares of kirti-kirti or, better yet (relative to risk reduction), parnaparnti. Although kirti-kirti hunting provides the possibility of a bonanza harvest and has a higher average return rate than parnaparnti hunting, it is associated with significantly higher variance ($n = 76$ and $575$ bouts, respectively, $CV = 2.9$ versus $0.81$, equality of variances F test, $F = 38.0$, $p < .001$; see table 2.1). Much of the difference between the two is due to the chances of failure: kirti-kirti hunters failed to acquire anything on 75 percent of the recorded bouts; parnaparnti hunters failed on only 9 percent of the bouts. The variance associated with parnaparnti hunting is also more predictable: hunters can monitor changes in efficiency associated with yearly, seasonal, and local circumstances through their own and others' daily returns. Such variation for kirti-kirti is often swamped by the daily stochasticity and difficulties of pursuing and capturing hill kangaroo (see Bird, Bliege Bird, and Codding 2009).

### Prediction 1

These differences have an important effect on the relationship between risk management, foraging effort, and harvest size. For parnaparnti hunting, longer foraging hours result in larger harvests (total kcal acquired regressed by total foraging time, $r = .38$, $p < .001$), whereas for kirti-kirti there is no such relationship ($r = .04$, $p = .73$). Relative to prediction 1, hunters can thus manage the risk associated with parnaparnti by adjusting their work effort and controlling distribution of their catch. We would expect, then, that the probability of sharing a catch from parnaparnti hunting would be less than that from kirti-kirti hunting. This is so in only a limited sense.

Kirti-kirti is shared on 100 percent of harvests; shares average 2,403 kcals ($n = 103$), distributed to an average of 9.6 other individuals per harvest. Parnaparnti is shared on 82.6 percent of harvests; shares average 648 kcals ($n = 52$), distributed to 2.5 other individuals per harvest. Compared with kirti-kirti, a smaller proportion of a recipient's parnaparnti take-home share is made up of food acquired by others ($n = 115$ and 125, respectively, $91 \pm .27$ percent versus $58 \pm .41$ percent, $p = .02$). However, because parnaparnti harvests are nearly always successful (9 percent failure rate), women share with others nearly every day they hunt. Kirti-kirti harvests are less successful (75 percent failure rate) but are shared with more people. Thus, the average number of others distributed to *per day* is the same for both parnaparnti (2.1 others per day) and kirti-kirti hunters (2.4 per day). Parnaparnti hunters share as frequently and to as many potential others as kirti-kirti hunters do over the long term. Because kirti-kirti hunting is much less reliable, this result is inconsistent with the hypothesis that differences in the sharing of the two resources are structured by concerns about reciprocity to reduce foraging risk.

### Prediction 2

To evaluate prediction 2, we estimated the long-term security risk of investing a share in a given recipient as the recipient's mean foraging efficiency (edible weight acquired per foraging hour before sharing) over *all* foraging bouts across *all* activities ($n = 1,196$). We then ranked all individual adult foragers for whom we had recorded at least ten bouts each ($n =$

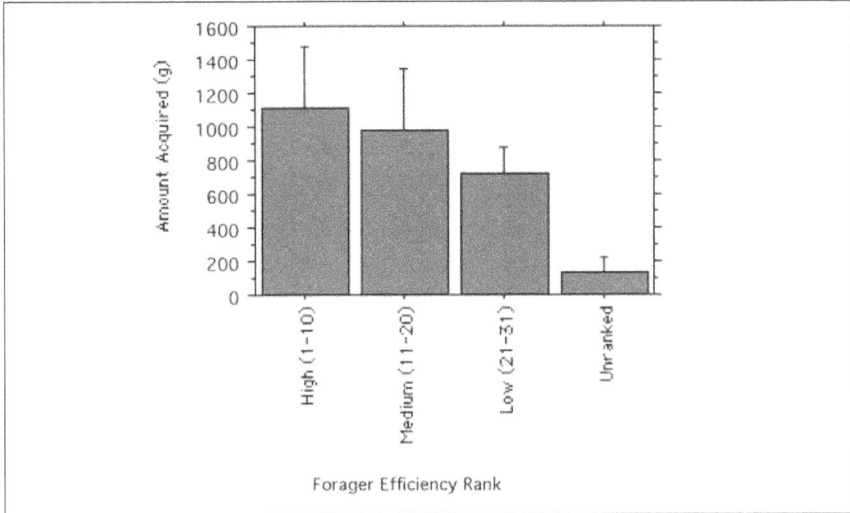

**FIGURE 2.3**

*Parnaparnti (sand goanna) hunting: amount acquired. Amount acquired is the mean edible weight acquired by a forager per parnaparnti hunting bout. Forager efficiency rank is the mean efficiency (edible grams per foraging hour) over all foraging bouts across all activities for the thirty-one individuals for whom we recorded more than ten foraging bouts. Unranked individuals are those for whom we recorded fewer than ten foraging bouts (see text). All error bars are standard deviation.*

31 individuals) by each individual's mean overall efficiency: high average efficiency (foragers 1–10), medium efficiency (foragers 11–20), and low efficiency (foragers 21–31). Unranked foragers—those for whom we had fewer than ten bouts recorded—are the biggest security risk: they either rarely foraged or were visiting from elsewhere. Note that lower-ranked foragers are less efficient, not necessarily low producers; as noted above, kirti-kirti hunting often fails but occasionally produces big bonanzas.

Figure 2.3 shows that when they participate in parnaparnti hunting, higher-ranked foragers, because they work longer, produce significantly larger harvests than those who are lower ranked or unranked (ANOVA, F = 16.0, p = .001). Distributions at dinnertime camps following parnaparnti hunts even out these asymmetries in acquisition: the average take-home share (edible weight hunters ended up with after all distributions were over) did not vary with hunter rank; high-ranked hunters received 822±620 grams, middle-ranked 961±766, and low-ranked hunters 801±543 (ANOVA, p > .500). Although consumption shares for unranked foragers

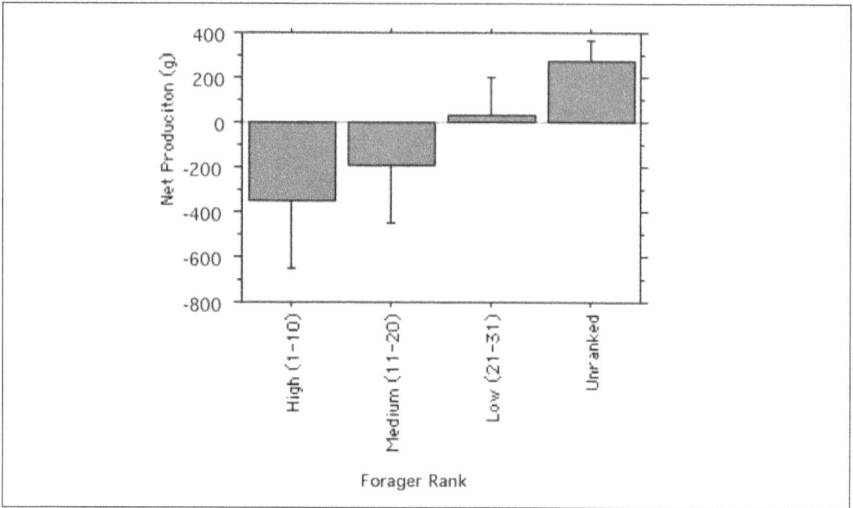

**FIGURE 2.4**

*Parnaparnti (sand goanna) hunting: take-home share minus amount acquired. Net production is the take-home share (total edible weight of a forager's share for consumption after primary distribution) minus the edible weight of all resources the forager acquired on the day of the parnaparnti hunt. Forager rank is as defined in figure 2.3.*

(455±460) are significantly lower than for all ranked hunters (p < .05 unranked versus high-, medium-, and low-ranked foragers), given that lower and unranked foragers work less and produce less when parnaparnti hunting, the fact that sharing is fairly even means that lower and unranked hunters consistently free-ride on the efforts of higher-ranked hunters. Figure 2.4 demonstrates this: high- and medium-ranked foragers produce more than they consume, whereas low- and unranked foragers produce less than they consume (ANOVA, F = 8.3, p < .001). The even outcome of sharing exaggerates asymmetries in production with consistent one-way flows from those who work harder to those who produce less.

For hunters to compensate for kirti-kirti hunting's increased risks, we would predict that (a) kirti-kirti hunters would receive a larger share of all resources acquired (including kirti-kirti and the more reliable parnaparnti) and (b) recipients who are a lower security risk (those who are highly efficient foragers over all activities) would be favored in distributions. Neither of these predictions is supported. On the days that kirti-kirti are acquired, a hunter's average postdistribution consumption share (edible weight of kirti-kirti and all other resources acquired by members of the

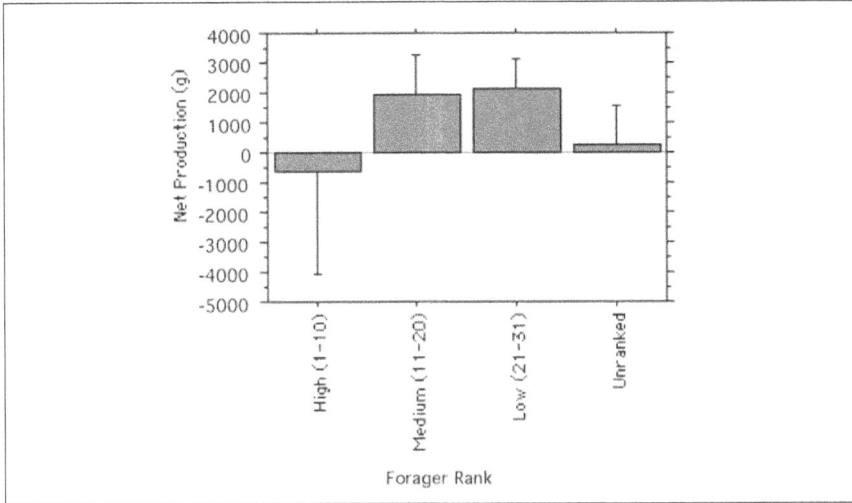

**FIGURE 2.5**

*Kirti-kirti (hill kangaroo) hunting: take-home share minus amount acquired. Net production is the take-home share (total edible weight of a forager's share for consumption after primary distributions) minus the edible weight of all resources the forager acquired on the day of the kirti-kirti hunt. Forager rank is as defined in figure 2.3.*

foraging party) is not significantly greater than the consumption shares of others present in the dinnertime camp ($1,551\pm1,691$ grams versus $1,849\pm1,606$ grams edible weight, respectively; $t = -.61$, $p < .500$). Hunter rank does not affect variability in postdistribution consumption shares: high-ranked hunters get $2,444\pm2,213$ grams, middle-ranked hunters claim $2,001\pm1,519$, and low-ranked $1,899\pm1,054$; $p > .500$. As with parnaparnti distributions, this makes for asymmetries in production: on average, high-ranked foragers produce and share more edible weight (all resources) than they receive following distributions of kirti-kirti (figure 2.5). This has a dramatic effect on *take-home* efficiency (grams *received* per foraging hours after distributions): kirti-kirti sharing serves to even out what would be asymmetries in production with one-way flows from high producers to low producers, which create asymmetries in the ratio of costs to benefits. More efficient foragers (grams *acquired* per foraging hour) have postsharing consumption return rates that are on average less than or equal to less efficient foragers (figure 2.6; $p > .350$). Low-ranked and unranked foragers gain the most by being present at a kirti-kirti distribution: their average return rates increase threefold. Sharing thus promotes free-riding on the efforts of efficient

41

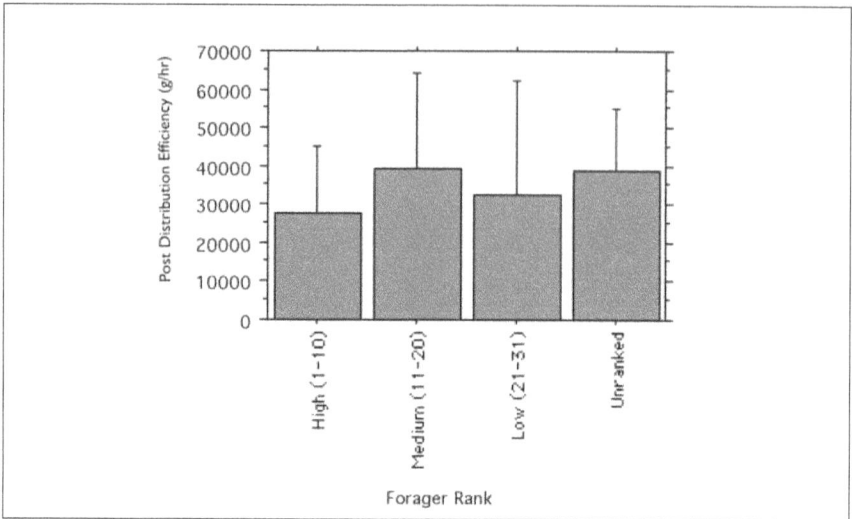

**FIGURE 2.6**

*Take-home efficiency following kirti-kirti (hill kangaroo) distribution. Postdistribution efficiency is the take-home share (total edible weight of a forager's share for consumption after primary distribution) per foraging hour per kirti-kirti hunt bout. Forager rank is as defined in figure 2.3.*

foragers, exaggerating differences between production and consumption rather than ameliorating them as risk-reduction reciprocity predicts.

### Prediction 3

Relative to prediction 3, we find no significant effect of coresidence or affinal relationships on distribution patterns at kirti-kirti or parnaparnti dinnertime camps. Coresidents and non-coresidents of kirti-kirti hunters receive an average postdistribution share of 1,736±1,102 grams and 1,370±998, respectively (t = −1.5, p < .200). Affinal kin (mother-in-law, father-in-law, spouse, or brother-in-law) of kirti-kirti hunters receive shares no larger than anyone else (1,215±1,007 edible grams for others versus 1,868±1,290 for affinal kin; t = 1.9, p < .100). For parnaparnti hunters, a coresident's take-home share is 481±339 grams versus 488±377 for non-coresidents (t = .08, p < .900). Affinal kin of parnaparnti hunters receive an average parnaparnti share of 507±394 grams. Others receive 459±355 grams on average (t = −.11, p < .800).

The overall sharing patterns are thus simply captured in how Martu describe their practices: shares in primary transfers (those at dinnertime camps) are distributed in a manner that ensures that all adults present, regardless of whether they produced or are likely to produce in the future, get an equal share. This pattern is certainly not what we would predict if hunters were concerned about controlling distribution to reduce production variance, and it leads us to question whether a lack of structured material asymmetries, and attendant mundane egalitarianism, results from reciprocity.

## DISCUSSION

Gould (1981, 1982) does a good job of articulating a common ecological explanation of food sharing and egalitarianism among desert Aborigines: reciprocal sharing serves to minimize risks in an inherently risky environment that constrains the development of hierarchy. The argument is that security in highly unpredictable environments rests not in storing goods for the future but in storing debt. Sharing serves as a means of storing social capital against which one can draw later during shortfalls. And because material resources are not stored, there is no basis for enduring wealth and social inequality. "The greater the degree of risk, the wider the extent of sharing. Conversely, the greater the opportunities for optimal harvesting with minimal risk…the greater the tendency for aggrandivized behavior" (Gould 1982:76).

Based on this argument, we would expect that a current share given is advanced payment for future shares to be returned. The results presented above suggest otherwise. Individuals do not bias shares toward potential reciprocators, and they receive shares whether or not they are likely to reciprocate, regardless of the degree of risk associated with the foraging activity. Martu share such that a consistently more productive hunter will gain less from others than he or she gives away. It could be that such inequalities in production are not sufficient evidence to reject the notion that individuals are sharing to reduce consumption variance associated with acquiring high-risk resources. But we think that this argument confuses the process of sharing with the goals of foraging. The sharing process involves flows from those who have to those who have not, eliminating variance in consumption across individuals on any foraging day. But this process does not involve eliminating variance in the costs of acquiring prey—individuals who pay a higher cost in time to get more are subsidizing those who pay less. The question then arises, if individuals are foraging for variable resources and managing variance with sharing, why produce more than anyone else? Although individuals may indeed be sharing to reduce present inequities in consumption (based on the prohibitive social costs of refusing demands, *sensu* Blurton Jones 1984, 1987; Peterson 1993; see below), the benefit of acquiring certain resources lies not in future portions received. If they are sharing to reduce their own variance in consumption over time, sharing would be inequitable, not equitable. The mystery may not be why people share but why some people produce more than others.

## WHY PRODUCTION INEQUALITY AND SHARING EQUALITY?

We suspect that Martu food sharing is so even because hoarding depends on the refusal to share. Although overt demands at distributions are rare, the pattern of Martu sharing conforms with what Peterson (1993) has termed demand sharing. As Myers (1986:113–116) describes for the neighboring Pintupi, Martu food sharing is an expression of shared identity; it emphasizes relatedness through generosity ("We share because we are all one family"). It is not considered offensive for people to hide portions of food or tobacco to reduce demands, but if asked, it is very rare for an adult to be able to refuse a demand. In food sharing among participants of a foraging party, everyone knows who acquired what, and asking for shares is rare because distributors make efforts to anticipate any potential demands. Under such circumstances, people who are less than generous would be considered less than human. As Martu say, they would be "like rocks," incapable of expressing compassion (*nyarru*). The mirtilya—elder men and women who are renowned for their hunting prowess and magnanimity—are said to be truly compassionate and human.

Such patterns are also predicted in what Blurton Jones (1984, 1987) has formally modeled as tolerated theft. Sharing is unconditional with respect to reciprocity, and goods flow from those who have more to those who have less, based on the social pressures to be generous ("resource holding potential"; Blurton Jones 1984). But if individuals present at dinnertime camps receive shares whether or not they give them, they can free-ride on the efforts of others. As Hawkes (1992, 1993) points out, the shared items are then like public goods, and working for them presents a collective-action problem. Where acquisitions are unsynchronized, it is better for the group if everyone shares more, but better for individuals to adjust their work effort around more reliable resources to acquire enough for themselves and share less. Wiessner (1982) and Sahlins (1972) provide clear examples of people limiting their work effort with concerns about the opportunities it will provide for others to free-ride. Under such conditions, where there are no sanctions against free-riders, what factors might maintain the inequality of work exaggerated by the equality of distribution?

## LINKS BETWEEN SHARING AND LEADERSHIP

[Sharing] does more than simply distribute the catch. It also doubles the rewards to the hunter by according him both social prestige as a good kinsman and meat when he takes his share from someone else's catch.

—Richard Gould, *To Have and Have Not*

Many, including the authors, have suggested that the signaling benefits of hunting and magnanimity may solve the collective-action problem engaged by sharing (see Hawkes and Bliege Bird 2002; Bliege Bird and Smith 2005 for review). The fact that among Martu, inequalities of labor are exaggerated by the equality of sharing is not anomalous if we assume that certain kinds of foraging variance are especially effective as honest displays of magnanimity. The extent to which individuals can provide "public goods" may thus serve to sustain the material egalitarianism of everyday life on one hand and the ritual gerontocracy on the other.

At first glance, the egalitarian nature of everyday social relations would seem to counteract the structured hierarchy of ritual ownership and performance, in which individuals compete to gain more knowledge in order to establish a gerontocracy of control over the younger generation's life histories, to gain ownership over dreams, dances, and sites of sacred significance. But maybe there is no real contradiction. The apparent social symmetry is not the result of the prevention of social competition but of social competition so strong and so universal that everyone must invest in it simply to stay in the same relative place on a positional treadmill.

The social distinctions that do arise are not those of material possession, in which individuals are marked by what they own or can claim, but of dispossession. Distinctions are made by the lack of attention to material ownership, the careless treatment of property that is the true sign of the competitive ascetic. All the renowned and generous hunters (mirtilya) we know are also the revered holders of the Law (ngurraru). In mundane contexts, mirtilya wear cast-off clothing, own nothing but their tools, deny nothing to anyone, claim no prerogatives, and seem to make no decisions for anyone else. The hierarchy of ascetics is based not on prerogatives claimed and power exercised but on honest performance of the opposite— on occasions when one might exercise power, one quietly demurs to another. Thus, the elderly *maparn* (healing ritual expert) sits quietly in the back of the vehicle, giving the "shotgun" position to a young man searching for bustard. If we make the mistake of assuming that the benefits of social status are to claim resources for oneself, we might erroneously ascribe greater status to the young man, who claims the highly desired, comfortable front seat, forcing the old man to sit cross-legged in the back on top of a plastic box full of tinned tuna. But it is the old man who has demonstrated his power, by refusing to claim the seat when he very well could have, who has given away the seat to the young man. Only those who "own" have the power to give, and giving is a signal of one's ownership. Ironically, only by demonstrating disengagement with property can one claim inalienable possession of it (Wiener 1992).

Among Martu, the mirtilya are revered for their hunting skills and generosity. Their magnanimity is acknowledged with some awe well beyond the network of kin that they associate with daily—their reputations are known throughout the Western Desert well beyond the Martu communities. The reputation is not maintained simply by giving: a mirtilya is a person who not only frequently gives but also frequently has things to give—a person who works harder than others so that surplus production can be distributed to all. The distinction, then, is not between those who own the least but between those who honestly demonstrate the most "disengagement"; those who do not simply produce little and consume it all themselves but those who sustain the largest differentials between what is acquired and what one actually consumes. The hierarchy that develops out of competitive asceticism is obscured simply because it has few immediate material components.

How does such a competitive regime become established? How do individuals benefit from such disengagement with property if not through enhanced control over resources and labor? Social signaling theory may offer a possible explanation for how such public-spirited altruism might actually benefit both the altruist and those who observe him or her. Under certain conditions, some foragers may seek costly strategies that carry with them inherent risk as a means of display (see Bliege Bird and Smith 2005) because being able to carry such risk and still succeeding, with an attitude that discounts future reliability (via storage or reciprocity), honestly displays qualities that are difficult to assess otherwise. When some begin to display thusly, it creates incentives for others to do likewise. If the display is embedded in acquiring unpredictable resources, escalating competitions can undercut hierarchy (Hawkes 2000).

We suggest that by focusing on high-variance resources, mirtilya hunters can be especially effective in honestly displaying their prowess and magnanimity—all hunters then need to compete to show these skills just to stay in the same place on a positional treadmill. That food sharing, and by extension the daily business of life, looks and feels so egalitarian may actually arise from competitions to provide public goods. This sharing as a costly public display accords with the modesty of the mirtilya hunters: talk is cheap when faking success is impossible, and success for unpredictable resources that are widely shared is costly. Being able to bear these costs without care for future reciprocity guarantees the validity of the signal.

The questions then remain, How is it that among Martu, with mundane egalitarianism, very real power over others is maintained under ritual circumstances? What are the consequences of being "mirtilya," and does this reputation translate into leadership or power over others in ritual contexts? We suspect that mirtilya reputations are an important component of establishing positions in the ritual hierarchy, including the most powerful ngurraru mentioned above. However, we do not yet know the extent to which being mirtilya is a requirement, whether all senior administrators of ritual and law are also mirtilya. Certainly, all mirtilya whom we know, both men and women, are also very powerful ritual leaders, but we do not yet have data to show whether the reverse is true. There may be other, related benefits to reputations of prowess and magnanimity. Elsewhere, among the Meriam, we have shown strong correlations between hunting prestige and reproductive success (Smith, Bliege Bird, and Bird 2003; see also Smith 2004). We do not know whether there are similar material or reproductive consequences of hunting reputations among the Martu.

Here we suggest that hierarchy in the mundane realm is obscured by the nature of social distinction—the fact that individuals gain not by hoarding more for themselves but by divesting themselves of resources and in so doing claim co-ownership of them. In a sense, everyone has the opportunity to gain this distinction, primarily because parnaparnti hunting is so predictable and productive and the materials by which production is achieved are so generalized. Paradoxically, this situation both promotes the widespread renown of individual hunters and discourages asymmetrical material hierarchy. However, not every individual has access to the secret/sacred knowledge that serves to mark position in the ritual hierarchy. Such knowledge is closely guarded, divulged only to those individuals who have paid the cost (initiation) to demonstrate their trustworthiness. Those with more knowledge thus have power over those with less. Some have argued that the two realms are linked, especially for men: men produce generously because in doing so they demonstrate their commitment to and concern for the Law and are then more likely to rise in the ritual hierarchy, pass the final stage of initiation, and marry their promised wives (Sackett 1979; Tonkinson 1988b). In that sense, then, some men may work more as a way to gain political and reproductive advantages through competition with other men. But what do women gain from generosity? We have suggested (Bliege Bird and Bird 2008; Bliege Bird, Codding, and Bird 2009) that in sharing with other women, they secure partners for cooperative hunting arrangements and specialize in different foraging activities, or between child care and foraging, and in so doing may enhance the survival and well-being of their children (see Wiessner 2002 for a similar argument on the benefits of generosity among the Ju/'hoansi).

## CONCLUDING COMMENT

We began this chapter by reviewing some common assumptions about the ecology of subsistence and dominance. Many have argued that enduring leadership requires wealth differentials and that when the accumulation of goods is limited by an unpredictable resource base, reciprocal arrangements are favored and more balanced social relations result. Based on an analysis of Martu foraging and sharing, we suggest another possible route: egalitarianism as a hierarchy of ascetics. We argue that without "disengaging" property (Tonkinson 1988a:550) through honest signals of ability vis-à-vis generosity, Martu hunters would quickly lose their place on the positional treadmill. The social distinction of generous Martu hunters is widely recognized and is clearly expressed in the lack of attention toward sanctioning nonreciprocators in everyday food sharing. Highly skilled, hardworking hunters generously give to all present regardless of whether those who receive are likely to reciprocate. These hunters are antileaders in mundane circumstances: they demonstrate little obvious inclination to speak for or control others in everyday life. We suggest that this situation is a display of their ability to bear the costs of magnanimity, an ability that in turn may underwrite tremendous power in ritual administration. Such circumstances favor the pursuit of distinction through costly ascetic performance, undercutting wealth asymmetries and at the same time promoting differential control of labor and production surrounding access to ritual hierarchy.

### Acknowledgments

Our heartfelt thanks go to the Martu, especially our family and friends at Parnngurr, Punmu, and Kunawarritji, for their tutelage, assistance, encouragement, hospitality, and unwavering tolerance. Many thanks to Peter Veth and Bob Tonkinson for introducing us to Western Desert cultures and to Brooke Scelza, Brian Codding, Kristen Hawkes, Polly Wiessner, Jim O'Connell, Jim Roscoe, Sarah Robinson, and Eric Smith for especially useful comments on and discussion of ideas in this chapter. An anonymous reviewer provided suggestions that significantly improved our framing of the analysis. We are grateful to all the SAR advanced seminar participants for their valuable input and to the editors for all their assistance and work in arranging such an engaging workshop. This study was funded with grants from the National Science Foundation (BCS-012781 and BCS-0075289).

**Note**

1. All errors are given as standard deviation.

# 3

# Women's Leadership

*Political Alliance, Economic Resources,
and Reproductive Success
in the Ecuadorian Amazon*

## Brenda J. Bowser and John Q. Patton

Leaders exist in all human societies. It is a truism of anthropology that authority is distributed according to age and sex in egalitarian societies and that positions of leadership are informal and situational. Therefore, leadership does not "emerge" in more complex societies without precedent. Rather, dominance hierarchies inherently and fundamentally structure the social fabric of all societies. The question at hand, then, is not "Through what processes do leaders emerge in societies where they did not previously exist?" but instead "What are the processes through which leadership emerges in different forms in different societies?" Studies of leadership in archaeology have tended to emphasize the acquisition of status and the control of strategic material resources. However, anthropological studies of cooperation and political processes remind us that if status hierarchies—relationships of differential power—form the warp of social fabric, then the weft is woven from relationships of kinship and alliance, and leadership in societies of all scales is dependent on building coalitions—that is, controlling social capital rather than material resources. Moreover, different people are likely to employ different strategies in developing, asserting, negotiating, maintaining, and contesting these relationships of power and alliance, as many archaeologists emphasize today (for example, see Arnold, chapter 6, this volume; Mills 2000; Stanish, chapter 5, this volume).

Previously, Bowser (2000) observed that indigenous women in Conambo, a community of horticultural foragers in the Ecuadorian Amazon, employ two strategies of alliance building and that these strategies may contribute to the status of a woman and her husband and enhance the well-being of her family. One strategy involves developing strong cross-coalitional alliances, working to build political consensus and to mediate conflict in a village divided into two ethnic factions, consistent with comparative data indicating that women intermediaries have greater access to positions of leadership cross-culturally (Ross 1986). The other strategy involves maintaining clear, strong relationships of alliance within a woman's own coalition rather than across factional boundaries. Further, these strategies have material advantages because women who have established strong cross-coalitional relationships benefit from the ability to exchange meat, obtain propagules (propagative stems) for their gardens and materials for decorating pottery, draw labor, arrange marriages, and establish fictive kin ties across the political divide. However, Bowser's case study also suggests that such intermediary strategies are risky and these "women-in-between" (to borrow Marilyn Strathern's term [1972]) may pursue such positions because their intracoalitional alliances are insecure.

Additional cross-cultural data indicate that women's leadership is associated with their control over economic resources (Low 1992) and, possibly, their strong female kinship ties and the presence of male kin (Yanca and Low 2004). In Conambo, women contribute the majority of calories to the family diet from their gardening. Postmarital residence is generally matrilocal during the early years of marriage, and many middle-aged and older women live geographically close to some of their adult brothers and sisters, even if they no longer live near their parents' households. According to these studies, these factors should favor women's leadership in Conambo, and more extensive kinship ties should correlate with women's greater status within the community.

In this chapter, we explore the two alliance-building strategies further to address some of the fundamental questions of this volume. The analysis allows us to evaluate the relative benefits of the various alliance-building strategies and the importance of control over material resources as factors in women's status and the emergence of women's leadership. First, we examine the social capital on which women's leadership is built, by examining the influences of kinship and political alliances on women's status. Second, we consider the economic and reproductive benefits of women who are viewed as important leaders in the community. Third, we examine the stability and heritability of women's leadership in Conambo. Fourth and finally, we consider how understanding the alliance-building strategies of women, especially political brokers between factions, may contribute to our understanding of how positions of leadership become institutionalized—or do not—over time. We conclude that lack of kin ties in a kin-based matrilocal society, resulting from aggregation of people from multiple ethnic and linguistic groups, is a major factor motivating women to build personal positions of political leadership, because they can draw upon those political ties, in the absence of kin ties, to gain greater access to productive and reproductive resources. We suggest that women's leadership, particularly in resolving political matters between factions, is accepted precisely because they are viewed by members of opposite factions as less subject to the influence of kin and therefore as more trustworthy. However, in this case, these personal positions do not provide the basis for heritable, institutionalized leadership, which elsewhere in Amazonia is supposed to be based on historical processes of the *longue durée*: the dominance of a kin group in numbers, as well as "genealogical superiority" (Heckenberger 2005), or descent from the original founders of a place. This fundamental contradiction—that political leaders who can bridge a political divide between multiple coalitions may be those least likely to be members of a dominant kin group—is a principle that may apply to both men and women. And it may help explain why the development of sociopolitical complexity may not simply be a natural outcome of population growth or aggregation—an organic response to scalar stress or a structural inevitability of the longue durée. Rather, extraordinary circumstances may be needed to catalyze the institutionalization of leadership and overcome the inherent instability of leadership in small-scale societies.

## BACKGROUND: WOMEN'S POLITICAL STRATEGIES IN CONAMBO

Women participate actively in political life in Conambo, particularly in consensus building and conflict resolution within the community, which is divided into two factions based on ethnic and political differences. Women and men organize themselves into separate gender-segregated domains of political life, and women's political networks are organized differently than men's (Bowser 2000, 2002, 2004; Bowser and Patton 2004, 2008). Some women build alliances that crosscut the political division of the village into two factions, and they act as mediators between these factions. Conversely, men's coalitions are more clearly delineated and tightly bounded, and these define the political division. Thus, women's political networks integrate the two factions, facilitating information flow, consensus building, and conflict resolution across the factional boundary. Women exercise their political influence in a variety of situations, such as tensions arising from heated words, fistfights, contested paternity, and bad marriages; decisions regarding newcomers' rights of access to community land and membership in the community; and blockades to prevent the entry of *petroleros* (oil company representatives) and other defensive responses to encroachment by outsiders.

The two factions function as self-governing, egalitarian, autonomous, but interrelated segments of one community. The upriver faction comprises predominantly Achuar people, and the downriver faction comprises mainly Quichua speakers of Zaparoan descent. Both factions are ethnically mixed as a result of marriage and political defections, and interactions are facilitated by a high degree of multilingualism. Their differences are rooted in different social memories of the histories that establish and validate each ethnic group's claims to the place, dating back to the community's formation about thirty-five years ago, although competing claims to territorial rights extend into deeper history (Bowser 2002; Bowser and Patton 2004, 2008; Patton 1996, 2000, 2004). Resolving conflicts between the two factions is a major focus of politics within the community. Both sides have attempted and failed cyclically to bridge their differences, to cooperate and coordinate economic, political, and social activities rather than operating as opposing, competing factions. Effective leadership arises for short periods, cooperation increases across the factional boundary, but ultimately the cooperative relationships dissolve. In this sense, Conambo, the largest community in the territory, with two hundred people and twenty-four households, may be viewed as transegalitarian, a place where people are trying to develop more complex organizational structures *a vivir bien, tranquilo*—to live well, tranquilly.

### Women's Leadership and Age

In small-scale societies, leadership is characterized as informal and situational, based primarily on age and sex. As a generalization, this is true in Conambo. At the same time, certain individuals in all societies are recognized as possessing and exercising more leadership qualities than other individuals, and such qualities distinguish certain individuals from others in the same age and sex categories (Brown 1976, 1991). In Conambo, a woman who has demonstrated leadership abilities over time is called an *amu* (in Quichua) or a *juun* (in Achuar). Men and women in Conambo say that such a woman is "more important" than others, a quality we refer to as "status" and "leadership." Above all, an important woman is recognized in terms of her maturity and her leadership role in political activities. An important woman helps organize consensus, solves conflicts between people, knows how to organize people, directs the actions of others, speaks well, and is persuasive.

Quantitative data show that women's status in Conambo increases considerably as they grow older, consonant with anthropological expectations and informants' statements (Bowser and Patton 2008). The status of young women and older women is highly predictable based on age. It rises rapidly during women's younger years and levels off late in life. However, the status of middle-aged women varies greatly. In other words, middle-aged women may be able to enhance or diminish their status through their own agency, whereas there is comparatively little chance of women affecting their status during youth and old age.

To quantify status, we asked fifteen women to judge the relative status of twenty-seven women in the community, including all twenty-four female heads of household and three coresident women (one widow and two young married daughters). We showed each informant photographs of the twenty-seven women, presented in random sets of three photographs, and asked each to identify the most important woman and the second most important woman in the triad using the emic terms *amu* and *juun*, which encode qualities of political leadership. We asked each informant to make comparative judgments of twenty triads for a total of 810 judgments. We calculated a status score by assigning two points to the woman ranked first in each triad, one point to the second-ranked woman, and no points to the remaining woman. We then summed these points.

Women's status increases as they grow older (figure 3.1). The linear regression correlation between women's status and age is highly significant ($r^2 = .75$, p = .00, N = 27), and the relationship between women's status and age is best predicted by the quadratic equation ($r^2 = .839$, p = .000, N = 27) and best represented by a curve (see figure 3.1). This means that women's status in Conambo rises steeply in their younger years and begins to level off in their older years.

We can distinguish three age groups of women: young women of low status, middle-aged women of variable status, and older women of high status. Figure 3.1 indicates that the status of younger and older women can be predicted fairly accurately by their age; the data points for these two age groups cluster closely along the lines generated by the regression analysis and the quadratic equation. However, the middle distribution does not follow either line as closely, indicating that the status of middle-aged women is less predictable by age than the status of women in other age groups. In

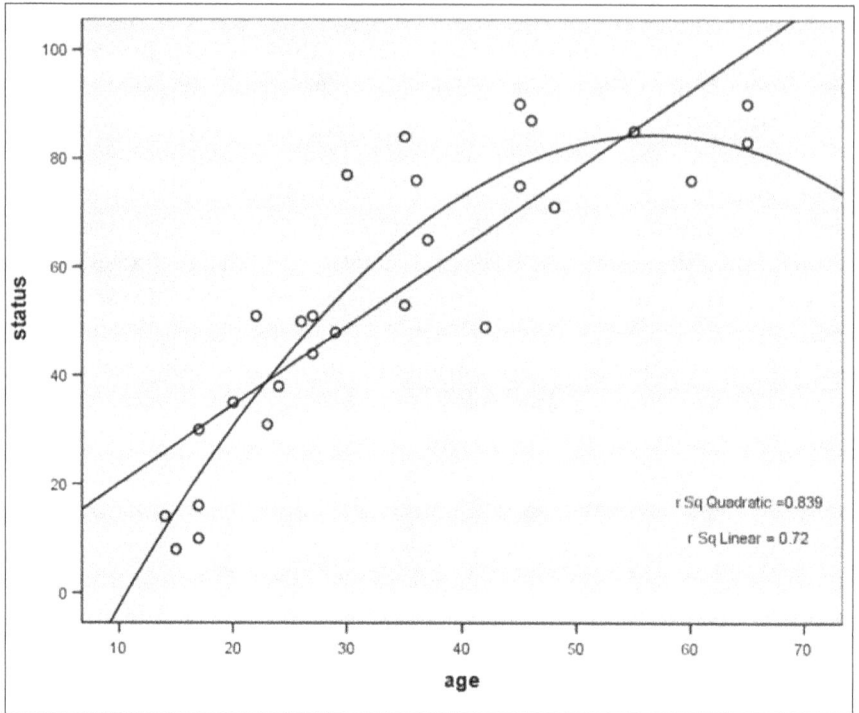

**FIGURE 3.1**
*Women's age and status in Conambo (1992–1993).*

fact, age is a poor predictor of status differences within this age group, and most middle-aged women have status that is higher or lower than expected for their age. Therefore, women in Conambo do not judge the status of middle-aged women based on age alone, and status differences among middle-aged women must be explained by other variables.

### Women's Alliances and Age

The preceding analysis shows that the status of middle- aged women in Conambo is influenced by factors other than age, suggesting that the agency of middle-aged women may influence their positions of importance in the village. Previous analysis of women's alliances shows that some women in Conambo are positioned as political brokers between the two ethnic factions (Bowser and Patton 2004, 2008). The following analysis of women's alliances shows that political centrality tends to occur during middle age, and it contributes significantly to the status of these women. Young women and older women tend to be politically peripheral.

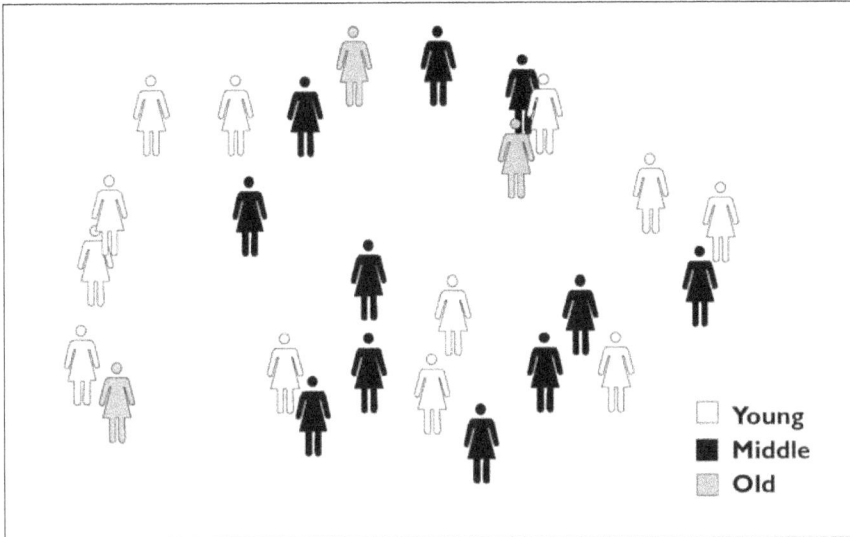

FIGURE 3.2

*Multidimensional scaling (MDS) of women's alliance similarities in Conambo (1992–1993). Each married woman is represented by an icon, coded by her age category. Closeness between icons indicates that women share similar alliances, and closeness to the center represents political centrality.*

For this analysis, quantitative measures of women's alliance strengths and similarities were applied from our previous analyses, which have been described elsewhere (Bowser 2000; Bowser and Patton 2004, 2008), to produce a multidimensional scaling (MDS) of women's alliance similarities. *Alliance strength* is a measure of the degree to which two women are likely to support each other during a conflict in the community, and *alliance similarity* is a measure of the degree to which two women share the same allies, based on women's judgments in a triadic similarity task used in network analyses. In effect, the MDS is a spatial representation of women's political networks in Conambo (figure 3.2). Each female head of household is represented by an icon, coded by her age category. Closeness between icons shows that women share similar alliances, and closeness to the center represents political centrality. Young women and older women tend to be peripheral. Many women in the middle-aged group tend to be central, though not all. These women define the political core of women's networks in the village. This MDS suggests a developmental cycle in which young women begin as politically peripheral members of the community, move toward the political core during middle age, then move back toward the

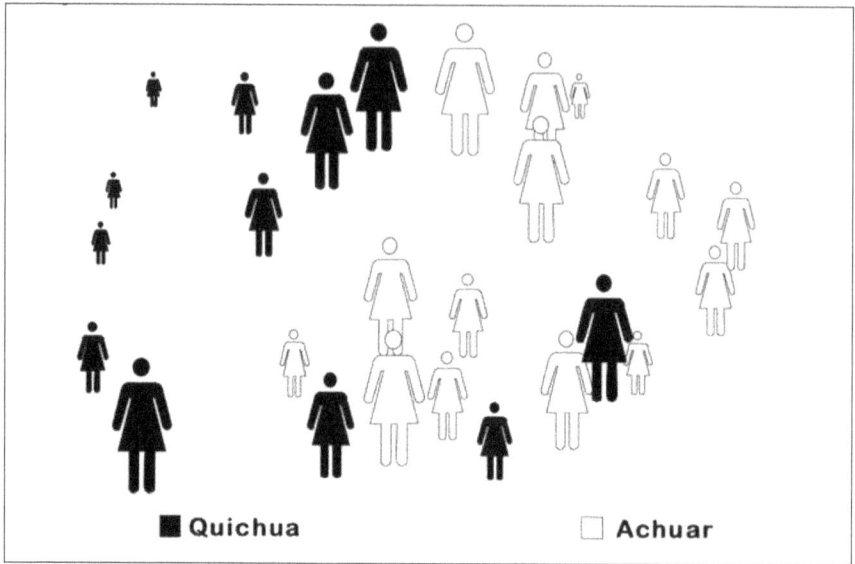

**FIGURE 3.3**

*The MDS from figure 3.2 is coded by women's political faction and status to show that positions of political centrality and status are intermediate between the Achuar and Quichua factions in Conambo (1992–1993). Larger icon size indicates higher status.*

peripheries as they become older and are displaced by middle-aged women.

Figure 3.3 is the same MDS, coded by each woman's factional membership, scaled proportionately according to her status, with larger icons representing higher status. It shows that positions of political centrality are intermediate between the Achuar and Quichua factions. Thus, in middle age, many women are not only politically central in the village but also political intermediaries between the two factions. These are positions of high out-group alliance similarity and low in-group alliance similarity.

Political brokers occupy positions of inherent tension and risk because women's stronger relationships across the political divide correspond with weaker relationships within their own factions. There is a highly significant negative correlation between a woman's in-group and out-group alliance similarities (r = –.704, p = .000, N = 27). However, these political broker roles are positions of high status. There is a significant positive correlation between a woman's status and her out-group alliance similarity when age is controlled as a variable (r = .461, p = .016, N = 27). In other words, a woman who develops extensive alliances across the political divide is likely to have higher status than expected for her age. Conversely, women with weaker out-group alliances tend to have lower status than expected for their age. Similarly, there is a highly significant negative correlation between a woman's status and her in-group alliance similarity when age is controlled as a variable (r = –.563, p = .002, N = 27). Thus, middle age is a time when women may enhance their status through their own agency by pursuing roles as political intermediaries.

## WOMEN'S LEADERSHIP AND ACCESS TO SOCIAL CAPITAL

In this section, we examine the social capital on which women's leadership is built. We identify the relationships of kinship, alliance, husband's status, years in residence, and household size that correlate with women's status. By analyzing women's alliances within their factions (in-group alliance similarity) versus women's alliances with members of the opposite faction (out-group alliance similarity) as separate variables, we evaluated whether different strategies of alliance building may contribute differently to the status of a woman. To examine how women may build a position of leadership that bridges the factional boundary, we analyzed out-group status (based on Quichua judgments of Achuar women's status and on Achuar judgments of Quichua women's status) and in-group status (based on Quichua judgments of Quichua women's status and on Achuar judgments of Achuar women's status) as independent variables. Because we were interested in why a woman may gain or lose status independently of her age, to consider women's agency, we controlled for age effects. The residual values from bivariate regression analyses of the relationship between status and age were used as measures of age-controlled status, which represent the degree to which a woman's status is higher or lower than expected for her age.

The results directly and indirectly support the hypothesis that women build positions of leadership as political brokers by building cross-coalitional alliances. Women who have strong alliances across the factional divide are judged by women of the opposite faction to have higher status, an index of greater leadership abilities, than other women of their age. Surprisingly, such women have few adult kin in Conambo (see bivariate analyses below), especially male kin in their own coalition. Possibly, women pursue this strategy in part to compensate for the lack of kin within their own coalitions. However, we suggest here that women with low kin relatedness are successful in building cross-coalitional alliances because they are viewed by the opposite faction as more impartial and fair, and therefore more trustworthy, than women with stronger kin ties and obligations.

A woman's leadership is judged within her coalition according to different criteria. A woman's in-group status is predicted mainly by her husband's status and to a lesser extent by her relationships of political alliance in the village. A woman's age-controlled in-group status (that is, whether her status is higher or lower than expected for a woman of her age from the perspective of other women in her faction) is predicted by her husband's in-group status, the size of her household, the strength of her alliances, and her husband's age-controlled status.

In the following subsections, we provide the results of the statistical analyses. We identify the relationships of kinship, alliance, and husband's status that correlate with women's status in bivariate analyses, and we model the relationships in a multivariate linear regression to eliminate the effects of colinearity.

### Women's Leadership and Kinship

Here we examine the influences of kinship on women's status in Conambo. Kinship is fundamental to tribal social structures. Matrilocality enhances the influence of kinship on women's social structures in Conambo in terms of boundaries, opportunities, and obstacles to the processes and strategies that influence women's access to social capital and positions of leadership.

We measured and analyzed women's kinship with other adults in the village in terms of kin relatedness. We measured kin relatedness using standard methods in behavioral ecology, as described in Bowser and Patton 2004. Closer consanguine kin were assigned higher kin relatedness values than more distant kin (parents, children, and full siblings = .5; half siblings, aunts, uncles, and grandparents = .25; full cousins, half aunts, and half uncles = .125; and half cousins = .0625). We measured and analyzed women's kin relatedness to all adults in the community, to male relatives, to female relatives, to members of their own coalitions, and to members of opposing coalitions. We examined status and age-corrected status in terms of all informant judgments (total), judgments of members of each woman's own coalition (in-group), and judgments of members of the opposing political faction (out-group). The bivariate analysis of the nine kin relatedness variables and six status variables is summarized in table 3.1. This analysis was repeated, with numbers of kin replacing measurements of kin relatedness, and is summarized in table 3.2. Influences of affinal kinship on women's status were measured and analyzed using the same sets of variables by replacing a woman's kin relatedness and number of kin with those of her husband.

Kinship has no significant influence on a woman's status within her coalition, but it does influence her status with out-group women. There are no significant relationships between any of the kinship and status variables

TABLE 3.1

*Women's Status and Kin Relatedness*

| | | Status | | | Age-Corrected Status | | |
| --- | --- | --- | --- | --- | --- | --- | --- |
| | | Total | In-Group | Out-Group | Total | In-Group | Out-Group |
| **Kin Relatedness** | Total | −.265 | −.044 | **−.461\*** | −.208 | .160 | **−.541\*\*** |
| | In-Group | −.288 | −.062 | **−.485\*** | −.225 | .151 | **−.560\*\*** |
| | Out-Group | .217 | .129 | .279 | −.165 | .015 | .267 |
| | Relatedness to Women | −.122 | .115 | −.353 | −.085 | .297 | **−.487\*\*** |
| | In-Group | −.122 | .115 | −.353 | −.085 | .297 | **−.497\*\*** |
| | Out-Group | NA | NA | NA | NA | NA | NA |
| | Relatedness to Men | **−.395\*** | −.241 | **−.504\*\*** | −.324 | −.052 | **−.499\*\*** |
| | In-Group | **−.439\*** | −.266 | **−.560\*\*** | −.356 | −.053 | **−.551\*\*** |
| | Out-Group | .217 | .129 | .279 | .165 | .411 | .267 |

\* p ≤ .05    \*\* p ≤ .01; N = 27

Correlations (Pearson's r) between women's status and kin relatedness.

in the judgments of in-group women. However, women with more in-group male kin are significantly under-ranked by out-group women (see tables 3.1 and 3.2). Women's total status is significantly and *negatively* associated with male kin relatedness within the community. This relationship is driven by the judgments of out-group women who ranked them lower in status as their kin relatedness with in-group men and the number of male kin increased. This relationship holds after age correcting women's status. There are no significant relationships between a women's status, average or age corrected, and her kinship with out-group men (measured as kin relatedness or number of kin). A woman's age-corrected status as judged by out-group women is significantly and *negatively* associated with kin relatedness with in-group women. None of the women in the sample had consanguine female kin in the out-group.

Affinal kinship has little influence on women's status in Conambo. Of the six variables of women's status, only one has a significant correlation with any of the eighteen variables of the husband's consanguine kinship in the community. Age-corrected in-group status is significantly associated with the husband's kin relatedness with out-group members (r = .394, p = .046, N = 26) such that women with closer in-laws (the husband's kin relatedness) have higher status as judged by in-group women.

This data pattern suggests that women with strong kin ties within their coalitions are less successful in acting as political brokers with out-group

TABLE 3.2

*Women's Status and Number of Kin*

|  |  | Status | | | Age-Corrected Status | | |
|---|---|---|---|---|---|---|---|
|  |  | Total | In-Group | Out-Group | Total | In-Group | Out-Group |
| **Number of Kin** | **Total** | −.200 | −.019 | **−.401*** | .032 | .345 | −.337 |
|  | In-Group | −.215 | .033 | **−.414*** | .006 | .322 | −.355 |
|  | Out-Group | .114 | .171 | .039 | .279 | .317 | .121 |
|  | **Female Kin** | −.131 | .078 | −.330 | .072 | .368 | −.294 |
|  | In-Group | −.131 | .078 | −.330 | .072 | .368 | −.294 |
|  | Out-Group | NA | NA | NA | NA | NA | NA |
|  | **Male Kin** | −.291 | −.073 | **−.479*** | −.032 | .284 | −.375 |
|  | In-Group | −.336 | −.118 | **−.517*** | −.102 | .224 | **−.427*** |
|  | Out-Group | .114 | .171 | .039 | .279 | .317 | .121 |

* $p \le .05$   ** $p \le .01$; N = 27

Correlations (Pearson's r) between women's status and number of kin.

members. Perhaps because their stronger kinship ties within their coalitions make it less likely that their political loyalty is negotiable and less likely that they will be impartial in community politics, out-group women are less likely to trust them. As a result, women with strong in-group kin ties are less successful in pursuing leadership strategies as political intermediaries.

### Women's Leadership and Political Alliances

We measured and analyzed twelve variables of political alliance: the woman's alliance strength (average, in-group, and out-group), her alliance similarity (average, in-group, and out-group), her husband's alliance strength (average, in-group, and out-group), and his alliance similarity (average, in-group, and out-group). These twelve alliance variables were compared with the six women's status variables (total, in-group, out-group, age-corrected total, age-corrected in-group, and age-corrected out-group) and are summarized in table 3.3.

A woman's *total status* is significantly correlated with the strength of her husband's alliances within the community. This relationship holds true for both in-group status and out-group status. None of the other alliance variables is significantly associated with total, in-group, or out-group status.

A woman's *age-corrected status* is significantly correlated with the overall strength of her alliances with other women in the community. This relationship is driven by her alliance strength with out-group women. In addi-

TABLE 3.3

*Women's Status and Alliance*

| | | Status | | | Age-Corrected Status | | |
| | | Total | In-Group | Out-Group | Total | In-Group | Out-Group |
|---|---|---|---|---|---|---|---|
| **Alliance** | **Strength** | .200 | .335 | .186 | **.498**\*\* | **.501**\*\* | .289 |
| | In-Group | .078 | .169 | −.027 | .045 | .189 | −.140 |
| | Out-Group | .176 | .151 | .179 | **.415**\* | .297 | **.381**\* |
| | | | | | | | |
| | Similarity | .052 | −.043 | .143 | −.042 | −.175 | .126 |
| | In-Group | −.286 | −.290 | −.245 | **−.563**\*\* | **−.469**\* | **−.439**\* |
| | Out-Group | .283 | .202 | .329 | **.461**\* | .258 | **.504**\*\* |
| | | | | | | | |
| | Husband's Strength | **.500**\* | **.523**\*\* | **.418**\* | .395 | **.440**\* | .219 |
| | In-Group | .303 | .311 | .260 | .066 | .111 | −.005 |
| | Out-Group | .392 | .345 | .396 | **.439**\* | .345 | .391 |
| | | | | | | | |
| | Husband's Similarity | .195 | .253 | .112 | **.416**\* | **.472**\* | .229 |
| | In-Group | −.200 | −.118 | −.265 | −.349 | −.183 | **−.405**\* |
| | Out-Group | .345 | .322 | .329 | **.666**\*\* | **.570**\*\* | **−.552**\*\* |

\* p ≤ .05    \*\* p ≤ .01; strength and similarity N = 27; husband's strength and similarity N = 24

Correlations (Pearson's r) between women's status and alliance.

tion, women with alliance patterns most similar to out-group women and least similar to women within their coalitions have higher age-corrected total status. Both in-group and out-group women assign greater status to women with lower in-group alliance similarities. The relationship between out-group similarity and age-collected status is driven by out-group women's judgments.

Correlations with the husband's alliances show a similar pattern. Women give higher total status to women whose husbands have greater alliance strength overall. Out-group women assign higher age-corrected status to women whose husbands have less alliance similarity to in-group men and less similarity to out-group men. Likewise, in-group women give higher status to women whose husbands have higher alliance similarity to out-group men.

The alliance data are consistent with the previous data sets supporting the argument that women gain positions of leadership by acting as political brokers. Age is a strong predictor of women's status in Conambo, but age is not a variable that women can control. The correlation between the alliance variables and age-corrected status indicates that women who

TABLE 3.4

*Women's Status and Husbands' Status*

| | | Status | | | Age-Corrected Status | | |
|---|---|---|---|---|---|---|---|
| | | Total | In-Group | Out-Group | Total | In-Group | Out-Group |
| **Husbands' Status** | Total | .872** | .872** | .776** | .555** | .606** | .299 |
| | In-Group | .600** | .716* | .404* | .444* | .670** | .046 |
| | Out-Group | .440* | .286 | .562** | .198 | −.028 | .361 |
| | Age-Corrected Total | .383 | .375 | .350 | .633** | .569** | .484** |
| | In-Group | .120 | .266 | −.056 | .403* | .604* | .056 |
| | Out-Group | .207 | .046 | .363 | .140 | −.131 | .374 |

$* p \leq .05$  $** p \leq .01$; N = 26
Correlations (Pearson's r) between women's status and husbands' status.

actively pursue strategies to recruit and maintain alliances across the political divide in Conambo achieve higher positions of leadership.

### Women's Leadership and Husbands' Status

Women's status and that of their husbands are highly correlated (table 3.4). The relationship between total status for wives and their husbands is highly significant, and this holds true after correcting for age effects. Women have significantly higher status relative to other women of the same age if they have higher-status husbands, and the opposite is marginally true (p = .053 for husbands' age-corrected status and wives' total status). Correcting for age for both wives and husbands (the lower right quadrangle in table 3.4) indicates that this relationship is primarily evident in the status judgments of in-group men and women.

These correlations do not indicate directionality of influence, and this relationship is likely to be bidirectional. In other words, a woman's status is likely to be influenced by her husband's status, and vice versa. One indication of the latter is that a woman's alliance similarity is associated with her husband's status. That is, a woman with a higher-status husband has greater alliance similarity with out-group women (r = .393, p = .047, N = 26) and lower similarity with in-group women (r = −.422, p = .032, N = 26). Thus, a man's status may benefit from his wife's role as a coalitional broker.

### Women's Leadership, Household Size, and Years of Residence in the Community

Household size is highly correlated with a woman's status in the community and her age-corrected status (table 3.5). This relationship is highly

TABLE 3.5

*Women's Status and Household Size*

| | Status | | | Age-Corrected Status | | |
|---|---|---|---|---|---|---|
| | Total | In-Group | Out-Group | Total | In-Group | Out-Group |
| Household Size | .622** | .605** | .569** | .643** | .599** | .480* |
| Age-Corrected Household Size | .368 | .362 | .333 | .670** | .603** | .525** |

* p ≤ .05   ** p ≥ .01; N = 24

Correlations (Pearson's r) between women's status and household size.

significant for both in-group and out-group status judgments. The relationship between age-corrected (women's age) household size and age-corrected status is also highly significant (total, in-group, and out-group) such that a woman with more children than expected for her age has greater status than expected for her age. The number of years a woman has been in residence in the community is not predictive of her status, but her husband's time in residence is highly significant (r = .511, p = .008, N = 26). This relationship holds for both in-group (r = .557, p = .003, N = 26) and out-group judgments (r = .404, p = .041, N = 26). Age-corrected status is significant for in-group judgments (r = 449, p = .021, N = 26) but not for out-group or total status.

### Multivariate Analyses of Women's Leadership and Access to Social Capital

Using all the significant social variables in the bivariate analyses yields a highly significant and predictive model of women's age-corrected status. In a multivariate stepwise regression with *women's age-controlled total status* as the dependent variable, age-corrected household size, the husband's out-group alliance similarity, and his total status (in order of contribution) made significant contributions to the model, accounting for 72.8 percent (R square) of the variation in women's age-corrected status (R = .853, p = .000). The other variables made insignificant contributions and were removed from the model. The three significant social capital variables in the model are influenced by women's actions. Age-corrected household size is a measure of a woman's reproductive success, which correlates with high significance to a woman's age-corrected status (see below) and is likely a reflection of her economic productivity (discussed in the next section). A woman's husband's out-group alliance similarity is significantly correlated to the strength of her alliances within the community ($r = .428$, $p = .037$, $N = 24$), and her husband's total status is predicted positively by her out-group alliance similarity ($r = .393$, $p = .047$, $N = 26$) and negatively by her in-group alliance similarity ($r = -.422$, $p = .032$, $N = 26$), another indicator of how women's roles as coalitional brokers influence their political standing within the community.

*Women's age-corrected in-group status* is predicted with high confidence by four social capital variables: husbands' in-group status, age-corrected household size, women's alliance strength, and husbands' age-corrected status. The model accounts for 76.6 percent (R square) of the variation in women's age-corrected in-group status ($R = .875$, $p = .000$). *Women's age-corrected out-group status* is predicted by women's out-group similarity, men's out-group similarity, and men's age-corrected out-group status (in order of contribution to the model; $R = .636$, $p = .000$). This model accounts for 63.6 percent (R square) of women's age-corrected out-group status. As with total status, the social capital variables that predict in-group and out-group women's status in the multivariate regressions are influenced by women's political actions. Positions of status are subject to strategic manipulation; specifically, these data support the argument that women who cultivate and maintain cross-coalitional alliances are more successful at securing positions of leadership in Conambo.

## ECONOMIC CORRELATES OF WOMEN'S LEADERSHIP

Here we consider the economic benefits of women who are viewed as important leaders in the community. We find that a woman's age-controlled status correlates significantly with the number of collective labor hours performed for the benefit of her household and that a woman's average status correlates significantly with the richness of her manioc gardens, which serves to reduce the risk of crop failure.

### Access to Collective Labor and Status

One of the measurable correlates of women's leadership is access to collective labor. Families accomplish large-scale, labor-intensive tasks, such as building houses, clearing land for new gardens, maintaining trails, and hauling large canoes from the forest (after completing the initial stages of production there), by inviting others to participate in festive work parties, or *mingas*. Both husband and wife invite guests, who are men and women from other households in the community. To calculate household access to collective labor, we attended forty-seven mingas held by fourteen households over a ten-month period. We recorded the number of guests, the work activities performed, and the number of labor hours worked, which ranged from 7 to 240 labor hours in one day. The greatest number of mingas were organized to accomplish work in women's gardens; the greatest number of labor hours were dedicated to men's canoe manufacture, especially canoe hauling, because canoe hauling requires more people and longer periods of work. For this analysis, a household's ability to mobilize collective labor is operationalized as the greatest number of labor hours recorded at a minga hosted by the household.

The importance of both women's and men's status in labor mobilization is evident, though women's status is more important than their husbands' status in predicting access to collective labor hours. A household's access to collective labor is predicted primarily by a woman's age-controlled status, which explains 41.2 percent of variation, and her husband's status, which explains an additional 18.6 percent, in the multivariate stepwise regression model (R square = .598, model significance = .000, N = 14). The model excludes the five other variables that correlated significantly with labor hours in the bivariate analyses: women's status, women's out-group status, husbands' out-group alliance similarity, husbands' age-controlled status, and women's age-controlled in-group status. None of the other kinship and political variables was associated significantly with access to collective labor in the bivariate analyses.

### Garden Richness and Status

A second measurable benefit of women's status is garden richness. Garden richness is a buffer against crop failure due to pests and diseases that plague specific varieties and may be encountered unpredictably in differing microenvironmental conditions. According to women in Conambo, richness reduces the risks of establishing new gardens following residential moves, a frequently employed conflict management strategy, or when a woman transfers varieties from an old garden to a new garden nearby. Additionally, women prefer different varieties for different reasons, such as yield, reliability, flavor, suitability for beer making versus cooking for meals, and storability in the ground before harvest.

Richness was measured as the number of folk varieties of manioc that a woman identified as present in her garden. During household surveys, we interviewed women twice, first to compile a list of named folk varieties cultivated by each woman and second to systematically ask each woman whether she cultivated any of the folk varieties named by other women but not named during her first interview. We obtained the names of folk varieties in both Achuar and Quichua, through separate interviews with multiple informants, to document exchanges of propagative stems across the factional divide between women speaking different languages. Such exchanges always involved changing the name of the folk variety and usually involved a literal translation, although sometimes an entirely new name was given. The number of folk varieties of manioc recorded in women's gardens in Conambo is comparable to those in studies among other closely related Amazonian groups (Boster 1984).

Women build garden richness by obtaining propagules of new varieties of manioc from other women, including their political allies. Women's political similarity to other women correlates significantly with the similarity of manioc varieties in their gardens, although the significance is marginal and the predictive value is extremely low (R square = .018, p = .054).

Garden richness is predicted by women's average status, which explains 44.7 percent of variation in a multivariate stepwise regression model (p = .001, N = 20). Because propagule sharing occurs among women, we analyzed the association of garden richness with household size and women's kinship and political variables, but not husbands' kinship and political variables. The model excludes nine other variables that correlated significantly with garden richness in bivariate analyses: household size, women's in-group status, women's out-group status, women's average political similarity, women's in-group political similarity, women's out-group political similarity, women's age-controlled status, women's age-controlled in-group status, and women's age-controlled out-group status. None of the other kinship and political variables is significantly associated with garden richness in the bivariate analyses.

## REPRODUCTIVE CORRELATES OF WOMEN'S LEADERSHIP

A third measurable benefit associated with higher status among women is reproductive success. Women with higher status have significantly more living children than lower-status women of the same age (r = .708, p = .000, N = 26). This relationship is stronger (more predictive and with a higher level of significance) than the relationship between husbands' status and the number of children they fathered (r = .489, p = .021, N = 22). This relationship between women's status and reproductive success indicates that the benefits women derive from high status, including access to collective labor and garden resources, are consequential and directed toward their children.

## STABILITY AND HERITABILITY OF WOMEN'S LEADERSHIP IN CONAMBO

Finally, we examine the stability and heritability of women's leadership in Conambo before addressing how understanding women's positions as political brokers between two factions may contribute to our understanding of how positions of leadership become institutionalized over time.

First, we consider how well a woman's age-corrected status in 1993 predicted her age-corrected status in 2006. That is, did women with high status compared with other women of their age in 1993 maintain this position in the long-term, suggesting that their strategies contribute to long-term maintenance of positions of leadership? The answer is yes. Concomitantly, women with low status compared with other women of their age in 1993 tended to have lower status in 2006 as well. There is a significant correlation between a woman's age-corrected status in 1993 and her age-corrected status in 2006 ($r = .768$, $p = .001$, N = 15).

However, we found no evidence that women's leadership positions are heritable by their daughters in this context. Women's age-corrected status scores in 1993 do not correlate significantly with their daughters' age-corrected status in 1993 or 2006 ($r = 263$, $p = .364$, N = 14).

## DISCUSSION AND CONCLUSIONS

Anthropologists have known for some time that women's access to positions of political leadership cannot be predicted directly from measures of sociopolitical complexity (Whyte 1979) or women's contribution to subsistence (Sanday 1972). Cross-cultural variation in women's political leadership cannot be predicted successfully using the same models that explain cross-cultural variation in men's political leadership (Ross 1983), and it is not well understood why this is so (Low 1992; Yanca and Low 2004). However, women's political leadership can be best understood cross-culturally as one of three interrelated dimensions of women's political activity, including "participation in community decision making in whatever public arenas exist in society," "participation in private arenas, irrespective of women's public role," and "access to political or quasipolitical positions of authority" (Ross 1986:846). This finding is consistent with long-standing arguments by feminist archaeologists and other anthropologists that a focus on the acquisition of formal positions of political power alone fails to recognize the importance of women's influence in other political activities, such as consensus building and conflict mediation, as well as the power they exert in domains not considered by anthropologists to be political, such as religious divination, which in reality has tremendous political implications because of the power to compel punishment by expulsion, murder, or execution (for example, Conkey and Spector 1984; Martin and Voorhies 1975; Nelson 2004; Strathern 1972; see also Bird and Bliege Bird, chapter 2, this volume; Wiessner, chapter 9, this volume). In a 1986 cross-cultural study, Ross found that women's political participation is found in societies in which political decision making is widely shared and occurs in private, not just public, places, a situation we have documented in Conambo, where the domestic context is a place where informal and formal political processes are carried out (Bowser 2000, 2002; Bowser and Patton 2004, 2008). Concomitantly, we identified a number of ethnoarchaeological indices of women's participation in political decision-making processes in people's houses in Conambo: the ubiquity of visiting areas that are large enough to accommodate public discourse; the ubiquity of large-scale painted designs on pottery vessels that are visible at public viewing distances; and the organization of domestic space, including the accessibility of "private" domestic spaces from exterior spaces and the permeability of boundaries between gendered spaces. In Conambo, these permeable boundaries enable women and men to participate jointly in political discussions and provide women access to men's political discussions while maintaining a division between the "public" visiting area where men sit and the more "private" kitchen area where visiting women sit (Bowser and Patton 2004).

Low (1992) proposes that women's leadership and formation of political coalitions should be found where women's political participation can serve to facilitate their control over economic resources, enhancing their reproductive success. In Conambo, this appears to be true. Women who exhibit stronger leadership qualities than other women in their cohort have more access to cooperative labor, richer gardens, and higher reproductive success. Yanca and Low (2004) further propose that women's leadership may be explained by women's kin relationships—particularly, strong female kin ties—as well as the presence of some male kin, based on a cross-cultural correlation between women's political leadership positions and sororal polygyny. The Conambo data suggest that this might not be true.

Women employ two strategies of alliance building, and these strategies contribute to women's positions of leadership, access to economic resources, and reproductive success. One strategy involves maintaining strong relationships of alliance within one's own coalition rather than across factional boundaries. This strategy contributes to strong in-group leadership, which is predicted mainly by husbands' status and less by women's relationships of political alliance in the village.

The other strategy involves developing strong cross-coalitional alliances, working to build political consensus and mediate conflict in a village divided into two ethnic factions. Women who have strong alliances across the factional divide are judged by women of the opposite faction to have higher status, an index of greater leadership abilities, than other women of their age. However, such women have few adult kin in the village, especially male kin in their own coalition. Indeed, women's male kinship contributes negatively to women's out-group status. Here we suggest that women with low kin relatedness are successful in building cross-coalitional alliances because they are viewed by the opposite faction as more impartial and therefore more trustworthy than women with stronger kin ties and obligations.

Possibly, women pursue cross-coalitional strategies of alliance building to compensate for their lack of male kin, who are potential allies within their own coalitions. However, this seems unlikely, given that male kinship does not correlate positively with any measure of women's status in Conambo in the multivariate models. Likewise, women's female kinship does not contribute significantly to women's status in the multivariate models, despite a strong matrilocal pattern of postmarital residence. Women's female kinship does predict meat transfers between households (Patton 2005), an economic benefit that may contribute to reproductive success.

Might women's strategies of building cross-coalitional alliances be processes through which leaders emerge in societies in which they previously did not exist? Might these positions of leadership change and become institutionalized over time? The data suggest that this is not the case. Women's pursuit of cross-coalitional alliances in Conambo is related to women's life histories. It appears to peak in middle age and wane as women reach the end of their reproductive years. To date, the evidence suggests that these positions are not heritable by a woman's daughters. Rather, this case suggests another reason for the inherent instability of leadership positions within segmentary societies.

# 4

## Privatization of Resources and the Evolution of Prehistoric Leadership Strategies

**Jelmer W. Eerkens**

Over the past century, the Owens Valley of eastern California and its historic and prehistoric inhabitants have been the subject of many anthropological and archaeological studies. A majority of these studies have focused on the "unusualness" of the Paiute people (for example, Bettinger and King 1971; Dyson-Hudson and Smith 1978) as described by Julian Steward in the 1930s (for example, Steward 1930, 1933, 1934, 1936, 1938). The Paiute were considered "unusual" hunter-gatherers for three reasons. First, although classified as Great Basin hunter-gatherers, they dug irrigation ditches and tended plants. Second, although they were considered to be politically and socially "simple," they had headmen and other inherited leadership positions. Third, families, villages, and districts owned and defended tracts of land. Indeed, the Owens Valley Paiute did not share these behaviors with other linguistically related Paiute and Shoshone people in the Great Basin—people often noted for their extreme social and technological "simplicity" (Thomas 1981).

Steward and many subsequent Great Basin anthropologists accounted for (or, more accurately, tried to explain away), these unusual practices as a product of environmental factors. Owens Valley was noted for its abundance of water (a fact not lost upon the city of Los Angeles, which constructed an aqueduct in the early 1900s to carry Owens Valley water to the growing city, putting farmers out of business and drying Owens Lake). Plentiful water and the higher resulting biomass in Owens Valley, it was argued, allowed inhabitants of this valley, unlike Paiute and Shoshone people in most of the Great Basin, to invest energy and time in other activities, beyond merely eking out a living from the harsh desert.

However, over the past thirty years, many anthropologists and archaeologists working in the region have come to embrace this unusualness rather than try to explain it away. In many social evolutionary models, the Owens Valley Paiute are represented as a society in transition, from foraging to agriculture, from politically simple to socially complex. Consequently, the archaeological record has received much attention as a means to study the very beginnings of these processes. This chapter continues in that vein, though it shies away from the notion of unilinear evolutionary models and "transitional" societies—that is, that groups of people not readily classifiable into one of several traditionally defined categories (for example, hunter-gatherer, pastoral, and agricultural) must be in transition between those endpoints (for similar critiques, see also Arnold, chapter 6, this volume). It follows on work by Bettinger (1982, 1983) and focuses on the development of small-scale leaders within Owens Valley Paiute society. The chapter begins with an examination of leaders and leadership as described by Julian Steward ethnographically. Subsequently, it turns to archaeological data from households to help illuminate aspects of economic inequality within villages, which are argued by extension to relate to the development of leadership.

## THEORETICAL BACKGROUND

The focus on "leaders" and "leadership" in this chapter and others in this volume is similar in many respects to that of earlier studies on the development of "social complexity" or "social hierarchies." The broader questions within these approaches are identical—namely, understanding how certain individuals come to gain unequal access to resources and, similarly, why or how others give up such access. The main difference is the social scale at which these questions are asked, namely, individuals versus more general societal developments. Importantly, this finer social scale necessitates an alternative methodological approach in data collection, focusing of course on individuals and their actions.

The difference in focus is likely the product of changes in archaeological theory, including both evolutionary theory and agency theory, which are increasingly interested in the behaviors of individuals to explain the archaeological record. Such changes in focus of course require attendant changes in the types of data we collect, particularly in this case the scale at which we collect them. Research on "households" in archaeology (for example, Ashmore and Wilk 1988; Flannery and Winter 1976) brings data collection down to a level commensurate with these theoretical models, as does bioarchaeological research on individual burials. The study below draws on these two sources.

In this chapter, the word *leader* refers to individuals with the power to make decisions on behalf of others and more specifically to those with decision-making power beyond the nuclear family. Within-family leaders (for example, adults versus children) have probably always existed in human societies, so it is really the extension of this power outside the family that is of concern. Certain individuals often use decision-making powers to gain unequal access to various kinds of resources (for example, information, material goods, religious practices, and political connections). Such goods can be used to further a leader's own agenda, especially increasing personal wealth and political influence, for example, by giving these goods away to create social and economic debt, often to be repaid with interest (for example, Earle 1978; Fried 1967; Harris 1985:235; Upham 1990). Thus, leaders are involved in frequent interactions with others in the local community and are usually also active in extralocal trade to gain access to more exotic materials.

The basic premise of this chapter is that leaders cannot evolve without major adjustments to the egalitarian social order. Leveraging religious systems to provide unequal access to decision-making power is one means by which this change can be accomplished (Bird and Bliege Bird, chapter 2, this volume). Another is to alter the rules that dictate public sharing and communal ownership over various economic resources, leading toward increasing levels of privatization (note that religion and ideology can be used to accomplish this also). Rules favoring egalitarian access to economic resources and public goods are present in some form in many small-scale societies and are often reinforced by a range of social-leveling mechanisms (Bird and Bliege Bird, chapter 2; Bowser and Patton, chapter 3; and Wiessner, chapter 9, this volume).

Without exclusive and restricted ownership of resources and the ability to control their distribution, it is difficult for aspiring leaders to leverage their greater production or differential access into anything unusual. Under such circumstances, there is little incentive to produce a surplus because it is readily consumed by others without requiring reciprocal repayment or accrual of social debt (Bettinger 1999; Shennan 2002). I refer to this process as freeloading. It is also difficult to gain access to exotic goods that aspiring leaders might use to mark their social position within societies, because the exclusive display of such goods is generally taboo and others might repossess them. As a result, economic units within such settings, usually households, tend to be redundant. Because goods are freely shared, all households tend to produce and have equal access to the same range of materials.

Privatization of resources, that is, restricting access or control over distribution to a small subset of individuals—in the extreme, a single person, is one solution to this issue. However, it would have been difficult for a family or an individual simply to begin asserting that some subset of resources previously considered to be public was now private. It is unlikely that individuals could have changed the rules on their own in this manner. Free-loaders in particular stand to lose the most under such rule changes and may be the most vocal about or resistant to potential change.

Instead, I argue that a common way to produce an owned surplus is to invest time and energy in a different kind of resource, one for which the rules about ownership have not yet been well defined (Eerkens 2004). Typically, the ability to access, process, and move such resources should be within the power of individuals or small groups of people and should not require communal or cooperative behaviors. Eventually, it might be possible to shift other resources, previously understood to be public, under the domain of private ownership. However, it seems likely that such shifting would have to happen slowly, over the course of generations, as the notion of privatized goods becomes established, commonplace, and easily translatable to other domains.

Furthermore, within this chapter, I argue that increases in population density and sedentism create social conditions that favor the erosion of public goods systems. Demographic conditions that force unrelated individuals to live close to one another in sedentary villages encourage free-loading behavior. For those wanting to overproduce, for example, to engage in long-distance exchange, the exploitation of new resources that can be individually controlled and privatized may be an efficient social solution. The technologies employed to exploit such resources are likely to include artifacts that can be produced at the individual or family level and do not require cross-family cooperation to operate. Although it is difficult to see the actual breakdown of this social order, the by-product of private ownership and unequal access to resources should be reflected in the archaeological record by decreasing redundancy between economic units or households in small-scale settings and new types of technologies that can be individually produced and used.

## LEADERS AND THE ETHNOGRAPHIC RECORD IN
## OWENS VALLEY

Julian Steward carried out the majority of his fieldwork in the Owens Valley during the late 1920s and 1930s. Although the Paiute had long been settled by the US government into small reservations and *rancherías* (small properties for homeless or landless Native peoples), Steward felt that he could collect accurate information on precontact lifeways from older informants. The use of such "memory ethnography" can be questioned on many grounds, and there are obvious examples of misinformation, such as informants reporting painting pots in black-on-white styles when not a single prehistoric example of local pottery is known to be painted in any color. Yet, lacking alternative primary sources of ethnographic data (though see Chalfant 1933 for additional information collected from local newspapers), Steward provides a historic anchor point for understanding the development of leadership.

As discussed earlier, the Owens Valley case has been interesting to anthropologists because all Great Basin peoples spoke one of three closely related Numic languages. Indeed, it is now generally accepted that a recent (within the last thousand years) migration of hunter-gatherer peoples out of the Southwest, near Owens Valley, accounts for the linguistic patterns in the Great Basin (Bettinger and Baumhoff 1982; Kaestle and Smith 1992). This migration is commonly referred to as the Numic spread. The implicit assumption of anthropological discussions referring to the unusualness of the Owens Valley case, then, was that this migration must have consisted of simple hunter-gatherers lacking marked positions of leadership. These groups remained simple elsewhere but evolved into more complex organizational forms in the Owens Valley region. The major question therefore was, what caused such unusual social organizations to develop in Owens Valley but not elsewhere in the Great Basin? Steward (1938) attributed these developments to the more favorable environments and subsistence opportunities in Owens Valley, particularly the increased availability of water and higher bioproductivity. Others have offered alternative viewpoints, such as access to resources and trading networks (for example, Bettinger 1982, 1983).

It is possible of course that the reverse could have happened—that complex hunter-gatherers spread across the Great Basin but evolved simpler social organizations as they encountered newer environments. Such a logic is inconsistent with social evolutionary models popular during the 1950s and 1960s that had human societies consistently evolving toward more complex forms over time (for example, Fried 1967; Service 1962,

1975). Such a scenario has not often been considered in Great Basin studies, nor will I discuss it further here, but it is related to an important assumption that underlies this chapter. Namely, I assume that the earliest societies in Owens Valley generally lacked marked positions of leadership and that leaders evolved only later in the course of prehistory. There is some indirect archaeological evidence to support this position, but much of it relies on analogies to other ethnographic cases.

At contact, Owens Valley Paiute groups maintained several social and political positions vested with important decision-making power. The most notable was the village headman. Headmen were "intelligent, persuasive leaders, though not always skilled hunters, fighters, etc.," who tended to inherit their positions through paternal relations (Steward 1933:304). Headmen would organize and control various activities, such as communal hunting or fishing activities (for example, rabbit drives) and war parties; make decisions about village social and political issues (for example, approving or vetoing witch killings); and set the date of, organize, and take charge of community fandangos (Steward 1933, 1938). Such fandangos, held in the fall, were several-days-long festivals during which individuals from neighboring villages were invited to dance, feast, gamble, and trade. Quantities of food were provided for guests, and a large brush enclosure approximately 100 meters in diameter was constructed for dancing. Headmen also oversaw the construction and maintenance of the village assembly house (typically 7 to 8 meters in diameter), though these structures were never used for serious rituals or ceremonies. Thus, the majority of headman decision making involved the gathering and synthesizing of information related to more public and communal activities.

Unfortunately, Steward did not specifically state the role of such headmen in exchange relations. Trading was clearly an important activity, and large quantities of goods were traded all around eastern California and over the Sierra Nevada into central California. Items typically traded included foods (acorns, pine nuts, seeds, and so on), salt, obsidian, beads, baskets, blankets, and tobacco. Bettinger and King (1971) suggest that headmen controlled all trading activities and that their political offices were supported by such a redistribution network.

Village headmen also had the power to appoint individuals to other positions of leadership. Such positions included, most notably, irrigator. This person would oversee construction and maintenance of irrigation ditches, including construction of the large diversion dam that required organizing about twenty-five men (Steward 1933:247). Parallel rows of smaller canals were constructed and maintained to bring water to small plots of land where bulbs and seeds of native plants were sown and harvested. As well, this person would make decisions about how water was distributed to various plots. This activity has not been the subject of much archaeological research but has led some anthropologists to suggest that the Owens Valley Paiute should not be classified as hunter-gatherers but as agriculturalists instead (Lawton et al. 1976). Classificatory monikers aside, this activity serves as another example of the unusualness of Owens Valley groups. With the possible exception of Fish Lake Valley, the next valley to the east, irrigation was otherwise unknown in the Great Basin.

Shamans also held considerable status and decision-making power in Owens Valley Paiute society and were always distinct from headmen (that is, an individual could never assume the duties of both headman and shaman). Shamans could be of either sex, were primarily healers and doctors, and helped organized some ritual events. Though shamans could also use their powers to do harm to others and were sometimes feared, village headmen had the power to organize killings of shamans who had overstepped their authority. Shamans were generally paid for their services. As an indication of how much respect people had for the healing powers of shamans, informants told Steward that many commonly available herbs were thought to be of little effectiveness unless administered or first touched by a shaman. Clearly, shamans had something of a monopoly over healing, a service performed for individuals rather than a communal activity. Some of Steward's informants suggested that shamanistic powers, hence shaman positions, were inherited patrilineally. However, it is clear that in some cases, shamans attained their positions through experience, usually dreams or visions that instructed them to claim such a position.

One other position vested with decision-making power was the owner of a rabbit net. Male elders owned and controlled the use of such nets, which were generally around 1 meter high by 20 meters long and required considerable investment of labor to construct. Steward (1933:253) noted that the plants required for the cordage did not grow in Owens Valley and had to be obtained from Shoshone territories to the south. The owners of such nets would organize and orchestrate communal rabbit drives in which large numbers of rabbits would be caught.

In sum, ethnographic leaders in Owens Valley held important decision-making power, particularly in the realms of economics, warfare, technology, and feasting. Outside of the special position of shaman, such powers did not apparently translate into religious or ritual activities. Thus, the separation of decision-making power with regard to economic versus religious realms or, alternatively, material goods and public services in the

case of headmen and irrigators versus immaterial goods (secretive information) and individual services in the case of shamans is clear (for com-
parison and contrast, see chapters 6, 8, and 11 by Arnold, Pauketat, and
Kantner, respectively, this volume). Leadership was often inherited patrilineally but not always, and it could be denied by the broader community
to individuals who were not considered "intelligent" or "persuasive." Thus,
the decision-making power held by leaders was often to the benefit of the
entire group, for example, in organizing large-scale activities from which
everyone gained through the communal rather than individual focus. At
the same time, leaders likely gained differential access to high-level information, prestige, and perhaps certain material resources as well.

## LEADERS IN PREHISTORIC OWENS VALLEY

Having described some of the leadership positions that Steward presented for the ethnographic Owens Valley Paiute, I now turn to the archaeological record. What evidence is there to support the presence of these
positions prehistorically, and what can we say about their development?

After examining the distribution of obsidian artifacts in central Owens
Valley, Bettinger (1983) felt that the archaeological record supported the
existence of suprafamily control over such resources and by extension suggested the presence of prehistoric leaders. It was unclear to him when
exactly such leaders developed, but he felt that they had some antiquity in
the region. He argued further that environmental explanations were
unlikely to account for such developments. Instead, he suggested that
unequal access to exchange networks was a promising avenue to explore as
a means to explain the development of leaders in prehistory (Bettinger
1983:55). Unfortunately, the nature of the data he collected (surface survey) did not allow him to address this issue at the scale of the individual.
Bettinger focused instead on higher-level band- or village-level societal
developments.

Following a brief description of the culture history of the region, the
remainder of this study follows on Bettinger's work. But rather than
regional-scale data, it turns on the analysis of burials and households in an
effort to understand the effects and behaviors of individuals.

### Owens Valley Culture History

The culture historical sequence in Owens Valley has been established
through survey and excavation (for example, Bettinger 1975; Bettinger
and Taylor 1974). Although important details remain to be worked out,
such as the establishment of leaders, the basic sequence has been repeat-

edly tested through excavation and has held up well. For this chapter, the most recent two thousand years of prehistory are of concern. Three widely recognized culture historical units fall within this time frame. Locally, these are referred as the Late Newberry (circa AD 1 to 500), Haiwee (circa AD 500 to 1400), and Marana (circa AD 1400 to contact).

Late Newberry patterns seem to be marked by residentially mobile populations (Eerkens, Spurling, and Gras 2008) moving in a north–south annual round that included the establishment of a number of base camps from which various logistical activities took place. It has been argued that a focus on large game hunting using atlatls, mainly for prestige-seeking males, characterized this period (Hildebrandt and McGuire 2002; McGuire and Hildebrandt 2005). According to Hildebrandt and McGuire, this prestige appears to have been parlayed primarily into differential access to mates rather than into decision-making power. Intensified hunting for large game, argued to be a low-caloric-return activity, was likely underwritten by women's increased devotion of time and labor to gathering activities. An increase in the number of groundstone tools around this time supports this notion. There is also ample evidence that obsidian production, primarily for producing bifaces, peaked at all the major obsidian quarries. Whether such production was for exchange or to support increased hunting activities is not definitely known, but the latter seems likely.

Haiwee (AD 500 to 1400) patterns represent a dramatically reduced settlement system, seemingly representing semi- to complete sedentism (Basgall 1989; Eerkens 2003b). The introduction of new technologies, such as the bow and arrow (Yohe 1998) and more casual flake cutting tools (versus bifaces), marks this period, though diets continue to be diverse, including large game, small game, piñon nuts, and some seeds.

The Marana period (AD 1400 to contact) is marked by continuing semi-sedentism and the introduction of new material technologies. A new type of projectile point is introduced, as are cooking pots, which were used to boil the increasing amounts of small seeds that were harvested (Eerkens 2004). There is also a marked increase in the density of groundstone and a focus on the harvesting of "green" piñon nuts—that is, cones that are not yet naturally ripened (Eerkens, King, and Wohlgemuth 2004). All of this indicates a heavy reliance on gathered resources and presumably very heavy demands on the time and labor of women. With the exception of some mass-captured animals, such as rabbits, hunting does not appear to have been particularly important, as seen in relatively low numbers of faunal remains. Indeed, the density of flaked stone chipping waste is generally quite low in domestic sites dating to this period.

**TABLE 4.1**

*Mortuary Data from Owens Valley*

| | Total | % with Beads | Average Beads | % with Points | Average Points | Other |
|---|---|---|---|---|---|---|
| Marana | 3 | 0% | 0 | 33% | 0.3 | |
| Haiwee | 7 | 17% | 0.5 | 83% | 3.7 | Milling stones, pipes |
| Newberry | 3 | 33% | 333 | 33% | 0.3 | |
| Pre-Newberry | 4 | 33% | 0.7 | 33% | 0.7 | Milling stones |

Note: Percentages and averages calculated only for those burials where information was available.

### Mortuary Data

As mentioned in the opening paragraphs, a major challenge in reconstructing and understanding prehistoric leadership strategies to find an archaeological signature that is consonant with the scale of leaders, namely, the individual. Worldwide, analysis of burials has been a common means to achieve this end. In Owens Valley, not only are burials rare, but also those that have been exposed during the course of archaeological work have been only minimally studied. A tabulation of all known burials in 2000 (Gilreath and Holanda 2000) listed only nineteen in the Owens and adjacent Rose valleys, spanning between 7000 BC and protohistoric times. Of these, seventeen could be assigned to one of the culture historical units discussed above. Table 4.1 summarizes the mortuary data.

Of the seventeen burials, twelve could be estimated for ontogenetic age, with ten estimated to be adults, one a child, and one an infant. There is very little information to indicate unequal wealth distribution in any of the time periods. With the exception of a single Newberry child buried with approximately one thousand marine-shell beads, most burials were associated with either no or a small number of grave goods. Excepting this one child, which may have received special treatment because of its age (rather than status), one is tempted to draw the conclusion that individuals were treated equally following death in all time periods. Equal burial treatment is particularly evident in the Haiwee period, which also has the largest sample size. Save one individual, all were buried with multiple projectile points.

Unfortunately, the small sample size of burials makes it difficult to say much more at this time. Indeed, a single rich adult burial in any of the periods could greatly alter our notions about the relative distribution of wealth.

## Household Data

Households provide a second avenue to examine patterns at a detailed social scale. Although it is difficult to tease out the behaviors of individual persons from domiciles, houses reflect the behaviors of individual economic units, likely akin to extended families (for example, Ashmore and Wilk 1988; Flannery and Winter 1976). Such a scale is more likely to highlight the behaviors of potential or aspiring leaders than analyses of entire sites or regions, precisely because small-scale leaders frequently draw upon the labor of kin to achieve certain political and economic ends (for example, Arnold 1993, 1995a, 2001c, chapter 6, this volume).

Unfortunately, sites and regions have generally been the focus of excavations and research in Owens Valley, largely because of the dominance of cultural resource management (CRM) archaeology. I do not intend to imply a failing or shortcoming on the part of CRM archaeology, only that the focus of CRM is somewhat different from that required for the approach followed here. CRM archaeology frequently turns on mitigating impact or disturbance to "sites" and generally focuses on that scale of analysis. Almost by definition, then, CRM archaeology is unlikely to focus on individual- or family-level data often required in neo-evolutionary and agency studies.

The number of excavated houses in Owens Valley is still relatively low because of the depth at which most are buried (0.5 to 2.0 meters) and the time it takes to properly excavate, analyze, and report such remains (for example, Basgall and McGuire 1988; Bettinger 1989). However, the sample available is worthy of a preliminary analysis into differential access to resources. To examine diachronic change in household access to material goods, I examine the distribution of goods in domiciles from three domestic sites from southern Owens Valley: CA-INY-30, CA-INY-3806, and CA-INY-3812 (see Eerkens and Spurling 2008). These sites are within 20 kilometers of one another near the shores of what, before water diversions by the city of Los Angeles, was Owens Lake. The former two sites have seen intensive excavation, and both contain multiple house floors and other domestic features (for example, hearths and pits), the basis of the comparisons. CA-INY-3812 was excavated briefly in the early 1990s, when a single large structure was found. In total, fourteen houses were excavated between these three sites.

In most cases, a single 1- to 2-meter-wide trench was dug across a house. Floor zones generally consist of a saucer-shaped, 5- to 10-centimeter-thick zone of compacted sediments with large amounts of charcoal and other organic debris. This and other evidence suggest that these archaeological features represent the remains of small- (2 to 3 meters in diameter) to medium-sized (5 to 6 meters in diameter) circular huts, with cane or wooden posts supporting a brush superstructure.

For this study, only artifacts found directly on or within 20 centimeters above a floor (thus within the house fill) were included. Because houses appear to have been occupied over multiple seasons and years and were likely cleaned of large debris at regular intervals, the majority of artifacts included in this analysis consist of smaller items, such as beads and pressure flakes, though larger groundstone, flaked stone, worked bone, and other artifacts are also found. These items represent artifacts missed during cleaning events and those remaining in the house after the final occupants left, never to return and reuse them.

All houses in the study have internally consistent age determinations placing them within the period of interest. As well, all are single component, dating to only one chronological period (Marana, Haiwee, or Newberry), and represent primary archaeological deposits. Additional structures from these and other sites in the region could have been included in the analysis but were eliminated because they have artifacts or age determinations consistent with multiple chronological periods (for example, both Marana and Haiwee).

I examined interhousehold differences between two types of nonlocal materials, obsidian and *Olivella biplicata* beads, and compared these materials with a sample of materials available in the more immediate area. Obsidian is derived primarily from sources within the Great Basin (to the north, east, and south of the sites in this study); *Olivella* beads come from the Pacific Coast, with chemical evidence suggesting production in southern California (Eerkens et al. 2005). Table 4.2 shows the obsidian data (derived from Eerkens and Spurling 2008), including the Shannon-Wiener Diversity Index (SWDI) for geochemical types and the frequency of highly exotic obsidians from geochemical sources greater than 100 kilometers distant.

It is clear from the table that Marana-period houses have not only higher overall geochemical diversity, indicating acquisition from a broader geographic range, but also greater interhousehold differences. Thus, some Marana households have very little (for example, structure 7) and others (for example, structure 6) very high geochemical diversity.

By contrast, Haiwee-period houses have virtually no geochemical diversity, with all but one flake from the Coso Volcanic Fields. Newberry houses display slightly greater geochemical diversity but still significantly less than Marana houses. However, when Newberry houses accessed obsidian, a

**TABLE 4.2**
*Obsidian Data from Owens Valley*

| Cultural Period | Site | Structure | Est. Size (m²) | ¹⁴C Date | SWD1 Obsidian | Percent Exotic Obsidian | Olivella Beads | Bone Beads | Ground-stone | Bone Tools |
|---|---|---|---|---|---|---|---|---|---|---|
| Marana | INY-30 | 1 | 11.3 | 310±70 / 470±70 | 0.79 | 0.03 | – | – | 2.5 | 1.5 |
| | INY-30 | 5 | 10.2 | 410±80 | 0.73 | 0.15 | – | 1.5 | – | 0.4 |
| | INY-30 | 6 | 14.5 | None | 1.19 | 0.20 | 1.6 | – | 1.6 | 2.0 |
| | INY-30 | 7 | 8.0 | 480±60 | 0.12 | 0.03 | 3.0 | 1.0 | 1.5 | – |
| | INY-30 | 8 | 9.1 | 270±70 / 470±50 | 1.05 | 0.10 | 4.9 | 0.9 | – | 0.3 |
| | INY-30 | 9 | 12.0 | 180±60 | 0.95 | 0.12 | 21.5 | 2.2 | – | 0.4 |
| | INY-30 | 10 | 12.0 | 330±60 / 390±90 | 0.97 | 0.25 | 0.1 | 0.6 | 0.3 | 0.3 |
| Haiwee | INY-3812 | 1 | 19.6 | 1,340±50 / 1,600±60 | 0.0 | 0.00 | – | – | 0.1 | – |
| | INY-3806 | 1 | 8.0 | 1,340±60 | 0.0 | 0.00 | – | – | 0.5 | – |
| | INY-3806 | 2 | 19.6 | 1,400±80 / 1,490±70 | 0.0 | 0.00 | 0.2 | – | 0.2 | – |
| | INY-3806 | 3 | 21.2 | 1,160±60 | 0.13 | 0.00 | – | 0.8 | – | 0.6 |
| Newberry | INY-30 | 12 | 15.9 | 1,530±80 / 1,860±70 | 0.75 | 0.30 | 0.2 | – | 0.5 | 0.6 |
| | INY-30 | 14 | 13.9 | 1,650±100 / 1,840±80 | 0.54 | 0.23 | 0.6 | – | 1.3 | 0.5 |
| | INY-30 | 15 | 18.1 | 1,460±60 | 0.43 | 0.13 | 0.1 | – | 0.3 | 0.9 |

Notes: *Olivella* beads, bone beads, groundstone, and bone tools recorded in numbers per square meter of house floor excavated.

higher percentage of it was from sources more than 100 kilometers away. Newberry inhabitants had ample access to distant obsidian, likely through high mobility on the part of male hunters (see Eerkens, Spurling, and Gras 2008), but the number of such distant geochemical types for any individual house was low (usually only one). Moreover, both Newberry and Haiwee houses show very little interhousehold differentiation, indicating that each household generally had access to the same acquisition networks as others.

Similar patterns are evident in *Olivella* beads. Marana houses show high interhousehold variance in the density of *Olivella* beads, with some displaying high numbers (for example, structure 9) and others low (for example, structure 10; structures 1 and 5 had no beads). By contrast, Newberry and Haiwee houses all have lower densities and more even interhousehold distribution.

Interhousehold distribution of artifacts that can be made from locally available materials, including bone beads, groundstone, and bone tools, tends to be much more evenly distributed among houses, even in the Marana period. This pattern holds for potsherds as well (data not shown), though generally only Marana houses have sherds (Eerkens and Spurling 2008; Eerkens 2004).

Interestingly, there is a slight correlation between obsidian source diversity and the density of *Olivella* beads during the Marana period, but the correlation is far from perfect. Thus, houses with the highest obsidian geochemical diversities do not necessarily have the greatest density of *Olivella*, nor do houses with the lowest obsidian diversities have the lowest counts of beads. This again points out the heterogeneity of Marana households. If we assume that these goods were largely moved via exchange in the Marana period, as would be suggested by reconstructions of mobility patterns (Basgall 1989; Eerkens 2003a; Eerkens, Spurling, and Gras 2008), then it further suggests that various households may have been acquiring these goods via discrete networks.

There is a further pattern in obsidian source diversity measures relating to house size during the Marana period. A strong and positive linear correlation exists between estimated house size and obsidian source diversity ($r^2 = .66$), shown in figure 4.1. If house size is an accurate predictor of the number of individuals in a household, then this correlation may indicate that larger households have bigger social networks, with a corresponding increase in access to goods from a larger geographic region. More detailed examination of the specific obsidian sources present within the houses indicates further that smaller houses had access mainly to the most proximate obsidian sources and larger houses had access to more dis-

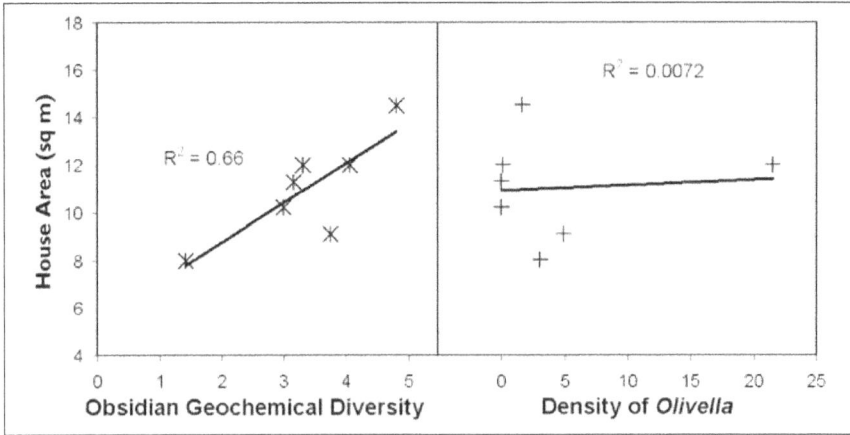

**FIGURE 4.1**

*House area versus obsidian source diversity and density of* Olivella *beads for Marana-period houses.*

tant sources. This pattern does not hold for *Olivella* beads, also shown in figure 4.1. A correlation between house size and the density of beads is much less clear ($r^2 = .01$). Even if we remove structure 9, the medium-sized house with the highest density of beads, the correlation between house size and bead density is not as strong ($r^2 = .23$) as with obsidian diversity.

## DISCUSSION

The studies above suggest sharp changes over time in both the overall intensity and interhousehold variability of exchange. These differences are quite pronounced in household data but are lacking in mortuary contexts. In particular, the results suggest marked changes around six hundred years ago, at the beginning of the Marana period. Before this time, households formed redundant units with relatively equal access to exotic goods, as represented by obsidian and shell beads. After this time, households seem to be quite independent of one another and exhibit considerable heterogeneity in access to exotic goods. In contrast, representation of more local materials is much more redundant over all time periods.

These results are very much in line with previous research (Eerkens 2003b, 2004) that demonstrates marked changes in subsistence activities, from a more generalized diet incorporating a range of foods to one focused on small seeds, also right around six to seven hundred years ago. I have argued that the shift toward seed-intensive economies represents a renewed focus on resources that are individually collected and individually processed using technologies that are also easily produced by small house-hold units. Families could have claimed such resources for private use more easily than communally collected resources, which would have been more openly and freely shared and hence easier to appropriate by free-loaders. Importantly, harvesting and processing seed resources individually rather than communally does not result in a decrease in return rate effi-ciency, unlike the hunting of most game and the processing by pit-hearth roasting of roots and tubers, communal activities that reduce many of the costs and increase overall return rates.

Furthermore, I have argued that processing and, especially, storing these resources also seemed to take place frequently within the domicile, out of view of others in the community. Greater visibility subjects such resources to greater scrutiny such that they might be claimed by members outside the household unit. The distribution of various artifacts across sites, especially potsherds (found primarily within houses), supports this notion (Eerkens 2004). I attributed these patterns to a movement away from open and pub-lic sharing to a more privatized and closed system (see also Wiessner 1982)—in other words, to a focus on the individual household as the basic unit of economic productivity rather than the village or some broader social unit.

The spatial distribution of obsidian sources and shell beads presented above suggests that this new focus on the household may have translated to other social institutions, such as access to exotic resource acquisition networks. Before the Marana period, households had equal access. After this time, some social units had greater and others only limited access to such distribution networks and presumably to the material wealth that moved through them. In the case of obsidian, such access appears to have been correlated to house size, though this pattern is less evident for beads. In contrast, there is currently no evidence to suggest that these changes were carried over in the treatment of the dead, though the sample size of Marana-period burials is so small (n = 3) that I would not yet lend great weight to this finding.

### Erosion of Egalitarian Norms

Moving back to the main question and purpose of the chapter, do economic nonredundancy and greater wealth inequality represent the evo-lution of leaders—that is, individuals with decision-making power over others? It is difficult to make this argument strongly. Although most individ-uals we recognize as leaders ethnographically have access to wide-ranging exchange networks, the reverse is not necessarily true. Economically inde-pendent households might display just as much disparity in access to exchange networks as leaders versus nonleaders, especially if family size plays an important role in dictating the number of exchange nodes a household has. Thus, it is quite possible that Marana-period households behaved independently of one another without any centralized decision-making power between them.

Indeed, this is the situation that Steward (1938) described in ethnographic times for much of the Great Basin, outside of Owens Valley and a few other regions. In those areas, Paiute and Shoshone were known for their emphasis on independent and highly mobile nuclear families that made decisions without consulting other social units (Bettinger 1983). Thus, unlike in Owens Valley, families did not have to pay any heed to any type of leader, Steward did not indicate that there would have been any disparity in exchange relations between such independent families. But without data to evaluate this possibility, it would be difficult to make the simple argument that disparity in exchange relations equals leaders in prehistoric Owens Valley.

What I would argue strongly is that by six hundred years ago, Owens Valley societies had removed one, if not *the major*, impediment to the development of leaders—the notion of equal access to exotic goods. Without being able to claim ownership over various resources, potential leaders have little incentive to overproduce and create a disposable surplus (Bettinger 1999). Such resources would be quickly absorbed by opportunistic freeloaders. Nor can leaders give away such surplus to accrue social debt, gain status, or enforce their decision-making will on others. In short, I would argue that without some notion of privatized goods, true leaders cannot evolve. Furthermore, the installation of an ideology of privatization is often driven by increases in population size and numbers of non-kin freeloaders. It is unlikely that aspiring leaders can get the majority of others to agree to such an ideology when applied to goods for which rules of sharing and public ownership are already well established. Instead, they are more likely to have it applied to new kinds of resources and technologies (material or immaterial).

In Owens Valley, the data suggest two possible interpretations of social conditions and evolution of leaders. First, following the establishment of a privatized goods system, small-scale leaders could have been asserting themselves six hundred years ago, and the disparity we see in exchange represents the material remains of such leaders. Alternatively, a privatized goods system could have been implemented around six hundred years ago to combat freeloaders. Leaders could have evolved out of this social milieu four hundred years later, during the protohistoric or early Historic period (circa two hundred years ago), when Steward recorded their presence.

I strongly suspect the former because I think that individuals are generally self-interested, prestige-seeking, and quick to take advantage of changing social situations to benefit themselves and their families, but this is largely my theoretical bias. In any case, addressing this issue will require the collection of additional fine-grained data from the archaeological record. In particular, we need to undertake a careful and spatially extensive excavation of a single-component protohistoric village to establish the archaeological signature of interhousehold difference during a period when we know leaders existed. Some protohistoric houses were excavated at CA-INY-30, as evidenced by the presence of glass beads, but it is difficult to segregate the prehistoric from the protohistoric materials at this site. As well, we need to know more about sharing practices between households and changes therein over time. Such data would provide a more direct measure of interaction than simply the redundancy of material culture. I am currently involved in research using ancient DNA to track the spatial distribution of carcass elements (for example, skulls, forelimbs, and hind limbs) from individual kills across these same archaeological sites. Such information should allow us to evaluate the degree of meat sharing between houses during different time periods, but it requires excellent site preservation and a large amount of work extracting DNA from a range of animal remains.

Finally, I do not mean to imply that certain individuals in earlier time periods did not enjoy certain social benefits based on their actions. Indeed, the successful prestige-seeking hunters of the Newberry period may have had differential access to mates and mating opportunities (for example, Hildebrandt and McGuire 2002; McGuire and Hildebrandt 2005). However, such status positions do not appear to have accrued any long-lasting material or economic benefits, other than additional mates and perhaps children, likely because all the proceeds of their labor were given away (a public goods system). It is only during the Marana period that any such status positions appear to have been formalized and marked by material differences in the archaeological record. As I have argued, this difference relates largely to resource ownership practices that shifted to a more privatized one.

### Possible Catalysts

What could have been behind the erosion of egalitarian notions in terms of access to nonlocal resources around six hundred years ago? To address this question, it would be nice to have a continuous distribution of sites spanning the shift. Unfortunately, the temporal range of sites investigated by archaeologists contains gaps, particularly between around AD

1000 and 1300, to which no houses have been dated. Thus, we have no analogous contexts from the period immediately preceding the shift.

Paleoclimate is often cited as a catalyst to such changes. However, two issues complicate evaluating paleoclimate as a catalyst for social change. First, there are many ways to measure paleoclimate (tree rings, lake-level cores, glacial moraines, pollen). Second, not only do these different signals measure different aspects of paleoclimate (maximum temperature, annual temperature variation, precipitation, frost-free days), but they also measure these things at different spatial scales (seasonal, annual, decadal, millennial) (see also Stine 2000). It is often unclear to which aspect and temporal scale humans adapt. More specifically, it is unclear how various facets of human culture respond to these different components of paleoclimate.

In terms of paleoclimatic records, Owens Valley is an ideal place to work. A number of proxy paleoclimatic sequences have been built on a range of data types. Perhaps most relevant to the current study, a core from Owens Lake, just kilometers from the sites investigated here, has been extracted and its paleoclimate reconstructed. This core records detailed paleoclimatic changes in the lake over the past one thousand years (Li et al. 2000). In this paper, the authors attempted to reconstruct patterns in precipitation and temperature, and although paleoclimate seems to have been fluctuating throughout all of prehistory, they identify several "periods" of more sustained conditions. In particular, they identify a period of relatively dry climate lasting from about AD 1000 to 1220, corresponding roughly to the Medieval Climatic Anomaly (MCA). Two shorter-duration wet events, around AD 1025 and 1125, fall within this earlier period. A second period, lasting from approximately AD 1220 to 1480, is marked by overall wetter climatic patterns, though a brief dry spell around AD 1400 is evident. The third period, between AD 1480 and 1720, is characterized as dry and cool, though it too displays a number of shorter wetter events.

Within this core from the lake, it appears that if anything the transition between the relatively egalitarian Haiwee and nonegalitarian Marana patterns took place within the midst of the second period, for which wetter conditions are implied. That the transition happened in the middle, rather than at the beginning or end of a climatic "era," is perhaps significant, suggesting that the changes are not necessarily knee-jerk reactions to climatic shifts. Instead, if paleoclimate was indeed a factor, then this implies that longer-term social evolutionary processes (over at least two generations) were at work.

Would the wetter conditions during this interval (AD 1220 to 1480) have meant higher natural resource productivity in the region? As Kantner has proposed (chapter 11, this volume), the evolution of leadership positions may take place within the context of "good" climatic conditions in which generation of surplus is possible. This may have happened in Owens Valley, but it is not clear that this need be the case. In particular, it is unclear exactly *how* overall increased rainfall would have affected natural resource productivity. The timing of rainfall (for example, winter versus summer) is very important in determining plant productivity. Furthermore, some plants important to human economies actually produce better during slightly drier conditions (Basgall 1999). Thus, making this argument will require more than just matching social changes to gross climatic ones, necessitating more detailed predictions regarding the dynamics between human social systems and climatic patterns (see Bettinger 1999).

A second major factor, often cited by archaeologists as a catalyst in fostering social change, is population pressure (for example, Carneiro 1970; Wright and Johnson 1975). Population levels are difficult to estimate, let alone the pressures such populations may have placed on local environments. The archaeological record of Owens Valley suggests increasing numbers of artifacts and sites in the Marana period (Bettinger 1999), and this certainly suggests greater numbers of people, but exactly how those artifacts and sites translate into population levels is difficult to evaluate. Moreover, we do not yet have the chronological control to examine changing population levels within the Marana period, though work in this area is taking place (for example, Eerkens 2003a).

It is tempting to argue that slightly wetter conditions between AD 1220 and 1480 may have increased the abundance of the ever-important (to local diets) seed resources, perhaps enabling populations to grow. Then, during the slightly drier and cooler conditions beginning around AD 1480, seed production decreased, putting more pressure on family units to work harder to make ends meet. Such conditions may have fostered an emphasis on privatizing food resources and heightened the importance of trade relations, especially for larger families. Such conditions may have enabled certain economic units to override traditional egalitarian norms, fostering a new era in which certain resources, especially seeds and exchange networks, came under the control of smaller social units. Out of this milieu, certain aspiring men may have been able to assert greater influence over decision-making processes at family and village levels. The extent of such decision-making power was undoubtedly limited, likely to economic transactions, as the ethnographic record suggests, but appears to have been at a level greater than at previous time periods.

## CONCLUSIONS

Based on theoretical arguments and ethnographic observations, we know that small-scale leaders hold certain decision-making powers over others within a local community, which they frequently use to gain access to surplus. Such surplus can be used in local redistribution or trade to create social debt and to gain access to exotic goods, making leaders well connected both within and outside the local village. However, none of this works if leaders cannot own and freely use such surplus on their own terms. Thus, a notion of privatized goods is a prerequisite for the evolution of leaders (see also Shennan 2002).

Ethnographic accounts from Owens Valley clearly show the existence of local leaders who organized and controlled various economic activities (Steward 1933, 1938) and had the "power and prerogative to make and enforce unpopular decisions" (Bettinger 1983:49). The archaeological record in this region demonstrates a clear shift in the distribution of wealth (for example, beads) and access to exchange networks around six hundred years ago. Before this time, households appear to have been redundant units, whereas after this time there is much greater variation between them. I argue that this shift marks the evolution of a privatized goods system (Eerkens 2004). I believe that these differences also mark the evolution of small-scale leaders or at a minimum created the social conditions that later led to their emergence.

At the same time, I would not push the influence of such local leaders too far. It is clear from the ethnography that family units were still fairly independent of one another (Steward 1933, 1938) and that they served important functions for larger social units such as villages. Leaders who overextended their decision-making powers or placed unreasonable demands on others would have quickly found themselves without a supporting cast. Offended families could have moved out of communities to new areas or could have banded together to remove the decision-making power of a leader. Thus, leaders must have provided some benefits to other families (for example, organizing various events or taking the heat for unpopular but necessary decisions) or at least not demanded too much, such that they were generally tolerated.

In any case, the Owens Valley study is an interesting one because it examines the evolution of leaders at the very incipient stages of their development. Many archaeological studies of leadership begin only with the analysis of social situations in which leaders are already well established and highly visible. In the Owens Valley case, it is clear both ethnographically and archaeologically that leaders were present but not dominant in local societies. Analysis of such incipient conditions allows us to better understand the more basic processes behind their ultimate evolution.

# PART II

*Pathways to Institutionalized Leadership*

# 5

## The Evolution of Managerial Elites
## in Intermediate Societies

### Charles Stanish

This chapter begins with some empirical observations from the ethno-graphic and historical record of intermediate societies. The primary obser-vation is that individuals of rank in nonstate societies (big men, chiefs, caciques) do not possess coercive power over the people they head and represent. What seems clear is that the group accords a substantial amount of ideological status and temporary ad hoc power to leaders or chiefs. The ideological power is recognition that certain situations require the use of authority. However, and this is significant, in normal circumstances, leaders rely on persuasion by various means to achieve collective goals and there-fore constitute a "managerial" elite and not an entrenched power elite as is found in state societies. A managerial elite can be defined as individuals who make decisions at the behest of the community for the benefit of the community. This is not to say that these leaders are not motivated by self-interest. Quite the contrary: leaders usually seek to aggrandize material resources and social prestige for themselves. However, in nonstate-level intermediate societies as defined in our advanced seminar, leaders cannot count on policing powers to enforce their will as leaders in state societies can. These kinds of leaders lack permanent authority, and their power is sit-uational. For simplicity, I refer to all these kinds of leaders as chiefs, rec-ognizing the controversy implied by the term. They stand in contrast to leaders in state societies who hold a monopoly of power. To be an effective chief, you have to keep your group together and keep factions cooperating. The most effective means of being a successful chief in the absence of coercive power is the creation of ritual and religious taboos that both reward cooperation and punish noncooperators.

My theoretical position is at odds at varying junctures with that of most of my colleagues in this fine volume. If one does not accept multilevel selection, as I do, then this theoretical position is untenable. Likewise, if one views the emergence of any kind of inequality as inherently negative, then this position is also unacceptable. If one argues that reproductive success is the only true measure of adaptive success, then this theoretical framework is flawed, because I maintain that other benefits in human society can likewise be a motivator for individuals to assume leadership roles. And finally, at the other end, if one advocates "kick[ing] in the front door of evolutionary theory," as my good friend Timothy Pauketat (2007) does, then my theoretical perspective is hopelessly retrograde, because I remain a staunch evolutionary anthropologist. In this light, I take this opportunity to thank my colleagues for their forbearance and constructive criticisms. I learned much in our days in Santa Fe, and their observations have, I hope, strengthened the quality of my argument.

## THE EVOLUTION OF COOPERATION

The empirical fact that leaders in intermediate societies lack coercive power in almost all circumstances has substantial theoretical implications. In classic evolutionary and cultural ecological theory, rank, power over others, and surplus are codeterminative. People do not accept rank and the extraction of surplus from their numbers unless they are forced to do so. Sahlins (1972:82) summarized the core theoretical position years ago. To create surplus, he argued, there are only two choices: you have to either get "people to work more or [get] more people to work.'" Following traditional logic, complexity (hierarchy) could develop only if the bulk of individuals in any society were compelled to act against their own self-interests and accept higher levels of sociopolitical integration in which elites extract surplus for their own benefit. Coercive theories of political and economic evolution, from internal or external factors, were the only viable ones under the theoretical constraint presented by the problems of human will and self-interest.

There is, however, a third way of increasing surplus that does not require coercion and that conforms nicely to recent work in evolutionary psychology and game theory. This is the creation of rudimentary economies of scale, in which people do not work more but work differently, in special-ized labor organizations (see Arnold 1993, 1996b). As described in detail below, a group can create surplus resources not necessarily by working more but by working differently *without* increasing its total labor input.

Such a theoretical stance is different from a focus on the evolution of culture, the evolution of society, and other evolutionary ways of looking at historical change. This game theory approach avoids the pitfalls of "total-izing" theories in which most aspects of life are ranked according to their selective value.[1] In the game theory framework adopted here, the key ele-ment is the political organization of economic production by cooperative groups of agents. The successful creation of cooperative labor arrange-ments in a competitive political landscape results in increasingly higher levels of cooperation. Other aspects of culture—language, art, kinship ter-minologies—are only marginally relevant to this process. In short, cultural evolution is redefined and refocused on the evolution of cooperation among human groups.

## GAME THEORY APPROACHES TO THE EVOLUTION OF COOPERATION

Classical game theory studies human interactions as two or more peo-ple compete for economic resources or some other social advantage. A game is a controlled experiment in which each player has control over his or her actions. Players adopt strategies to achieve a positive "payoff." Payoff is the result that accrues to the individuals of the game. Strategies are courses of action and reactions to the parameters of the game and to other players' actions designed to maximize a player's payoff.

Classical economic and game theories assume that people are gener-ally rational and knowledgeable. *Rational* is a loaded term. In classical eco-nomic theory, it means that all people in all places and times will always evaluate benefits and costs of any action in similar ways and adopt the opti-mal strategy. People are considered to be ego-directed, acting in their self-interest. These assumptions are also common in many kinds of theory in anthropological archaeology that have been used in the past to explain the emergence of complexity.

However, real life is substantially more complex than the assumptions that underlie classical economic theory. The intent of modern game the-ory is to model as precisely as possible actual social interactions, taking into account the empirically observed behavior of people. As a result, new means of modeling human interaction have been refined and modi-fied to better reflect actual social life. The results of this work have been surprising and provide processual archaeology a means to incorporate individual behavior in cultural evolutionary theory.[2]

A key assumption of classical economics that has been challenged is precisely this notion of economic rationality and ego-directed behavior. Classical economic assumptions about human rationality simply do not conform to the empirical reality of human sociality. It is now abundantly clear from evolutionary game theory experiments, such as the Iterated Prisoner's Dilemma and an iterated Ultimatum Game, that people are not rational in the classic economic sense. They are adaptive in an evolutionary sense as used by theorists such as Robert Axelrod. As he describes it, "in complex situations, individuals are not fully able to analyze the situation and calculate their optimal strategy. Instead, they can be expected to adapt their strategy over time based upon what has been effective and what has not" (Axelrod 1997:14). Most significantly, this and other game modeling indicate that individuals acting in self-interest can create organizations of substantial complexity that mimic structuralist explanations in history and anthropology.[3] Finally, a large body of research indicates that people are not always ego-directed; under certain social circumstances, people act in prosocial, costly ways.

Adaptive individuals are therefore "smart" individuals who are not genetically locked into predetermined behaviors but rather are agents who can alter their strategies literally overnight. There are, of course, limits to such flexibility, given the culturally constrained repertoire of potential behaviors available. Nevertheless, humans are vastly capable of adapting behaviorally to altered circumstances. There is usually more than one "rational" outcome to any social interaction, and people are capable of altering their strategies in response to new conditions, both cultural and natural. Cultural norms also alter the strategic calculations of people in any society. Two groups of people faced with identical circumstances often choose different actions, and both actions may be completely "rational" insofar as they permit the individual and group to reproduce socially and biologically. This observation is a cornerstone of cultural anthropology and, as we will see, a cornerstone of understanding the evolution of cooperation. With the adoption of this fundamental anthropological assumption, game theory can now be used to model the vast range of human cultures throughout the world in space and history.

### Experimental Data

A number of games that illustrate the nature of strategic human interaction have been created. These data provide the baseline for archaeologists to model the emergence of complex society.

*Prisoner's dilemma (PD).* The PD is one of the classic games in the history of the discipline. In this game, people are placed in a situation in which cooperation will be an optimal outcome for the players—for example, two prisoners placed in separate cells. However, each individual could do better or "less worse" than the other by being the first not to cooperate or to "defect": if each prisoner keeps quiet, they both can go free, but if one talks, he or she partially gains at the expense of the other. The experimental data clearly indicate that defection is the norm in the regular PD, as people cannot trust their fellow players not to defect.

This game is a type of "tragedy of the commons" situation, in which individuals acting in self-interest benefit themselves in the short term but hurt the group and eventually themselves in the long term. In other words, if each individual chooses a maximization strategy, everyone eventually loses more than would have been gained by cooperation. The situation can also be characterized as a conflict between group versus individual rationality; those who act rationally as individuals do worse than those who act rationally as a group.

The one-time PD offers great insight into a particular kind of ideal social situation. However, it poorly reflects the dynamics of social life. When time and learning are added to the mix—that is, when an evolutionary component is included—the results of the PD dramatically change.

*Iterated Prisoner's Dilemma (IPD).* The simple, one-shot PD game shows that the best strategy is always to defect, even though mutual cooperation would provide a better payoff. In a more complex experiment, the IPD, the game is played over an extended period of time by the same players. The IPD is a powerful game. As one of its most creative practitioners has noted, "what the [Iterated] Prisoner's Dilemma captures so well is the tension between the advantages of selfishness in the short run versus the *need to elicit cooperation from the other player to be successful in the longer run*" (Axelrod 1997:6, emphasis added).

A key element of this variation is that players must have some assurance that they will meet the people they are interacting with on a consistent basis. This alters the cost-benefit calculation from the simple PD, in which defection is the norm, to a situation more reflective of human social interaction. In running simulations of the IPD, Axelrod (1984) found that the highest payoff for players was a simple strategy called Tit-for-Tat. The strategy was simply to cooperate on the first move and do whatever the other player did on each subsequent move. Cooperation emerges between competing individuals because cooperation is in each player's self-interest. A simple "social history" of the players develops, and this is the basis for reciprocal behavior over time. The IPD demonstrates that cooperation can develop between selfish agents and that coercion need not be present for hierarchy to emerge among autonomous agents.

### Adding Punishment and Social Histories: The Ultimatum Game (UG)

The UG is one of the most powerful means of understanding the nature of human interaction and studying deviations from expectations of classical economics. The UG consists of two kinds of players: proposers and responders. Each proposer is given a quantity of money. He or she can offer part or all of that amount to a responder. If the responder accepts the offer, both players can keep the divided amount. If the responder declines, neither player receives any money.

Rational-actor theory is quite clear in what the obvious choice is for the responder: he or she should accept any amount of money because there is virtually no cost to him or her and at least a marginal benefit. However, in practice, responders are willing to give up "free" money if the offer is not deemed "fair." Nowak, Page, and Sigmund (2000) ran a series of simulations using an iterated UG. They discovered that there is an "irrational" human emphasis on fairness in games that most approximate social reality. By *irrational*, they refer to what would be expected in an economic exchange in which each actor seeks to maximize resources. Cultural norms affect the amounts that people consider fair, but in all experimental studies, people do not behave as rational economic agents. In fact, people tend to be both irrationally cooperative and irrationally vindictive under experimental circumstances that most closely approximate social life (Fehr and Schmidt 1999). People in all cultures so far evaluated will punish defectors, even at a cost to themselves, as seen in Henrich and others 2005, a report on a cross-cultural assessment of the UG. This work demonstrates that there is clear variability in the way in which norms of fairness and punishment work but that

> [subjects] care about fairness and reciprocity and will sacrifice their own gains to change the distribution of material outcomes among others, sometimes rewarding those who act prosocially and punishing those who do not. Initial skepticism about such experimental evidence has waned as subsequent studies involving high stakes and ample opportunity for learning have repeatedly failed to modify these fundamental conclusions. (Henrich et al. 2005:797)

The irrational behavior included the punishment of cheaters; people were ready to hurt cheaters even at a cost to themselves. When information on players' reputations was included, cooperation emerged as an evolutionary stable strategy. Nowak, Page, and Sigmund found that without information on players' reputations, evolution always leads to the predominance of economically rational actors—that is, offering little and rejecting nothing or offering high and accepting little. However, with the addition of players' social history, "fair" strategies will dominate. The ability to remember what a fellow actor will do and pass this information on to others is critical, and it represents the adaptive capacity of human beings. They summarize their results: "When reputation is included in the Ultimatum Game, *adaptation favors fairness over reason.* In this most elementary game, information on the co-player fosters the emergence of strategies that are *nonrational, but promote economic exchange*" (Nowak, Page, and Sigmund 2000:1774, emphasis added).

Other work demonstrates the importance of punishment as an adaptive strategy. Bowles and others (1997:2–3) note that "important forms of cooperative behavior are commonly observed" both in controlled observations and in the laboratory. The traditional rational-actor model is insufficient. They note that people are traditionally "irrationally pro-social," a behavior that does not conform to economic maximization models as found in classical economics. They also note that defection (also referred to as free-riding) "is significantly alleviated if there is an opportunity for costly retaliation" (Bowles et al. 1997:5). Retaliation costs outweigh the costs of cooperation in long-term runs. They note that the experimental evidence supports the proposition that "if costly retaliation opportunities are combined with communication opportunities almost no defection occurs and, therefore, no resources are wasted for retaliation" (Bowles et al. 1997:5–6). They argue that "a predisposition to cooperate and [a predisposition] to undertake costly punishment are probably related phenomena," and they refer to these as "reciprocal fairness."

Gintis (2000:2) and Gintis and others (2003) refer to this phenomenon as strong reciprocity, defining it as a predisposition "to cooperate with others and punish non-cooperators, even when this behavior cannot be justified in terms of self-interest, extended kinship, or reciprocal altruism" (2000:2). Gintis contrasts "strong" reciprocity with its "weak" counterpart. The latter is known in the literature as reciprocal altruism. He argues that reciprocal altruism is too weak to explain the evolution of cooperative behavior because when a group is threatened, the optimal behavior for self-interested agents is defection: "[P]recisely when a group is most in need of prosocial behavior, cooperation based on reciprocal altruism will collapse" (Gintis 2000:6). Again, in this model, the role of punishment is central to the evolution of cooperation in a group of self-interested individuals.

This behavior is opposite to what one would expect from classical economic assumptions about rational and ego-directed human behavior, but it is an empirically verified and theoretically sound observation in social science that simply cannot be ignored (see Bowles and Gintis 2003b; Boyd et al. 2003). This idea is based upon the acceptance of altruistic punishment and group selection, a position I view as theoretically sound. Following Fehr and Fischbacher (2003:790), "[w]hen punishment of non-cooperators and non-punishers is possible, punishment evolves and cooperation in much larger groups can be maintained." Any model of cultural evolution, in my view, must incorporate what I now accept as an empirical reality, based upon this large body of data.

All this work has provided us with a new assumption about the normative social behavior of humans, called *Homo reciprocans* (Bowles and Gintis 2002). In this model, people have a

> propensity to cooperate, they respond to the cooperation of others by maintaining or increasing their level of cooperation, and they respond to defection on the part of others by retaliating against the offenders, even at a cost to themselves, and even when they cannot reasonably expect future personal gains from such retaliation. (Bowles et al. 1997:4–5)

Perhaps the key phrase for archaeological work immediately follows: "Rather, [*Homo reciprocans*] is a conditional cooperator whose penchant for reciprocity can be elicited under the proper circumstances" (Bowles et al. 1997:4–5). The work of archaeological research is to define those "proper circumstances."

## BECOMING A LEADER: BUILDING COOPERATIVE LABOR ORGANIZATIONS THROUGH RITUAL, STRATEGIC REDISTRIBUTION, AND FEASTS

From an economic anthropological perspective, three criteria must be met for this model to be successful in archaeology. First, there must be an economic mechanism that corresponds to the theoretical model. That is, the cooperative labor organization must provide greater benefits to each individual than he or she could receive by working alone. Furthermore, the benefits received must be sufficiently large to compensate for the loss of autonomy of the communal production. Second, there must be a social mechanism that can maintain this labor organization—defection must be punished, and the benefits to the cooperators must be guaranteed. Third, we need a theoretical mechanism that can account for the development, maintenance, and spread of successful labor organizations over time.

### Criterion 1: Economic Specialization and Economies of Scale

For the first criterion, I offer the economic mechanism of rudimentary economies of scale in intermediate societies. As mentioned above, it is almost always assumed in classic evolutionary models in archaeology that the evolution of rank entails huge economic costs to commoners. In this view, to increase surplus production and thereby create the economic organizations and material conditions for rank and hierarchy to develop, there must be an increase in the total amount of per capita labor from the vast majority of the population.

This assumption permeates contemporary theoretical literature, but it is wrong. It is quite elementary to have an increase in economic production without an increase in per capita labor input. In economic terms, this situation is known as an economy of scale, in which individual laborers carry out specialized organized tasks to achieve an economic output instead of creating the product individually. An economy of scale can occur in two ways. First, labor organizations create economic efficiencies from specialized production mainly by eliminating redundant tasks. That is, these organizations produce much more wealth for the same amount of labor than do societies in which the household is the highest level of cooperative labor organization. Second, there are many tasks that require a minimum number of workers to be feasible. These kinds of nonlinear "threshold" activities are possible only where complex labor organizations exist and can be successfully maintained.

As early as the late eighteenth century, the political economist Adam Smith (1937[1776]) outlined the basic phenomenon of economies of scale. He provided the now classic argument that economic specialization (division of labor) by workers properly organized produces far more in the same amount of time than individual laborers can produce on their own. Smith used the example of the production of metal pins, one of the simplest commodities he could find to illustrate the phenomenon in the late-eighteenth-century industrialized world. Making pins is actually less complicated (in the sense of requiring minimal technical knowledge) than making many objects in preindustrial societies, such as the fineware pottery discussed by Vaughn in chapter 7, this volume, fancy canoes, and metal objects throughout the ancient world. Pin manufacture in eighteenth-century England is therefore a good analogy for many kinds of labor organization in premodern economies, such as many of those discussed in this volume.

Smith identified about eighteen distinct tasks associated with pin production. In one factory, ten workers produced forty-eight thousand pins in a day. Individually, these workers could have produced only a fraction of this amount in the same time. Increasing the number of individual, nonspecialized workers (those who produce the entire pin by themselves) increases production arithmetically. Increasing the number of specialized workers (those with just one task, no matter how technically simple) increases production at a much greater rate. That is, this more complex organization will result in greater productivity at the same level of labor input and without a concomitant change in technology. This phenomenon, in which a specialized work organization produces more than the sum of individuals working alone, is what Smith called "the productive powers of labor" and represents gains through efficiency of task specialization.

In Western economics, an economic efficiency through specialization is defined when the cost of one produced unit decreases as the capacity to produce the unit increases. In premodern economies, the same general phenomenon is evident, albeit in a more rudimentary form. Economic efficiencies can be achieved when individuals task-specialize and take advantage of situations in which a marginal increase in labor cost produces a disproportionately large increase in output. This phenomenon works for any economic activity in which there are a number of distinct tasks, including the preparation of special foodstuffs, alcoholic beverages, and artisan goods. In short, surplus can be increased in an economy of this nature not by getting people to work more but by getting them to work differently as specialized producers. Again, to anticipate a criticism, it is significant for modeling the evolution of rank that all these "specialized" tasks are not qualitatively different from the "nonspecialized" ones—that there is nothing technically new to learn. *What is new is the organization of the labor, not the nature or intensity of that labor.*

The second type of specialized preindustrial economic production is one that allows people organized above a household level to conduct activities that are not possible for an individual household alone. Unlike the first kind of specialized organization, which exponentially increases production through the arithmetic increase in numbers and organization, the second kind is characterized by a density-dependent task that requires a certain number of people. The number of people required is substantially larger than that available from a household organization. When that number is reached, a threshold is broken. New possibilities open up. A very simple example would be making canoes out of large trees. Given the weight of a tree to fell and transport, the task requires at least a dozen people. Bowser and Patton, in chapter 3, this volume, note that one of the economic consequences of women's leadership is the opportunity for "large-scale, labor-intensive tasks, such as building houses, clearing land for new gardens, maintaining trails, and hauling large canoes from the forest." With fewer than twelve people, the task is impossible. A group that amasses the minimum necessary will be able to carry out the task.

The ability to get people to work differently and to maintain this new labor organization is the key to the evolution of ranked political economies. Even though a rudimentary economy of scale is economically efficient, it entails laborers' loss of autonomy over production. Wiessner (2002:235; chapter 9, this volume) makes this important point: "[E]galitarianism is the outcome of complex institutions and ideologies created and maintained by cultural means which empower a coalition of the weaker to curb the strong." Egalitarian societies do not maximize economic resources as much as they protect the autonomy of individuals and households against possible coercive aggrandizers. In demanding "fairness" and reciprocity, groups utilize the repertoire of egalitarian social practices that have served humanity for so long, even at an economic cost to themselves. This social phenomenon—economically irrational but culturally quite rational prosocial behavior—is the principal constraint that must be overcome. The intense competition between emergent elites seen in the ethnographic literature is inherent in this process. Elites compete for non-elites to join their factions. They fight against the centrifugal forces of household-level resistance to political authority. In short, when aggrandizers are able to overcome the inherent limits of nonstate economies, they are able to create more complex political economies. In game theory terms, the limits include non-elite resistance to the loss of autonomy, irrational prosocial behaviors by faction members engaged in costly punishment, competition from other aspiring chiefs, and competition from outsiders. When aspiring managerial elites are successful, the result is the evolution of intermediate or chiefly societies. At its base, the evolution of complex societies can be seen as nothing more than the evolution of more complex cooperative labor organizations.

What is the basic means by which aspiring managerial elites can be successful? Given the discussion above, the answer must be found in social mechanisms that can bring together a group of autonomous actors to create a successful economy of scale.

### Criterion 2: Ritual and the Evolution of Cooperative Labor Organization

The second criterion for a successful theoretical framework in archaeology is punishment of defectors to cooperation and reward to cooperators by means of feasts. I propose that ritual beliefs such as taboos and magic provide the "punishment" mechanisms necessary for this model to work. Ritually embedded feasting provides the material benefits that prevent defection by members of the group and compensate for the loss of autonomy in noncooperative labor arrangements.

A review of the ethnographic literature indicates that an emphasis on ritual is a persistent theme in intermediate societies.[4] Most importantly, ritual provides a series of benchmarks by which members of a cooperative group fully understand when they will receive their payoff for laboring in a specialized organization; ritual and taboo also reinforce norms of fairness and reciprocity. Ethnographers and historians have documented many kinds of ideologies, rituals, and ceremonies throughout the world's cultures in space and time. The kinds that interest us here are those that affect production and exchange. Ritual provides guarantees to all members of the labor organization that they will receive a fair share of their production. It furthermore provides sanctions against noncooperators and prescribes the social rewards individuals will receive for cooperating over a long period of time. Ideology, with its concomitant ritual, is the social means by which elites guarantee the exchange of surplus wealth and thereby keep that organization alive.

Firth's ethnography of the Maori exemplifies the cross-cultural pattern of the critical role that religion and ritual played in production and exchange of surplus. Firth divided all communal work into two types. One type was made of people all doing the same task, and the second type was characterized by a specialized division of labor. He is emphatic that in the second type of the specialized work, "the people had to comply with a definite set of magical regulations" (Firth 1967:232). These regulations in effect constitute ritual in the service of specialized labor organization, in this case a rudimentary economy of scale that was vastly more economically efficient than the former.

Malinowski also noted the pervasive nature of magic and ritual in Trobriand economic production, both of basic foodstuffs and of prestige goods obtained by trade or manufactured in more complex specialized labor organizations: "Among the forces and beliefs which bear upon and regulate garden work, perhaps magic is the most important.... [T]he magician has to perform a series of rites and spells over the garden, which run parallel with the labour, and which, in fact, initiate each stage of the work" (Malinowski 1961[1922]:59).

To keep the group working together in a specialized labor organization, the individual laborers must be guaranteed that they will receive their fair share of their production at the end of what can be a lengthy process. Firth (1967:306) talks about the essential role of the chief in "the apportionment of a common product among the members of a working party." It has to be fair. It has to be based on notions of reciprocity and ritually sanctioned redistribution. One of the necessary conditions for a successful economic organization in any ranked society is an ideology of reciprocity that guarantees equitable redistribution of production. In other words, these ideologies keep productive groups together and sanctify the allocation systems mediated or controlled by the elite.

Punishment of free-riders (see Eerkens, chapter 4, this volume) is one of the hallmarks of the conditional cooperator in evolutionary game theory. In moderately ranked societies, the right to punish people is not vested exclusively in the chief. However, when punishment does occur, it is usually described by Western observers as an act by the chief. I would argue that a more careful reading of the ethnographic descriptions indicates that in reality the chief is merely expressing the will of the community. Malinowski (1961[1922]:64), for instance, notes in his observations that "[p]ower implies not only the possibility of rewarding, but also the means of punishing. This in the Trobriands is as a rule done indirectly, by means of sorcery. The chief has the best sorcerers of the district always at his beck and call." Chiefs have the power to punish, but only with the assistance of religious specialists. Because religious specialists themselves often form part of the elite or are attached to other elite, the authority to punish is limited by consensus of community. Even the seemingly coercive power of chiefs is at base a persuasive process.[5]

### Feasts

All societies have feasts. Feasting is one of the most common features of collective human behavior. However, competitive feasting among leaders in intermediate societies is different. It is a form of gifting conducted with the explicit goal of obligating people in the future. By accepting the feast giver's goods and food, the participant is obligated to provide something of value in the future. Feasting is a mechanism that satisfies the second criterion listed above: it provides material and social benefits to the participants in a more complex cooperative group. The politically astute hosting of feasts represents perhaps the key tactic in the successful creation of cooperative labor organizations.

In most cases in the ethnographic record, the value reciprocated is labor. Dietler (1996) argues persuasively that one of the most important roles of drinking feasts in small-scale premodern societies centers on the mobilization of labor through "work-party feasts." Dietler refers to these as "entrepreneurial feasts" and notes that political and social power is "continually being renegotiated and contested through competitive commensal politics" (Dietler 1996:93; see Dietler and Herbich 2001). Competitive feasting and elite-directed ceremony are found throughout the world in the ethnographic literature of ranked prestate societies. In fact, they are ubiquitous.

As is well known in the ethnography of "Big Man" societies, successful feasting and ceremony serve to build up a number of reciprocal obligations. As these obligations add up, entire households can directly or indirectly be drawn into larger work units. The classic ethnographies illustrate how feasting is directly tied to chiefly authority and economic activity. Oliver's (1949:14) ethnography of the Solomon Islanders reads like a textbook on how rank is established through competitive feasting in which a leader acquires pigs from his faction and builds a "clubhouse" where all the men of his group meet to make decisions.

Likewise, in *Primitive Polynesian Economy* (1975:223), Firth notes that feasts occur in times of economic abundance: "A chief will hold a [major] feast only if the crops have been good that season, and if he has accumulated large reserves." Why do the chiefs hold the feasts in the first place if they are so costly? For Firth, the answer was almost self-evident:

> A Tikopia chief [also] plays an important role in ceremonial feasts outside the series specifically associated with him as just described.…Only chiefs, their near relatives and wealthy elders can afford such a gesture…[and] as the…primary feast giver is thus usually a chief, he is able to command on general grounds a large supply of food and also reaps the major prestige of the event" (Firth 1975:229–230)

The answer of course is prestige: his people (the chief's clan) become a focus of interest and acquire prestige for a good feast. This prestige, according to Firth, is imbued with authority. This authority, even in a society in which households and villages are virtually autonomous politically and economically, can be utilized to control people's behavior.

### Criterion 3: Economic Selection

> Those societies that grew and became better organized were advantaged in individual wealth and economic and military

power, and tended to conquer, absorb, or be imitated by smaller and less well organized societies.

—Peter Richerson and Richard Boyd,
*Institutional Evolution in the Holocene*

The third criterion is a theoretical mechanism that can account for the development, maintenance, and spread of successful labor organizations. It is what I refer to as economic selection. The concept of economic selection borrows from natural selection in evolutionary biology but goes beyond it to incorporate human adaptive behavior and group or multilevel selection. Economic selection is quite simple: it postulates that in any particular physical and social landscape, only a limited number of optimal labor organizations can develop. In a competitive social environment, people will create or emulate the most successful ones, and the least successful will disappear. As Richerson and Boyd say it, successful labor organizations conquer, absorb, or are imitated.

The multilevel selection position is of course controversial. In the advanced seminar, I enjoyed discussions with John Kantner, who has argued for a traditional Darwinian model of natural selection favoring the emergence of leadership out of egalitarian societies. In this view, "natural selection is believed to favor competitive and economizing individuals who maximize the net benefits of their behavior" (Kantner 1996:43). Kantner argues that the control of resources allowed a coercive leadership to arise in the American Southwest, as seen in sites such as Chaco. Where we do agree is that game theory analyses indicate that competition over resources in such a cultural context will result in the emergence of a single individual or faction that constitutes an elite. The degree of coercive power enjoyed by such an elite remains the point of interesting contention.

In short, how does a chief persuade people to work in the absence of coercive means of organizing labor in intermediate societies? There is a whole host of traditional and social pressures that compel people to work. However, in the end, the answer is that in one form or another, people are materially compensated for their labor by their faction heads. In the advanced seminar, Jeanne Arnold described how Chumash chiefs own property and pay specialists for their services. These payments differ from those in more complex economies, but they are payments nonetheless. What seems "natural" in our Western market society seems odd for someone living in a society in which feasting and ritual dominate the economic process. Yet, precisely these kinds of ritualized work and consumption are key to the success of intermediate societies. This pattern holds throughout the literature in a huge diversity of cultures and historical contexts among intermediate societies. Becoming and being a chief requires immense work and constant adaptive decision-making to keep factions together.

## A BRIEF ARCHAEOLOGICAL EXAMPLE

There is unfortunately insufficient space in this chapter to outline what I believe to be an appropriate epistemology of verification in archaeology and other historical sciences (a slightly fuller explanation can be found in Stanish 2008). Suffice to say that I reject the New Archaeology hypothetical-deductive approach of Carl Hempel and instead embrace the modifications of logical positivism of Karl Popper and his followers. We cannot, in my opinion, test models of cultural laws. Rather, as with paleontology and other historical sciences, we must adopt Popperian approaches that use actual empirical observations to develop logically coherent models that provide "best fit" explanations for the historical record. For archaeology, we create models from historical and ethnographic data to explain, in the most parsimonious way, the archaeological record. The theory offered in this chapter provides one such explanatory framework.

Beginning around 1400 BC, people in the Titicaca Basin of southern Peru and northwestern Bolivia (figure 5.1) began to create "special" spaces in quantity.[6] People had inhabited the region for at least seven millennia, but only during the middle of the second millennium BC did large permanent settlement develop around the region. In many of these settlements, people started building square or slightly rectangular rooms, with prepared clay floors and drainage canals and probably adorned with small stone monuments called *huancas*. These "special" places were found all around the region, with many sites containing two or more (see Hastorf 2003; Janusek 2004). Evidence suggests that these were places of feasting ritual, places where a larger group would come together on a periodic basis.

In other sites, people constructed large platforms that loomed over the habitation areas. Plourde (2006) has documented a massive set of terraces on the site of Cachichupa, in the northern Titicaca Basin, that was constructed in one brief period of archaeological time. The platform area was large enough to accommodate the entire population of the village and more. The people dug a large pit and filled it with more than a dozen broken fineware pots that were then buried. Habitations were constructed below the platform. Unlike those in many other villages in the region, the houses were constructed in a formal manner. As at Chiripa (Hastorf 1999, 2003; Plourde 2006) and other sites, the houses were built in large squar-

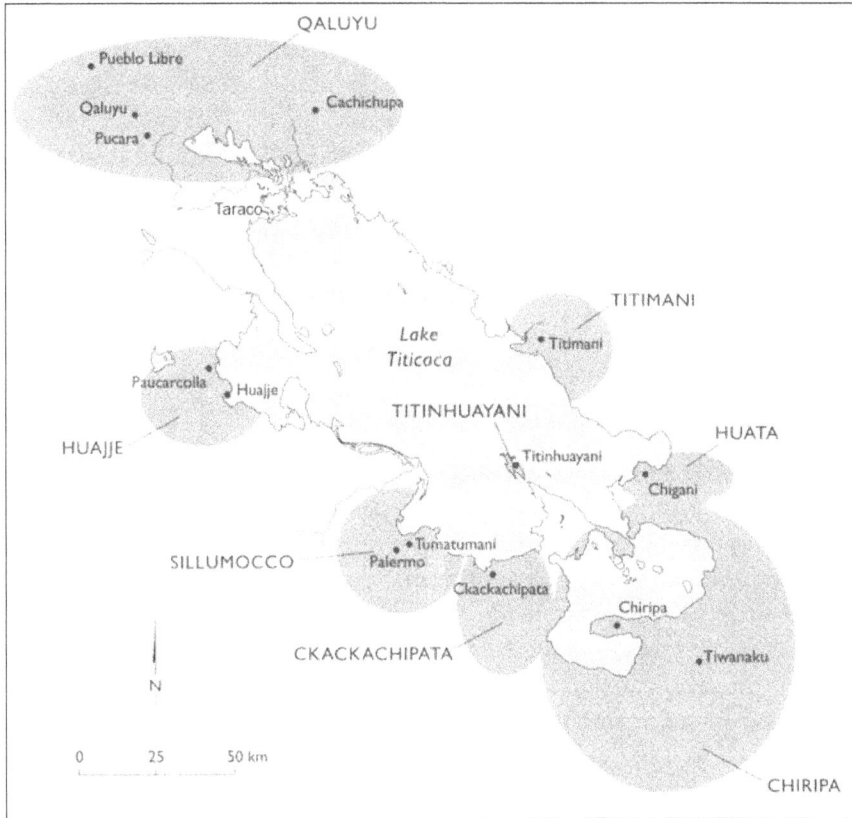

**FIGURE 5.1**

*Formative-period political centers, Titicaca Basin. Map by Charles Stanish.*

ish compounds surrounding a plaza area with a sunken court and mono-lith in the middle.

Central places of substantial complexity developed by the middle of the first millennium BC and continued up to around AD 200–400. At the beginning of this period, we see evidence for leadership as discussed in the advanced seminar: intermediate societies with leaders who had to per-suade, not coerce. By the end of this period, coercive mechanisms were in play in the region, resulting in the one and only state society in the Titicaca Basin, that of Tiwanaku.

These centers contained architectural elaborations of the earlier special places. The people of the region developed an artistic and religious canon that was replicated around the region. The key elements of this canon included a raised area above a squarish sunken court and an enclosure area demarcated by a low wall. Monoliths were collected in the sunken courts. These three architectural elements occur in almost all sites where public architecture is found. Likewise, these central places had compounds of domestic architecture oftentimes surrounding smaller plazas or courts.

Once developed, this cultural pattern spread throughout the region rapidly, covering almost all the lake edge settlements and extending up the major rivers. The rapid spread of this organization represents an example of economic selection: when these organizations developed in the northern and southern regions, adjacent polities were quickly absorbed or imitated these successful practices. An agent-based model of Titicaca Basin settlement growth and consolidation (Griffin and Stanish 2007) indicates that four variables can explain the bulk of variation in at least settlement growth and decline: access to eastern and western trade routes, competition between groups, migration, and agricultural potential. The model is an explicit test of economic selection and demonstrates that the concept works both theoretically and empirically.

Virtually all the major settlements of this period, circa 500 BC, were located on key nodes in the extensive trails and roads in the region. Qaluyu, Pucara, Taraco, Tiwanaku, and dozens of others are located in areas where roads or well-worn trails converge. Although there is little systematic research to date, evidence suggests some forms of craft specialization taking place in these centers. This work includes at least obsidian object manufacture, pottery making, stoneworking, and andesite axe production in organizations that took advantage of economies of scale, the effective organization of task specialists.

The archaeological data from the intermediate societies in the Titicaca Basin can be understood within the framework developed in this chapter. Certainly, as Pauketat in the advanced seminar and others have noted for such constructions (see Hastorf 2003), the special places and later elaborate architecture and religion associated with them surely had (and have) multiple meanings for the people who created, participated in, and later observed and reflected on them. But the architecture and religion also had some concrete political and economic utility. There are no elaborate and "private" spaces in the settlements before the emergence of coercive mechanisms in the first millennium AD. The raised areas or pyramids, sunken courts, platforms, and enclosures are visible to the entire community. One can easily see how norms of fairness are "built" into the architectural landscape. Unlike the palaces or enclosed temples of state societies, the architecture in this period literally screams openness and visibility in that any redistribution and regulation were in view of all. Communal activities would have taken place in the open, in the plazas, or in sunken courts. There were no roofed structures of any sufficient size to conduct communal activities—all roofed structures were very small houses. Almost any kind of ritual procession would have been open for anyone to witness (though see Hastorf [2003], who sees some of the small rooms as restricted areas of ritual).

Ritual, as seen in the Yaya-Mama complex of stonework, trumpets, flat-bottomed bowls, and other accouterments, developed in the first millennium BC. I have noted elsewhere (Stanish 2004) that this religious tradition, first identified by Chávez and Mohr-Chávez (1975), contains a coherent set of "readable" symbols that unify a pan-ethnic ideology. We do not know what these symbols mean, but they most certainly represent some kind of materialized ritual (in the sense used by Vaughn, chapter 7, this volume) that marked time, events, and probably feasts.

All the commodities that we know of—obsidian, pottery, stonework, and axes—are amenable to efficiencies in productivity through task specialization. The location of the central places indicates that one settlement determinant was access to exotic goods, a proposition confirmed by the agent-based model referenced above. In short, the architecture, location, religion, and art of the central places in the Titicaca Basin between 1400 and circa 200 BC suggest a landscape in which leaders, in concert with the people in their communities, created cooperative labor organizations that successfully competed with their neighbors. The public space ensured a ritually sanctioned location for redistributive feasting marked by a calendar of rites that guided the economic and spiritual life of the villagers. Participants in these rituals had a focus on which to develop a sense of comunitas (Hastorf 2003) that promoted working in task-specialized labor. Commodities came in, either by down-the-line trade or by caravans organized by the leaders. These commodities were transformed into valuables that were redistributed internally and ex-changed externally in what would fuel this ever-increasing process of political consolidation.

The work of Elizabeth Klarich (2005) brilliantly illustrates this process at the central place of Pucara in the northern Titicaca Basin. She demonstrates that the initial occupation of the site "supports the use of inclusive or corporate strategies by early leaders." The pampa in front of the terraces was linked with the entire site area and was an "open, public space" with no evidence of restricted movements (Klarich 2005:261). Foodstuffs and possibly other commodities were produced and consumed in quantity in this area. During the middle and final periods of the site, coercive mechanisms are manifest archaeologically by the reduction in importance of the pampa area and the erection of walls and other barriers to free movement. Furthermore, the former small sunken court area at the base of the terrace that was originally open from the pampa was now restricted, most likely inhabited by an elite with entrenched authority. The first steps to the evolution of a coercive state took place at the end of this period, but it was a process that was never completed. The site was largely abandoned before such a state-level, class-based system could be initiated.

In short, the ritual and political centers that developed in the Titicaca Basin before state development contain the elements by which leaders and their factions could mobilize people into task-specialized production. The open nature of the special areas manifests notions of fairness in that activities, redistribution of goods, and decision making are visible to all. Rituals that were centered on perhaps ancestor worship (Hastorf 2003) most likely also coincided with cycles of production, consumption, and redistribution as seen in contemporary highland Andean society today. Leadership, fairness, a transformation of work, and group adherence to norms of appropriate behavior permitted cooperation on a scale not previously witnessed in the region. The successful groups that were able to perpetuate these organizations led to concentrations of economic and political power in these centers, which dominated the Titicaca Basin in the mid-first millennium BC.

## CONCLUSIONS

One of the great questions in anthropological archaeology is why, after several thousand generations of successfully living in nonhierarchical societies, modern humans let a subgroup of their society control key decision-making powers. For two generations, cultural evolutionary theorists have tried to model this change as a coercive process in which elites gradually usurped power from non-elites as an unavoidable trade-off: higher levels of sociopolitical complexity were seen to be the least distasteful option for the bulk of the population in a context of resource stress or competition from other groups. Most of the participants in the advanced seminar see the emergence of leadership as ultimately negative for people in nonleadership positions. Eerkens (chapter 4, this volume) phrases it well when he rhetorically asks "how certain individuals come to gain unequal access to resources and, similarly, why or how others give up such access." This is certainly a reasonable position within a long and respected theoretical tradition; it is clearly justified in complex state-level societies in which political elites assume policing powers and other forms of subordination, both material and ideological, over the rest of the population. However, I argue that emergence of leadership positions in the kinds of intermediate societies discussed here enhanced *both* the leaders and individuals in the group as a whole. In game theory terms, it is not a zero-sum game. Individuals in the entire group benefit from coordinated cooperative labor organizations in that societies can produce more material resources from the same amount of labor and can compete more successfully against other, less organized groups. The key cost for individuals in the group is control over the production *process* and therefore the ultimate disposition of the resources. Overcoming this cost by creating rituals that guarantee reciprocity is the key goal of aspiring leaders. It is a tenuous process at best; the ethnographic record is replete with instances of people leaving cooperative labor organizations and rejecting control by managerial elites. When it is successful, however, the cooperative group is able to grow materially at the expense of other groups, increase its size and therefore its economic efficiency, and force changes in the cultural landscape; other groups must either emulate the organization or face absorption by the more successful one.

Given this position, if we reconceptualize the problem as not one of cultural evolution in the broad sense but one of the evolution of cooperation in game theory and economic anthropological terms, we arrive at some rather interesting results. We can address the question best phrased by Vaughn in chapter 7: "Why would people cooperate with their own subordination in noncoercive circumstances?" Using ethnographic, historical, and archaeological data analyzed from a game theory and evolutionary game theory perspective, one can demonstrate that the emergence of a noncoercive "managerial elite" is an optimal outcome for the entire population in settled village societies of a minimum population size.

Work in a number of disciplines, including evolutionary game theory, evolutionary psychology, and anthropology, indicates that the assumption of the pure ego-directed and rational individual in groups is not always warranted. In real-life situations, people act in ways that are irrationally prosocial, valuing fairness in economic interactions and willing to engage in costly punishment of cheaters. That this phenomenon is cross-culturally valid appears to be supported by a large amount of observational and experimental data. This being the case, the way in which we model the emergence of complex society must take this into account. The evolution of culture, from this perspective, is the evolution of cooperation that occurs among individuals in small groups that overcome or take advantage of these phenomena.

In anthropological archaeology terms, the evolution of cooperation from small egalitarian village societies to more complex ones is effectively the development of simple chiefly societies. Given the new work on the normative behaviors of humans in groups, this process must be modeled as one in which coercion is absent before the development of much more complex state societies. For chiefs to emerge, they must work within the constraints discovered by the experimental work described above. Fairness, reputation, and costly punishment characterize the social environment in which chiefs emerge. For an emergent elite group to be successful, it must adopt strategies that work within this environment.

The means by which chiefs achieve their position are based upon the strategic use of resources created by complex labor organizations. Feasts, magic, taboo, labor, and chiefly success are inextricably intertwined. Successful chiefs instinctively recognize the imperative to be fair and generous to their faction members, or they would be soon without much of a faction beyond their kin.

In a context of relatively high population densities and other critical exogenous factors, new economic organizations that are more competitive than "egalitarian" social organizations will spread quickly over a landscape.[7] They will be successful precisely because they provide greater economic resources for the entire population, both collectively and individually. People are willing to trade off a small amount of autonomy in control of nonsubsistence resources for the benefits of substantially heightened production and consumption of prestige goods and some other commodities. Ethnography teaches us that keeping politically autonomous extended families working together in cooperative organizations is the key political goal of noncoercive elites. Strategies such as competitive feasting, the creation of rudimentary economies of scale, and the adoption of political ritual that schedules the production of commodities and the reciprocation of goods, all embedded in ritual, constitute the means by which successful chiefdom organizations emerge and are sustained.

### Notes

1. For the purpose of this chapter, I refer to game theory *approaches* in the broadest sense, including evolutionary game theory and classical game theory.

2. By *processual archaeology* I simply mean the type of archaeology that is self-defined as a comparative social and behavioral science that seeks to understand regularities in human behavior across space and time (Stanish 2008).

3. This is an esoteric point that deserves to be mentioned at least in passing.

Classic structuralist theories of history seek to understand the underlying and subconscious structures of human society that explain the "surface" behavior of peoples across space and through time. Cross-cultural regularities in this tradition can be understood as the manifestation of deeper structures of human social realities. Recent advances in game theory, in contrast, suggest that similar cross-cultural patterns of behavior may be the logical outcome of the interactions of strategic and adaptive individuals in groups and do not necessarily reflect any deeper structure. That is, what appear to be the manifestations of mysterious "deep structures" may in fact be understood as a logical outcome of individuals following simple rules of learned and adaptive behavior. These rules emerge from trial and error among cognitively modern humans and are passed on through generations as culturally transmitted social mores and values.

4. A superficial explanation is that the Western ethnographers, locked in their positivist epistemologies, focused on those aspects of non-Western societies that made them appear to be "primitive" to satisfy the covert or overt malicious political and social demands of their own societies. An alternative explanation is that their firsthand observations were in fact generally accurate. I assume the latter for professional ethnographers such as Raymond Firth, Bronislaw Malinowski, Margaret Mead, and others of their stature.

5. The Maori ethnographies of Firth provide additional examples of how magic and ritual are integral in economic production. Firth (1959:245) states unequivocally and in numerous passages that "[m]agic, in fact, in one shape or another, permeates all the economic life of the native."

6. Mark Aldenderfer (1991) has discovered the earliest probable "public" space, dating to the third millennium BC, at the Asana site. He interprets it as a communal dance ground.

7. This entire chapter begs the deeper theoretical question of *why* strategic chiefly behavior can emerge in the first place. From the economic anthropological and game theory perspective here, the underlying shifts of the cultural landscape that permit this process are exogenous factors, such as an increase in population densities and an altered physical environment. This broader theoretical issue must remain the subject of other publications, given the space limitations in this chapter.

# 6

# The Role of Politically Charged Property
# in the Appearance of Institutionalized Leadership

*A View from the North American
Pacific Coast*

**Jeanne E. Arnold**

Simple forms of leadership are ubiquitous. Parents and elders in small-scale societies provide training, protection, and sustenance for younger inexperienced members of their social units. They also make decisions of many kinds and in return enjoy access to underlings' labor. I characterize this as a formative, kin-based, and essentially apolitical form of leadership. Among tribal or Big Man groups, as expanding societies develop more substantial communities and invest in more extended social webs and resource networks, effective or charismatic adults might lead by providing these services for larger numbers of people. Such leaders are likely to reap benefits from their positions and to make demands on followers as well. These are politically constituted forms of leadership, but tribal leaders and Big Men lack permanent authority and operate situationally and sequentially, as has been documented in several areas worldwide (Arnold 1996a, 1996b, 2000b; Roscoe 1993; Saitta and Keane 1990; Spencer 1993; Wiessner, chapter 9, this volume). Often these are heterarchical systems within which independent ceremonial leaders, war leaders, curers, hunt leaders, and councils of elders provide limited leadership concurrently within distinct social spheres or where communal leadership prevails. Offspring in these cases do not inherit rights to take the mantle of leadership, and followers can retract their support if leaders "mislead."

The earliest emergence of what we may distinguish as *institutionalized* power and leadership is an exceptionally important juncture in the political evolutionary process. By institutionalized political leadership, I mean *inherited leadership* and leadership with *sustained and renewable control over non-kin labor*, attributes we typically first associate with chiefs and simple chiefdoms. The shifting relationships between leaders and followers in a cross section of societies, particularly leaders' ability to control the labor of unrelated people, have been shown to be instructive in understanding developing political trajectories. I have sampled evidence from a range of ethnographic sources around the globe to show that the process by which leaders manage to gain power is intimately related to their emergent ability to secure the use of a broad spectrum of labor and to sustain that use across multiple situations, such as ceremonial events, craft production, seasonally intensive food acquisition, and warfare (Arnold 1993, 1996a, 1996b, 2000b). This is what I call renewable and reinforceable control over non-kin labor, and we see such powers consistently in chiefdoms and more complex political formulations. In contrast, this kind of relationship does not occur in tribes or Big Man societies, in which sustained control over labor is limited to extended kin and (sometimes) fictive kin. A focus on the labor process and labor organization in societies clustered around the Big Man–chiefdom transition thus, I argue, allows us to both identify and explain the significant political shift entailed in the appearance of institutionalized leadership, marked by hereditary chiefs. The construction of this explanation for the appearance of chiefdoms draws on many world areas (for example, Ames 2001; Arnold 2000b; Hayden 1997; see also Stanish, chapter 5, this volume).

However, the present discussion focuses less on labor and much more intensively on exploring the coevolution of institutionalized leadership and the privatization of crucial forms of property. In this chapter, I explore the idea that the development of a narrow range of types of valued property and the inheritance of that property—particularly costly technologies, crucial resource-extraction areas, and specialized intellectual property (knowledge)—are key to understanding how a formal succession of rights to leadership roles can emerge. I argue that incipient control of such property precedes and fosters the institutionalization process, although it may also be crucial in signaling and sustaining leadership. Leaders in power may also effectively manipulate many other more ordinary types of goods, including treasured foods, exotics, ceramics, and small valuables, but these stand apart from the largely indivisible, exclusive, and politically charged kinds of property I focus on here.

The material underpinnings that herald success in the development of institutionalized leadership remain underproblematized, at least in my own work to date and in that of most theorists investigating political evolution in prestate societies. Ownership of property entails fundamentally important, socially recognized rights to material or intellectual property, and it has for decades been examined with regard to empires and states (Earle 2000) and modern society (Carruthers and Ariovich 2004). A renewed focus on various kinds of property—and specifically what roles they play in the *earlier* stages of political evolution—seems long overdue.

A brief historical review reminds us of several common assumptions about the relationship between ownership of property and the evolution of political economies. Using the foundational constructs of Karl Marx and Lewis Henry Morgan, Engels (1972[1884]) wrote at length about the origins of the family and the development of private property. Generations of materialists in the twentieth century—scholars and laypersons alike—followed their several leads. In simplest terms, Morgan, Marx, and Engels embraced a dominant connection between the ownership of private property and the presence of advanced agrarian societies. Engels argued that before the advent of robust agricultural systems, wherever the matrilineal clan (gens) was still the primary economic unit, property such as houses, fields, clothing, tools, and weapons was governed by the gens, and inheritance was simple and largely communal. For example, clan ownership of land was clearly recognized in gens-organized prestate Greece, where the landscape was "divided up" (Engels 1972[1884]:171) but property was not held by "private" family units. Indeed, Engels asserted, the nuclear family as such did not exist and thus could not own property privately. He argued that American Indian groups—including farmers such as the Iroquois of the eastern woodlands—were organized by these principles.

But when early societies began to domesticate herd animals and to accumulate wealth (in the form of animals and their products) on a larger scale, matrilineal descent reckoning awkwardly left the inheritance of the paternally controlled herds to the father's birth clan rather than to his children. The solution to this problem, Engels theorized, was the dissolution of corporate or matrilineal social structures and the establishment of paternal laws of inheritance and the monogamous nuclear family, wherein children could inherit the property of their fathers. This change resulted in "the victory of private property over primitive, natural communal property," which in his view co-occurred with the emergence of the state (Engels 1972[1884]:128, 170). Such a system was driven by the desire to concentrate within the nuclear family the wealth that came to be prized as the greatest good in society. Thus, early economies without farming had no ownership of property (Engels 1972[1884]:87–92), and horticultural societies (those without domesticated animals) owned property only collectively and communally. Later on, in Engels's view, farmers who also husbanded animals devised new rules of kin reckoning and developed the very first private property and, ipso facto, the state.

Other early influences on the field (for example, Childe 1942, 1951: 61–71) asserted that humans began to "control nature" at the start of the Neolithic revolution. Farming economies were the first to develop control over food supplies in the form of significant surpluses, which in turn led to population growth. Closely linked to these firsts were the development of storage facilities and regular trade relationships, paving the way for manipulations of foods and products, formal leadership, and eventually the rise of civilization. Childe's work is often read to mean that in the absence of domestication and cultivation, there was no way for nonfarmers to augment food supplies, assert control over resources, or expand their communities, because any improvements in hunting technologies or techniques, for example, would result in overtaxing wild populations rather than possibly engendering surplus and storage. The clear implication is that forager-collectors were simply not accumulators of surplus, did not store foods and goods, were not owners of resources or facilities, and therefore were not—and could not be—politically complex. Childe's narrative renders hunter-gatherers without trappings of ownership, property, or political will. This is much the same conclusion that can be drawn from Engels's work.

Perhaps it is not startling that anthropology has barely budged from this position during the past half century. In the zeal to generalize about non-farmers in order to explore the complexities of states and civilizations, scores of textbooks and overviews of sociopolitical evolution, from 1940 to the present, have endorsed such stereotypes. These sources generalize about an egalitarian ethos and mobile lifeways among hunter-gatherers that lead to scant property accumulation, no ownership of territories, no inherited rank, little or no formal leadership, and so on. Corporate lineages with their collective ownership of property are almost universally linked in these overviews with farming and herding societies, not forager-collectors. Although the economic anthropologist Melville Herskovitz (1940:313–349) rejected many of these false associations some seventy years ago and provided a rich selection of counterpoints about rank and property drawn from a wide range of ethnographic cases, his insightful lessons were not taken to heart. Most of our colleagues continue to ignore the lives of nonfarmers when describing the evolution of status differentiation, the appearance of ownership and hereditary inequality, and the emergence of leaders on a comparative or global scale (for example, Haas 1990).

This is a perspective I have described elsewhere as agricentrism (Arnold 1993, 1996a:82–88). Agricentrists rigidly correlate emerging farming life-ways—never hunting-collecting economies—with the beginnings of organizational complexity, sedentism, storage, property, leadership, and power. Even today more than a few archaeologists endorse this strict agriculture–complexity linkage (for example, Smith 1993). Yet, research on complex hunter-gatherers around the globe exposes glaring deficiencies in such views. It is clear that some hunter-gatherers, primarily along resource-rich coastlines, were sedentary and lived at exceptionally high population densities (for example, the Calusa of Florida and the Chumash of California). Many groups harvested and stored enormous quantities of food and had delayed-return economies (for example, the salmon-based societies of the Northwest Coast). Compelling evidence exists for specialization, intensive trade systems, hereditary inequality, legitimate chiefs, and even slavery among hunter-gatherers (Ames 2001; Arnold 1996a, 2001b; Coupland 2006; Graesch 2004; Hayden 1997; Marquardt 1988; Prentiss and Kuijt 2004).

We are in a good position therefore to employ data from complex hunter-gatherers in North America to examine ownership and leadership (Arnold 2001b, 2004; Hayden 1997; Prentiss and Kuijt 2004; Sobel, Gahr, and Ames 2006). At this point, such an exploration is necessary because the model that dominates the discipline—that formal leadership, inequality, and property ownership occur only in agricultural societies—is empirically incorrect and has led to a consistent failure to critically analyze leadership and property in a full and appropriate range of cases. This situation has seriously hindered our chances of tracking how politically important property and centralized leadership are associated, because we look in only some of the places those phenomena occur. Space limits me here to empirical consideration of two complex hunter-gatherer groups, the Tlingit and the Chumash. I use ownership of key technologies and associated political evolutionary developments among the Chumash as a more extended case study. I also briefly revisit ideas I developed earlier regarding the central role of opportunistic behavior in the emergence of leaders (Arnold 1992, 1993, 2001b).

## OWNERSHIP OF PROPERTY AND TECHNOLOGY

Property of certain kinds is obviously politically charged and can be used to create and alter relationships of power. Costly technologies essential for transportation and communication, for instance, and esoterica crucial for ritual performances may provide uniquely favorable opportunities for aspiring leaders to shape political processes and gain control over group labor. Technologies often serve as arenas "for the negotiation of social power" (Dobres and Hoffman 1994:233–234) and are thus quite relevant to discussions of political evolution and emergent leadership (see DeMarrais, Castillo, and Earle 1996).

Privatized valued property in prestate societies was clearly not confined to herder-farmers (see also Eerkens, chapter 4, this volume). Here I draw on a detailed consideration of examples from two areas of western North America: the Northwest Coast and California. Among the Tlingit of the Northwest, there is ample evidence for lineage-based ownership of property, as well as individual ownership of property of many types (Kan 1989). This became especially evident during the course of significant ceremonial events such as memorial potlatches, which were given by clan leaders on behalf of deceased clan members and were among the Tlingit's most important ceremonies. Although the frequency of Tlingit potlatching increased somewhat during the postcontact nineteenth century, the events themselves did not change radically in character or become wildly competitive, as they did among the Kwakiutl (Kan 1989:29). Thus, historically observed patterns appear to reflect traditional practices. Tremendous amounts of property (food and objects) were transferred and consumed during potlatches, but the symbolic dimensions of articles at hand largely overwhelmed the purely material significance of the shifts in ownership of objects. In the complex intermingling of people and possessions, the objects carried metamessages about power, rank, rights, and values (Kan 1989:209). Virtually everything presented by hosts or guests at potlatches began as exclusive property, whether it was salmon held in a household's stores or prized furs, coppers, or blankets. Some of it, perhaps many foods, may have been classified as clan property, but the ethnographic record is rarely clear on this point. If foods were gathered and processed by households, ownership may have resided there rather than at the lineage/clan level, although such a distinction might have disappeared as materials were aggregated for presentation. But many of the valued manufactured items presented at feasts were unambiguously recognized as the property of families or individuals.

The leaders of the hosting clan and other lineages within the Tlingit matriclan asserted rights to display crests, claim titles, and perform special songs, dances, and speeches during the execution of the ceremonies. These kinds of intangible property were among their most important possessions, crucial to affirming power and prestige, and some could be won or lost during competitions at the potlatches (particularly if the deceased held a position for which political succession was in doubt). The host often gave furs as welcome presents to guests, but eventually, during the long ceremonies, the hosts attempted to dominate and lower the relative status of guests by overwhelming them with gifts. So many prized items were bestowed that guests could not carry them all; so much food was provided that guests had to regurgitate; and fires were deliberately made so hot that the plank-house roof caught fire. The point was to create indebtedness and loss of honor among the guests (Kan 1989:231–233). Of course, when those guests later served as hosts at the next memorial potlatch, they reciprocated in kind.

Guests were treated not only as a group but also as individuals whose specific rank and status affected where they were seated, how they were announced, and which gifts they were given. Property was linked intimately to status. So-called *aristocratic gifts* circulated only among the highest-status Tlingit elites during potlatches, more or less on a separate plane from other gift exchanges (Kan 1989:238). These included—in descending order of value—significant personal property such as engraved native-made "coppers," slaves, Chilkat blankets, and abalone ornaments. The first two originated outside the Tlingit world, in encounters with non-Tlingit that could be controlled by the clan leader-elites. Both are explicitly identified as the personal property of those elites, not lineage property (Kan 1989:245). Most importantly, chiefs used both of these unique forms of property and the sheer mass of property to reinforce rank, maintain reputation and honor, and solidify prestige and leadership. What appeared to be struggles over wealth during potlatches were ultimately about the symbolic capital that elites used to solidify rights as leaders as they simultaneously honored the ancestors and expressed respect.

Northwest Coast groups varied considerably in terms of potlatch customs and the range of occasions for which potlatches were held. Among the Kwakwaka'wakw (Kwakiutl) and Nuu-chah-nulth (Nootka), for example, because a chief passed his name and title to an heir during his lifetime, there was no competition for succession during mortuary potlatches, and a death was only one of many reasons to host a potlatch. Other occasions included births, namings, puberty rites, and marriages. It is clear that considerable individual and family property, much of it closely tied to reinforcing social hierarchies, changed hands during these events. Kwakwaka'wakw chiefs' property ownership encompassed crucial resource-collection areas, as well as houses, crests, masks, names, songs, and narratives, and it is reported that ritually sanctioned foods were also closely controlled by leaders (Wolf 1999:91). Kwakwaka'wakw myths reinforce the point that inequalities have always infused the society; chiefs have existed forever, and they have always owned resource areas (Wolf 1999:103). Herskovitz (1940:341) and Boas (1921) realized that Kwakwaka'wakw leaders' ownership of ordinary property and invaluable property—particularly crests, titles, and resource-collection areas such as prime fishing sites—was central to their being. People viewed inherited leadership and property ownership as entirely naturalized. The ethos of profound social inequality and selective exclusivity of ownership of certain politically charged property found among the Tlingit, Kwakwaka'wakw, and other complex Northwest Coast groups was much like that of the Chumash of southern California.

Ethnographic documents show that property rights were fundamentally important in Chumash society (Blackburn 1975:77). In characterizing the Chumash worldview pertaining to ranking and property, Blackburn (1975:49) writes that the whole society was hierarchical: "There exists a palpable feeling of class consciousness that permeates most social relationships." Political and economic statuses were well defined and associated with wealth, prestige, and social privileges. Several kinds of property and status (including some political offices) were inherited matrilineally, although chiefs' families resided patrilocally and passed along rights and property patrilineally. Individuals or families owned economically significant forms of property, such as strings of shell-bead money (*abalorio*), and considerable social distance existed between poor and wealthy families (Blackburn 1975:50–51).

> Inequalities in abilities, potentialities, and social prerogatives are assumed to be both innate and inevitable. Some beings are simply inherently superior to other beings. Similarly, differences in social rank and prestige are proper and natural, since they are based on biologically and socially inheritable differences in supernatural power and esoteric knowledge. A person inherits his status in a hierarchical society and universe just as he inherits the skills and qualities necessary to the proper performance of the role. (Blackburn 1975:70)

Many kinds of property were recognized, and ownership of these things was normal and unquestioned. A few specific examples illustrate this. The chief (*wot*) was acknowledged as the owner of costly items and an orchestrator of people. He underwrote feasts through control over community stores of food, he accumulated goods from the people (and was supported by them), and he could send them to war. In short, he controlled both labor and property (Blackburn 1975). The chief may also have routinely maintained a granary for acorns at his house (Johnson 2001:63). Provincial chiefs, who appeared to have legitimate multicommunity control, hosted feasts and wielded influence over large areas. Visitors from other provinces brought offerings of foods and goods to the feasts (Hudson et al. 1981:11). High-ranking women were often independent owners of property and wealth (Blackburn 1975:56). Both ritual gear and intellectual property were of great importance. Hudson and others (1981: 100) specify that "the chiefs owned the ritual paraphernalia used in ceremonies" and their control of supernatural knowledge was crucial given that "success or failure was directly linked to [their] relative knowledge and use of power" (Hudson and Underhay 1978:43). A balanced Chumash universe was never due to luck or chance but required active intervention by ritual leaders using key proprietary tools such as cult paraphernalia. This link to ritual gear further highlights the critical foundational role of property for emergent power and leadership.

As has been demonstrated by means of ethnohistoric and archaeological data, the Chumash who occupied the northern Channel Islands (figure 6.1) were manufacturers of a formalized shell-bead currency that functioned as a standard of value for countless transactions across much of southern California over the course of at least five centuries (circa AD 1300–1819), extending into the early postcontact era (Arnold 1992, 2001b; Arnold and Graesch 2001; Blackburn 1975). Bead manufacturing villages on the northern Channel Islands contain millions of chert microlithic drilling tools and millions of shell beads in various stages of production that together attest to the impressive scale of this specialized islands-centered industry. Excavations at specialized craft-producing villages there have yielded hundreds of thousands of analyzed specimens and by-products (Arnold 1987, 2001a, 2001b; Arnold and Graesch 2001; Arnold and Munns 1994; Arnold, Preziosi, and Shattuck 2001; Graesch 2004). The frequent and calculated use of shell-bead money for purchases of goods, foods, and services is well documented. For instance, ethnographers recorded that people had to pay significant amounts of bead money to have their children initiated into the elite religious 'antap society (Hudson et al. 1981:100). Chiefs used shell money to purchase feathers for important ceremonies (Blackburn 1975:narrative 16). The mythological being Coyote purchased boards to make a plank canoe and bought red milkweed to make fishing line. Coyote also paid money to aggrieved neighbors in restitution for their possessions (for example, mortars) broken by his

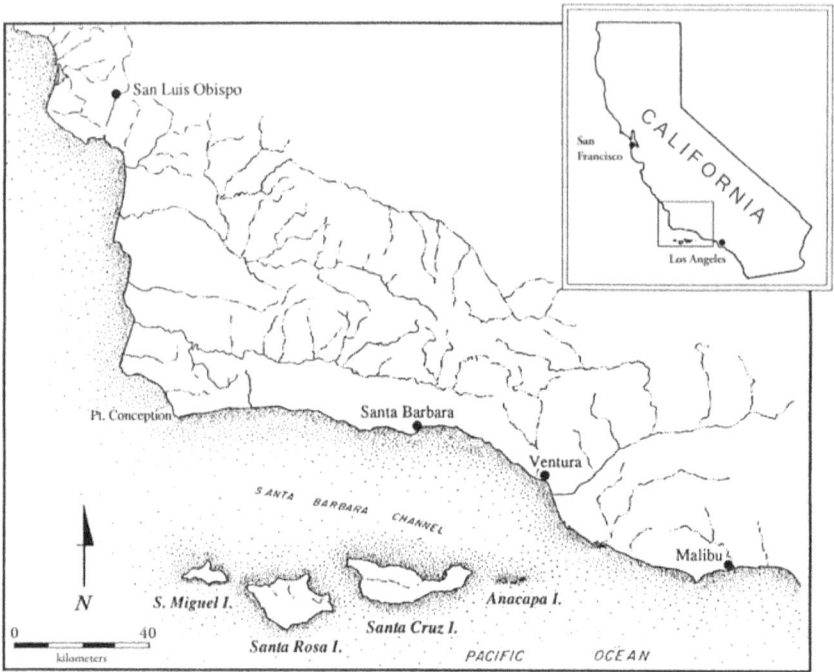

**FIGURE 6.1**

*The territory of the Chumash of southern California. Map by Jeanne E. Arnold.*

mischievous son (Blackburn 1975:narrative 32). And a nephew paid his uncle a measured string of shell money for passage in the uncle's wooden plank canoe from the mainland to Santa Cruz Island (Blackburn 1975:narrative 19).

Moreover, the first day of the Chumash winter solstice ceremony was given over to the monetary payment of all debts incurred during the year, and the presiding chief and the ceremonial assistant (*paha*) took a percentage of the money changing hands (Hudson and Underhay 1978:63). All the people gathered to witness and reconcile these debts (compare this ceremony with the Tee in New Guinea; see Wiessner, chapter 9, this volume), which had to be satisfied in full with shell money (Hudson et al. 1981:56). This was an activity separate from people's offerings made to support the execution of ceremonies at summer or winter solstice events. Also, wots who sponsored ceremonies or families who needed specific ritual dances to be performed had to pay money for the services of ceremonial dancers, often paying through the paha (Hudson et al. 1981:69).

## PROPERTY AND POLITICAL MANIPULATION

Once we see the ubiquity of prized and privately held property of several sorts among these nonfarmers (see also Eerkens, chapter 4, this volume), we can turn to how property has been used strategically to create or maintain leadership. My approach is to consider explicitly how aspiring leaders take action with these types of property. I expect to see that three key classes of property—*costly technologies, crucial resource-collection areas*, and *special intellectual property*—are the most politically charged property types and harbor the greatest potential to underwrite emergent power and leadership in a wide range of cases. All three have salience in the archaeological record.

### Ordinary Property and Politically Significant Property

For the Chumash, we can identify a long list of ordinary types of property that were privately held but likely had a rather limited effect on political evolution, including most clothing, weapons, containers, procurement tools, tule reed boats, foods, houses, decorative beads, and even shell-bead money. Such items were important and valuable in their own right but potentially attainable by all. Money itself is a very special case. Chumash people of high rank typically had disproportionate amounts of shell money, but because it was accessible to anyone, it was not symbolically exclusionary. At the other end of the spectrum are several classes of family or individual property that had great political significance among the Chumash because of their rarity and value. These were (1) the oceangoing plank canoe, unquestionably their most costly technological object; (2) certain crucial and circumscribed resource-collection areas (for example, isolated sources of high-caliber materials for specialized production); and (3) certain kinds of rights and knowledge, often of the ceremonial or supernatural variety, plus associated paraphernalia.

Selected other Chumash items were highly prized but I believe not so exclusive in a political economic sense. These included rare personal ornaments of stone or shell; swordfish, which could be caught only from large plank canoes; exotic goods symbolizing connections to distant allies, such as carved soapstone ollas from the southern Channel Islands; and very large and costly fishing nets. Such objects were valuable to the Chumash (compare the Chilkat blankets or abalone ornaments of the Tlingit elite) and were probably out of reach for most people, but it appears they were occasionally distributed to commoners, perhaps to create social debt. In such contexts, these kinds of property undoubtedly held importance for ensuring loyalty and reinforcing alliances. We have good evidence that swordfish was occasionally shared across households and villages by canoe owners, probably both to indebt recipients (Noah 2005) and to display generosity (see also Bird and Bliege Bird, chapter 2, this volume). Costly signaling theory assigns value to this kind of practice, and it would have been an effective way to reinforce rank and social differences.

Alternatively, such items *might* have been acquired by non-elites through purchase—possibly without political strings attached—although at great expense. However, despite their high labor value and symbolic value, these items were of a different character than the three property types I have identified as special and exclusive (above). The archaeological record shows that small numbers of rare ornaments, various swordfish cuts, and exotics such as soapstone vessels sometimes entered the property rosters of ordinary Chumash households. In contrast, the three most treasured classes of property would theoretically never have been deeded or dispensed to commoners, and there is no evidence to suggest that they were. Although this distinction may seem subtle, it is important.

To generalize and summarize, I propose that in all political evolutionary sequences of societies approaching or reaching chiefdom thresholds, a few selected classes of property are essential for deep-rooted *political manipulation*. The first group consists of rare material property that was neither physically divisible nor dispensable to commoners, including the most costly and sophisticated technologies. Examples include such inherently indivisible items as Chumash redwood plank boats and the rarest of Tlingit aristocratic gifts, their slaves and their engraved (precontact-era) coppers. The second group consists of crucial resource-extraction areas (quarries, beaches, mines, wells, often improved by constructed facilities) that were essential for specialized production or exchange enterprises. Examples include costly fishing platforms at prime salmon-harvesting locations along the mid–Fraser River in Canada (Hayden 1997), prized stone sources, and beaches where redwood driftwood crucial for making boats accumulated in southern California. The third group comprises special secular, supernatural, or ceremonial knowledge (intellectual property) that provided holders with inalienable rights. I want to be clear that I would not expect each property class to have played a major political role in all cases. I also do not suggest that all people who acquired such property were chiefs— some, assuredly, were ritual leaders who did not always extend their control into political spheres—but I do propose that the people who became chiefs consistently manipulated one or more of these classes of property. This is an archaeologically testable proposition.

Several other variables merit attention. Property must be heritable to perpetuate inequality and contribute to the building of institutionalized leadership, with the corollary that selected material items must be of types not normally destroyed during mourning ceremonies. Property by definition has the effect of excluding others, but as noted above, many classes of items that were owned were not possessed exclusively by leaders. Thus, they held far less symbolic importance in the political evolutionary process. Many items in any given society are common; that is, they are found redundantly in the population and across most or all ranks. Property categories that most people can obtain (such as arrows, mortars, houses, and ordinary clothing) are not politically exclusionary.

Elaborate crafted goods such as ceramics are an interesting property type to consider in this light. The prized Nasca polychromes of Cahuachi described by Kevin Vaughn (chapter 7, this volume), for example, were clearly distributed by elites—but widely, such that many people came to own them. They represented a newly complex production technology and effectively materialized and reinforced Nasca leadership, but I suspect that their dispensation did not foster the *emergence* of that leadership. My own tentative explanation, based on the framework introduced above, would be that the emergence of local leadership at Cahuachi may have been rooted in the control of ritual intellectual property associated with (possibly) exclusive ownership of the location where the Nasca River reemerged in that region's extremely arid landscape. In this admittedly simplified view of a complex case, the polychromes and their water-associated symbols materialized the region's new sociopolitical relationships after they arose. See Vaughn's chapter 7 for his meticulous assessments of the ceramic iconography, ceremonialism, water, and other relevant variables.

Special clothing may also serve as an important symbol of established political office, but chiefly regalia and vestments alone almost certainly cannot play a *formative* role in political evolution. Rather, special categories of dress come into being following the institutionalization of leadership and from that point forward may be exclusively held.

Power differences emerge not from coming to own piles of ordinary property—beads, baskets, cloaks, feathers, or pots—but from controlling and orchestrating labor through the use of special knowledge (see Kantner, chapter 11, this volume) or controlling highly exclusive property such as engraved coppers and plank canoes, which traditionally an ordinary member of society could never acquire. The control and manipulation of information and things can evolve into the power to govern or exploit people (Carruthers and Ariovich 2004), but very few classes of property have the gravitas to fit the bill; the property must be unusually

**FIGURE 6.2**

*Chumash fishers in a plank canoe. Drawing by Jon Standley. Used with permission, from* The Origins of a Pacific Coast Chiefdom: The Chumash of the Channel Islands, *edited by Jeanne E. Arnold, University of Utah Press, 2001.*

costly, complex, or rare. This begs the question, from where do these tangible properties come? I suspect that they have complicated multistepped developmental trajectories during which, for example, difficult extraction or construction techniques are experimented with and eventually refined (Arnold 2007) or within which complex ritual performances (Pauketat, chapter 8, this volume) come to be associated with esoteric knowledge and secret paraphernalia. If this is correct, such property must be of a type to allow owners to *exclude* others from certain activities, and it should allow owners to develop *control over other people's labor.*

## CASE STUDY: CHUMASH OWNERSHIP

Specific references to property ownership among the Chumash can be identified from Blackburn's (1975) rich corpus of more than one hundred oral narratives and selected other sources. Many kinds of objects are mentioned, but overt references to their ownership are uncommon, perhaps because, as discussed earlier, private ownership was pervasive and "natural." Most cases relate to the expensive plank canoe (figure 6.2). In Blackburn's narratives 23, 26, and 28, we find four cases: (1) a canoe owned by a chief's daughter; (2) a canoe owned by the mythological cormorant and pelican, taken out to sea at the direction of Sl'ow, a chief; (3) three canoes apparently owned by Sl'ow; and (4) a canoe owned by or used by nephews of Sl'ow. According to Hudson and otherrs (1981:14), Fernando Librado, an informant to ethnographer John P. Harrington, had an ancestor named Sulupiauset who owned a plank canoe and is reported to have "built the first canoe on the islands and taught the people there how to use it." We also find reference to ownership of redwood canoe boards. Narrative 32 tells of an old man who owned canoe boards that he sold to Coyote. These examples clearly illustrate a narrow range of ownership of a costly technology, all linked to chiefs (see also discussion below).

Critical resource-collection areas are noted in narrative 27: some coastal dwellers owned a specific shoreline where stranded whales came ashore, implying enormous bounty. From another account, it is apparent that ownership of resource-extraction areas by Chumash chiefs was important because inter-Chumash hostilities could erupt in competition over fishing zones or "trespass through another chief's territory to collect acorns or seed[s]" (Johnson and McLendon 1999:36). However, I found no ethnographic reference to ownership of (known) critical immovable resources such as asphaltum mines on the mainland coast and massive chert quarries on Santa Cruz Island. This does not mean that quarry zones were not owned or restricted loci; they very likely were, but there are no references in the narratives to these or many of the region's production industries. For example, sources provide no accounts of the archaeologically well-documented, exceptionally large-scale chert microblade manufacturing activities on the Channel Islands (Arnold 1987, 2001b; Arnold, Preziosi, and Shattuck 2001). This is likely because local tool-production processes changed shortly after historic contact and well before Harrington's interviews took place. Iron needles were substituted for chert microdrills in the manufacture of shell disk beads after the 1819 abandonment of Santa Cruz Island, and chert drills were no longer made. Thus, Harrington's informants in the early 1900s never observed people making or using chert drills and rarely observed anyone making shell beads.

Nonetheless, we know from considerable archaeological evidence that formal specialized production was occurring on a grand scale. Many millions of microdrills and shell beads were made during a few centuries by craftspersons exclusively on the Channel Islands. We can infer that some level of control of the unique raw material source—blocky cherts located in a concentrated band of quarries on eastern Santa Cruz Island—was key in this process. Otherwise, the exclusive craft production enterprises on the islands could have been easily compromised, something that could not have been risked when the islanders were making a form of currency. I provide considerable evidence that a virtual monopoly on chert microlith and shell-bead production was indeed established (see Arnold 1987; Arnold, Preziosi, and Shattuck 2001). Distributions of Santa Cruz Island chert debitage shifted dramatically around AD 1150, from widespread (and modest in scale) at regional sites to spatially restricted on eastern Santa Cruz

Island, and knapping activities came to be focused almost entirely (99 percent) on microdrill making. This shift indicates the onset of limited access to the quarries after the manufacturing of a more robust, standardized microdrill type became critical in the specialized bead-making industries.

Schortman and Urban (2004) discuss how the manufacture, distribution, and restricted uses of craft products frequently contribute to the development of political power. Among other factors, they suggest that the link between the degree of control over crucial raw materials and elite involvement in stimulating craft production is especially strong. As I argue above, this makes good economic sense. Thus, the emergence of intensive craft production may signal one kind of strong property ownership, particularly if the raw material collection areas are for the production of prized crafted goods rich in symbolic content. Emerging leaders may be instrumental in fostering specialization through manipulation of the labor *and* the property rights involved.

In the Chumash area, where formal craft specialization was pervasive (Arnold 1987, 1992, 1995b; 2001b; Arnold and Bernard 2005; Arnold and Graesch 2001; Arnold and Munns 1994; Arnold, Preziosi, and Shattuck 2001; Graesch 2004), I expect that specialized microblade makers must have had rights to the circumscribed chert sources; specialized bead makers must have had guaranteed access to a patchwork of rich shell-collecting loci; and canoe makers, who were part of a highly skilled, exclusive craft guild (Hudson, Timbrook, and Rempe 1978), must have been able to assert collection rights at prime driftwood beaches. Regrettably, as noted, the narratives are virtually mute on the subject of raw materials ownership in Chumash territory. Various specialized occupations are noted ethnographically (canoe maker, fisher, shell-bead money maker, fishnet maker; Blackburn 1975; Johnson 2001:59), but related resource ownership is not explained. Despite this gap in our documentation of property and leadership, Johnson (2001:60–62) has been able to identify many occupational roles and villages of origin for specific Island Chumash individuals, whose lives he traces by means of the Harrington notes and the local mission and census records. The list includes many elite occupations and leaders, such as princess, chief, shaman, canoe maker, and 'antap member.

Prestige goods theory holds that the ownership of certain kinds of craft goods, typically those rare and prized, can be used to gain power and dominate others. When prestige goods are made largely for circulation among elites and such property is strongly linked with elevated status, elites can create significant debt by occasionally dispensing them to lower ranks. Because these may be the kinds of potent symbols "that make social life possible" (Schortman and Urban 2004:192), the dependencies created can be profound. But, as noted earlier, when these items circulate in growing numbers among commoners, their political salience is diminished, and I question whether the goods so chosen by elites had the potency to be used to *create* new forms of leadership (and followership). I suspect that leaders held in reserve the most treasured kinds of property that were the spring-boards for their own political ascendancy. Moreover, far more empowering than simply owning prized goods is the control of the production or distri-bution processes. Many archaeologists will likely agree with the contention that at least one route "to political control…lies through monopolies over the fabrication of objects that convey, in emotionally compelling ways, sociopolitical values that work to the advantages of the monopolists" (Schortman and Urban 2004:193).

Embedded in this kind of control is the specific technical *knowledge* required for complex manufacturing processes, such as sewn-plank canoe making and difficult ceramic firing techniques (Schortman and Urban 2004:191). Intellectual property of this kind is quite politically charged. A few classes of ceremonial and supernatural knowledge, including religious and astronomical wisdom and proprietary songs, dances, speeches, and crests, are also fundamentally important in tracing political evolution, and I present evidence for this below (see also chapters 7 and 8 by Vaughn and Pauketat, respectively, this volume). Because ownership and creating indebtedness of various kinds are key to reinforcing power relations in many documented cases, I suggest that these may also be crucial in establishing those relations.

## CHUMASH POWER AND LEADERSHIP

> The Chumash political structure had a supra-village level, headed by a "big chief" who ruled the district from a capital vil-lage. One capital was *Syuxtun*, whose chief had authority over some thirteen rancherias.
>
> —*The Eye of the Flute*, edited by Travis Hudson and others

The Chumash were among the world's most politically complex hunter-gatherers, and several lines of evidence indicate that the Island Chumash were organized as a simple chiefdom after AD 1300 (Arnold 1992, 2001b, 2004). Archaeologists tend to talk in generalities about the ethnohistoric evidence regarding forms of leadership in this region, but several disparate sources are rich with details that may help us more fully understand power, authority, and property. I assemble these data below and closely compare them to unpack the evidence.

Hudson and Underhay (1978) describe Chumash political structure in depth, based on observations recorded originally by explorer Juan Rodriguez Cabrillo in 1542 and augmented by Harrington's informants, who were Chumash elders born in the early to mid-1800s. Cabrillo reported that the mainland Santa Barbara Channel area consisted of two major political provinces, one ruled by a woman whose capital town was Syuxtun (Santa Barbara) (Hudson et al. 1981:101; Wagner 1929). Each province included many towns and villages. These communities were each under the political control of a captain (wot). A larger council of wots governed the province, with one man or woman serving as the "big chief" (*paqwot*), or principal ruler. The community of the paqwot became the political capital for the province and served as the center for political, economic, and ceremonial activities (Hudson and Underhay 1978:27).

Other provinces and their respective leaders existed on the islands and along the more westerly coastal areas (Hudson et al. 1977). The "island province" was a large one, with the chief and capital at Liyam on Santa Cruz Island overseeing more than twenty good-sized villages and a population of at least twenty-five hundred at contact. Hudson and Underhay count potentially four additional mainland provinces with capitals at major population and trading centers. Altogether, at least two political units were identified near Santa Barbara, two more at Ventura, and one at Malibu. These—or some combination thereof—may well correspond to polities that we today would call simple chiefdoms. Arnold and Green (2002) have noted that such geospatial areas and populations are consistent with the scale of historically documented chiefdoms around the world and thus suggest that, for instance, the southern mainland area (the Ventura to Malibu groups, all of whom spoke Ventureño Chumash) was likely a separate simple chiefdom from the Island Chumash group. Distinctive Chumashan languages differentiated the Santa Barbara, Ventura-Malibu, and Island zones, among others, requiring multilingual speakers to conduct trade and govern many social interactions. Independent territories (Hudson and Underhay 1978:28) were actively defended against outside intervention, and wars were sometimes waged (Johnson 2007).

A few specific narratives related by Fernando Librado to Harrington help to illustrate these political structures. Hudson and others (1981:15) report that one "big chief," or paqwot, oversaw all of Santa Cruz Island. He had a daughter who, when she was born, was named by the '*alaqlapch* (shaman-priest) and destined to "become ruler of the four islands." When she grew up, she was pronounced "princess of the islands" by many people, but others on the islands objected and a civil war ensued. With peace restored, she was declared wot of all four northern islands. Her name was Luhui (Encarnacion). According to a second narrative, a man named Kwaiyin, a powerful wot on the mainland, was instrumental in forming the *siliyik*, or Chumash council of officials, consisting of twenty religious ('antap) leaders led by Kwaiyin (Hudson et al. 1981:17). The duties of the various members of the governing body were outlined, and they reportedly then dispersed to live at three large capital villages and other important communities, although Kwaiyin maintained political control over the whole mainland coast and islands (Hudson et al. 1981:18). Hudson and others (1981:100) summarize: "The chiefs and other secular officials had political authority over villages and groups of villages, and both cooperated and competed with their political counterparts through intermarriage, warfare, and trade." It is important to note that the chiefs and 'antap overlapped in restricting access to important knowledge, some of which was secular and some ritual. As Johnson and McLendon (1999) point out, there is a subtle mix of historical and mythological accounts in Fernando's Kwaiyin story, but his descriptions of political structure appear coherent and consistent with other data.

Succession to the office of chief is described in a way that allows for varying scenarios. It appears that new chiefs were typically selected and groomed by current leaders. Often they chose sons or other relatives, but not always. The 'antap leadership (called "the twenty") was a frequent source of potential new paqwots when a relative was not suitable, and the endorsement or approval of that group was important in the process (Hudson et al. 1981:21, 99–102). Most of the twenty were also village-level leaders or economically important people in their communities, such as canoe builders, fishers, and dancers (Hudson et al. 1981:25–28).

Members of the regionwide 'antap organization controlled much of the society's important ritual knowledge. Several 'antap members were found in every large village—among them the wot of the village—and according to Harrington (Hudson and Underhay 1978:29), a council of twenty senior ritual leaders represented all 'antap members at the provincial level, conducting high-level rituals and perhaps advising the province chief. Twelve of these twenty exclusively held the esoteric knowledge and thus had the power to control human interactions with the celestial and social worlds and to maintain balance in the universe. The twelve lived dispersed in towns across the province, and some were likely the political wots of their communities. Hudson and Underhay (1978:29) specify that "the 'antap owned and used all ritual paraphernalia, cured illness, [and] maintained the essential cosmic balance." Their paraphernalia (crystals, charm stones, plummet stones, sacred pipes) and the associated ability to cure illness, control the weather, predict the future, and contact beings in other worlds constituted ownership of important objects and knowledge. Chumash astronomer-priests (*'alchuklash*) were 'antap leaders with specific duties related to celestial powers, reducing peril for the people, and altering the course of the future by influencing the cosmos. They were feared and respected. Astronomer-priests and shaman-curers were paid for services (Hudson and Underhay 1978:35–37) and were at least part-time specialists. *Tomol* (plank boat) makers and owners also exclusively controlled a complex repertoire of secret knowledge surrounding the proper building and operation of canoes.

Hudson and others (1977:4, 11) speculate that the 'antap organization originated no earlier than the AD 1500s, but Corbett (2004) provides archaeological evidence for the first appearance of large bone whistles comparable to types used historically in 'antap ceremonies. The bone whistle data suggest that this organization had its origins during the AD 900 to 1100 era. I believe that 'antap membership and attendant special knowledge may have brought enhanced power to emerging political leaders during the AD 1100–1200s.

These various accounts document what Harrington's informants remembered and what Cabrillo understood from his attenuated observations in 1542, but it is important to consider alternative readings of the data. Johnson and McLendon (1999:30, 33) suggest that Hudson and Underhay may have overstated the case for provinces or federations and paramount ("big") chiefs among the Chumash, although they allow for the possibility. They suggest that, for the conservative purpose of documenting sociopolitical affiliation for federal NAGPRA claims, the fundamental Chumash political unit was the village, and our knowledge of higher-level sociopolitical groupings is less certain. But they reinforce the notion that the chief of Syuxtun, a man named Yanonali, claimed authority over thirteen regional towns from Goleta to Carpinteria (a resource-rich territory extending 40 kilometers) at the time the Santa Barbara Presidio was established. Several historic documents, together with Johnson's marriage network analysis, indicate the continuance of that political arrangement in subsequent years (Johnson and McLendon 1999:35). The parallels between this assertion and other accounts naming Syuxtun as a capital and identifying ten to twenty linked towns in various provinces around the region suggest that there may have indeed been such political territories.

Further historic evidence indicates that chiefs had real power and influence, including the so-called paramount chief of Santa Cruz Island,

Sulwasunaytset, father of the princess of the Island Chumash, who herself allegedly had authority over all four islands (Johnson 2001:64–65). Relatives of these individuals (Cecelia Leqte and others) were known to settle near Santa Barbara Mission around 1819. They were the very last people to leave the islands because, it was suggested, they had the most to lose from submitting to the authority of the missions. In 1819 Leqte's husband, Jose Crespin (Sudon) Kamuliatset, was chief of Liyam, the capital town of Santa Cruz Island, and he also left the island in the last group. There were reportedly three other town chiefs at other large villages on Santa Cruz Island during the 1810s.

The specificity of these accounts about power, knowledge, and inequalities in Chumash society, as well as the repeated distinctions drawn between paqwots and wots and capital towns and other towns, sways the balance of evidence toward the suggestion that there were chiefs with multicommunity authority, constituting a series of several simple chiefdom territories. Still, the nature of Chumash sociopolitical power remains an open question subject to new ethnohistorical and archaeological discoveries. For present purposes, I assume that wots and paqwots were formalized positions with political authority, bolstered by links with ritual authority, and were not roles misinterpreted by observers. We may not know precisely what all their powers were, but we are in an improved position to explore the kinds of property that could serve as a platform for emergent political leadership.

## DEVELOPMENT OF POLITICALLY CHARGED PROPERTY: IMPLICATIONS FOR LEADERSHIP

In Historic-era intermediate societies such as the Chumash, Calusa (Marquardt 1988), and Pacific Northwest groups (Ames 2001; Coupland 2006; Martindale 2006; Sobel, Gahr, and Ames 2006), ownership of a few special classes of property appears to have contributed disproportionately to the prestige, power, and economic standing of established leaders. Thus, the invention or manipulation of such potentially politically charged property may be a primary mechanism by which individual leaders first emerged as active agents. Scanning relevant data on the Chumash, the great importance of key property associated with the sea—their sophisticated plank boats, or tomols—attracts our attention. Virtually all the prominent Island Chumash men (those identified in the mission and ethnographic eras as chiefs, the "council of twenty," or Brotherhood of the Tomol members) were involved in canoe building and fishing expeditions with canoes (Johnson 2001:63).

Elsewhere I have traced the history of the development of the plank canoe (Arnold 2007; Arnold and Bernard 2005). It was by a large margin the most valued property in that society, owned by few people. These sleek watercraft were swift and could "fly on the water" at a pace of 7 knots (Hudson, Timbrook, and Rempe 1978:136). They were composite craft made of dozens of drilled and sewn planks, requiring considerable engineering knowledge and roughly five hundred person-days to make. This exceptional labor investment was compounded by the need to make the canoes with rare and costly materials, such as drift redwood logs from northern California and a caulk of high-caliber asphaltum from mines near mainland Santa Barbara. For a discussion of other construction details, see Arnold 1995b, 2007 and Hudson, Timbrook, and Rempe 1978.

Evidence of exclusivity and individual ownership of plank canoes is found throughout the ethnographic record and in the oral narratives of the Chumash (Blackburn 1975; Hudson, Timbrook, and Rempe 1978). Tomols were not lineage/corporate property, but possessions of wealthy individuals. "Only a rich man owned such a canoe, and sometimes he might own several. The well-to-do people used to order canoes, having them made at their own expense" (Hudson, Timbrook, and Rempe 1978:39). Owners clearly were in full charge of their use and profited personally from providing passage and moving goods across the channel (Hudson, Timbrook, and Rempe 1978:136, 155). Canoe owners had "wealth, status, prestige, and economic power" that set them apart from ordinary villagers, and they were members of the organization known as the Brotherhood of the Tomol, sharing in the ownership of proprietary, carefully guarded ritual knowledge about these prized canoes (Hudson, Timbrook, and Rempe 1978:155). On the question of limited or exclusive ownership of this valuable property, there is no doubt.

Moreover, private ownership was strongly correlated with political power and formal leadership in Chumash society. Owners of canoes wore waist-length bearskin capes as a mark of distinction (Hudson, Timbrook, and Rempe 1978:145). Although not every canoe owner was a wot (a village-level chief or higher chief), it seems that every wot on the coast had one or more tomols, and the highest-status owners could be linked with unusually elaborately decorated canoes. For instance, the "princess" of the northern islands owned a tomol with fancy shell inlay and painted motifs, along with unique "ear" forms at the prow and stern (Hudson, Timbrook, and Rempe 1978:107).

Uses of canoes included controlling trade by moving great cargo loads between the islands and the mainland, carrying passengers who needed to travel across the channel or between islands, capturing fish daily, periodically deepwater fishing, and moving people or goods along the mainland shore (Arnold 1995b, 2001b; Hudson, Timbrook, and Rempe 1978:125). "They carry cargo whenever they cross to the islands and when they return," according to Hudson, Timbrook, and Rempe (1978:131). Many types of goods, including seeds, acorns, baskets, asphaltum, and plant fibers (for fishing line and nets), were transported from the mainland to the islands. Shell beads, redwood driftwood, fish, and shellfish were among items shipped from islands to the mainland (Arnold 1992; Hudson, Timbrook, and Rempe 1978:135). The larger tomols could carry up to twelve people, including the crew. Cargo capacity exceeded 1,900 kilograms. These watercraft were also used for showy displays and for acquiring prized open-ocean fauna such as swordfish. It can easily be argued in fact that although the tomol resolved many basic practical challenges for the elite coastal Chumash, such as food acquisition and movements of people and goods, most uses of tomols were at the same time politically charged demonstrations of power and status, reinforcing social distinctions and creating social debt. Meanwhile, ordinary daily food provisioning by coastal non-elites occurred mostly at the shoreline or from the simple, inexpensive, small tule reed boats owned by many commoners.

I contend that many centuries before contact, material control over the making and operation of the plank canoe could have stimulated differences in sociopolitical power and created a foundation for Chumash leadership. We need only consider what the chief's position would have been like without this technology—or what it would have been like if this technology had been ubiquitous. Indeed, it seems entirely reasonable to say that without the canoe, the paqwot position might not have existed, an argument that finds support in the absence of chiefs and big chiefs among the northern Chumash (north of Point Conception) and groups farther north (toward Big Sur), who did not use tomols in that area's rough open-coast waters. Recorded accounts of paqwots and their political provinces halt at the northwestern margin of the Santa Barbara Channel, matching the distribution of tomols.

In an imagined scenario without plank canoe technology in the core Chumash area, aspiring leaders would have had no ability to control the labor or products of specialized shell-bead producers on the islands, manipulate social information from distant coasts, govern cross-channel trade activities, or fish intensively in the open ocean. They moreover could not have captured or distributed swordfish, controlled access to bulky exotics such as soapstone vessels from the southern Channel Islands, produced income by supplying transportation, or marshaled key resources for ceremonies. These were most of the primary mechanisms by which historic chiefs asserted their power and authority, created obligations, amassed wealth, and signaled their capabilities. Without plank canoes or with everyone in possession of them, they would have been left with little that was exclusively theirs to control, and Late- and Historic-period Chumash society as we know it simply would not have existed. The criteria noted earlier—that politically charged property should be costly and exclusive and should foster the ability of rising leaders to control non-kin labor and to exclude people through various means from central or powerful activities and roles—are well met by the plank canoe.

Direct and indirect archaeological evidence indicates that the developmental sequence for the tomol unfolded between about AD 500 and 1000, marked by a long process of experimenting with construction materials and canoe form and size to address very demanding performance requirements (see Arnold 2007). I believe that it took much of this period for the development and refinement of this sophisticated watercraft—that is, for it to arrive at its full size and 2-ton cargo capacity and to operate safely and reliably on the open ocean. It also took a long time for sufficient numbers of these craft to be operating such that a network of small-time traders, boatwrights, and other incipient specialists could emerge around the channel region, perhaps under the orchestration of rising leaders.

## CONCLUSION

The case of the plank canoe serves as a useful model for examining the role of special kinds of privatized material and intellectual property in the emergence of formalized leadership more generally. This is particularly so because the development of the tomol simultaneously embodies the privatization of a costly technology and certain proprietary knowledge in both ritual and secular domains, as well as the ownership of several kinds of exclusive resource-collecting loci (for example, asphaltum mines and drift-redwood–rich beaches). Space here does not allow, but it will be important to begin to investigate closely the impacts of other kinds of exclusive ceremonial knowledge and resource-extraction properties on emergent leadership in California and elsewhere.

Clearly, the canoe helps to illuminate the course of economic and political development in the Chumash realm. Elsewhere I argue that leadership is predicated on gaining control of the labor of non-kin in enterprises such as (but not limited to) intensive craft production, often when unique ecological or organizational opportunities arise (Arnold 1993, 1996a). In the Chumash case, aspiring leaders shepherded the florescence of the region's massive microblade and bead-making industries, which eventually had hundreds of participants across multiple communities. They also began to underwrite the costly and skilled tomol-making specialization, perhaps most pointedly during periods of documented demographic shifts (abrupt aggregation near reliable streams) and climatic stresses, such as sustained droughts starting around AD 1050–1150 (Arnold 2001a, 2001b). After several decades during which human health was compromised because of apparent food and water scarcities, widespread benefits emerged with the development of increased cross-channel trade facilitated by the operation of plank canoes throughout the region. This was a classic case of the emergence of opportunistic leaders operating under less than optimal climatic conditions, fostering a new political economy (Arnold 1992, 1993, 2001b). Although competition may have been intense for ownership of the best raw materials and skilled labor, there was apparently also significant cooperation among followers, an inference we can make given a regionwide absence of appreciable evidence for coercion during the Late period.

Control over access to the chert quarries on the islands was also implemented around AD 1150 (Arnold 1987, 2001b; Arnold, Preziosi, and Shattuck 2001). The intensive production of shell-bead currency on the Channel Islands that emerged from these developments was of tremendous economic and symbolic importance. Shell-bead money greased the wheels for much of the trade that ensued in the southern half of California over the next five centuries. It is highly likely that the opportunistic leaders involved in facilitating bead making and trade were also plank canoe owners. Ownership of the only watercraft that could safely and regularly cross the channel made these other activities and processes possible. If costly canoes, shell-money-making specialists, and the several kinds of ownership entailed therein had never materialized, other property and practices no doubt would have arisen in the region, but it is not clear what might have constituted an alternative basis for sharp disparities in status and a foundation for institutionalized leadership there.

Acknowledging that complex hunter-gatherers could indeed store food, amass property of many kinds, and build institutionalized political leadership, we can more holistically search for cross-cultural parallels in the role played by ownership of special, politically charged property types in underwriting and stimulating the emergence of chiefs with formal authority and sustained control over labor. Cases from western North America point to the importance of the ownership of costly and sophisticated technologies and certain kinds of crucial resource-collection areas, including those linked with transportation, exchange, and specialized production systems. Clearly, special in-tellectual property such as technical, ceremonial, and supernatural knowledge also underwrote institutionalized leadership. Such property should be implicated in the emergence of chiefly elites among the world's other complex hunter-gatherers; future archaeological investigations must be developed to assess this possibility. More broadly, I propose that some combination of these three classes of property constitutes a foundation for the evolution of institutionalized leadership and a formal succession of rights to chiefdom-level leadership roles for all economic bases, including agriculturalists and pastoralists. I encourage comparative analyses from a full range of intermediate societies to test this proposition.

### Acknowledgments

Generous support for research on the Channel Islands of California has come from the National Science Foundation (BNS 88-12184 and SBR 95-11576) and from the UCLA Academic Senate. Logistical support for field research has been provided by the UCLA Cotsen Institute of Archaeology, the University of California Natural Reserve System, and the Santa Cruz Island Reserve, which is located on property now owned by the Nature Conservancy and encompassed by Channel Islands National Park. I thank the participants in this SAR advanced seminar for their stimulating contributions to our deliberations about the nature of leadership and archaeological signatures of leadership. Special gratitude is extended to the co-organizers of the seminar, John Kantner, Kevin Vaughn, and Jelmer Eerkens.

# 7

# Emergent Leadership in Middle-Range Societies

## *An Example from Nasca, Peru*

### Kevin J. Vaughn

Leadership had emerged in the pre-Hispanic Andes by the third millennium BC (for example, see Haas and Creamer 2006; Shady Solís 2004), but the ways in which it was established and maintained varied considerably over time and by geographical area. Building on previous papers (Vaughn 2005, 2006), here I focus on the transitions to permanent leadership in Nasca, Peru, during the first millennium AD. I argue that permanent leadership first emerged in the region during this era. This leadership was based on ritual feasting and was reinforced in group ceremonies and the circulation of ideologically charged crafts. One of the key factors in the persistence and permanence of leadership positions was the ability of leaders to effectively materialize an ideology through polychrome ceramics. I explore how individual leaders attained their positions by looking at the long-term trajectory of this emerging leadership and by evaluating both the contexts (environmental, historical, and social) in which this leadership emerged and the ways in which this leadership may have been enabled and resisted by other members of society. Specifically, I evaluate data collected through regional studies of craft economies and household organization that reveal insights into how and why other members of society allowed their decision-making power to be co-opted. Ultimately, I argue that the inequality resulting from this leadership was based less upon physical coercion and discrete economic resources and more upon a broadly shared ideology.

This chapter begins with a consideration of leadership, how leaders might emerge in various sociopolitical contexts, and how they sustain their positions in the face of possible resistance. In the past, I have focused on political economies and how emerging leaders build and maintain wealth. Here I expand that argument and specifically focus on three interrelated factors that individuals use to establish and maintain leadership: feasting, ritual, and materialization. To illustrate this discussion, I use Nasca in the Early Intermediate period (circa AD 1 to 750) as an example. My focus here is not to evaluate the *first* evidence for emergent leadership in the Andes or even the *most important* instance of emergent leadership in the Andes. Instead, by considering the Nasca region, I focus on the processes of emergent leadership and attempt to elucidate how archaeologists may better understand these processes. I turn to an introduction to the environmental and archaeological setting and then discuss the evidence for cycles of leadership in the Nasca region.

## LEADERSHIP AND LEADERS

It is an anthropological truism that all societies, from the most egalitarian to the most stratified, have some form of leadership. Forms of impermanent and situational leadership exist in even the most "egalitarian" of societies (Aldenderfer 2005; Bird and Bliege Bird, chapter 2, this volume; Wiessner 2002, chapter 9, this volume). *Permanent* positions of leadership are not ubiquitous, however. Indeed, permanent leaders emerged only in certain times and places, and many small-scale societies—ones that seem to have composed the majority of human history—lack these positions. A key issue for archaeologists, then, is understanding the mechanisms by which these kinds of leaders emerge where they previously did not exist. To paraphrase Rick, I define permanent leadership as having the following characteristics: (1) decision-making authority is systematically ascribed to an individual; (2) judgment on whether to obey or follow that individual "is based on the perceived position" of the leader; and (3) this perceived position has a "widespread level of legitimacy" (Rick 2005:76).

To attain this position, leaders mobilize broad support across social groups (that is, beyond immediate kin) to enable these social changes. Previously, I have considered these kinds of social changes in the context of emerging political power (Vaughn 2005). By my definition, permanent leaders have political power in that they are in a position to make decisions for others. Particularly germane to the development of political power in the pre-Hispanic Andes are political economies—that is, the ways in which people and groups control and manipulate the production, distribution, and exchange of wealth (Vaughn 2006). Key are the mechanisms by which emerging leaders mobilize a surplus, as these individuals can face significant obstacles in small-scale and middle-range societies. Specifically, commoners from whom leaders may attempt to extract wealth own the means of production in these societies. This ownership places them in an advantageous position over a potential leader and creates a situation in which a potential leader must convince them to give up some of their autonomy and any previous egalitarian ethos that may have existed.

In these situations, aspiring leaders or interest groups (such as corporate groups or factions) tend to manipulate the political economy (1) by accumulating prestige goods through alliance networks and exchange, (2) by intensifying production (especially crafts production) through either charisma or kinship ties, or (3) by using some combination of these strategies (Vaughn 2006). This is no small task, however, because exchange and alliance networks that focus on prestige goods are difficult to monopolize; the procurement of these goods takes place outside a potential leader's sphere of persuasion. Furthermore, middle-range societies face significant obstacles to increasing production precisely because potential leaders are tethered to other individuals by kinship obligations (Wolf 1982, 1990) and because household modes of production tend to be resistant to production increases (Stanish 2003).

Building on a model first proposed by Stanish (2003, chapter 5, this volume), I argued that an effective way for emerging leaders to mobilize surpluses is by hosting feasts that emphasize public ritual and incorporate a materialized ideology. Here I wish to expand on the importance of public, ritually laden feasts because they potentially provide social contexts in which emerging leaders can coalesce political power so that their positions become permanent. By no means do I suggest that this is the *only* pathway by which leaders can coalesce political power, but I argue that it can be an *important* pathway in certain sociopolitical contexts.

## FEASTS, RITUAL, AND MATERIALIZATION

Feasts of course are "public ritual events of communal food and drink consumption" (Dietler 2001:69). Much ink has been spilled over feasts in the past decade of archaeological discourse. The bulk of this literature points to the importance of feasts as an impetus for sociopolitical change because they afford opportunities for sponsors to display their generosity by distributing food and wealth, thereby enhancing their social prestige and gaining political capital (see, for example, Dietler and Hayden 2001; LeCount 2001; Mills 2007; Rosenswig 2007; Walker and Lucero 2000). Political capital is gained and social prestige is enhanced by the creation of reciprocal obligations between sponsors and guests through the gifting of food, drink, and material goods.

The importance of feasts is not just that they provide the settings for public rituals and give feast sponsors the opportunity to display their generosity. They provide an impetus to articulate regional exchange systems, and they provide a mechanism for labor intensification (Dietler 2001:69; see also Junker 2001; Lucero 2003; Spielmann 2002; Stanish 2003, 2004). Critical also is that feasts are important in providing the social and economic impetus for emerging leaders to promote a "sense of solidarity, inclusiveness and equality" (Walker and Lucero 2000:132) and simultaneously (and paradoxically) promote inequality by accumulating more material and social capital.

Multiple examples of feasts in the ethnographic and archaeological record demonstrate they are important arenas for public rituals, provide mechanisms for labor intensification, and can provide an impetus for exchange and promoting solidarity. An exhaustive summary is neither appropriate nor necessary here. Instead, I briefly mention two ethnographic examples that illustrate how leaders can simultaneously garner support and elevate their position relative to other members of society by sponsoring feasts.

Junker (2001:271) describes sixteenth-century Spanish accounts of feasts in the Philippines as an important feature of the political economy of Philippine middle-range societies. Feasts of "ostentation, merit, or vanity," as they were called, were associated with elite rites of passage such as birth and marriage and with life-crisis events such as death and illness. Feasts were also important prefaces to critical events of the political economy such as trading expeditions, harvests, warfare and raiding, alliances, and chiefly succession. In orchestrating feasts, a chief was able to accumulate wealth by drawing on the labor of his constituency and then redistribute that wealth in ritually charged social arenas; his ostensible generosity "emphasized his role as a superior kinsman and strengthened the often tenuous bonds that held together political coalitions" (Junker 2001:271). Feasts were also arenas in which chiefs would give valuables such as porcelain bowls and metal gongs to elite participants, thereby securing alliances and political relationships. Indeed, though there was great variety in the way feasts were conducted, as well as in their scale and complexity, for the purposes of this discussion, there were two features common to *all* feasts in the sixteenth-century Philippines: (1) *social prestige was always conferred upon the feast's sponsor*; and (2) *valuables were always exchanged among elites*.

Whereas the Philippine example shows that feasts were social arenas in which exchange took place and elites benefited, other examples demonstrate the importance of labor intensification. At "work party feasts," for example, a group or individual sponsors a feast in exchange for labor on a specific project. This kind of feast was common cross-culturally (see Hayden 2001), and one of the most well-known examples was in the indigenous Northwest Coast of North America (Perodie 2001). There, feasts were frequently orchestrated for the purpose of post carving and raising and house building. Labor was provided by the family of the sponsor, as well as by other households, and many work party feasts were intracommunity events (Perodie 2001:195).

These examples suggest that feasts provide one setting for the intensification of production and for the exchange of valuables and other kinds of goods that could potentially circulate regionally. The key point here is that the ultimate benefactor of these kinds of feasts is the feast sponsor and that these events may be one of the critical social avenues through which aspiring leaders can actually mobilize a surplus. Additionally, all participants in these ethnographic examples of feasts are negotiating these new structured relationships, and in large part *it is the feast participants who enable this ostensible generosity*.

Although both ethnographers and archaeologists demonstrate that feasts provide the potential arena for these kinds of changes, a fundamental paradox remains for aspiring leaders in middle-range societies. Specifically, given potential resistance to these kinds of changes, how are aspiring leaders able to convince other people that it is in their best interest to ultimately support the leaders' endeavors? In other words, why would people cooperate with their own subordination in noncoercive circumstances? A cursory review of the anthropological literature suggests that incipient leaders often turn specifically to manipulating public ritual closely tied to religious ideology to make their efforts appealing to others (Aldenderfer 1993, 2005; Lucero 2003; Potter 2000b; Schachner 2001).

Bawden (2004:119) provides a useful definition of ideology as "that special formulation of social discourse that promotes the interests of its advocates in the wider community." The most important aspect of ideology is that it creates a means to justify developing inequalities because of unequal exchange and production relationships, especially in societies in which physical and economic forms of power are lacking (Earle 1997).

Although ritual can be a conservative force that expresses asymmetrical social relations, it can simultaneously serve as a dynamic force that acts to reproduce and transform those social relations (Aldenderfer 2005; Dietler 2001; Hastorf 2001; Rick 2005:71). By performing ritual, "actors not only continue to be shaped by the underlying organizational principles of those practices, but continually re-endorse them in the world of public observation and discourse" (Ortner 1984:154). Of course, the flip side to this is that public ritual provides an arena for these new relations to be contested. After all, public ritual by definition requires an audience, and the audience actively enables and engages the public ritual (Inomata 2003, 2006).

Rituals in sedentary agricultural societies are often linked to agricultural cycles and can be effective means "for negotiating power relationships at all levels." The rituals are important in creating these social asymmetries, but also critical are the items produced for and used in these contexts. These items can include ritual attire, paraphernalia, and objects depicting important religious symbols that are enacted or displayed in rituals. By giving ideologies physical form through "a codified visual symbolism" (Bawden 2004:119), items used in ritual contexts serve as a constant reminder of one ideology's primacy over others. As is well known in archaeological discourse, DeMarrais, Castillo, and Earle (1996:16) call this process the materialization of ideology.

The materialization of ideology is a critical component of structuring unequal social relations in societies in which ideology is a significant source of power, because it provides a tangible way to manipulate beliefs and "to guide social action" (Earle 1997:10). Materialization of specific ideologies is important to emerging leaders in power building because an elite extending its ideology "through materialization promotes its objectives and legitimacy at the expense of competing groups" and through materialization, ideology is made a "significant element of political strategy" (DeMarrais, Castillo, and Earle 1996:17). Most importantly, materialized ideology, whatever form it takes, integrates and legitimizes this new socioeconomic formation.

Materialization takes many forms, from small portable objects to large monuments to events such as communal and ceremonial feasts. The forms taken by individuals are critical in the efficacy of ideology as a source of social power. DeMarrais, Castillo, and Earle (1996:17) suggest that there are four principal forms of materialization: ceremonial events, symbolic objects and icons, public monuments and landscapes, and writing systems. Each varies in terms of a person's access to resources and the strategies by which they are used to materialize ideology. For example, monumental architecture and ceremonies can serve to integrate and define disparate populations, and symbolic objects and icons can be used as emblems of office or as highly portable vessels that display the principal symbolic motifs of an ideology. Because archaeologists deal with material things, this focus on materialization can provide us with direct access to the strategies used by people in their efforts to co-opt positions of leadership.

By no means do I pretend this to be an exhaustive summary of the factors responsible for emerging leadership. I simply wish to highlight aspects of feasting, ritual, and materialization that are important contributors in the emergence of permanent positions of leadership. To illustrate the importance of these factors, I now turn to the South Coast of Peru and focus on the emergence of leadership in Nasca. In the context of Andean prehistory, Nasca is one of many pre-Inca "civilizations" to have emerged independently, and although aspects of Nasca are well known, archaeologists are just beginning to understand the processes that led to its emergence.

## ARCHAEOLOGICAL CONTEXT

The South Coast of Peru is well known for the development of indigenous complex societies, beginning with the Paracas and Nasca cultures and ending with conquest by the Inca Empire in the late fifteenth century. Paracas and Nasca are best known for their elaborate material cultures of textiles and polychrome pottery. The latter, along with the Moche, were labeled "mastercraftsmen" in an important treatise on ancient cultures of the Andes (Sawyer 1968).

The South Coast of Peru includes the modern department of Ica and the Acarí Valley to the south (figure 7.1). The heartland of Nasca society was the Río Grande/Ica river system. The Nasca region in general is characterized by dry desert, with rivers that originate high in the Andes cutting across the landscape like green stitching on tan cloth. The most important—and limited—resource within this terrain was, and still is, water. The water regimen along the southern coast is very unpredictable. Generally speaking, the amount of perennial water that feeds the rivers of the drainages decreases and becomes more unpredictable as one moves from north to south. Overall, the South Coast desert environment is marginal and appears to have limited population growth until later prehistory because of an inadequate economic base. Some scholars have suggested that the marginal environment prevented highly complex societies from ever developing in the region (Silverman 1996:99).

Here my focus is on the southern Nasca region (SNR; figure 7.1). Admittedly, part of this focus is research bias, as this is where I have conducted my investigations over the past decade. However, this restricted

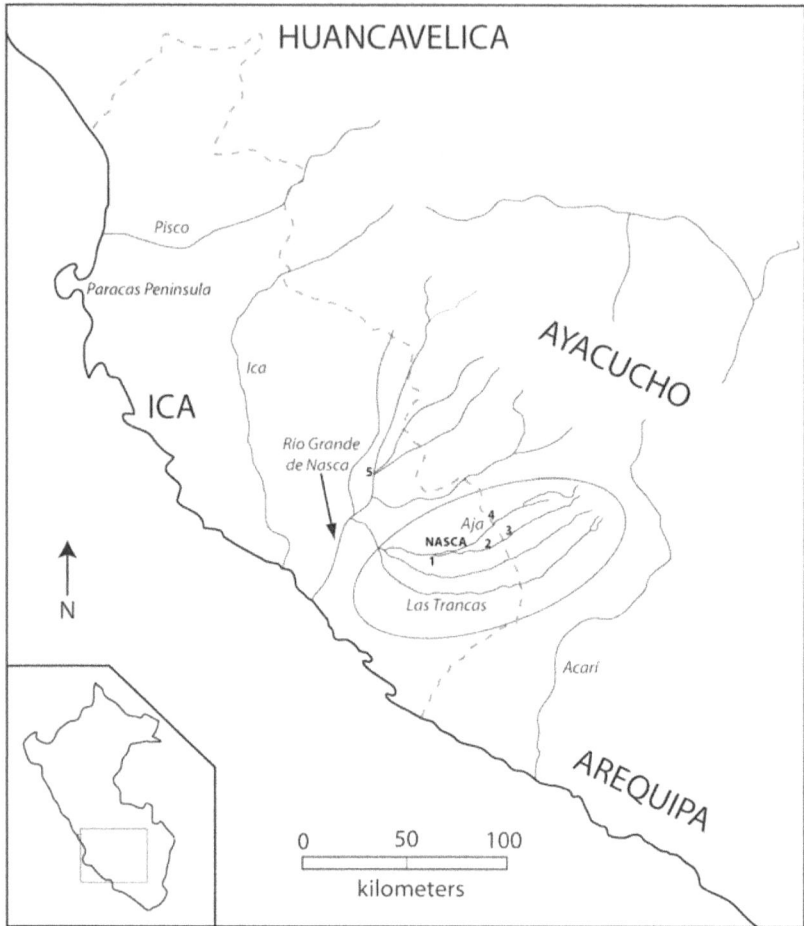

**FIGURE 7.1**

*The South Coast of Peru comprises the modern department of Ica (dotted line) and the Acarí Valley. The Nasca heartland contains the Río Grande de Nasca and Ica drainages, including their tributaries. The focus of this chapter is the southern Nasca region (SNR), which is demarcated by the square. (1) Cahuachi, (2) Marcaya, (3) Upanca, (4) Uchuchuma, (5) La Muña. Map by Kevin J. Vaughn.*

region also seems to have been the center of emergent leadership in Nasca from early in prehistory, and, as I will argue, it was the center of permanent leadership in the first millennium AD.

Contributing to the scarcity of water in the region, the SNR has a unique hydrological system characterized by "influent streams" (Schreiber and Lancho Rojas 2003). These rivers are characterized as such because of the transmission loss in river volume as the water flows into the lower foothills because of deep valley alluvium. This situation causes the rivers to flow partially on the surface, and at the base of the foothills, where the alluvium is deep, the rivers are reduced to a trickle until they appear to drop completely below the surface. These rivers then reemerge (indeed they "reappear") in the lower valleys of the region after running dry for dozens of kilometers.

Historically, reconstructing paleoenvironmental conditions on the South Coast has been something of an indirect endeavor. Based on settlement patterns, Schreiber and Lancho Rojas (2003) have stated that there were cycles of wetter and drier periods during the first millennium AD, with major desiccation occurring in the fifth and sixth centuries. Additionally, authors frequently invoke ice-core data from Quelccaya (Thompson et al. 1985)—high in the southern Andes of Peru—to infer that there was a major drought in the region during the sixth century (Carmichael 1998; Schreiber 1998). These archaeologists suggest that significant changes in Nasca prehistory during this century may have been due to deteriorating environmental conditions (Carmichael 1998; Schreiber 1998:263; Schreiber and Lancho Rojas 2003:156).

Recently, based on sediment and geomorphological analysis of desert loess, Eitel and others (2005) have reconstructed broad environmental conditions in the region, for the first time giving archaeologists access to this kind of data specific to the South Coast. They see an overall increase in desiccation beginning at 200 BC (their start of the Early Intermediate period) and lasting through AD 1000 and characterize this period as one of the driest ever during the Holocene. The importance of this reconstruction is that the emergence of Nasca society seems to have occurred during a period of increasing desiccation. I return to this point below.

## EVIDENCE FOR LEADERSHIP IN NASCA

Archaeological and (especially) art historical studies on the South Coast have traditionally focused on the impressive material culture of Paracas and Nasca. Paracas is most famous for multicolored textiles, some of the most elaborate in the pre-Hispanic New World, and Nasca is most renowned for colorful polychrome pottery. Over the past several decades, archaeologists (especially) have attempted to rectify this particularistic focus on material culture by focusing on settlement survey and on scientific excavations of ceremonial centers and habitations. Following the traditional Andean chronological scheme devised by John Rowe and his students in the mid-twentieth century, archaeologists generally divide the region's chronology into a series of alternating horizons, defined by pan-Andean integration and "intermediate periods" when that interregional integration collapses (table 7.1). Because the prehistory of the Nasca region has been summarized elsewhere (Schreiber and Lancho Rojas 2003; Silverman and Proulx 2002), here I focus on specific junctures in time that speak to emergent or sustained leadership. I begin this discussion with a consideration of the evidence of leadership in the Early Horizon (circa 800 BC to AD 1) and then move to my principal focus, Early Nasca (AD 1 to 450). Archaeologists have generally understood leadership in Early Nasca to be based on ritual feasting that was reinforced in group ceremonies and the circulation of polychrome pottery bearing a materialized ideology. I discuss the emergence of this leadership, as well as its collapse, to demonstrate the fluidity of the positions that developed in the first few centuries AD.

## EVIDENCE FOR PRE-NASCA LEADERSHIP

The Early Horizon represents the first extraregional integration of the Andes in prehistory. This integration came in the form of the well-known religious cult based in the northern highlands at Chavín de Huantar (Burger 1992; Rick 2005). The South Coast manifestation of the Chavín phenomenon is known as the Paracas culture. Excavations by Julio C. Tello on the Paracas Peninsula made this culture famous by revealing elaborate textiles known as the Paracas Necropolis and Cavernas traditions. Paracas is most famous for spectacular textiles, and textiles are believed to have been the principal vehicles for Paracas ideology, as well as symbols of Paracas authority (Paul 1990). The source of these textiles is apparently in the Paracas Peninsula, far to the north of the SNR.

Toward the latter part of the Early Horizon, there is a substantial increase in settlements in the Nasca region (Cook 1999; DeLeonardis 1997), and the SNR appears to have witnessed a sizable increase in population as well. Van Gijseghem (2006) suggests that the SNR—because of the effects of demographic growth to the north—acted as a frontier zone and provided a new cultural landscape for migrant populations. Furthermore, he believes that this initial colonization promoted a social milieu of competition for prominence between lineages and groups in a previously unoccupied cultural landscape (Van Gijseghem 2006). One locus of this competition was at Cahuachi.

Cahuachi is located in the Nasca Valley, about 20 kilometers downstream from the modern town of Nasca (see figure 7.1). Apparently, part of the early emergence of Cahuachi's importance was related to the sacred character tied to its location on the cultural landscape. The site is found in a unique position, where water reemerges in the riverbed, which upstream

TABLE 7.1

*Andean and Regional Chronology*

| Horizons and Intermediate Periods | Local Period | Culture | Nasca Phases | Paleoclimate* | Approximate Dates |
|---|---|---|---|---|---|
| Late Horizon | Inca | Inca | N/a | Arid (N < 50 mm) | AD 1476–1532 |
| Late Intermediate | Tiza | Tiza | N/a | Semiarid (N = 150–200 mm) | AD 1000–1476 |
| Middle Horizon | Loro | Loro, Wari | Nasca 8, MH 1–2 | Arid (N < 100 mm) | AD 750–1000 |
| | | Late Nasca | Nasca 6–7 | | AD 550–750 |
| Early Intermediate | Nasca | Middle Nasca | Nasca 5 | Arid (N < 100 mm) | AD 450–550 |
| | | **Early Nasca** | **Nasca 2–4** | | **AD 1–450** |
| | | **Proto Nasca** | **Nasca 1** | | **100 BC–AD 1** |
| Early Horizon | Formative | | | | |
| | | Paracas | | Arid (N < 150 mm) | 800–100 BC |
| Initial Period | Initial | Initial | | Semiarid (N < 250 mm) | 1800–800 BC |
| | | Late Archaic | | | 3000–1800 BC |
| Archaic | Archaic | Middle Archaic | | Semiarid | 6000–3000 BC |
| | | Early Archaic | | (N < 250 mm) | 10000–6000 BC |

*Environmental data from a recent study by Eitel and others (2005) are included to contextualize major environmental changes in the region.

is dry for many kilometers. Silverman (1993:305) has noted that today the site is known by locals as a place "'*donde aflora el agua,*' where the water comes to the surface." As Schreiber and Lancho Rojas (2003:156) note, the direct association of Cahuachi with water reemerging to the surface can be no accident in this dry desert landscape.

Cahuachi had previously been the locus of temporary settlements (Isla Cuadrado 1990), but several lines of archaeological evidence suggest that Cahuachi became a regionally important settlement during this time. First, in the Paracas phases, populations began to settle permanently at the site, as excavations by Strong in the 1950s revealed Late Paracas domestic dwellings here (Strong 1957:13). Second, the site apparently gained ritual importance in the region. This is seen in several examples of nonresidential architecture, such as the so-called Step-Fret Temple (Orefici 1988) and massive caches such as large cloth deposits found in excavations.

Third, recent work has suggested that the site began to emerge as a locus for the production of "Nasca 1 blackwares" (Vaughn and Van Gijseghem

2007). These are highly burnished, short black bowls with a very fine paste and very little temper. Iconography on blackwares is minimal and abstract, if present at all. Along with Van Gijseghem, I have argued that this was the beginning of what could be called the Nasca cult at Cahuachi, in which early leaders orchestrated ritual feasts using blackware bowls as serving vessels in concert with other ritual paraphernalia (especially elaborate textiles). Blackwares, however, were also produced in other regions of the SNR, based on compositional analysis (Vaughn and Van Gijseghem 2007), and Van Gijseghem (2004) has suggested that the "cult" at Cahuachi is but one of many competing groups in the social environment of the Late Formative.

However, something happened in the region that clearly triggered an increasing importance ascribed to Cahuachi. Eitel and others' (2005) data suggest increasing desiccation by the beginning of the first millennium. This date corresponds to the beginnings of Early Nasca culture. One key technological change was a shift from the use of postfired organic pigments to prefired mineral pigments on ceramics (Menzel, Rowe, and Dawson 1964). This was a major technological breakthrough and enabled Nasca artisans to create rich vibrant colors on their polychrome pottery. It appears that as soon as this innovation was made, drastic changes occurred throughout the region. I turn to these changes below.

## EARLY NASCA: FEASTING, RITUAL, AND MATERIALIZATION

Nasca, the most well known of the indigenous cultures to have developed in the region, emerged at the beginning of the Early Intermediate period and was a loosely allied "confederacy" of chiefdoms (Silverman and Proulx 2002) supported by a mixed agropastoral economic base. The majority of people in Early Nasca lived in small rural villages in the upper valleys, where permanent water was available (Vaughn 2004). The small villages were autonomous in terms of their subsistence economy, but the entire region was integrated into a wider social realm through an economy involving the production, circulation, and consumption of polychrome ceramics and through group rituals and feasting undertaken at Cahuachi (Vaughn 2004).

Building on previous practices initiated in the Early Horizon, the center of power in Early Nasca society was Cahuachi, which during Early Nasca became a primary ceremonial center for the region. Archaeological studies over the past few decades have demonstrated that Cahuachi served as the center of a regional Nasca cult and the focus of pilgrimage (Silverman 1993). Very few archaeologists (for example, Isla Cuadrado and Reindel 2006; Schreiber and Lancho Rojas 2003; Vaughn 2004) consider Cahuachi to be an "empty" ceremonial center, as previously characterized (Silverman 1993). Instead, reconstruction of activities undertaken at Cahuachi suggests a hyperceremonialism focused on rituals and feasts orchestrated by Early Nasca leaders. Some archaeologists go so far as to suggest that there was a large permanent population at the site (Isla Cuadrado and Reindel 2006: 396). Unfortunately, few publications have resulted from extensive excavations undertaken in recent years, so it is difficult to test this hypothesis.

How did the Early Nasca leaders establish themselves? Given the marginal environment in these lower valleys, it is highly unlikely that early leaders of Nasca were able to monopolize agricultural resources. Farming during this period was limited to floodplain agriculture and relied on annual flooding of the influent streams.[1] Furthermore, there is little evidence for large storage features implying agricultural surplus in Early Nasca villages (Vaughn 2004). At Cahuachi, the evidence for large storage features is not completely clear. For example, a series of rooms excavated at the site by Silverman (1993:302) provides some evidence for centralized storage facilities. According to Silverman, though, these were not used for storage of subsistence goods but instead for storage of ritual paraphernalia. Silverman believes that vessels found alongside walls and sealed in floors indicate small-scale efforts to store foodstuffs, but in her limited excavations, she did not find large, formal, or centrally located storage facilities (Silverman 1993:340).

In any event, whether or not there was large-scale storage at Cahuachi, certainly the economic base in Nasca was tenuous. Within this fragile economic milieu, the actual location of Cahuachi must have been important to emerging power in the region (see Arnold, chapter 6, this volume, for a discussion of the importance of control over resource areas).

The use of coercive force may have been limited in Nasca also. This statement should be qualified and requires a slight digression into a discussion of a cultural feature in Nasca known as trophy heads, as they are often invoked when attempting to understand the role of violence in Nasca society.[2] Trophy heads were decapitated heads, removed from the body after death and elaborately prepared to be displayed and carried. After decapitation, the foramen magnum was widened so that soft internal tissue could be removed from the brain case. Lips and eyelids were sewn shut, a hole was drilled through the frontal bone, and a carrying cord was passed through this hole.

An ongoing debate in Nasca archaeology revolves around the role of trophy heads in Nasca society. Some (for example, Proulx 1971, 2006) believe that trophy heads are material evidence for warfare; others (for example, Carmichael 1994) believe that they are symbolically linked to fertility. I have tended to side with the "symbolic" argument, not to deny the existence of violence in Nasca but because trophy head imagery appears with great frequency on iconography and there is a clear demonstrable link between the heads and agricultural fertility. It is clear now, however, that a simple dichotomy fails to adequately explain trophy heads and their role in Nasca society.

Analyses of trophy heads from cemeteries suggest that Early Nasca heads include those of males, females, and children (Forgey 2006; Kellner 2002; Williams, Forgey, and Klarich 2001). Based on mtDNA analysis, individuals whose heads were taken appear to be members of the Nasca Valley (in this case within the SNR), not of a foreign population (Forgey 2006). If trophy heads were the result of organized warfare, we would expect young males to make up the demographic profile of trophy heads and would expect trophy heads to be a distinct external population. Because trophy heads are made up of males, females, and children from within the SNR, some (including the author; see Vaughn 2005) have argued that trophy heads are not related to organized warfare. The demographic profile of a mixture of males, females, and young children is a typical ethnographic profile of small-scale raiding parties (Cameron 2008), suggesting that this may have been one manner in which the heads were obtained. Thus, the lack of an abundance of young males in the sample does not preclude violence or coercive force. By Middle and Late Nasca times, however, trophy heads are mostly from young males, suggesting that the scale of organized violence within the Nasca region changed in composition over time (Forgey 2006).

To move from osteological evidence to that of imagery, iconographically there are clear links between trophy heads and the growth of critical crops such as maize (numerous motifs actually depict plants growing directly out of trophy heads). Trophy heads are conceptualized by some archaeologists as part of a "life to death continuum" in which blood from decapitated heads was necessary for human and plant fertility (Carmichael 1992). It appears, then, that no matter how they were obtained, actual trophy heads were related to some concept of human and plant fertility, as well as ritual renewal, and had some sort of power as ritual objects (Conlee 2007). That trophy heads were used in some kind of ritual context is supported by the archaeological evidence of numerous caches of trophy heads found throughout the Nasca region (see Browne, Silverman, and García 1993; Forgey 2006; Williams, Forgey, and Klarich 2001 for summaries). Furthermore, in evaluating the trophy heads, Forgey (2006:105) demonstrates that wear patterns on the heads suggest prolonged use after they were prepared. It is difficult to reconstruct exactly how they were used after they were prepared, but I believe that whatever power they may have held must have been transferred to whoever used and displayed them.

Overall, then, there is little evidence for monopolization of scarce agricultural resources in Early Nasca, and the use of coercive force, even if limited to small-scale raiding, seems to have been closely tied to ritual display. Indeed, a large part of the power of Early Nasca leaders was based on their ability to control and manipulate the ritual realm. Leaders in Early Nasca appear to have been ritual specialists who gained their status through public ceremonies and prestige building tied to ritual and esoteric knowledge (Silverman 1993:338; Silverman and Proulx 2002). Sociopolitical leadership does not appear to be highly centralized in Early Nasca society, as there is little evidence for institutionalized stratification based on settlement patterns and analysis of burials (Carmichael 1988; Schreiber and Lancho Rojas 2003; Silverman and Proulx 2002; though see Isla Cuadrado and Reindel 2006 for a different view).[3] Instead, leadership was probably highly flexible and involved political acts and display (Silverman and Proulx 2002:247). These political acts were integrally related to the association that aspiring leaders had with agricultural fertility, and this ideology was communicated in major group ceremonies and feasting events. These may have been performed throughout the Nasca region, but clearly the most important of these events took place at Cahuachi.

Agricultural fertility and the importance of water pervade every aspect of Nasca material culture. Contextual analysis of Nasca polychrome pottery with natural motifs of animals such as killer whales, fish, and birds; agricultural produce such as chili peppers, beans, and maize; geometric figures; and supernatural creatures suggests that "almost the entire corpus of Nasca iconography is a sacred, interrelated visual system with its referents tied to the dominating themes of water and propagation" (Carmichael 1998:224). In addition to trophy heads, the well-known Nasca geoglyphs (Nasca Lines) were also a material manifestation of the central concern with agricultural fertility, water, and propagation. The Nasca Lines are straight lines, trapezoids, and monumental figures created on the desert floor by sweeping away oxidized rocks to reveal the lighter desert sand. They were most likely manifestations of the worship of mountain gods (*apus*) who controlled important weather-related phenomena, including clouds, lightning, and rain, in traditional Andean belief systems (Reinhard 1988:365). Using ethnographic and ethnohistoric evidence, Reinhard argues that the geoglyphs themselves were pathways used in rituals related to religious practices enacted to ensure that water would be provisioned for people and their crops (Reinhard 1988). Most anthropologists concur with this view (for example, Lambers 2006; Silverman and Proulx 2002).

Concepts of human and plant fertility appear to have been enacted in large public ceremonies and feasting. If we turn to ceramic iconography, there is evidence to suggest that large ceremonies involving feasting were a key aspect of Nasca ceremonial life. For example, Townsend (1985:125, fig. 7) reports a bowl that depicts some kind of agricultural ceremony. According to Townsend (1985:125), the ceramic artisan "intended to represent a costumed figure such as those who appeared in the public plazas, and perhaps also in agricultural fields, to celebrate the great annual feasts of the Nazca region." In another example, Carmichael (1998:224, fig. 13) describes a particular double-spout bottle depicting a scene with an individual holding a panpipe surrounded by ceramic containers and people playing musical instruments. Carmichael interprets this scene to be a festival. Still other iconographic examples show groups of people playing musical instruments such as drums, rattles, and panpipes and carrying agricultural implements and products such as digging sticks and the plants themselves (Proulx 2006).

Archaeological evidence supports this interpretation of Nasca iconography and demonstrates that large ceremonial feasts took place at Cahuachi. For example, in some of the earliest scientific excavations at Cahuachi, William Duncan Strong (1957:31) reported finding "broken panpipes, llama remains, bird plumage, and other apparently feasting and sacrificial materials." Valdez (1994) reports on excavations carried out at Cahuachi in 1986. The excavations, located near Strong's earlier excavations, revealed abundant food remains including maize (*Z. mays*), beans (*P. lunatus, P. vulgaris*), and camelid bones from all parts of the animal, suggestive of a brief feasting episode (Valdez 1994). Silverman (1993; also see Silverman and Proulx 2002) interprets most of the material remains at Cahuachi to periodic pilgrimage and feasting, and Orefici (1993; Orefici and Drusini 2003) suggests that most of the activities taking place at the site were related to public ceremonies.

These ceremonies most likely involved rites that welcomed the annual harvest and the renewed flooding of rivers each year to provide water for fields (Vaughn 2004). As previously described, Cahuachi is located where water from the Nasca River emerges from the ground, and the site's placement on the landscape had a strong association with water, fertility, and the agricultural cycle. It is not difficult to imagine that those individuals who sponsored feasts and ceremonies tied to agricultural cycles and who associated themselves directly with places on the landscape related to fertility and water would have established positions as intermediaries between the natural and supernatural worlds (see Pauketat, chapter 8, this volume, for examples of religious figures who consolidated leadership in native North America).

There is yet another component of these ritual events that I wish to explore. If these ceremonies were critical events in which political acts were carried out, materialization of this religious authority would have made it possible for individuals or groups sponsoring these feasts not only to establish and reinforce their positions but also to broaden their access to additional social groups. The monuments at Cahuachi and the ceremonial feasts were important forms of materialization. However, another important form, one that was highly portable and could serve to remind people on a daily basis of elite-serving ideologies, was polychrome ceramics.

The role of polychrome pottery as the principal medium of Nasca ideology has been reported extensively in the Nasca literature (for example, Carmichael 1998; Proulx 2006; Sawyer 1961; Silverman and Proulx 2002). Its role in ideology, however, extended beyond simply depicting the important themes of Nasca religion. Polychromes were actually central to feasts and ceremonies because they were the principal vessels in which food and drink were served (Vaughn 2004). Indeed, they are the most common vessels appropriate for serving found at Cahuachi (Silverman 1993), and they were integral parts of feasts such as those described by Valdez and Strong. Thus, it is clear that polychrome pottery was the most important *ritual paraphernalia* used by sponsors of feasts in Early Nasca and that it played an essential role in the materialization of symbols related to ritual knowledge possessed by early leaders. Ultimately, then, I suggest that by linking themselves directly to these symbols, those who controlled the iconography of the polychromes, depicting agricultural and fertility themes, would have had yet another way of establishing themselves as intermediaries between the natural and supernatural worlds.

Given our expectations, then, one way in which emerging leaders attempt to extend their influence in a society such as Nasca is by attempting to control and manipulate symbols that are directly tied to ideology. To test this theory, I, along with colleagues, employed geochemical sourcing combined with an analysis of clay and pigment variability in the region to trace the source of Nasca polychrome pottery production. In multiple analyses, we concluded that Cahuachi was the source of the majority of polychrome ceramics used at residential sites in the SNR (Vaughn et al. 2005, 2006; Vaughn and Neff 2000, 2004). Indeed, Orefici and Drusini

(2003:144) report evidence for pottery production at Cahuachi consisting of kilns, production-related materials such as paintbrushes, caches of pigments, and unfired clay, indicating that production took place at the site. These studies demonstrate that one particular artifact that materialized ideology was directly associated with the activities of leaders taking place at Cahuachi, suggesting that the production of this important material good was critical to the development of their positions at the site.

The flip side to this proposition of course was consumption. If public ritual with sponsors and an audience provides an arena for new social relations to be contested, then the consumption of goods bearing materialized ideology should provide clues to whether other members of Nasca society engaged in and enabled these public rituals. Indeed, evidence from excavations of domestic sites throughout the SNR demonstrates that polychromes from their source at Cahuachi were widely distributed throughout habitation sites in the SNR. For example, at three primarily Early Nasca sites—Marcaya, Upanca, and Uchuchuma (see figure 7.1)—they make up nearly 60 percent of the vessel assemblage and are the principal serving vessels at the sites (Vaughn 2005). With the exception of a few vessel shapes (head jars and "cupbowls" specifically), polychrome bowls and vases enjoyed unrestricted distribution to households, regardless of their status (Vaughn 2004). Despite this wide distribution, polychromes are compositionally homogeneous, suggesting a restricted locus of production and contrasting with Early Nasca wares that are compositionally heterogeneous (Vaughn et al. 2006).

Based on this work, we can conclude that the emerging Nasca "craft economy" depended on centralized production of polychromes and was controlled by early leaders, with ritual feasting the most important mechanism by which these individuals of Nasca distributed pottery. Furthermore, the consumption of the pottery was widespread in Nasca society. What is critical for the purposes of this chapter is that the corpus of recent evidence suggests that *Early Nasca leaders were responsible for materializing important icons of Nasca ideology.* They were responsible for the production of the vehicles for this ideology and for their distribution in feasts—events also laden with social and political meaning. What is particularly telling is the widespread consumption of Nasca polychromes throughout the SNR and, I suspect (though this has yet to be verified through excavations), throughout the Nasca region as well. In other words, given that these vessels were used in day-to-day Nasca domestic life, the majority of people in Nasca actively engaged and promoted these leadership positions.

Illustrating the fluid nature of leadership, the importance of the icons of Nasca and the mechanisms for this leadership extended beyond just the Nasca region. For example, in the Moquegua Valley, Goldstein (2000) reports that local elites engaged in long-distance exchange with contemporaneous Nasca leaders. These "intermediate elites" associated themselves with distant powers to enhance their own precarious positions within their own societies. Ultimately, Goldstein argues, elite interaction and the consumption of exotic goods were important elements in the rise of chiefly power in the region.[4] Closer to the SNR, Valdez (1998) makes a similar argument for local leaders in the Acarí Valley, as does Silverman (1997:445) for the development of Carmen society in the Pisco Valley.

To summarize, Cahuachi appears to have gained some importance by the latter part of the Early Horizon. At that time, the residents constituted one of several competing groups in the SNR. By Early Nasca, however, leaders at Cahuachi had established regional importance, and the site had become a primary ceremonial and pilgrimage center. What were the sources of these changes? Though the data are not precise enough at this juncture in research, I suspect that regional environmental desiccation may have been a factor. More importantly, though, the technological changes in pottery production, *specifically those that allowed for prefired mineral-based pigments*, must have been a major factor enabling leadership to become more permanent.

During the Early Horizon and the florescence of Paracas culture, textiles served as ritual attire and display objects (Paul 1990) and also to materialize ideology. Although there is a direct link between the iconography of Paracas textiles and Nasca ceramics (Sawyer 1997), during Early Nasca, ceramics became much more important as a medium for religious motifs. This is not to say that textiles were not elaborate and important in Early Nasca (for example, see Frame 2003–2004). However, a sharp decline in their use is seen during this period. Sawyer (1997) has proposed that this decline in textile use was due to production becoming too time-consuming (for example, it took more than an estimated twenty-nine thousand hours to produce only one Paracas textile [Paul 1990:32]). Silverman (1993) suggests that the shift from the use of textiles to the use of pottery was due to the growth of the Cahuachi cult and the need for ritual pottery.

I agree with this position but believe that there is more: in Early Nasca, a more portable and efficient means of materializing ideology was necessary to *maintain the prominence of the cult based at Cahuachi*. Ceramics offered several advantages over textiles as materialized ideology. Both are potentially portable, but elaborate ceramics are far more *efficient* to manufacture than elaborate textiles, especially after fuel and the raw materials needed for pottery production have been collected.[5] A skilled group of potters can potentially make many more pots than a group of equivalently skilled weavers, enabling this materialized ideology to reach more social groups. Because of an economy of scale (see Stanish, chapter 5, this volume, for an extensive discussion of economies of scale), the labor involved in making an additional pot by a group of potters or even a single potter is relatively trivial, but this is not the case with multiple elaborate textiles.

The efficiency in pottery manufacture when compared with textile production results in a critical difference: it allows anyone who controls this technology to attain a "widespread level of legitimacy," one of the characteristics of permanent leadership that I outlined previously. Furthermore, ceramics are not just more efficient vehicles for materialized ideology. They serve a very practical purpose, because they can be used as vessels for both food and drink: the critical ingredients of successful feasts and ceremonies. Thus, polychrome ceramics were the critical ingredient in the emergence and maintenance of the permanent leadership of Early Nasca leaders. They were portable, they materialized ideology, they were used in public rituals, and they reached a broad audience who in turn brought them back to residences throughout the hinterland, where they were used in daily life.

## CHANGES IN NASCA LEADERSHIP

The pattern I describe above seems to endure through the mid–fifth century AD (corresponding to the beginning of Nasca phase 5), and then something happened again in the Nasca region. Perhaps because of the extended drought documented from Quelccaya, settlements began to aggregate into much larger habitations, iconography drastically changed to incorporate new substyles, and for the first time the subsurface water in the dry middle valleys was accessed by underground aqueducts called *puqios*. A severe drought would have had an enormous impact on the control that Nasca leaders retained, especially if their power was derived from access to supernatural knowledge associated with agricultural fertility. If a drought caused agricultural productivity to fail, leaders who served as intermediaries to the supernatural world would have lost much of their authoritative role.

Carmichael (1998:225, fig. 14) proposes a model of Nasca 5 ceramic production from this possible drought and subsequent societal changes. In this model, he suggests that stress caused by a severe drought would have fostered accelerated ceramic production because those who manipulated Nasca ideology were forced to reinvent icons. The increased competition in ceramic production would have resulted in experimentation and innovation. The scenario proposed by Carmichael fits well into the model that I outline for Early Nasca. The hyperceremonialism at Cahuachi peaked in Early Nasca during a time when the entire region was suffering from desiccation. This situation must have made Early Nasca leadership much more tenuous. The prestige associated with leaders living at Cahuachi collapsed with environmental degradation and resource depletion in Nasca 5. This collapse forced a realignment of the existing system, and the cyclical transient "office" that was held by Nasca leaders became vulnerable to competitive rivalry, perhaps resulting in a power shift to other aspiring leaders.

Indeed, Cahuachi, though still used as a ceremonial center, seemed to lose much of its importance in Nasca 5, and this change appears to have resulted in a power shift to the north in Palpa. There, a large site called La Muña (see figure 7.1), with civic-ceremonial architecture and a large mortuary complex with elite burials, was established in Nasca 5 (Isla Cuadrado and Reindel 2006). One heavily looted tomb measuring 13 meters deep was clearly the burial of a very important individual. Though looted, remains in excavations included gold, fine ceramics, and textiles. This is the only site of its kind on the South Coast during this period, and although data are still forthcoming, the site suggests that permanent leadership had shifted again in the region.

Ultimately, the scenarios I propose are subject to testing and future archaeological work. I believe that the importance of this study, however, is that through detailed archaeological investigations, we are able to trace the development of leadership in one particular region in the Andes. Leadership was part of the Andean landscape for several millennia before it became permanent on the South Coast. Permanent leadership in Nasca, because of a tenuous agricultural regime and relatively limited coercive force, was always closely tied to feasting, public ritual, and an efficient, broadly distributed materialized ideology that was incorporated into daily life.

### Notes

1. Some extensive agricultural terracing in the upper valleys of the region is associated with Upanca, an Early Nasca site (Vaughn and Linares Grados 2006), but it is unclear whether the terracing was used during this period. Some preliminary work has been done at the terraces, but their chronology is difficult to assess (although there are some Early Nasca ceramics on the surface of the terraces). Schreiber (1999) believes that the terraces were used by the Wari Empire, and she is currently directing a project to test that working hypothesis. Until work is completed at the terraces, it remains unclear how they fit into the wider political economy of Nasca.

2. Obviously, the label *trophy head* implies that the head was taken in warfare. To avoid this assumption, some authors prefer less loaded terms, such as *disembodied heads* (DeLeonardis 2000) or *severed heads* (Conlee 2007). Here I use the term *trophy heads* only to avoid confusion.

3. The evidence that the authors put forth for stratification is primarily based on burial data in Middle Nasca. The evidence in Early Nasca is unclear.

4. There is no specific evidence to suggest whether these Moquegua leaders were interacting directly with leaders at Cahuachi or obtained exotic goods through down-the-line exchange. Given the small quantities of Nasca ceramics in the Moquegua region, quite possibly the latter is true. The point, however, is still that these intermediate elites were associating themselves with distant powers.

5. Previous studies suggested that clay for pottery was collected near Cahuachi (Vaughn and Neff 2004), but fuel sources have not been determined. Huarango (*Prosopis chilensis*) trees grow in the valley bottom today, and even with protracted desiccation, they were surely present in the past as well.

# 8

# Of Leaders and Legacies in Native North America

## Timothy R. Pauketat

> Probably every Indian tribe, north and south, had its early hero god, the great doer or teacher of things.
>
> —James Mooney, *The Ghost-Dance Religion and Wounded Knee*

> Whether prophets sprang up only in response to the peculiar conditions resulting from the presence of the whites it is impossible to say....It is quite possible that conditions similar to those developing from the occupancy of America by Europeans had occurred in pre-Columbian times when one tribe was hard pressed by another.
>
> —Paul Radin, *The Winnebago Tribe*

To a considerable extent, leaders lead by consent. That is, by definition, leaders must have followers who concede to their authority in order to have the authority to lead. Thus, the relationship between leadership and a community of followers is key regardless of one's theoretical vantage point or case study. Various contributors to this volume recognize this essential social fact (especially Bowser and Patton, chapter 3 and Kantner, chapter 11). Some contributors view it in a "brokered" or top-down fashion, as with Kusimba and Kusimba's discussion of administrative councils (chapter 10; see Kantner, chapter 11, this volume). Others in this volume understand the "pluralistic" or bottom-up character of some consensus building, as with Vaughn's, Eerkens's, Wiessner's, and Bird and Bliege Bird's respective considerations of communal feasts, fandangos, social exchanges, and forager decision making.

Of course, consensual relationships between leaders and followers are not restricted to certain times or places within the human experience, although they do take different forms under varying historical conditions, distinctions that underwrite notions that elites in middle-range societies are "managerial" or "emergent" rather than all-powerful (see Stanish, chapter 5, and Vaughn, chapter 7, this volume). That is, consensus building existed in all times and places in the past, and it still exists today in both brokered and pluralistic terms (Kantner, chapter 11, this volume). Understanding the relationship between leadership and consensus formation in these terms is as relevant to explaining today's ruling elites and governments as it was in the appearance of the first hereditary leaders in the ancient past, making the relationship between authority and consensus an ongoing historical process (Pauketat 2007).

In this chapter, I examine the relationships between leaders and consensus formation through the lens of community, highlighting the material and religious dimensions of the community-formation process in Historic and pre-Columbian-era native North America. To expose the means whereby communities and institutionalized leaders are mutually constructed around authorities, I draw on certain notions of materiality, object agency, and personhood (see Fowler 2004; Gosden 2005; Knappett and Malafouris 2008; Meskell 2004). I also draw freely from case material that has very little to do with the first appearance of inherited leadership positions or centralized authority in native North America. However, by doing so, I argue for a general explanation of the historical processes behind the emergence of leadership.

After a brief consideration of theories of community, agency, and personhood, I review the characteristics and life histories of a number of well-known native North American leaders from the seventeenth through twentieth centuries AD. I argue that these prominent historical figures *and the materiality of community building* shed considerable light on ancient historical processes involving what we imperfectly identify as the institutionalization of leadership. To make this case, I turn in the second part of the chapter to a consideration of Mississippian-period leaders from AD 1050 to about 1600, pointing to recent evidence indicating that the social construction of narratives was synonymous with the institutionalization of the practices of leadership and the transformation of community identities through experiences of great places (figure 8.1). In the end, I return to a couple of Historic-period examples to show how would-be authorities might emerge from particular histories of leaders and community building.

## FROM IMAGINED COMMUNITIES TO SOCIAL PERSONS

Since the 1960s, explanations of the relationship between leaders and communities have focused on understanding the institutionalization of

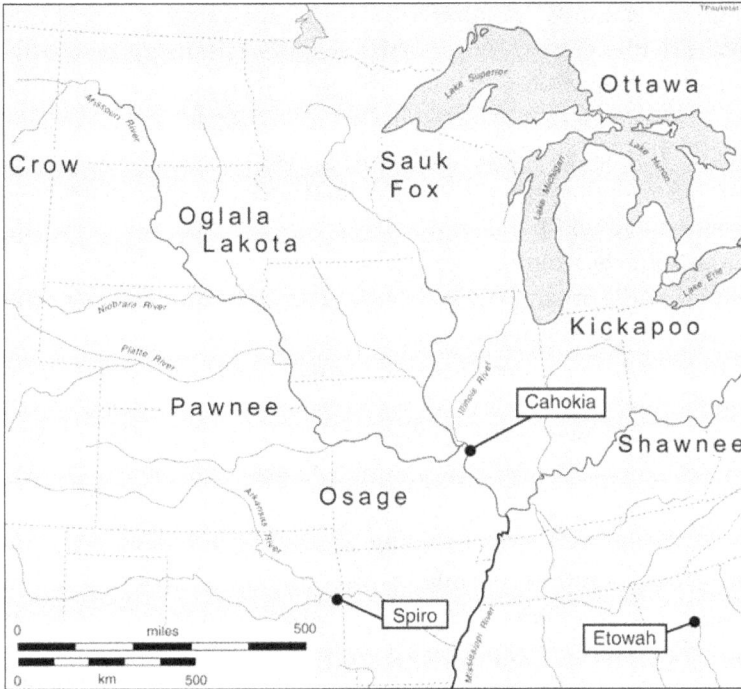

**FIGURE 8.1**

*Locations of Cahokia, Etowah, and Spiro, along with other indigenous nations mentioned in the text. Map by Timothy R. Pauketat.*

leadership, as if it could be separated from the historical formation of communities or corporate ideologies (compare Clark and Blake 1994; Hayden 1995 with Pauketat and Emerson 1999; Saitta and Keene 1994). Initially, explanations took opposing positions: there were integrative or managerial models that espoused bottom-up views, in which leaders arose owing to organizational necessity, and there were political or coercive models that understood leaders to create themselves in more proactive, self-aggrandizing ways (see Brumfiel and Earle 1987; Fried 1967; Service 1975). More recently, the varying emphases on leaders or communities have been collapsed into single models characterized by alternative leadership strategies: selfish, network, or apical versus collaborative, corporate, or constituent (for example, Beck 2003; Blanton et al. 1996; Mills 2000; Pauketat 1994; Stanish 2004).

Most of these approaches are based on a view of communities as "natural" organizational phenomena (Isbell 2000, following Anderson 1983).

From such a natural-community (or "building-block") perspective, communities are thought to be irreducible features of human social organizations that exist everywhere and serve essential integrative functions that articulate basal household or family groups with the larger society (see Pauketat 2007). In explanations based on natural-community viewpoints, communities are the petri dishes wherein leadership institutions grow (for example, Muller 1997).

An imagined-community view posits that communities are not simply or even primarily organizations. Instead, communities are dynamic identities (connected to common experiences, places, and memories) that are susceptible to being more or less inclusive, politicized, commemorated, reinvented, and scaled up or down (Isbell 2000; Pauketat 2000a). This alternative vision of community does not reject the "reality" of communities and their basis in social interaction but instead recognizes that the interactive reality means that communities are subject to continuous renegotiations of interests and the social production of memories whenever people gather together, encounter one another, or interact within the landscapes of experience. Community is a dimension of all social engagements and is produced, experienced, or invoked to variable extent in every social act (Pauketat 2008b). One's village, neighborhood, or ceremonial center might instantiate community, but so might meetinghouses, public plazas, battlefields, the Internet, or individuals who embody the ideals and principles of the collective.

Given this viewpoint, it is not a stretch to envision various sorts of communities whose ideals—which is to say, their organizing principles—undergird and also precede community authorities. That is, certain people embody or project a community's ideals or identities more or better than others. Such community leaders, who might alter the ideals even as they promote them, could emerge in part because they fit some preexisting sensibilities. In ancient times, such principles were very much rooted in one's ancestry and kin ties (see Fowler 2004; Gillespie 2001). The spirits of the dead or other supernatural beings, or their representations or associated physical manifestations, could be understood as the community's symbolic core. From shamans to kings, some leaders were powerful because they assumed the position of ancestors, superhuman beings, or otherworldly powers (for example, Clark 1997).

## AGENCY AND PERSONHOOD

How do we get powerful legitimate authorities in the first place? To explain, it is necessary to begin with two theoretical assumptions. First, ephemeral leaders of one kind or another always exist, owing to force of personality or the exigencies of history (see Eerkens, Stanish, Arnold, Vaughn, chapters 4, 5, 6, and 7, respectively, this volume). Second, across pre-Columbian North America (and in most preindustrial societies around the world), agency was not located solely in the human body; powers, spirits, and other supernatural forces that animated life were located in things, substances, and intangible phenomena (wind, light, heat, and the like).

With the second assumption, I also mean to invoke a particular view of agency stemming from the works of Gell (1998), Latour (1999, 2005), Strathern (1988), Wagner (1991), and others that holds as uncommon fully autonomous human "individual" agents (outside certain modern Western contexts). That is, the ability to motivate people or other biological organisms to act—which is to say, have agency—is not one solely owned or entirely embodied by human beings or even other living organisms. It is instead shared by a variety of organisms, inanimate things, unseen forces, and spaces.

Stated another way, agency—the ability to bring about a consequence or cultural change—is dispersed, shared, or distributed (see also Chapman 2000; Knappett and Malafouris 2008; Meskell 2004). This is not to suggest that inert objects have a historically independent ability to act or effect change. Rather, such objects or other organisms, inanimate things, unseen forces, spaces, and landscapes are "nodes" in historically constructed webs, networks, fields, or arenas, at the heart of which are human beings (Gosden 2005; Meskell 2004). The broad implications of understanding leadership in such "actor network" terms (Latour 1999) are much the same as in the relational terms of a contemporary sense of "practice theory" and "landscape archaeology" (Ashmore 2004; Joyce and Lopiparo 2005; Pauketat 2001b). That is, when human beings act in this world, they engage or implicate interests, identities, narratives, and entire social fields. For this reason, all agency is actually a negotiation with and between the people, places, and things of one's experiences and memories.

The point is not a semantic one, but a profoundly processual issue that determines the starting points for our inquiries about leadership. First and foremost, it means that leaders, to be leaders (that is, agents with the power to lead), must somehow be vested with agency that is otherwise dispersed within society and beyond. That is, they cannot necessarily strategize to grab power in ways that step outside their cultural contexts or landscapes. Instead, grabbing power is a collective process of centering a dispersed social field in a place or person.

Persons are, in fact, idealized agents who embody some larger social identity or community sensibilities (Gillespie 2001). That is, such persons are the embodiments—living, dead, animate, or inanimate—of community identities (see Fowler 2004; Gell 1998; Gillespie 2001). They may not be located in one place, thing, or human body (following Strathern's [1988] distinction between "individuals" and "dividuals" and Wagner's [1991] discussion of "fractal" persons). At certain scales, the ways in which identities are personified—let us say, by gathering causal properties unto themselves—are tantamount to political centralization. Thus, that which some might envision as the institutionalization of leadership could instead be seen as the personification of community identities or ideals.

Such notions of agency and personhood have the virtue of better fitting historical characterizations of native North American cultures. This is particularly true of the animistic qualities of American Indian religious beliefs. In many American Indian cosmologies (as with many people around the world), the worlds of the living and the dead, or the cultural, natural, and supernatural, were and are not separate bounded spheres of human experience. As described historically, seen and unseen supernatural forces imbued this world and impelled human actions. Among various midwestern, Plains-Prairie, and southeastern groups, for instance, the mysterious life force called *wa-kan-da* by Siouan speakers and *kawaharu* by Caddoan speakers inhabited substances such as fire, water, air, and earth (see Bailey 1995; Fletcher and La Flesche 1992; McGee 1897; Powers 1977; Radin 1990; Wissler 1974[1934]). Moreover, ancestor spirits inhabited certain places or things, and the living engaged the dead in these places or through these things. In some cases, the things and not the living human bodies—such as sacred posts among the Mississippians and their descendants—*were* persons (see Hall 1997; see also Kelly 2006; Pauketat 2008a; Pauketat and Alt 2005).

## SOME AMERICAN INDIAN LEADERS

The history of American Indian peoples since first European contact is replete with leaders of all sorts and stripes (see Hoxie 1996). There are political, military, civil, and religious leaders, or combinations thereof, variously termed sachems, elders, captains, werowances, caciques, and shamans. Some were willing leaders who sought power. Others were accidental leaders thrust into history by circumstance. Some might be said to have led heterarchical segments of society; others were apical persons in social or political hierarchies (following Crumley 1995). Some achieved their positions in life; others we are told were ascribed those positions at birth. Few were probably simply one thing or the other. Instead, they were some combination of a few or all of the above produced during and after the fact of being a leader.

This will be evident through a cursory review of some well-known Historic-era leaders. Unfortunately, any review of American Indian figures drawn from recent history will necessarily be biased because of the short-comings of historiographic accounts. For my present purposes, I do not attempt a systematic overview, which may be impossible. I also do not limit my review to certain types or historical contexts of leaders, or even to official leaders at all (for example, Pocahontas), in part to make the point that leadership was an emergent property of particular individuals. In addi-tion, I seek to highlight four general observations about historical figures in different contexts by drawing freely if loosely on some of the better-known characters from the past four centuries across native North America (see table 8.1). For present purposes, I ignore the larger history of these actors, many of whom rose to historical prominence through their engagement with or against Euro-Americans.

I also do not discuss a whole list of historic figures whose positions were inherited, including many southeastern rulers, male and female, whose authority would be undermined by colonial events. In part, this is because hereditary leaders are not as well known today, except perhaps for the Virginia Algonquian ruler Powhatan (who did actively pursue a political and cultural legacy, aided by his daughter). For instance, generations of sachems in the Northeast are poorly known outside particular encounters with or memorials to Euro-American dominance (such as when the head of the Indian leader dubbed King Phillip was mounted on a pike at Plymouth for twenty-five years). Perhaps in certain contexts, their very suc-cess gave them a peculiar sort of historical anonymity.

Sometimes their names correspond to those of their predecessors, to gods and spirits, or to entire peoples. For example, a host of Osage chiefs in the eighteenth and nineteenth centuries were named Pawhuska, which is also a place-name in modern-day Oklahoma (Rollings 1992). Like-wise, the name Powhatan stood for a leading person, a town, and a people (Rountree 1989). Lastly, one "mythical" hero character, Pawhukatawa, was talked about among the Skidi Pawnees "almost daily in 1835"; yet another Skidi Pawnee chief took on the persona of Pawhukatawa and was pho-tographed as him in 1868 (Hyde 1974:195; see also Grinnell 1961).

Perhaps of greater historical significance than hereditary authority was the active pursuit of legacy, or what might more reasonably be called the construction of one's narrative. In some sense, such a construction of legacy may have constituted the "institutionalization" of leadership. And in

TABLE 8.1

*Select Native North American Historical Figures\**

| Historical Figure | Century | Identity | Leadership | Vision? | Predecessor? | Media? |
|---|---|---|---|---|---|---|
| Black Elk | Early 20th | Lakota | Religious | X | X | X |
| Black Hawk | Early 19th | Sauk-Fox | Military | | | X |
| Cheez-Tah-Paezh | Late 19th | Crow | Religious, military | | | X |
| Cochise | Late 19th | Apache | Political, military | | | |
| Crazy Horse | Late 19th | Oglala | Religious, military | X | | |
| Handsome Lake | Early 19th | Seneca | Religious | X | | X |
| Hiawatha | 16th | Mohawk | Religious, diplomatic | X | | X |
| Joseph | Mid-18th | Nez Percés | Civil, military | | X | |
| Kenekuk | Early 19th | Kickapoo | Religious | X | | X |
| Nakai-Doklini | Late 19th | Apache | Religious, military | X | | X |
| Neolin | Mid-18th | Delaware | Religious | X | X | X |
| Patheske | Mid-19th | Winnebago | Religious | X | | |
| Plenty Coups | Late 19th–20th | Crow | Political, military | X | | X |
| Pocahontas | Early 17th | Powhatan | Diplomatic | | X | X |
| Pontiac | Mid-17th | Ottawa | Political, military | | X | |
| Quanah Parker | Late 19th–20th | Comanche | Civil, military | | | |
| Redbird Smith | Late 19th | Cherokee | Civil, religious | | X | X |
| Red Cloud | Late 19th | Oglala | Political, military | | | |
| Roman Nose | Late 19th | Cheyenne | Political, military | | | |
| Sacagawea | Early 19th | Shoshone | Diplomatic | | | X |
| Seattle | Early 19th | Salish | Military, diplomatic | | | X |
| Shawnee Prophet | Early 19th | Shawnee | Religious | X | X | X |
| Sitting Bull | Late 19th | Lakota | Political, military, religious | X | | X |
| Smohalla | Late 19th | Wanapum/ Yakima | Military, religious, diplomatic | X | | |
| Tavibo | Late 19th | Paiute | Religious | X | | |
| Tecumseh | Early 19th | Shawnee | Political, military | | X | |
| Wovoka | Late 19th | Paiute | Religious | X | X | X |

\*From Hoxie 1996 and Mooney 1973

this regard, I will make the four general observations concerning the present overview of historical characters.

## FOUR OBSERVATIONS

The first observation of the Historic-period characters begins with their diversity as a group. Pontiac was a political-military leader but not a religious figure; Wovoka was a cultic personage; Pocahontas was neither, but perhaps a diplomat of sorts (with emergent if unrealized potential). As leaders or storied characters, they may be described as more or less political, military, diplomatic, civil, or religious. The first observation is this: *there may not have been one pathway to power or prominence.* Moreover, I do not sense that achieved or ascribed status was rigidly observed in many of these cases. The same might even be said of many supposed hereditary rulers in the American Southeast, some of whom assumed the mantle of authority, some of whom were elected by councils, and others of whom probably usurped control and legitimated their authority after the fact (see Anderson 1994; Muller 1997).

A second observation is also apparent: among those listed in table 8.1, *religious figures were as likely—perhaps more so—to alter the cultural histories of other native peoples or to "consolidate" leadership authority as were more overtly political leaders or war captains.* The cultural legacies of particularly skilled or aggressive warriors or war chiefs—say, Black Hawk, Red Cloud, Roman Nose, and Cochise (Sauk-Mesquakie, Oglala, Cheyenne, and Apache, respectively)—seem contingent to an extent on how they mixed religion with warring. It is probably significant that more than half the cases listed in table 8.1 involved people who claimed to have had visions that enabled or encouraged them to lead in certain ways (see Irwin 1994; Mooney 1973). Such visions, which often were manifest in the personal characteristics of the visionary or were verifiable in his successful prophetic predictions, trumped any claim to authority based on other personal or inherited qualities. People whose war-making prowess was based in some part on their religious experiences or followings include highly regarded, nearly legendary, and certainly remembered individuals such as Sitting Bull and Crazy Horse, Chief Seattle, Keokuk, Plenty Coups, and Popé, of the Lakota, Coastal Salish, Sauk-Mesquakie, Crow, and Tewa peoples, respectively (Hoxie 1996).

A good example of how life experiences, including religious ones, were mobilized by leaders to construct their own personae is seen in Cheez-Tah-Paezh of the Crow:

> Without any special prominence in his tribe until the summer of 1887...he participated in the sun dance of the Cheyenne, and showed such fortitude in enduring the dreadful torture that he was presented by the Cheyenne with a medicine saber painted red, in virtue of which he took the title of Sword-bearer. This naturally brought him into notice at home, and he soon aspired to become chief and medicine-man. Among other things, he asserted that no bullet or weapon had power to harm him. What other claims he made are not known, but his words produced such an impression, it

is said, that for a time every full-blood and half-blood among the Crows believed in him. (Mooney 1973:706–707)

Perhaps similar to such religious warrior-leaders were well-known political-military leaders whose life experiences were linked to other religious movements or cult figures. These would include Chief Joseph of the Nez Percés, Pontiac of the Ottawa, and Tecumseh of the Shawnee. Chief Joseph was influenced by the cultic shaman Smohalla (see "Discussion," below); Pontiac linked his political vision of an intertribal league with the nativist prophecies of the Delaware cult leader Neolin; and Tecumseh parlayed his Shawnee brother's prophecies into wide-reaching political alliances (Dixon 2005). Indeed, many of those in table 8.1 had a prominent predecessor—be it a parent, a teacher, or a superordinate ancestor—from whom legitimacy might be claimed at the time or after the fact.

However, the most influential leaders of the recent historical past were cult leaders who rejected violence. The Paiute cult visionary Wovoka, building on a legacy of western revitalistic movements in the second half of the nineteenth century (including that of his predecessor Nakai-Doklini), was at the heart of the Ghost Dance that culminated in the first confrontation at Wounded Knee (Kehoe 2006; Mooney 1973). The one-time social outcast Kenekuk, who later became the "Kickapoo prophet," likewise rejected violent solutions to early-nineteenth-century American Indian problems (Herring 1988). So too did Redbird Smith of the Cherokee and, much earlier, Hiawatha, whose own religious awakening reportedly led him to promote new variants of traditional Iroquoian mourning practices and adoption rites (Woodward 1963). Another visionary, Tecumseh's physically and socially challenged misfit brother ("the Shawnee Prophet"), was a most influential leader (but a poor war chief; see Edmunds 1983).

There were many religious figures, shamans, and cult leaders who may have built on the legacies of one another. Naming oneself or one's town after an ancestor or ancestral being (for example, Black Hawk, Tecumseh, Pawhuska, and Pawhukatawa) exemplifies such legacy building, but so too do the thick histories of religious movements in certain regions. An example is known from the Delaware Indians:

> Neolin...was certainly not the first or only prophet to claim to have communed with the Great Spirit. As early as 1737...a shaman had appeared before the Indians of the Susquehanna Valley, castigating them for trading their furs for rum....More than a decade later the missionary John Brainerd learned of the teachings of a Delaware woman who claimed to have spoken

with the Great Power....Still later, another Delaware prophet, named Papoonan...scolded his people for growing "proud & Covetous, which causes God to be angry...." Another Delaware shaman, called Wangomend, drew a chart for his Susquehanna followers that was very similar in content to the map Neolin would later create. (Dixon 2005:95–96)

However, legacy building is not as simple as perpetuating a tradition, leading me to make a third observation: oftentimes, as in Wovoka's Ghost Dance, Handsome Lake's "code" of conduct, Quanah Parker's peyote practices, and Neolin's or Kenekuk's native–Christian hybrid (Paiute, Iroquois, Comanche, Delaware, and Kickapoo, respectively), *the various religious reinventions syncretized the religious beliefs of one group with those of another native or Euro-American group* (Dixon 2005; Hagan 1993; Kehoe 2006). That is, such nativist movements or revitalizations were community-building and culture-making phenomena par excellence. They repackaged or reinvented traditions in very active, charged, and dynamic ways. And although the listed examples might include some historical anomalies, all practices, performances, and promotions of tradition in the past did (and do today) the same thing at varying scales and to varying degrees (Pauketat 2001a).

The scale and degree of culture making or reinvention are linked to a fourth and final observation based on the native North American leaders: *a lasting cultural legacy was contingent on the materiality and spatiality of the promulgated narrative.* Their ideas were realized in practice. The Ghost Dance, for instance, was literally incorporated into the beliefs of people through coordinated bodily movement and sensuous, highly emotional experiences in communal gatherings. There were even specific shirts made to be worn for the rituals (figure 8.2). Likewise, Hiawatha's political-religious exhortations to confederate, as well as those of Tecumseh in later years, were embodied in the production and distribution of wampum belts. Cheez-Tah-Paezh of the Crow wielded a magical sword (Mooney 1973:706). The Delaware Prophet, Neolin, drew road maps to heaven and "made copies to circulate among all the tribes" (Dixon 2005:93).

Perhaps similarly, the Shawnee Prophet's cultural productions took place at specially constructed places, the last and most famous of which was Prophetstown, Indiana (Sugden 1997); the ceremonies and objects of Redbird Smith's revitalized Ketoowah society took place at "Redbird Smith Place" (Woodward 1963:8). And though Kenekuk's blend of native and nonnative religious practices were not so centralized, they did involve the disposal of medicine bags, abstinence from alcohol, and the production and distribution of a new form of "prayer stick" by the Kickapoo Prophet

**FIGURE 8.2**

*Arapaho Ghost Dance shirt (from Mooney 1896:plate CIII).*

himself (Herring 1988). The spread of the peyote cult in many parts of the eastern woodlands had similar all-pervasive consequences, including forgetting old ways and practices by eliminating their materiality; people disposed of their personal medicine bundles (Radin 1963[1920], 1990; Stewart 1987). The Shawnee Prophet (Tenskwatawa) had encouraged a similar phenomenon in the early 1800s such that "the shores of Lake Superior...were strewn with these medicine bags, which had been cast into the water" (Mooney 1973:679).

The narratives of such revitalizations were actively commemorated or practiced via material culture, bodily movement, and the experience of places, but other means of spreading the word or remembering the words of these leaders were also responsible to some degree for building the legacies of these characters. Oration was among the most common and potent, if ephemeral. Combined with some means of broadcasting, inscribing, or recording one's words, oration or eloquence in speech was especially important in creating one's persona: Tecumseh and the Shawnee Prophet traveled and preached widely in search of allies and converts; so too did

Smohalla of the Wánapûm (closely related to the Yakima and Nez Percés). Nopkehe of the Catawbe is remembered today as a gifted speaker and compromiser; Pocahontas's wit and youthful wisdom enabled her to act as a political diplomat at home and abroad; various leaders traveled to Washington or had speeches transcribed by the press; modern rail and telegraph communication spread the word of the Ghost Dance; Sitting Bull performed for a year in Buffalo Bill Cody's circus; so too did Crazy Horse's cousin Black Elk, an Oglala holy man (Brown 1989[1953]; Hoxie 1996). Others were commemorated in still other ways: innumerable monuments and dollar coins continue to construct Sacagewea's place in American history (Howard 1971); Black Hawk produced an autobiography (1994[1916]); portraits were painted for posterity; Chief Plenty-Coup of the Crows donated his stately home to the public, an idea he got after visiting Washington's Mount Vernon (Linderman 2002[1930]).[1]

## MISSISSIPPIAN HEROES AND HEROINES

In the Historic era, American Indian leaders took many forms. Of course, the circumstances that brought certain forms of leadership to the fore were complex and historically contingent, with religious leaders in particular having widespread effects, syncretizing and reinventing the practices of multiple groups (and drawing their influence in some measure from predecessors). Particularly influential characters were at the heart of large-scale movements that possessed a materiality or were emplaced in the cultural landscape and collective memory in ways that redefined community. With these generalities in mind, I turn to the Mississippian period (AD 1050–1600), when particular masculine and feminine characters emerged to personify political-religious movements and ultimately to rule over greater "macro-communities" (Pauketat 2000a, 2007).

Of course, Mississippian leaders were most certainly not the first in ancient North America. Indeed, throughout much of ancient history in eastern North America, leaders of various sorts are evident, presumably as part of larger social and political formations that archaeologists recognize as complexes or phases tethered to specific places and often mound-construction practices (Milner 2005). Some of the better instances were impressive ceremonial and town centers, from Watson Brake and Poverty Point in Louisiana to the Scioto Valley Hopewell in Ohio. Archaeologists have long debated whether such complexes were communal or hierarchical; are to be called tribes, chiefdoms, or confederacies; and were led by achieved or ascribed leaders (Pauketat 2007; see Carr and Case 2005; Gibson and Carr 2004; Sassaman 2004, 2005).

Recent approaches to the study of these complexes and periods have adapted historically oriented theories that recognize the contingent relationships between places, practices, objects, and persons. In our studies of Cahokia, Emerson and I have argued that the rapid foundation of this place circa AD 1050 involved political and religious negotiations of varied interests and reinventions of community and polity that played out in regional space and everyday lives (Emerson 1997; Pauketat 1998, 2000a, 2000b; 2004b, 2005; Pauketat and Emerson 1999). The dynamic also included immigrant groups, some of which might have supplied young women for Cahokia's "mortuary theater" (Alt and Pauketat 2007; see Alt 2002, 2008; Emerson and Pauketat 2002; Fowler et al. 1999; Kehoe 2002).

That mortuary theater, especially as seen in Cahokia's Mound 72, was carefully performed on special occasions and appears designed to reference particular memories, powerful cultural narratives, supernatural powers, and ancestral persons (for a range of interpretations, see Alt and Pauketat 2007; Brown 2003; Emerson and Pauketat 2002; Hall 2000; Kehoe 2002; Porubcan 2000). Long- and recently dead men, women, and children were interred in discrete events in this and other mortuary mounds. The first of the Mound 72 events was the decommissioning of an ancestral temple and the removal of its associated oversized marker post. Atop the former post pit were interred the bodies of twenty-two immolated women, the first of several such sacrifices in this one mound. Also included was the interment of the shroud-wrapped bodies of a pair of men on and under a "beaded blanket," accompanied by presumed retainers, sometime after the temple decommissioning. The various bodies appear to have been carried to the spot and buried with the remains of others and with a set of distinctive objects (arrows, chunkey stones, beads, copper-covered rods).

Although interpretations vary, Robert Hall (1997, 2000) suspects that the various male and female interments in Mound 72 indicate the practice of world-renewal and spirit-adoption rites like those seen in the eastern Plains or Mexico at contact, played out here in exaggerated form. Like him, I suspect that these mortuary events were great, staged, cosmological and political dramas that also for the first time engendered people in ways previously unknown in North America, even as they celebrated select memories over others, emplaced a (particularly political) creation story at Cahokia, and, most importantly, located otherwise dispersed superhuman powers and ancestral spirits in the bodies of particular Cahokians at Cahokia (Alt and Pauketat 2007). Elsewhere, I summarized the creation story this way:

> Analysts have recognized the parallels between the Mound 72

burials and general themes that run through the folklore of eastern Woodlands Indians. Native people frequently told stories of an Earth or Corn Mother and a male hero or pair of twin-brother heroes (Hall 1997). Earth Mother, sometimes associated with the Evening Star, gave people maize, her body issuing forth the sacred crop in some manner. She lorded over the other evening stars, while the Morning Star was the sovereign of the early morning sky. Various Plains and Mississippi valley people believed that the Morning Star had had intercourse with the Evening Star, a union signified by arrow iconography (or perhaps the chunkey game sticks and stones gendered male and female, respectively)....Meanwhile, the Morning Star, or his cognate a great falconoid Thunderbird who resided in the sky realm, also assumed a human form. In the legends of Siouan-speaking peoples...he was called "Red Horn," a heroic man... sometimes able to change himself into an arrow in games....Two twin boys were born to Red Horn, at least one of these from the union with an underworld giantess, if not Earth Mother herself, before Red Horn was subsequently killed...[and later] resurrected [by one of the sons]....

We can understand the beaded burial complex in Mound 72 to have retold and recast the legend, if not also the related story of Earth Mother, this time embodied by corpses and cultural objects. The cast were all assembled there: twin falconoid men, chunkey players...an executed foursome...and possible Earth Mother sacrifices. With them were other pieces of the story. (Pauketat 2005:203–204).

Moreover, I have also argued that this mortuary theater doubtless involved the living as much as the dead, because clearly someone was on hand to bury the bodies and, as obviously, the immolation and burial of people were probably theatrical events meant to be seen by many (Pauketat 2006). Conceivably, the bodies laid out in Mound 72 and other such mortuary mounds around Cahokia were props in a mortuary theater that ultimately starred—consistent with the historically retold legend of Red Horn or Earth Mother—the living cult heirs apparent of those lying dead on the stage of Mound 72. Such living heirs—various leaders, diplomats, priests, and the like—may have included both men and women, despite the fact that most sacrificial victims were young women (Fowler et al. 1999). But as heirs or reincarnates, they were narrativizing in ways that recast the dead, if not also the living, as heroic persons. Presumably, they were doing this in front of large diverse audiences that included recent immigrants, all of whom were participating in the formation of some greater community identity (Pauketat 2006).

Certainly, the accoutrements in these burials might have been props in a staged event or citations to cultural ideas or supernatural forces (see Brown 2003; Pauketat 2005). For instance, particular interments, the numbers and layers of bodies in any one pit or tomb, and the shape and orientation of the mound itself seem to reference the night sky and the duality or directionality of the cosmos. Bundled arrows with different colored tips, among other things, also point (literally) to solstitial sunrises and sunsets (Pauketat 2006). In addition, the alternating layers of light- and dark-colored earth used to bury the dead seem to cite the nonhuman powers of sky and earth, if not also the cultural identities of the people who deposited the earth (based on analogies with other Eastern Woodlands Indians; see Alt and Pauketat 2007; Pauketat 2008a).

In its theatricality and schematic layout, Mound 72 is duplicated by other now destroyed mortuary mounds around Cahokia (Alt and Pauketat 2007; Kelly 1994; Pauketat 2004a). Mound 72 and the other Cahokian mortuary mound practices appear to have been mimicked in certain ways by far-off people (Hall 2000; Pauketat 2004a). Farther afield, other Mississippian places are known to have comparable, if less elaborate, theatrical emplacements of cosmological forces through mortuary spectacles. The best known of these is at Spiro in Oklahoma. There, the "Great Mortuary" appears to have been a staged event that among other things might have been intended to create a legacy for the dead in ex post facto fashion (Brown 1996).

Another example is known from the Etowah site in central Georgia (King 2003, 2004). The burials of Mound C appear to have included people who impersonated a masculine superhuman character similar to Cahokia's Red Horn or Morning Star god-man:

> One of the most commonly represented supernatural beings in the Etowah corpus is the Morning Star or Birdman....That the Birdman is not of this world is demonstrated by his (or her) possession of clearly both human and raptor physical characteristics. (King 2004:159)

> Even more intriguing is the possibility that at least some of the SECC goods buried in Mound C graves reference a mythology

that was not even local to northern Georgia and were, indeed, over a century old when they were finally buried in Mound C. James Brown continues to construct a compelling case that some of the embossed copper plates and cutouts in Mound C burials...originated...at Cahokia....That foreign style and mythology served to charter the power of Etowah's Middle Mississippian elites, and it was...[associated] with a mythological place in the Mississippian world: Cahokia. (King 2004:160, 163)

The similarity between Cahokia's and Etowah's masculine heroic narratives and the transmission of a "foreign style" across such space and through time might not be surprising when one considers that, besides deeper historical connections across the East, Cahokia was larger and earlier than all other Mississippian complexes (Pauketat and Emerson 1997). Just how Cahokians did project their narrative is worthy of a second look, as it speaks directly to the historical processes whereby leaders and legacies are constructed.

## THE CONSOLIDATION OF MISSISSIPPIAN AGENCY

Given my earlier noted theoretical predilections and the ethnohistoric information that agency was dispersed in the ancient Eastern Woodlands and Plains, there is little reason to believe that the pre-Mississippian peoples of the mid-continent conceived of themselves as a society of "individuals" in the Western sense of that word. In fact, there are art-historical and archaeological reasons from the Woodland period (150 BC–AD 1050) to infer that rocks, plants, earth, fire, and animals were treated as if they were animate forces. For instance, supernatural or spiritual forces, when depicted, invariably appear as zoomorphic or abstract, with the occasional anthropomorphic image, usually interpreted to depict a shaman or a deceased ancestor (for example, Penney 2004; Seeman 2004).

I suspect that this is precisely because isolated human beings were seldom thought to be embodied agents or whole persons (Fowler 2004; Gillespie 2001). Rather, their agency was partial. Even after the Mississippian period, when the "superhuman characters" might have emerged from Cahokia and beyond, supernatural powers were seldom vested entirely in human bodies. I have previously summarized the animistic tendencies of the people (Pauketat 2008a):

Various indigenous Plains-Prairie creation stories from the recent Siouan and Caddoan past feature gendered supernatural forces and superhuman characters (Dorsey 1997; Hall 1997; McCleary 1997; Radin 1948; Townsend 2004). Among other things, fire, ashes, and light-colored earth seem to have presenced the sun or, more commonly, the sun-carrier or "fire-bringer"—a "Thunderer" god-man also known as the "Morning Star." Dark earth, corn, water, and perhaps refuse signified earth the creator, creation, and the Evening Star or her god-woman cognate most often known as "Corn Mother." In some accounts, the Morning Star was said to have been responsible for carrying the sun into this world, an act of daily regeneration. In these or others, the Evening Star or Corn Mother gave the world corn and mothered at least one of two twin heirs-apparent, the latter at one point reincarnating the father after retrieving his head or bones from otherworldly "giants" or from the netherworld (for example, Radin 1948).

Fire, earth, water, and certain feathers, tobacco, and paint (made from earthen minerals) were believed to possess agency. They were "spirits" or, in Jason Jackson's (2003) terms, "witnesses" because they could inform the deities that which people on earth had been doing (see Bailey 1995; Dorsey 1997; Fletcher and La Flesche 1992; Jackson 2003; Radin 1990; Salzer and Rajnovich 2000; Swanton 1942, 1985, 2001). Men and women made offerings both to earth and fire, or the Evening and Morning Stars, including crops, buckskins, tobacco, and, sometimes, human beings.

It may be that the earliest lasting merger of human beings and supernatural forces in eastern North America happened at Cahokia. It was here that the gods became flesh and dwelled among the people (Emerson 2003). There are no better expressions of this merger than in the series of carved three-dimensional objects that Thomas Emerson (1997) has called Cahokia redstone figures and figurines. As he and his colleagues have argued, these carved sculptures depict priestly or shamanic superhuman characters, including Red Horn or Morning Star and Earth Mother (see Emerson et al. 2002, 2003; see also Brown 2004). The redundant association of religious practitioners, gods, ancestors, plants, and gendered human forms is unmistakable (figure 8.3).

Importantly, many of these objects, though made at Cahokia, were distributed across the Midwest and South or were carried to other far-off

**FIGURE 8.3**
*Cahokian sculpted figure pipe, found at Spiro, Oklahoma, of "Big Boy" wearing a cloak or cape. Photograph courtesy of University Museum, University of Arkansas, "Resting Warrior" (cat. no. 47-2-1).*

places (Emerson et al. 2002, 2003). And interestingly, the same pan-eastern distribution seems to characterize a limited subset of other Cahokia-made objects: chunkey stones, shell beads, projectile points, distinctive ear ornaments, and a particular decorated pot (Alt and Pauketat 2007; Emerson and Pauketat 2008; Pauketat 2004a). I have previously pointed out that, besides showing up in Mound 72 with the beaded burial of the two men, these objects may be "pieces" of ancestral memories and heroic stories (more conventionally seen in Mississippian iconography [Brown 2004; King 2004]).

This heroic legend was one aspect of the stories that seem to have been told through the theatrical mortuary spectacles at Cahokia's Mound 72, in

Spiro's Great Mortuary, and in Etowah's Mound C. Through such spectacles of the dead, the Mississippians associated supernatural powers—the sky, earth, sun, and ancestors—with specific living characters to produce persons who embodied some new scaled-up community identity by locating the powers of the universe at these great sites. This remade the dead into iconic heroes and converted the living into their reincarnations, celebrated down through the generations because of their powerful ancestors and the supernatural forces emplaced in specific locations on earth.

Given the lack of pre-Mississippian antecedents, it seems unlikely that the first dead bodies in the earliest mortuary mounds at a place such as Cahokia were those of rulers of the same sort that second-generation leaders would have been. Thus, the results of the elaborate Mississippian mortuary practices described above could be said to be an "institutionalized" set of ideas—a Mississippian narrative—that was subsequently reinvented (reinstitutionalized?) by later generations and at other places. However, institutionalization of this sort was synonymous with a series of communal negotiations wherein particular leaders and followers manipulated memories and constructed narratives of social persons with special agentic powers. Such narratives, or some semblance of them, seem to have been redistributed to other localities, say, from Cahokia to Etowah, where leadership was again renegotiated among local people.

## DISCUSSION

In the admittedly complex world of the Mississippians, the construction of leadership narratives happens through the creation of great ceremonial centers where "political communities" or "mega-communities" were constructed through spectacles involving ancestral and supernatural powers (Pauketat 2000a, 2007). In some Mississippian mortuaries, we can see that the first hereditary leaders were dead leaders whose descendants claimed legitimacy through ritual "projections into a nebulous past" or the citations of "heroic ancestors" (Clark 2004:213). At first glance, Historic-period developments might not seem comparable to the early Mississippian world, but there are commonalities that deserve a second look.

Among the Historic-period examples, because *there may not have been one pathway to power or prominence*, a character's leadership potential was contingent on his or her life history. *Religious figures were as likely—perhaps more so—to alter the cultural histories of other native peoples or to "consolidate" leadership authority as were more overtly political leaders or war captains.* Legitimate authority was sanctioned by supernatural powers, and leaders with lasting authority necessarily were not only religious in character but also communal. They recombined and gathered together powers (of their predecessors or otherwise dispersed agents) in a central place or person and forged new communities of followers. Such gathering and consolidation are revealed in performances in which *the various religious reinventions syncretized the religious beliefs of one group with those of other groups.* Appeals to one's local community were one thing, but significant power seems to have been synonymous with the ability to pull together and reinvent the religious beliefs of diverse peoples, whether we are talking about Wovoka's Ghost Dance or Cahokia's Mound 72.

The final common ingredient in the Historic-era leaders-to-legacies process involves the material and spatial dimensions of community building. *Lasting cultural legacies were those that broadcast their narratives and inscribed landscapes.* Whether or not leaders were translated into lasting authorities was a matter of creating a community of followers who identified with the organizing principle, which was not a leader as much as a common ideal (which served as a platform for leaders). This common ideal might be embodied by sacred objects or mnemonic devices—prayer sticks, wampum belts, dance shirts, road maps to heaven—or it might be commemorated through sacred places (dance grounds, Prophetstown, Redbird Smith Place). That is, significant communities of followers developed as religious movements around narratives that were in turn experienced at special places and through supernaturally charged material objects gathered together or animated for effect.

Under the right conditions, perhaps best exemplified by the Mississippian peoples, such a process can lead to communities of followers that transcend localities. It is important to note, however, that such things happened even relatively late in the Historic period. For instance, one such case involved Smohalla, a cult-figure and "chief of the Wánapûm, a small tribe in Washington [related to the Yakima and Nez Percés], numbering probably less than 200 souls," adjacent to a natural congregating point along the Columbia River that offered "abundant opportunity for the teaching and dissemination of his peculiar doctrines" (Mooney 1973:716–717). He was schooled in Catholicism during his youth, and "*the rapid spread of his doctrines among the tribes of the Columbia materially facilitated their confederation* in the Yakima war of 1855–56" (Mooney 1973:718; emphasis added). Although Smohalla did not achieve his political goals at the time, later events were to see him transformed into an even greater prophet.

Another historic example of a greater macro-community that grew up around a leader was the well-known case of Tecumseh. Tecumseh, whose name translates into "meteor" (or "comet") or "celestial panther," was an imposing warrior, the son of a Shawnee chief, and the brother of the Shawnee Prophet. About 1807 and at "40 years of age," he "had already thought out his scheme of uniting all the tribes in one grand confederation to resist the further encroachments of the whites" onto Indian lands of the American Midwest and mid-South (Mooney 1973:683). At religious gatherings headed by his brother, Tecumseh took the opportunity to promote his views of unity, turning "what was at first a simple religious revival" into a "political agitation" that turned "the apostles of the prophet" into the "recruiting agents for his brother" (Mooney 1973:683):

> In the spring of 1807 it was estimated that at Fort Wayne fifteen hundred Indians had recently passed that post on their way to visit the prophet, while councils were constantly being held and runners were going from tribe to tribe with pipes and belts of wampum.... The next spring great numbers of Indians came down from the lakes to visit Tecumtha [sic] and his brother, who, finding their following increasing so rapidly, accepted an invitation from the Potawatomi and Kickapoo, and removed their headquarters to a more central location on the Wabash....The new settlement...was known to the Indians as Kehtipaquononk, "the great clearing," and was an old and favorite location with them [later to be called Prophetstown]. (Mooney 1973:684)

Unfortunately for Tecumseh's vision, when Tecumseh was traveling across the South and Midwest in November 1811 to promote his confederation plans, Governor William Henry Harrison sacked Prophetstown. The place and the native fighting force were decimated, thus ending Tecumseh's young confederacy.

It is difficult to know what would have happened in either the Smohalla or the Tecumseh case had events turned out differently. Had the confederations of peoples held together, one might easily envision ceremonial gatherings in which the greater community of followers, increasingly unified around dance-cult or wampum-belt ideologies, may have accommodated the transfer of leadership to heirs, perhaps in some ways like the mortuary theater of the great Mississippian centers. Had something like that happened in the historic cases, archaeologists would identify them as instances of the institutionalization of leadership. Clearly, though, both accounts are similar in ways to the Mississippian cases. Powerful leaders emerged through historical chance and through political-religious movements that consolidated diverse beliefs and unified communities of followers.

## CONCLUSION

A general argument could be made that the emergence of hereditary leadership was a recursive historical process that involved leaders and communities mutually constructing authority. Making such an argument rests on understanding the historical details: how did such developments play out through time and across transregional space? But making such arguments and answering such questions also entail rethinking how we understand agents of change in our models and how the institutionalization of leadership and the consolidation of authority were synonymous with the personification and reimagining of community identities.

In the end, my argument for the emergence of leadership begins and ends with community. For this reason, it parallels the points made elsewhere by Arnold and Vaughn (chapters 6 and 7, respectively, this volume), especially to the extent that material culture and ideology are caught up in the relationships between leaders and communities. It also picks up on the importance of ritual and religion in the historical development of authority, a point made by Stanish (chapter 5) and others in this volume. Unlike others in this volume, however, I do not see the need to prioritize the accumulation or privatization of material wealth in an explanation of leadership (see Eerkens, chapter 4, and Arnold, chapter 6, this volume). Moreover, from my starting point, I argue that institutionalization was not a front-loaded process. It did not lead to leaders in easily predictable ways. Rather, it was a historical process of becoming whereby certain leaders or other prominent characters, present in virtually all societies, were socially, which is to say, consensually, constructed as the heroic persons, apical ancestors, and embodiments of variably scaled corporate identities, sometimes after the fact.

Of course, given such an argument, we must recognize that that which could be constructed and emplaced from dispersed agentic objects, bodies, and places could be deconstructed, displaced, and redistributed later. The memories of and narratives constructed about persons remain malleable, which probably explains why great ceremonial places correlate with the consolidation of personhood and official leadership positions and why the names of gods, peoples, and successions of hereditary leaders correspond. Even the powerful Mississippian centers with their supposed institutionalized leadership offices did not last. As King (2003, 2004) notes for Etowah, even seemingly central founding narratives can fall away, evaporating as part of the overall demise of a place and its hereditary leaders. Legacies too, it seems, live and die by consent.

### Acknowledgments

I am indebted to the volume's leaders, John Kantner, Kevin Vaughn, and Jelmer Eerkens, and am grateful for the opportunity to participate in the School for Advanced Research advanced seminar and to contribute to this volume; the volume editors greatly improved the present chapter. I am equally appreciative of the community of scholars who came together at SAR in Santa Fe, a place that fosters scholarship in ways few others can.

### Note

1. Perhaps the most recent and accidental of cases that exemplify such a principle would be the commemoration of the actions of Ira Hays, a Pima Indian involved in the second flag raising on Iowa Jima, as commemorated in photo, song, and film.

# PART III

*History, Process, and the Evolution of Leadership*

# 9

## The Power of One? Big Men Revisited

**Polly Wiessner**

Kanopatoakali, the great Tee Cycle organizer of the Kalia clan and descendant of a long line of influential *kamongo* [leaders], was on his clan's ceremonial grounds in 1934 when the first party of Europeans came into central Enga. The news that the mythical white-skinned sky people had descended to earth and were traveling through Enga had already spread far and wide, and so their arrival was anticipated. One of their huge dogs urinated on Kanopatoakali's legs and the grass on which he was standing. When they had passed, he gathered the grass, wet with urine, killed a pig, and held a ritual for the sky people to commemorate the event that he believed was a sign of good fortune. (Suilya Kanapatoakali, Wakumale village, 2005)

How wrong Kanopatoakali was, for the white men were to bring goods and opportunities that would unleash competition and make it possible for almost any man to become a kamongo. His sons and grandsons would lose their inherited privilege and engage in fierce competition for name and fame. For the first time in their history, the Enga were to experience the Big Man model (Sahlins 1963) of the unbridled aggrandizer so celebrated in anthropological models of what David and Sterner (1999) have called "the straight jacket" model of cultural evolution.

Neo-evolutionary schemes progressing from band to Big Men to chiefdoms to state (Fried 1967; Sahlins and Service 1960) are based on the notion that equality is the blank slate of nature upon which social complexity is written and as such can provide the starting point for studies of cultural evolution. Accordingly, it is inequality that most social theorists have sought to explain; once the slate of egalitarianism is written upon by hierarchy, equality drops out of consideration and hierarchy reigns. However, recent studies in primatology and evolutionary biology indicate that hierarchy, not equality, is most deeply rooted in our phylogeny and "egalitarian" tendencies entered the behavioral repertoire later in our evolution (Boehm 1993, 1999). Thus, it is not surprising that both hierarchical and egalitarian institutions coexist in all societies and constitute strong forces in the emergence of social complexity.

Archaeological studies conducted over the past few decades have greatly broadened views of social complexity and its emergence. They have shown that some of the most intricate social, political, and religious systems are structured as heterarchies rather than as hierarchies (Ehrenreich, Crumley, and Levy 1995) and that power and influence can be achieved in different ways: through wealth in people, wealth in things, and wealth in knowledge (Guyer 1995; Guyer and Belinga 1995). What is clear from these studies, though not explicitly stated, is that social complexity is the product of the interaction between hierarchical and egalitarian institutions in a society, not the replacement of equality with hierarchy. Here I first explore egalitarian and hierarchical institutions and interaction between the two. Then I turn to a case study among the Enga of Highland New Guinea to show how the interplay of hierarchical and egalitarian institutions led to the emergence of institutionalized social inequality in precolonial Enga history and that with a new era of economic and social opportunity after contact with Europeans, underlying relations of equality resurged to produce the classic Big Man model (Godelier and Strathern 1991; Roscoe 2000b; Sahlins 1963). Finally, I question what aggrandizers can accomplish through "the power of one" (Arnold 1993, 1995a; Earle 1997; Hayden 1995) and the proposition that complex systems of exchange can arise and thrive under conditions of unbounded competition.

## ON EQUALITY AND HIERARCHY

Hierarchy involves relations ordered by rank that may be fixed or fluid, achieved or ascribed, and based on many different criteria. High-ranking individuals are the ones most frequently in the focus of attention and the recipients of social esteem. Those on top enjoy privileged access to resources and to influence or power over others. Room at the top is limited. Rank positions are usually not attained through individual effort alone, but with the help of coalitions of supporters or cultural conventions that ascribe leadership. High-ranking individuals provide benefits to group members. The existence of a hierarchy may reduce competition so that those lower down in the hierarchy can devote their energies to enterprises other than social or political competition. Hierarchies may thus benefit the majority.

Egalitarian relations are characterized by "reverse dominance hierarchies" (Boehm 1999) in which coalitions of the weaker level the stronger so that all group members enjoy equal access to natural and social resources, status positions, and autonomy of decision making. Following Fried's (1967) classic definition, in egalitarian societies there are as many positions of leadership as there are qualified individuals to fill them. Leaders may lead, but followers may or may not choose to follow. Egalitarian institutions foster autonomy of decision making, recognition of moral equality, and an attitude of respect and appreciation for the abilities of others. (See Bird and Bliege Bird, Bowser and Patton, and Eerkens in chapters 2, 3, and 4, respectively, this volume, for further discussions of egalitarian societies.)

Both egalitarian and hierarchical institutions can be extremely repressive and ridden with tension. Those on top of hierarchical institutions may abuse power and appropriate disproportionate amounts of resources for themselves and their kin. In contrast, in egalitarian systems the more ambitious are subject to constant scrutiny and harsh leveling (Boehm 1999; Kelly 1993; Lee 1993; Wiessner 2004). Both egalitarian and hierarchical systems must be constantly maintained, although in cooperative enterprises people may voluntarily assume equal or unequal status.

The predisposition to form hierarchy appears to be more deeply rooted in human phylogeny than does a preference for equality. The great apes, our closest primate relatives, live in hierarchically organized societies, and informal hierarchies appear in children's play groups around the age of three in different cultures (Hold 1976). Finally, striving to create status differentials appears in some form in all cultures (Wiessner and Schiefenhövel 1996), and fundamental human organizational structures such as the family and kinship systems are based on relations of inequality (Feinman 1995; Flanagan 1989; Jones 2003). Unlike nonhuman primates, for whom hierarchy is primarily established through physical dominance, humans achieve inequalities through prosocial currencies such as the ability to mediate or organize defense, ritual, and exchange (Eibl-Eibesfeldt 1989; Wiessner 2006). Humans have been shown to have an aversion to bullying (Boehm 1999) and unfairness (Wiessner 2005); however, there is little evidence to suggest that humans have a deeply rooted preference for egalitarian social systems.

## VARIATION WITHIN EGALITARIAN AND HIERARCHICAL INSTITUTIONS

Systems of equality and inequality take different forms (Robbins 1994). All egalitarian institutions involve potential equality—that is, individuals are ascribed equal status and resources at the starting point. Some egalitarian institutions demand equality of outcome as well, restraining the capable and ambitious from acquiring more material resources, political influence, or social regard than others. Others stipulate potential equality but encourage the capable to excel and achieve higher status on the condition that they continue to provide benefits to the group. These are sometimes called trans-egalitarian societies. In no egalitarian institutions can the capable infringe on the autonomy of others, appropriate their labor, or tell them what to do.

The dividing line between transegalitarian institutions and hierarchical ones is not a clear one. Two criteria might be used: whether or not potential equality is upheld—that is, whether the children of higher-status individuals start life in a privileged position, with greater access to land, spouses, material goods, or social status—and whether influential individuals are permitted to accumulate the products of their achievements or are forced to distribute them widely.

Within hierarchical systems, inequality may be achieved or ascribed, and hierarchies may be fixed or flexible (see Kusimba and Kusimba, chapter 10, this volume). Position can be obtained in numerous ways—through accumulating wealth in people, wealth in knowledge and social skills, or wealth in things (Guyer 1995; Guyer and Belinga 1995). Wealth in people and wealth in knowledge provide important paths to prestige in many prestate societies; when wealth is assembled, it is usually distributed to strengthen or expand social ties.

## COST AND BENEFITS OF EQUALITY AND HIERARCHY

Egalitarian institutions are extremely effective for reducing the transaction costs of exchange—assessing value, protecting rights, and enforcing agreements (North 1990) on a number of accounts. These standardize the costs of social exchange by providing important information about others: that they are equals. It is not necessary to work out relative social standing with every interaction; individuals can help one another knowing that as equals they can ask and receive when in need. With egalitarian institutions, people do not fear that assistance given will be used to dominate, fostering the trust for delayed exchange. Egalitarian institutions allow all adults to participate in the enforcement of social norms, reducing the costs of social control. Finally, they facilitate the mobility necessary for intergroup cooperation because hierarchies do not mesh easily. Owing to these advantages, all societies maintain some egalitarian social institutions to facilitate cooperative enterprises. Their drawbacks include reduced incentive for surplus production when all produces must be shared, cumbersome decision making, and members choosing to vote with their feet (Eerkens, chapter 4, this volume).

Transegalitarian institutions avoid these drawbacks. However, when favorable environmental conditions permit surplus production limited only by labor, runaway competition can result, leading to political instability. Consequently, activities that benefit the group and require continuity in social ties and transmission of knowledge to organize, such as ritual, are often institutionalized, even when leadership in other realms of society remains predominantly egalitarian. I will return to this point.

Benefits of flexible hierarchical systems include increased incentive for surplus production, stronger leadership, efficient decision making, and more powerful representation in intergroup relations. Benefits of institutionalized hierarchies include organizational efficiency, reduced internal competition, and less energy expended on the race to the top. For individuals, institutional hierarchies can give preferential access to resources with little competitive struggle. The drawbacks of institutionalized hierarchies can include stagnancy from reduced competition, reduced cooperation, poor leadership, and abuse of power by those on top.

Anthropologists most frequently classify societies as egalitarian or hierarchical according to what they perceive as the dominant institutions; however, in all societies, egalitarian and hierarchical institutions coexist. For example, all societies have age hierarchies, and most societies have institutionalized inequality between the sexes. Hierarchy and equality may also have temporal dimensions—for example, age sets in which all members of a cohort are equal and proceed together to the next rung in the hierarchy as they move through the life cycle. Other societies have alternating periods of equality and inequality. Equality prevails in daily life and facilitates exchange; hierarchical structures are called on in times of emergency or when the cooperation of large groups is required (Harrison 1990; Tuzin 2001).

The relations between institutions of hierarchy and equality and their implications for the development of complexity are what I explore in the following case study among the Enga of Papua New Guinea (PNG).

## THE ENGA

The Enga of Papua New Guinea are a highland horticultural population well-known in the anthropological literature through the works of Feil (1984), Lacey (1975, 1979), Meggitt (1965, 1972, 1977), Talyaga (1982),

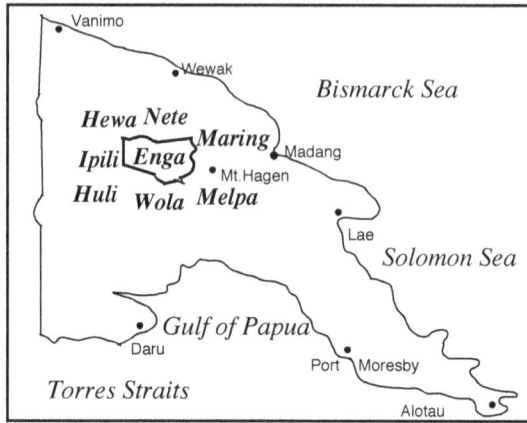

**FIGURE 9.1**

*Location of the Enga province in Papua New Guinea. Map by Polly Wiessner.*

Waddell (1972), and Wohlt (1978), among many others. Today the Enga number some 350,000 (figure 9.1). Their staple crop, the sweet potato, is used to feed large human and pig populations and is supplemented by other garden foods and forest products. The Enga are divided into nine mutually intelligible dialect groups (Brennan 1982) that share important economic, social, political, and religious orientations.

The Enga have a segmentary lineage system of phratries or tribes, with one thousand to six thousand members divided into constituent exogamous clans, subclans, and lineages (Meggitt 1965). Two axes of kinship organize Enga social and political relations. One is composed of agnatic kinsmen who compete for leadership within the group but support one another as equals in building houses and gardens, making bride wealth payments, defense, raising war reparations, and so on. The other comprises maternal and affinal kin outside the clan who supply crucial wealth for exchanges and support in times of strife. Men's interests are largely directed to the politics of land, social networks, and, above all, ceremonial exchange. Women devote themselves primarily to child rearing, gardening, and pig husbandry; they are also active in maintaining intergroup ties.

## THE DATA

The data presented here come from Enga historical traditions of one hundred tribes collected by Polly Wiessner, Akii Tumu, Nitze Pupu, Pesone Munini, and Alome Kyakas between 1985 and 2006. Historical traditions (*atome pii*) extend from approximately 1650 until the present (Wiessner 2002;

Wiessner and Tumu 1998).[1] Historical traditions are held distinct from myth (*tindii pii*) in that they are said to have originated in eyewitness accounts. They contain information on most aspects of Enga life. Accompanying genealogies allow events to be placed in a chronological framework.

The period covered by historical traditions was one of rapid change. The earliest traditions describe the population of Enga as diverse, with people practicing subsistence strategies that varied by altitudinal zone, from hunting and gathering in the high country to shifting horticulture in the rugged valleys of western Enga to sedentary taro horticulture in the fertile eastern valleys. A thriving exchange economy uniting groups in all niches revolved around the circulation of stone axes, cosmetic oil, salt, plumes, and shells. Pigs receive little note in early traditions.

With the introduction of the sweet potato along local trade routes some 350 years ago, constraints on production were released, and it became possible to produce a substantial surplus of wealth "on the hoof" in the form of pigs (Watson 1965a, 1965b, 1977). Immediate reactions to the arrival of the sweet potato differed by area; however, historical traditions from all areas report shifts in population distribution (figure 9.2), a population growth of approximately 1.1 percent per annum, and the expansion of ceremonial exchange and religious ritual in response to mounting social and political complexities (Wiessner 2002; Wiessner and Tumu 1998). Three large networks that can be counted as systems of ceremonial exchange arose (figure 9.3): the Kepele cult network of western Enga, the Great Ceremonial Wars of central Enga, and the Tee Cycle of eastern Enga. Bachelors' cults and ancestral cults circulated widely during the period and did much to standardize norms and values among Enga dialect groups and with neighboring linguistic groups.

Looking back in Enga history is like looking to the horizon from a high ridgetop; the nearest ridge is in focus, but the rest fade one by one into the mist. I begin the discussion of hierarchy, equality, and complexity on the mistiest ridge of time, just before the introduction of the sweet potato, with a sketch from eastern, western, and central Enga. Later I restrict the discussion to central Enga.

## LEADERSHIP IN THE EARLY GENERATIONS OF HISTORICAL TRADITIONS

Life in the early historical traditions of Enga was played out in a sparsely populated landscape, with men making considerable efforts to find spouses, establish exchange partnerships, recruit new group members, and gather people for social events. The trade of axe stone, salt, and items

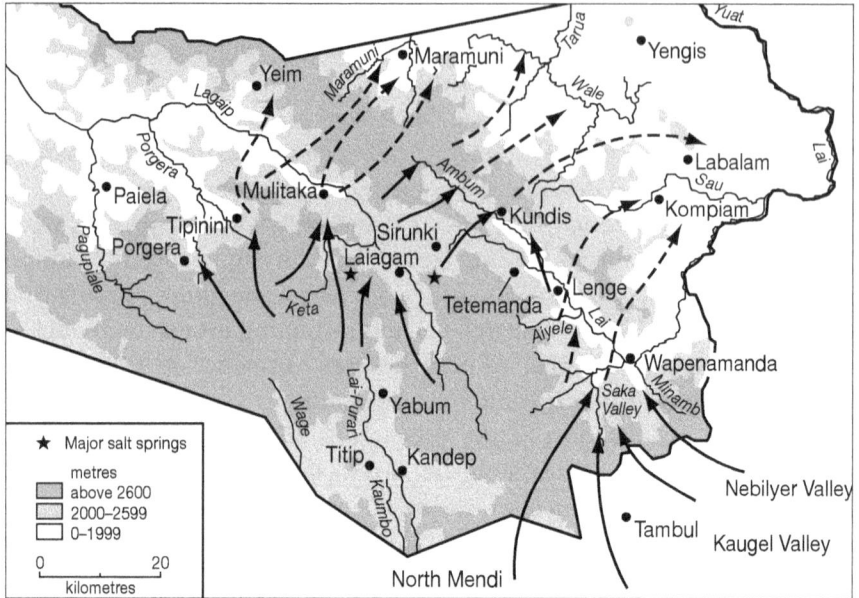

**FIGURE 9.2**

*Schematic representation of major migrations in Enga after the introduction of the sweet potato.*
*From the earliest generations of historical traditions until approximately the fourth generation*
*before present, we recorded 270 migrations of entire clans or large segments of clans. Map by*
*Polly Wiessner.*

for self-decoration worn at social and ceremonial events, such as cosmetic
oil, shells, and plumes, lies at the heart of many early traditions. Three
themes dominated Enga social relations at that time, as they continue to do
today. The first was potential equality and mutual respect expressed in the
proverbs "You need a man [a person]" and "Anybody can become a
wealthy man [kamongo]." The idea that any man could work hard and
become wealthy was the motor behind productive efforts throughout Enga
historical traditions. The second contrasting theme modifies the first: "A
good tree bears good fruits, and a sickly tree bears poor fruits." From earliest historical traditions, some people are mentioned as being more capable than others, and there was an expectation for at least one gifted son to
succeed the father. The seeds of both hierarchy and equality were thus
deeply rooted in Enga tradition.

A third theme running through Enga history is inequality between the
sexes, with men monopolizing the public realm and women exerting
strong influence in the private realm (Kyakas and Wiessner 1992). Men are

said to have gone to great lengths to win brides who could serve as companions, cook, bear and raise children, and, very importantly, forge affinal ties. Women moved across clan boundaries to and from their natal clans and were in a position to privately investigate possibilities for ceremonial exchange or secession of hostilities. In myth and legend, women are attributed with spreading cults throughout Enga (Wiessner 2004).

Early historical traditions mention that leaders assembled group members, mediated disputes, provided food for public occasions, organized trade, and negotiated war reparations to allies. Leadership appears to have been based on different criteria for hunters and gatherers inhabiting the high country of the west and horticultural groups of the east. In the west, major events included tribewide gatherings for the initiation of boys and feasts after hunts or harvests of pandanus nuts that drew people from surrounding areas. Great cassowary hunters were attributed with magical powers and high status. Traders received renown and were said to be "wealthy," though they travelled too widely to exert substantial influence at home. Ritual experts were powerful, feared, and respected within their realms of expertise, and their powers were passed from father to son. This situation is important because later, when ritual and exchange became integrated, control of ritual had long been in the hands of certain families and could not be appropriated by aspiring secular leaders.

In eastern Enga, by contrast, hunters received little attention. No initiations were held, and ritual was performed only at the level of small local groups. Status was attributed to those who managed the salt–axe stone trade and to local Big Men who mediated conflict, assisted others with wealth, and organized public gatherings such as funeral feasts and war reparations to allies. In central Enga, where the fertile lower valleys meet the high country, emphasis was on hunting, ritual, war reparations, and the salt–axe stone trade, bringing a diversity of leadership positions.

The following is a description of a leader, a kamongo from the Yakani tribe of central Enga:

> Wambi's first public distribution of wealth was during this war
> reparation exchange. All other members of the Timali clan also
> gave out pigs, but Wambi gave away more than others. His row of
> pig stakes was longer than the rest. There was nothing exciting
> or dramatic about Wambi's first Tee exchange. For example,
> Wambi and his men did not sing any boasting songs, he did not
> wear any intricately woven bird of paradise feathers on his wig,
> and he did not make eloquent speeches....Although Wambi was

the leader of our clan, according to what my grandfather said, his leadership was fairly weak. He did not have strong influence but merely made comments and suggestions. (Kopio Toea Lambu, Yakani Timali clan, Lenge, 1991)

There are some indications in early historical traditions that key positions in the organization of the stone axe–salt trade from eastern Enga to central Enga may have been passed from father to son. Outside this major trade route, trade links were organized through local kinship ties.

Warfare was a strong force throughout Enga history and served to break up groups that had become too large to cooperate, redistributing people over the landscape and establishing the balance of power necessary for ceremonial exchange to flow across boundaries (Wiessner 2006; Wiessner and Tumu 1998). Nonetheless, the names of great warriors are rarely recalled in historical traditions, perhaps because wars were fought sporadically, offering only temporary fame, and because prowess in warfare was not easily transferable to success in economic activities. The limited influence of Enga warriors contrasts with many societies in the eastern highlands of PNG that were perpetually at war, allowing great warriors to hold a continuous reign.

In summary, early Enga historical traditions indicate that leadership was weak and influence distributed among men with a variety of skills. The age hierarchy was informal, and ascribed status for men applied in the realms of ritual expertise and organization of the central trade axis. Enga men within a clan competed, but they deferred to the most skilled and they bonded into a cohesive force for events that required the presentation of a strong unified group. The inequality between men and women, exogamous marriage, and the strong private influence of women in their natal clans allowed enterprising men to draw support from a variety of other clans through polygynous marriages. Tensions existed between ideals of potential equality and the expectation that the sons of the gifted would replace their fathers. Potential for change was there.

## POST–SWEET POTATO DEVELOPMENTS: BACHELORS' CULTS

The sweet potato was introduced into Enga from the northwest during a period of famine. Subsequently, groups inhabiting higher-altitude areas moved to land in the lower valleys that they acquired from affines, and they settled down to agriculture. In many cases, as groups adjusted to the new social landscape, it was not long before the newcomers came into conflict with their hosts. The sixth to seventh generations before present saw the periods of greatest turmoil and most vicious warfare in precolonial Enga history.

In central Enga, where some of the largest and most vicious wars took place, the informal age hierarchy appears to have been challenged by youths, perhaps because of their fighting skills, at a time in history when larger fighting forces were being mounted. In response, elders instituted formal bachelors' cults (*sangai*) to replace informal individual rites of growth with formal "initiations." Bachelors' cults were presented to youths in appealing terms: through symbolic sexual contact with a sacred woman during secret cult rites, all young men—good-looking or ugly, wealthy or poor—would be transformed into handsome, mature, and capable men (Wiessner 2004). Bachelors' cults bonded peers for life, placing loyalty to clan "brothers" above interindividual competition. They put younger men firmly into the grips of elders, molded disciplined cohorts that could be organized to assemble large fighting forces, and kept young men out of the marriage market until they were mature and responsible clan members. Bachelors' cults were exported from central Enga to western and eastern Enga (Wiessner and Tumu 1999). Their sacred objects and rites were sold from clan to clan following the logic of Enga exchange that distribution, not retention, leads to prosperity. And so it did, for the cults eventually homogenized ideas about ideals for men and relations between the sexes throughout Enga, facilitating the expansion of ceremonial exchange networks based on marriage ties. And very importantly, they formalized inequality between older and younger men and potential equality for all men of a cohort. The latter became a driving force in Enga history, for it encouraged every man to work hard and strive to become wealthy.

### The Great Ceremonial Wars

The sixth to seventh generations saw a number of vicious wars in central Enga that departed from conventional wars in that they involved entire tribes or pairs of tribes and their allies rather than single clans (Wiessner and Tumu 1998). They continued for years or even decades, until vast tracts of land of up to 160 square kilometers were vacated. Victors invited friends and allies to help fill the land gained. The losers fled to the northeast, where they displaced scattered communities of people from other linguistic groups and prospered. Much other than fighting transpired during these wars. Larger groups formed for collective action, bachelors' cults spread in efforts to create homogeneity, and large war reparation exchanges were held for allies slain in battle. Marriages and bride-wealth exchanges solidified alliances, as did war reparations for slain allies. The spread of both bachelors' cults and cults for the ancestors standardized norms and values and provided occasions for large gatherings. When the wars ended, there was a void. Reasons for coordinated action and ceremonial exchange evaporated, and with the displacement of major tribes, the map of trade and exchange was disrupted.

The Great Ceremonial Wars of central Enga were born out of the desire to perpetuate the positive aspects of large-scale warfare in central Enga and eliminate the destructive ones. It appears that the organizers of the former great conventional wars, or their sons, were called on to use their social and political ties to generate events emphasizing display rather than devastation and fighting:

> The Great Ceremonial Wars were planned and planted like a garden for the exchange that would follow. They were arranged when goods and valuables were plentiful and when there were so many pigs that women complained about their workloads. Everybody knew what they were in for, how reparations were paid for deaths, and what the results would be. They were designed to open up new areas, further existing exchange relations, foster tribal unity, and provide a competitive but structured environment in which young men could strive for leadership. These qualities of the Great Wars made them differ from conventional wars, which disrupted relationships of trade and exchange, causing havoc and sometimes irreparable damage. The distributions of wealth that took place after the Great Wars brought trade goods from outlying areas into the Wabag area on the trade paths initially established by the salt trade.
> (Ambone Mati, Itapuni Nemani clan, Kopena, Wabag, 1987)

Great War episodes were fought about once a decade between entire tribes or pairs of tribes that were "the owners of the war," with intermediary tribes hosting men from the respective sides. The hosts provided their guests with food, water, entertainment, and frontline fighters. The timing and location of Great War episodes were first negotiated by fight leaders (*watenge*), leaders chosen from participant clans for their ability to plan the Great Wars, put on spectacular public performances, and organize the ensuing exchanges. For weeks before the battles began, people from the hosting tribes on both sides received warriors in their houses and made preparations, sang, danced, and brewed the fighting spirit.

On an appointed day, hundreds of warriors, or in later generations some two thousand warriors, appeared on the battlefield in full ceremonial regalia. Watenge engaged in flamboyant ritualized competition and announced a formal beginning to battle. Watenge were considered fair targets for humiliation—for example, warriors sought to capture or steal their plumes—but they did not participate in serious combat, for they were the men who would orchestrate the Great War exchanges at the end of battle. Fighting took place in a designated zone on the land of the hosts, so no land could be gained or lost. By day, warriors fought in front of hundreds or thousands of spectators while women sang and danced on the sidelines. By night, they ate, drank, talked with their hosts, and courted their hosts' daughters. Death rates were low. The battle continued for weeks or months until the watenge called an end to the fight and ceremoniously cast their arms into the river. In these "fights without anger," there were no winners or losers. No land could be gained or lost, no damage was inflicted on property, and no deaths were avenged.

Following the battle, the owners of the fight, hosts, and allies initiated a series of massive and festive reciprocal exchanges of pigs, cassowaries, goods, and valuables. The owners of the fight slaughtered hundreds of pigs and roasted them in earthen ovens. Hosts and allies awoke at dawn and traveled from clan to clan, collecting gifts of pork from the families they had hosted. These exchanges continued for three to four years, transforming the new relationships between hosts and hosted into enduring exchange partnerships.[2]

There was something for everybody in the Great Wars. Young men and women, as well as older men seeking polygynous marriages, had opportunities for display and courtship:

> When they [the warriors] first arrived, they would bring food for a few days, but after that they were fed by people of the hosting clans. It was a great occasion—many of the girls from the surrounding communities would come and entertain us. Of course, this meant that some of us would eventually end up marrying them. In the evenings, we would dance with the girls, and this was the situation in every household where the warriors slept. All nights were social nights; we had lots of fun with the girls. We courted them by night and went to fight during the day. It was exciting and fun. (Yopo Yakena, Malipini Kamaniwane clan, Kaeyape, 1986)

Mature men and women were drawn to exchange events where they could gain reputations for wealth distributed by individuals and clans. What counted was who did well in exchange, not in battle. Everybody feasted and everybody celebrated. The relationships between host and hosted were turned into exchange partnerships, giving every family a chance to broaden its ties and providing incentive for increased pig production.

Elders say that the position of watenge was inherited from the onset of the Great Wars for a number of reasons. First, the sons of watenge inherited the social connections and tactical knowledge necessary to organize these great events. Second, the public on both sides sought continuity for effective leadership. Third, opponents called on men who were known quantities, the capable sons of former watenge, to present themselves as representatives of the rival side. Of the five Great War leaders on whom we have sufficient genealogical information, all had fathers who were watenge. Three had both fathers and grandfathers who were watenge; for the other two, information on grandfathers is lacking. All were married to daughters of watenge from other clans involved in the Great Wars.[3]

In the context of the Great Wars, leadership in Enga became conditionally inherited. Sons of Great War leaders followed their fathers, if and only if they were capable. In a sense, leadership still resided in the flow of goods and services, as well as in inherited positions.

> It is said that unproductive fruit trees do not bear good fruits but that only good and healthy trees do. As such, it was always the son of a watenge who became a watenge. A man could have many pigs and be a wealthy kamongo and look good in the Great Wars, but these things would not win him the title of watenge. There was nothing a man could do to rise to this position. It was always the son of a watenge who became a watenge....We insisted upon this because he would be from a reputable family and therefore well brought up and exposed to the leadership qualities of his father and grandfather.[4] (Ambone Mati, Itapuni Nemani clan, Kopena, Wabag, 1987)

Between Great War episodes, watenge served as clan leaders in internal and external affairs.

### The Tee Ceremonial Exchange Cycle

The Tee Cycle was a massive system of enchained exchange of wealth that moved through eastern and central Enga. It had three phases. The first phase, the *saandi pingi*, involved the informal presentation—from men in the east to partners to their west—of gifts of small pigs, axes, salt, tree oil, and shells that were intended to "pull" the *mena tee pingi*, the phase of the main gifts. When a sufficient number of initiatory gifts had reached the westernmost clans, the phase of the main gifts began; large pigs, pearl shells, and other valuables traced the path of the saandi pingi from west to east. This phase was one of great display, competition, and excitement. When the pigs reached the easternmost clan, approximately half were slaughtered, and sides of cooked pork were sent westward in the *mena yae pingi*, which followed the steps of the main gifts. One cycle took approximately four years to complete; the next would send the main gifts in the opposite direction. The organization and timing of the Tee Cycle required significant skills in planning, persuasion, oration, and management of the flow of wealth. Because the Tee assembled a large amount of wealth in one place at one time, it served as a system of finance for other enterprises, such as war reparation exchanges and bride wealth.

The Tee Cycle, which included some thirty to fifty thousand participants at first contact, had modest beginnings (Wiessner and Tumu 1998). Like the Great Wars, it was set off by population movements from the high country to fertile lower valleys of eastern Enga. The new migrants had their own connections for obtaining axe stone from the western highlands and threatened the control of Enga tribes involved in the central axis of the trade. In response, kamongo in the Saka Valley constructed a new system for raising wealth; they invested in alliances to foil the plans of their rivals from immigrant groups. As the legend goes, they sent messages and initiatory gifts to their partners along well-established trade routes, asking them to provide wealth in the form of pigs and valuables on credit rather than by traditional barter. When wealth arriving along these chains of finance reached Big Men in the Saka Valley, they invested it in marriages or other alliances. These were investments in the sense that they promised long-term exchange and mutual support. Returns from these investments, together with wealth from home production, were used to repay creditors in a public festival. Through the concatenation of former trade partnerships, chains of finance were constructed to form the skeleton of what was to become the Tee Ceremonial Exchange Cycle.

The Tee was ingenious in that it allowed leaders to elicit finance on credit from people who were beyond the usual bounds of kinship reckoning. Finance through Tee chains thus partially decoupled economics from kinship, its protocols, and etiquette. Formal public wealth distributions conferred prestige on managers of wealth and fostered trust in their competence. Finally, skillful manipulation of chains of finance maximized the amount of wealth arriving in one place at one point in time, giving recipients the financial clout needed to engage in larger projects.

Tee festivals are said to have clung to the major east–west trade route for two to three generations. In the fifth generation before present, the Tee Cycle spread as surrounding groups realized that they too would have to participate if they were to compete in almost any area of social and political life—for example, arranging strategic marriages or raising wealth for war reparations. Nonetheless, the emerging Tee Cycle remained small in scale in the early generations. If one man could distribute seven to ten pigs, he was considered a wealthy man—kamongo (Wiessner and Tumu 1998:169).[5] Tee distributions were low-key and did not arouse a great deal of attention or greatly increase incentive for pig production. As the Tee routes expanded, leaders in key tribes in the trade axis kept the Tee Cycle within their control by passing on their positions to their capable sons and by intermarrying their sons and daughters. Inheritance of leadership in the early Tee Cycle does not appear to have been contested, perhaps because organizing enchained exchange was a time-consuming job, involved dangerous travel, and depended on far-flung social connections with a history. Clan members could benefit from leaving the job to the experienced.

The early Tee Cycle had the almost unlimited potential to assemble wealth to meet social and political agendas, but it lacked the excitement of a large competitive event to stimulate production.[6] The Great Wars, by contrast, gathered people from a vast area, defined sides, and engaged opponents in events involving dramatic competition and opposition. However, they lacked the Tee's chains of finance. It was not long before the Great Kamongo (*kamongo andake*) in central Enga, who participated in both systems, saw the potential of the Tee Cycle for financing the Great War exchanges and for investing the wealth that flowed out of them. In combining the two, he linked what Feinman (1995) has called a network strategy, with almost unlimited potential to assemble wealth, to a corporate strategy that had the benefits of assembling people in dramatic events. The subsequent history of the Tee Cycle is complex (see Wiessner and Tumu 1998:chapter 11). Within the next three generations, the Tee Cycle expanded in almost every dimension and developed into a regular three-phase cycle of enchained exchange that encompassed much of eastern and central Enga.

As the two systems merged, rituals were circulated to facilitate the coordination of the Tee Cycle and the Great Wars. Around the fifth generation, the bachelors' cults added elaborate emergence ceremonies, which became events to gather people to plan the Tee Cycle. Around the same time, the Kepele ancestral cult was imported from western to central Enga, where it was developed into a five-phase event to meet the needs of coordinating the Great Wars with the Tee Cycle and was renamed Aetee. The

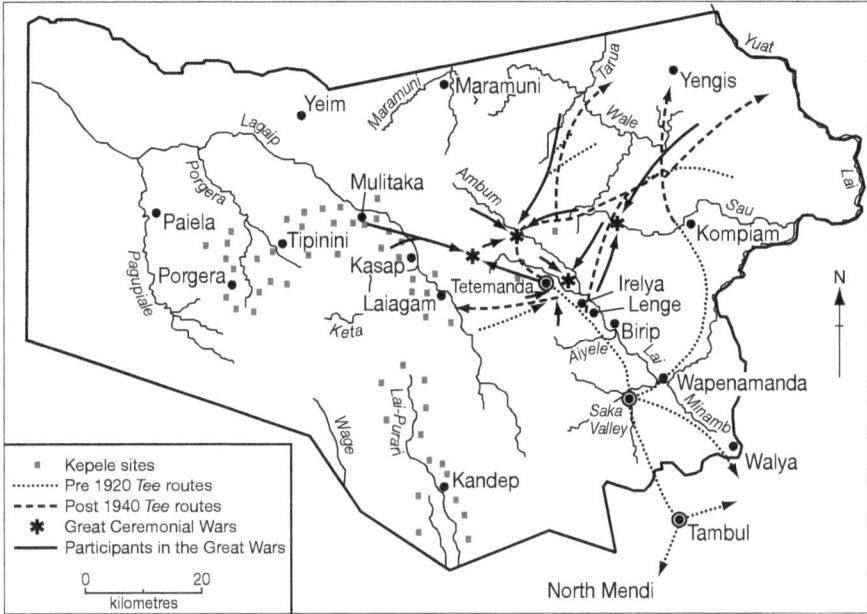

**FIGURE 9.3**

*The Tee Cycle, the Great Ceremonial Wars, and Kepele cult networks. Map by Polly Wiessner.*

Aetee and Tee Cycle involved alternating expressions of equality and inequality. Equality of all men and group prosperity were prominently expressed in Aetee ancestral rites. Subsequently, individuals were challenged to go out and engage in individual entrepreneurial tactics in Tee exchange to increase their own reputations and the overall wealth and status of the clan. Variations of both the Aetee and bachelors' cults were imported by clans in the east to serve similar purposes. These rituals, carried out in association with the Tee Cycle, transformed it into a more prominent and dramatic event, reaffirmed group loyalty, and made men willing to forfeit portions of their own agendas for group interest.

By the early twentieth century, the Great Wars had grown to great proportions and had become cumbersome to organize and difficult to coordinate with the Tee Cycle. The managers of both systems realized that it would be expedient to discontinue the Great Wars and to replace their exchange networks with the Tee Cycle. Three of the four Great Wars were discontinued early in the twentieth century; the last episode of the fourth Great War was fought in the late 1930s or early 1940s. New routes were added; the "river of Tee," with its many tributaries, flooded (figure 9.3).

## CONVENTIONAL WARS AND WAR REPARATIONS

The Great Ceremonial Wars and the Tee Cycle did not put an end to tribal warfare. Smaller conventional wars continued throughout Enga history and persisted until the present. However, their role changed through time, from splitting groups and spacing belligerent neighbors to creating a matrix of equality and trust among clans so that enchained exchange could flow across boundaries (Wiessner 2006). Rules were instituted to contain warfare, and war reparations, which were formerly paid only to allies, were extended to enemies so that groups could fight, make peace, and restore balance though the exchange of wealth. The complex politics of making peace and organizing war reparations greatly strengthened leadership throughout Enga.

## HIERARCHY AND EQUALITY ON THE EVE OF CONTACT WITH EUROPEANS

Relationships between equality and inequality in the full-blown pre-contact Tee Cycle were complex. At the top were the Great Kamongo or Tee Cycle managers, whose positions had been passed on in their families for generations.

> In recent times, after the coming of the white men, the sons of nobodies can become a Great Kamongo. This was not so in the past. Daughters of Great Kamongo were given to sons of Great Kamongo in marriage. This was done for many reasons. The most obvious ones are to maintain their prestige and status quo and the economics of the Tee Cycle. Strategic information in relation to the pig exchange system and personal security while traveling was accessible to those on top. Furthermore, members of a clan and those outside of clan borders gave honor and respect to a Great Kamongo.... If someone for the first time wanted to display his wealth and take part in public debates [concerning the Tee], he was ridiculed and frowned upon. In contrast, since the introduction of money, people from nowhere may become kamongo. (Tumu Lapinyo, Wapai clan, Akoma village, 2006)
>
> A son of a Great Kamongo was only expected to succeed his father in the event of his father's death or when he became old.... The son of a Great Kamongo was in a better position to succeed his father because he had the knowledge of how to

**TABLE 9.1**

*Status of sons of Great Kamongo*

Sons of Great Kamongo who:

| Status | Number | Percent |
|---|---|---|
| Became Great Kamongo | 32 | 38% |
| Became wealthy men | 11 | 13% |
| Became ordinary men | 41 | 49% |
| Married the daughters of kamongo | 38 | 45% |

Marriages were arranged by parents. Men were married at the age of twenty-five to thirty and women between fifteen and twenty. Underrepresented here are Great Kamongo who left no sons, or no capable ones.

> become a kamongo and people already expected him to do
> so.... The father did not specifically choose a son to succeed
> him. It came as the result of a natural process. As time went on,
> a Great Kamongo's children grew up and developed certain
> attributes. When the people saw these, they began to conclude
> that a certain son would certainly succeed his father. (Suilya
> Kanopatoakali, Kalia clan, Wakemale village, 2006)

In 2006 we conducted interviews with sons or grandsons of past, prominent, precontact Tee leaders. The results are given in table 9.1. Of the sons
of Great Kamongo who survived to adulthood, 38 percent followed their
fathers and became Tee Cycle organizers. Thirteen percent became
wealthy and were considered kamongo but did not have the charisma or
skills in mediation and oration to become Great Kamongo. Nearly half of
the sons of Great Kamongo became ordinary men. Forty-five percent of the
sons of Great Kamongo, the capable ones, were married to the daughters
of kamongo in other clans.

Nobody could name a Great Kamongo who lived before contact with
Europeans and came from an ordinary or poor family. Nine reasons were
given for inheritance of leadership by capable sons: (1) The sons of Great
Kamongo had access to knowledge that others did not have. They acquired
this knowledge by accompanying their fathers on trips to organize the Tee
Cycle. (2) The sons of Great Kamongo inherited social connections and
Tee partnerships that were strengthened by a long history of exchange. (3)
Great Kamongo married their sons and daughters to the children of Great
Kamongo for their first marriages, keeping knowledge and influence

within a limited circle. (4) Travel was dangerous owing to interclan warfare. Only those who had long-established networks for protection could travel widely and safely. Some Tee managers traveled through fifty to one hundred clans over a period of one to two years to organize Tee Cycles. (5) Great Kamongo silenced aspiring rivals from ordinary families when they tried to talk Tee in public. (6) If aspiring men tried to speak in other clans, the Great Kamongo would send word down the line to have associates ask them, "Who do you think you are that you can stand up and speak of the Tee Cycle in public?" (7) The public looked to the capable sons of Great Kamongo to follow their fathers. (8) Great Kamongo in other clans preferred to work with the families of well-known leaders. (9) Great Kamongo attracted more followers to work in their households: war refugees, bachelors, spinsters—both kin and non-kin—who became "servants" (*kendemane*), young people who came to work in the households of Great Kamongo in exchange for education and contributions to their bride wealth (Wiessner and Tumu 1998).

As in the Great Wars, inheritance of leadership applied to capable, interested, and honest sons. Should a Great Kamongo cheat, his partners would band together and end his career; a clean reputation was everything. Finally, kamongo held no privileged access to the spirit world; the inheritance of positions of ritual leadership that had deep roots in Enga history barred kamongo from entering this realm. Even the greatest of kamongos were buried in the same fashion as ordinary men.

Interestingly, inherited leadership seems to have its origins at a time when the population was sparse and exchange systems in their infancy, perhaps because benefits were small in relation to efforts invested to incite widespread competition and it was easier to obtain consensus concerning representation in small groups than in larger ones. As exchange systems grew, leaders who had inherited their positions maintained their advantage.[7]

Beneath the Great Kamongo or Tee Cycle managers were lesser local kamongo, men who were intelligent, raised pigs, gained wealth and local influence, and married several wives. These men also played roles in organizing local events within the clan. There was competition between the lesser kamongo for name and wealth within their subclans or clans, although for important decisions they deferred to the Great Kamongo out of group interest.

> This does not mean that people of lesser importance did not raise pigs or possess other items of wealth. They had wealth and were intelligent. But they could not assume leadership at the top

because those already in the class would not permit them in. Even if a man was not an advocate for the Tee Cycle or an orator, he could still be recognized as a kamongo. A man was a local kamongo relative to the number of pigs he had. The title *kamongo* was spoken to motivate and encourage people to breed pigs. The term was used to motivate the ordinary man to produce pigs and be a kamongo, but not to the level to rival the Great Kamongo. (Tumu Lapinyo, Wapai clan, Akoma village, 2006).

The success of the Tee Cycle and Great Wars thus depended on three factors. The first was leadership by a limited circle of managers at the top who had inherited the position, knowledge, and social connections necessary to organize episodes of the Tee Cycle with efficiency and continuity over time. Without such stability, the great exchange networks would have fallen to destructive competition, as they did during the colonial era. The second was widespread open competition between potential equals below the top for recognition as lesser kamongo. Without such competition, which drove production in the broader population, those on top would not have had the huge amounts of wealth to manage. The third was willingness of clansmen to set aside their own agendas and pull for united clan performance during Tee festivals.

Finally, the inequality between men and women contributed to the development of complexity. The marriages of Great Kamongo's daughters to Great Kamongo's sons sealed alliances between Tee Cycle managers at the top; additional marriages of polygynous kamongo to the daughters of ordinary men maintained the flow of wealth between the top and the bottom. Women, seen as "apolitical" and nonthreatening actors, often returned to their natal clans and felt out the climate for the first rounds of Tee negotiations, paving the way for more formal negotiations by men. In a very few cases, exceptional women took over their fathers' or deceased husbands' positions. The most notable example was Takime. The daughter of an exceptionally powerful Great Kamongo, she married a Great Kamongo of the Wapai clan (Kyakas and Wiessner 1992).[8] When her husband was killed in warfare, she refused offers for remarriage, even though her sons were toddlers, and took over her father's role to become one of the most influential Great Kamongo of her time. She paid bride wealth for eleven "female husbands" and then married these women to men of her choice. All of them worked to increase the wealth of her household. Her wealth, uniqueness, and contribution to the welfare of her clan are said to have won the respect of men.

In summary, during decades before colonial influence, the dynamics created by the interaction of hierarchy and equality made the great exchange systems possible and, with them, institutionalized inequality.

> This is another word of wisdom. A son of a Great Kamongo should marry the daughter of a poor man, and vice versa (in addition to marrying the daughters of other Great Kamongo). The poverty of one becomes a liability to the other, and the prosperity of one becomes a blessing to the other. This is the way wealth was distributed and spread to many families. If wealth had circulated among the Great Kamongo only, then economic activities like Tee exchange would not have functioned effectively. The middle-class kamongo and those at the bottom also participated in Tee exchange by giving away pigs. So a village received a good name because many at the bottom participated in Tee exchange. Really, nobody was poor. Everyone had at least one or more pigs. In our culture, there was a social hierarchy; on one end of the spectrum were the wealthiest, and on the other end were the ordinary. They were not poor and not wealthy. If they had been all equal, society would have come to a standstill. There would have been no respect or regard for one another [explained later as meaning that people would not defer to others in positions of authority with the knowledge, wealth, and social ties to make important decisions]. (Waisa, Yakane Kalia clan, Wakumale village, 2006)

## THE COLONIAL ERA AND THE NEW "BIG MEN"

Despite first contact with Europeans in the 1930s, the impact of the Colonial Administration and missions in Enga took hold only after World War II. Great changes took place in warfare, the Tee Cycle, religious practices, and the economy, and all of these changes had an impact on leadership. First, the Colonial Administration rapidly established the Pax Australiana throughout Enga.[9] Under conditions of peace, the Tee moved rapidly into outlying areas; the multiplicity of feeder routes made its organization and timing extremely complex (see figure 9.2). Second, capable men, regardless of family status, could be hired by the administration or work for the missions. Because the Great Kamongo and their sons were fully occupied with traditional activities, it was often ambitious young men from families in the middle or lower ranks who were attracted to work for foreigners. Men employed by patrols used steel axes, metal shovels, shells, and other wealth obtained from Europeans, to procure brides and large pigs from wide catchment areas outside the sphere of the Tee Cycle. They then pulled the clans of their spouses into the Tee Cycle, creating new feeder routes to suit their own designs. Third, the administration further formalized positions of leadership in Enga by appointing *luluiais* and *tutuls.* Luluais were Great Kamongo from the top who represented clans or tribes; tutuls were young men with linguistic skills appointed to assist them (Gordon and Meggitt 1985). These young men who communicated directly with colonial administrators gained substantial influence. Fourth, the introduction of metal shovels and steel axes greatly increased agricultural production, allowing more people to contribute larger amounts of wealth to the Tee Cycle. Fifth and finally, with the ban on warfare imposed by the Colonial Administration and the abolishment of ancestral cults by the missions, fewer enterprises tied people together at the clan level. Self-interest increased, and willingness to sacrifice for the group decreased, making the Tee a more individualistic event.

New positions, sources of wealth, education, and conditions of peace and prosperity enabled men who had formerly competed for the position of lesser kamongo to break into the circle of Tee Cycle managers at the top. When social barriers prevented them from doing so, they constructed their own feeder routes into the Tee and made alliances with other wealthy, aspiring lesser kamongo in clans along Tee routes. Through these alliances formed parallel chains of Tee partners that vied to control the flow and timing of wealth in the Tee Cycle to their own advantage (see Feil 1984). The Tee Cycle departed from its former three-phase cycle as competing chains launched their own initiatory phases and boycotted those planned by rivals. When the top strata of inherited Tee Cycle managers were in control, there was little destructive competition in the Tee Cycle. But with competing chains of self-made Tee Cycle managers, no holds were barred. Deceptive tactics were used: wars were initiated to block phases of the Tee Cycle launched by competing chains, murders committed to disrupt the flow of wealth, rumors spread to foil the plans of others.

This turn of events is not surprising. The concept of potential equality of all men had long been a part of Enga culture, and competition had always simmered beneath the top levels of leadership. With changes brought about by the Colonial Administration and new avenues to wealth, the bottom and middle broke into the top and competition was runaway. In some contexts, individuals even did Tee alone.[10] When prestigious positions at the top were no longer ascribed by inherited family status but were open to all, the pursuit of prestige became a goal in and of itself, favoring the aggressive personality that is often associated with Big Men. The Great Kamongo lost their hold, and the Tee Cycle began to fragment as a result of intense competition. The last cycle was held in 1978–1979 (Wiessner and Tumu 1998).

## IMPLICATIONS FOR ARCHAEOLOGY

Models for the emergence of complexity have been built on two assumptions. The first is that equality, the blank slate of nature upon which social complexity is written, gives way to hierarchy in highly competitive Big Man or "transegalitarian societies." The second is that in Big Man societies, aggrandizers, through pursuing personal gain, are able to build and sustain complex economic and ritual systems (Boone 1992; Earle 1997; Hayden 1995) that are the forerunners of chiefdoms. Let us take a closer look at each assumption.

There is no solid theoretical basis for setting equality as the starting point; this assumption has roots in analogies transposed from a handful of modern-day forager societies, such as the !Kung Bushmen, assumed to be representative of the Paleolithic (Wilmsen 1989; Wobst 1978).[11] Even among these model "egalitarian societies," there are institutionalized hierarchies based on age, between the sexes, or in ritual power.[12] On theoretical grounds, there is reason to expect that both hierarchical and egalitarian institutions with ideologies to support them should be present in all societies. Both are deeply rooted in human phylogeny, and both can greatly reduce the economic and social transaction costs of exchange in certain situations.

The interaction between egalitarian and hierarchical institutions and changing environmental and historical circumstances plays a critical role in the development of complexity. For example, on one hand, institutionalized hierarchy among the Enga was necessary to organize the Great Wars and Tee Cycle with efficiency and continuity over generations; on the other hand, widespread competition between lesser kamongo drove production and the growth of large exchange systems. The fact that ritual power was institutionalized from the onset of Enga historical traditions meant that the Great Kamongo could not appropriate ritual power to enhance their influence. Gender inequality allowed important matters such as peace and exchange to be first explored by women, who were defined as nonthreatening "apolitical" actors. The key question for any students of complexity is not "Why did hierarchy replace equality?" but rather "How was each force expressed in a society at a certain point in time, and how and why did the relation between the two change over time to create more complex societies?"

The second assumption—that men compete constantly to pursue agendas that further their own personal gain—does have theoretical roots in evolutionary biology and in neoclassical economics. But how far can an individual move a system toward complexity? The classic aggrandizer is often seen as able to manipulate others by extending assistance or by coercion, debt, contract, deceit, and marginalization to build the vast and competitive systems of ritual, warfare, and exchange that precede chiefdoms. But is it really possible for complex exchange systems to arise and expand under the destructive forces of competition? The Enga case suggests that it is not and that such systems cannot be built during short lifetimes but require inherited knowledge, authority, and connections for stability.

Inherited leadership in the sphere of complex exchange systems appears to have existed in surrounding PNG highland societies as well. To give a few examples, Gitlow (1947:35) described the Melpa, Enga's eastern neighbors (see figure 9.1), as having an upper class of chiefs who passed their power on to their elder sons and composed about 8 percent of the male population. These men orchestrated the community for *moka* (ceremonial exchange) and controlled the most prestigious items. Other early missionaries similarly describe class stratification (Ross 1936; Vicedom and Tischner 1943–1948; Wirz 1952a, 1952b).[13] For the Mendi to the southwest, the work of Mawe (1985) suggests that there had been institutionalized leadership, which had vanished by the time Lederman (1986, 1990) conducted her studies. Among the Mendi, leadership was symbolized by owning the most highly valued item in Mendi society, the *somb*, a valuable constructed from shells. Mawe (1985) described the somb owner as "the head of all ordinary rich men." Somb owners were representatives for the group in external relations and married many wives. Capable sons inherited the somb from their fathers, and the daughters of somb owners were preferably married to men who owned a somb. Among the Huli to the southwest of the Enga, ritual power was inherited and locked within a very limited circle of powerful ritual experts. The Huli were middlemen in the trade between the Papuan Plateau, from which tree oil and other valuables came, and groups to the north such as the Enga, the source of salt and stone axes. The Huli themselves had no exotic goods to contribute to the trade, but they exported complex ritual to control the trade from north to south, placing ritual experts as key figures in economic relations (Ballard 1995).

Finally, what is usually overlooked in Big Man models is that the very survival and success of an individual are dependent to a large degree upon being a member of a strong cooperative group. Men who compete on a daily basis put aside competition and immediate self-interest, defer to the most capable, and cooperate as "brothers" to pursue group agendas (Tiger 1969).[14] Men not only identify with their groups but also derive feelings of personal achievement from "team successes" or identification with team leaders or superstars. Accordingly, they will make sacrifices for group success. These were the sentiments that drove cooperation in both the Great Wars and the Tee Cycle. Without such cooperative interest, which modified the diverse personal interests of the players, it is unlikely that any aggrandizer could have seduced, enticed, bribed, or compelled group members to cooperate in large financial and political enterprises (see chapters 5 and 6 by Stanish and Arnold, respectively, this volume). It is in events for bonding groups that principles of equality and hierarchy often mesh to align the goals of those at the bottom, middle, and top of society. To continue the quote from Waisa cited earlier:

> A top kamongo did not do things entirely on his own. The people who were in the middle class also supported him in Tee exchanges and other smaller payments. For example, when staging a traditional dance [*sing-sing*], the top Great Kamongo danced in the foreground, and the people of lesser status danced on either side of the line. Each person dressed according to what he or she could afford in terms of birds of paradise feathers and other traditional attire. This diversity made the dance spectacular and magnificent. So the fabric of society tied together the top-level kamongo, the middle kamongo, and those at the bottom.

Fortunately, events to bond and align male interests—powerful tools in the emergence of complexity—are visible in the archaeological record (Dietler and Hayden 2001), though they are often interpreted as occasions for aggrandizers to show off, manipulate, or present a facade of equality in the face of real inequalities. However, more often than not, they may be the very places where hierarchy and equality mesh, complement each other, and provide a window into the more sophisticated dynamics of social complexity. It is in such events that archaeologists may be able to understand the dynamics of hierarchy and inequality.

## Notes

1. See Wiessner and Tumu 1998 and Wiessner 2002 (electronic appendix) for an in-depth discussion of our methodology and of oral traditions as history.

2. See Clark and Blake 1994 and Fox 1996 for a similar case of the association of sportive events with consolidation of power.

3. See Wiessner and Tumu 1998:289–290 for further description of the importance of inheritance of leadership in the Great Ceremonial Wars.

4. "Son" was broadly defined to include nephews if a watenge had no suitable sons.

5. The term *kamongo* means "to increase in wealth," according to Enga elders. A kamongo could have wealth in knowledge, people, or things—preferably all three—but had to translate it into material wealth. Ritual experts and conventional war leaders were not considered kamongo.

6. In some historical traditions, it is stated that kamongo began to encourage their fellow clan members to engage in the drudgery of pig rearing to increase the wealth and reputation of the clan.

7. For twenty years, we were so guided by the Big Man model that we did not question it, even though there was ample evidence to do so. These findings from our recent intensive research on leadership refute what we have published elsewhere, that inherited leadership came about in response to public demand to curb runaway competition as exchange networks expanded and the population grew and that the Tee Cycle did not involve inherited leadership.

8. We estimate that Takime was born around 1911. Her active years in the Tee Cycle were from about 1935 to 1965.

9. Peace was established quickly, in part because the initial means to repress warfare were brutal and in part because the Enga could see the advantages of peace for Tee exchange.

10. For example, Feil describes a Tee festival held alone by a man named Kepa in the 1970s because others in his clan could not manage to coordinate their giving with his. He concludes his description with the remark that "a Tee is a man's individual statement about his financial ability and the value he places on his Tee partners" (Feil 1984:195–196).

11. Even the Ju/'hoansi (!Kung Bushmen), so renowned for equality, have socially recognized hierarchies of respect based on age, with the young deferring to the older in talk regarding decision making and ritual. The amount of fame that healers can obtain is unlimited, and healers are never leveled for talking of their visions during trance healing or talking of their successes.

12. An exception is provided by Australian Aboriginals, whose hierarchies are said to make them the marsupials of hunter-gatherer societies.

13. For further discussion about stratification among the Melpa, see Feil 1987.

14. The emotional and social capacity of men to set aside competition, band, and bond, first presented in the work of Tiger (1969), is brilliantly shown for ninety-six societies in the volume from the Cologne exhibit Manner Bande und Manner Bunde (Welck and Konig 1990).

# 10

## Leadership in Middle-Range African Societies

### Chapurukha M. Kusimba and Sibel B. Kusimba

Structural/functionalist ethnographers recognized early the importance of acephalous or middle-range societies in Africa. Acephalous societies lacked hereditary leadership and rarely displayed obvious distinctions in status or wealth (Fortes and Evans-Pritchard 1958; Wiessner 2002, chapter 9, this volume). Distinct offices were vested in groups of people—including councils of elders, lineage elders, and age sets—rather than in individuals. These ethnographic cases have recently become grist for the archaeologists' mill as comparative data (for example, McIntosh 1999b).

Although anthropologists described the functions of acephalous or middle-range societies using many African case studies, they often ignored the flexibility in leadership offices, styles, types, and domains that can occur in these societies, probably because these emergent forms of leadership rarely led to structural change. For our part, it is the flexibility of leadership in acephalous societies that is most interesting (see also chapters 2, 6, and 9 by Bird and Bliege Bird, Arnold, and Wiessner, respectively, this volume). In some cases, local groups are organized into segments or nested hierarchies that provide a mechanism for supralocal organization in the face of broader threats, such as warfare (Southall 1999). Leaders might emerge in these times, but usually their temporary authority fades. In other cases, age sets or secret societies crosscut lineage organization and add another layer of social organization (Mair 1961). Although social organization does not mean leadership, it is true that in all societies, social organization provides the means through which individuals act to make decisions and that in all societies, leaders act through social institutions. This interface between social structure and agency is where we can understand the emergence of leaders.

The anthropological interest in "middle-range" societies stems from what they can bring to the understanding of how complex societies emerge (Pauketat, chapter 8, this volume). Earlier, neo-evolutionary models in archaeology focused on centralization, political control, and external environmental factors in the making of complexity (see an excellent review in Brumfiel 1992). Middle-range or acephalous societies in Africa offer numerous examples of very different kinds and functions of power. In African societies, power is of many kinds, including religious or ritual power and political or coercive power. Furthermore, authority or power is often vested in a variety of social groups, from secret societies to councils of elders and segmented lineages, which tend to forge authority through consensus building but which also resist the centralization of power (McIntosh 1999b). Recurrent themes across sub-Saharan Africa are the varying concept of power, prestige, and authority from one society to the next and the varied types of offices of power that existed in a single society. These forces discouraged the consolidation and centralization of power and authority.

## POWER AND INEQUALITY IN AFRICA

The notion of social, economic, and political power and how these are attained, maintained, used, and abused in acephalous and hierarchical societies continues to be debated by anthropologists (for example, Blanton 1998; Blanton et al. 1996; Clark and Blake 1994; Cowgill 2004; Drennan 1991; Feinman 1995, 2001; Hakansson 1998; Wiessner 2002). Archaeologists now widely recognize that

> individuals in societies are not merely a cog in a cultural wheel but [are] active participant[s], whose actions produce and reproduce culture. Different individuals in a society may pursue the same or different goals by a variety of means. Thus, it is the activities of individuals within a particular geographic and historical context that produce, reproduce, and change culture. Among the goals that individuals may pursue are wealth, status, and power. (Robertshaw 2003:156)

An admittedly essentialist view holds that those individuals who attain their goals—accumulators, aggrandizers, strivers, and entrepreneurial elites (Clark and Blake 1994; Hayden 1995; see Feinman 2001:155; see also chapters 5, 7, and 11 by Stanish, Vaughn, and Kantner, respectively, this volume)—are usually driven by self-interest (Earle 1997). The desire for wealth, status, and political power is the foundation of societal inequality and its institutionalization (Price and Feinman 1995). To attain these goals, individuals will use social, economic, military, and ideological power (Blanton et al. 1996:2; Earle 1997:5–10; Mann 1993). However, in many acephalous societies, those with a quest for power can achieve a diversity of offices or types of social, political, ritual, and religious power. In Cameroonian kingdoms, for example, power had more to do with the social prestige afforded to someone who was generous and could feed people. Power also referred to specialized knowledge to bring rain, cure disease, and so on. Different offices were responsible for these different spheres of knowledge and for ritual versus political authority. Power was thus decentralized, although the kings and special societies were linked in legitimizing myths (Asombang 1999).

The debate on the evolution of social complexity has moved away from a focus on increasing centralization as first proposed by Kent V. Flannery (1972) in his seminal paper *The Cultural Evolution of Civilizations*. Several competing, alternative, theoretical trajectories, including hierarchical, heterarchical, and social agency, have been proposed (Crumley 1995; Drennan 1991; Ehrenreich, Crumley, and Levy 1995; McIntosh 1998; Renfrew 1974; Robb 1999; Saitta 1999).

Many archaeologists have contributed to this debate, yet it is fair to say that the perspective offered by Richard Blanton and his colleagues in their seminal 1996 paper in *Current Anthropology*, "A Dual Processual Theory for the Evolution of Mesoamerican Civilization," has been the most influential in shaping the tone on the evolution of the social complexity debate in the past decade (table 10.1). In this and subsequent papers, the authors proposed that the dichotomy between distributive and authoritative power and collective and diffused power was the product of network and corporate power modes (Blanton 1998; Blanton et al. 1996:2; Feinman 1995, 2001). Network strategies are commonly founded upon exchange relationships between individuals from different ethnic groups and involve long-distance trade networks in prestige goods; they are wealth financed (D'Altroy and Earle 1985; Earle 1987; Kristiansen 1991:22). Individuals use wealth acquired through their exotic networks to gain social status and authoritative and distributive powers in their own societies. In network strategies, leaders place more emphasis on personal prestige, wealth, and power. Elite glorification; self-interest; control of wealth-creating resources, including local and regional exchange networks, princely residences, and burial; specialized manufacture; and restricted access to prestige goods generally accompany network strategies.

Two major avenues through which elites acquire power when using network strategies are patrimonial rhetoric and prestige goods systems. Patrimonial rhetoric fosters ties by emphasizing corporate membership among individuals and groups—for example, clans and extended families—and institutionalizes distributive power through organizations such as gender hierarchies and conical lineages. The prestige goods system attracts followers by creating demand for prestige goods and then controlling their production, exchange, and distribution (Blanton et al. 1996; Feinman 2001:155). To maintain control of prestige goods systems, elites often promote or sponsor the production of labor-intensive or technically complex items because in these contexts, they may employ their distributive and authoritative power to harness social and economic resources to which others do not have access (Brumfiel and Earle 1987; Robertshaw 2003). The prestige goods system promotes technological innovation in the production of exotic goods rather than agricultural tools and other instruments of staple production (D'Altroy and Earle 1985). How do elites maintain monopoly over long-distance relations with other elites? By using a symbolic vocabulary that "facilitates cross-cultural exchanges and reaffirms the elite's legitimacy vis-à-vis other elites" (Blanton et al. 1996:5).

Corporate strategies are collective rather than individual strategies (see table 10.1). Elites who use collective power strategies create "group-oriented chiefdoms" (Renfrew 1974). Corporate-based strategies emphasize integrative communal activities and rituals, including public construction, food production, and large cooperative labor tasks, through which social segments are woven together. These strategies and the ideologies behind them suppress economic differentiation and deemphasize access to personal wealth (Feinman 2001). Corporate-based societies are financed by the production of a surplus of staple goods, such as food crops, rather than prestige goods (D'Altroy and Earle 1985). Elites promote an ideology of corporate unity by appropriating surplus production to construct monuments to ancestors or gods, with whom only they can communicate directly on behalf of the people (Feinman 2001:157; Renfrew 1974:83). Elites' ritual and ideological power enables them to exercise political, spiritual, and economic control of their societies.

What circumstances favor elite application of network over corporate strategies, and vice versa, to gain control over resources? According to Blanton

TABLE 10.1

*Tendencies of Network and Corporate Modes*

| Network | Corporate |
| --- | --- |
| Concentrated wealth | More even wealth distribution |
| Individual power | Shared power arrangements |
| Ostentatious consumption | More balanced arrangements |
| Prestige goods | Control of knowledge, cognitive codes |
| Patron/client factions | Corporate labor systems |
| Attached specialization | Emphasis on food production |
| Wealth finance | Staple finance |
| Princely burial | Monumental ritual spaces |
| Lineal kinship systems | Segmental organization |
| Ostentatious elite adornment | Symbols of office |
| Personal glorification | Broad concerns with fertility, rain |

After Feinman 2001:160

and others (1996:7), "there is a loose association of the corporate strategy with environmental situations providing the potential for substantial agricultural development and of the network strategy with the marginal environments." In marginal environments, trade in prestige goods and development of an international style may be a more feasible power strategy than any attempt to promote appropriate surplus production of staples. Although, theoretically speaking, polities founded upon the two kinds of power strategies are likely to be structurally antagonistic (Blanton et al. 1996:7), in practice both network and corporate strategies can be found in all societies, albeit in varying degrees, with one or the other dominating (Feinman 2001; Robertshaw 2003; Strathern 1969, 1982a).

## THE IMPORTANCE OF TRADE IN SOCIETY

In all societies, trade is a vital means of distributing risks, establishing flexible social ties, and mediating local scarcity and seasonal resource crises (Wiessner and Tumu 1998; see also Wiessner, chapter 9, this volume). Trade items often play a crucial role in establishing and signaling differences in wealth (Oka and Kusimba 2008). Trade was one of the most significant factors in the development of social complexity in Africa (Connah 1987; Fattovich 1997; Hall 1991; Huffman 1996; Kusimba 1999a, 1999b; Pearson 1998; Pwiti 1997). As we gain access to more archaeological examples, we are learning more about the complex means through which ancient African societies exchanged trade items, goods, services, and ideas.

Trade enabled interacting partners to gain access to nonlocal resources. Trading partners ensure the constant flow of trade through fair trading rules and regulations. In ancient societies, these rules were expressed in many ways, including gift exchange, affinal kinship ties, and intermarriage (Strathern 1969, 1982a; Terrell 1986; Terrell and Welsch 1997; see also Wiessner, chapter 9, this volume). Alliance networks of exchange can enable a handful of interacting partners to control the main arteries of trade, such as rivers, ports, and foreign merchants (Arnold, chapter 6, this volume). For example, a handful of coastal elites and hinterland chiefs and kings controlled the bulk of long-distance trade in East Africa (Hakansson 1998; Jackson 1971; Kasfir 1992; Stigand 1913; Thorbahn 1979; Wakefield 1870). These networks enabled Swahili coastal merchants to supply international market demand for ivory. At the same time, rare prestige goods such as Chinese porcelain, expensive fabric, and glass beads were restricted to the elites as symbols of power, status, and wealth (Kusimba 1999a, 1999b).

Besides the exchange of valuables, trade enables the exchange and movement of ideas. Interacting partners, usually merchants, play an important role in the spread and incorporation of new ideas in society. For example, Islam became established as a religion of elites on the Swahili Coast no later than the ninth century but became a religion of the masses in the thirteenth century (Pouwels 1987, 2000).

Trade in rare, highly desirable prestige goods almost inevitably requires control and management of exchange networks. Elites may conquer an area of desirable resources—arable land, cattle, precious metals, obsidian, or ivory, for example—and bring it under political control (Kusimba and Kusimba 1999; see also Stanish, chapter 5, this volume). If successful, they sometimes gain control of the region's wealth and also its labor to help exploit resources. European colonies in Africa and the Americas were exploited not only for raw materials but also for cheap human labor (Blaut 1994; Ringrose 2001; Rodney 1969). However, political control also required that the infrastructure be developed and that skilled and loyal administrators be deployed to ensure that the resources reached their destinations. The other solution is for chiefs to negotiate with their counterparts to secure access to and protection of trade routes and free trade. They develop networks of alliance and friendship formalized through elite marriages, gift exchange, and ritualized kin networks (Johnson and Earle 1987; Renfrew 1974; Schortman and Urban 1992; Terrell and Welsch 1997; Wiessner, chapter 9, this volume).

In *How Chiefs Come to Power*, Timothy Earle (1997) argues that proximity to the centers of authority determines an individual's social and political rank and status and ultimately his or her access to economic and ideological power: "Cultural relationships of kinship determine rights and obligations that represent power over people, and political individuals manipulate these relationships (by strategic marriages, adoptions, godfathering and the like) to centralize and extend power" (Earle 1997:5). Elites achieve power by monopolizing the production, procurement, and distribution of a wealth-creating resource. Resources that successfully become endowed with economic power tend to be rare, so their ownership elevates the status of the owner. One way of controlling access to a power-laden rare item is to control the system of production and distribution. If the desired item is locally available, one can control its supply and demand by exercising control of craft specialists. If the desired item is nonlocal, however, one can gain control by monopolizing the process of procuring it. Elites therefore can gain control of local spheres of knowledge and its production by financing crafts or becoming patrons (real or symbolic) of a particular craft in order to commission production of a particular wealth- or status-creating item (DeMaret 1985a, 1985b; Kusimba 1996; McNaughton 1988). Also, elites can monopolize long-distance sources by building and maintaining networks of power through alliance building and friendships. Such friendships often foster elite competition for access to desired items (Malinowski 1984[1922]; Terrell and Welsch 1997).

## THE RISE OF LEADERSHIP: AN AFRICANIST PERSPECTIVE

Africa is a huge, ecologically and geographically diverse continent. In precolonial times, territorial, politically centralized states existed in many regions (Vansina 1966:155–156). In other regions, the sociopolitical landscape was more complex; the closely interacting societies with loose boundaries and overlapping means of interaction can be called mosaics (Kusimba and Kusimba 2005). Mosaics adapted to ecological diversity; problems and solutions regarding survival were varied. The knowledge of these solutions was an important resource that could be shared or withheld, and permeable social boundaries were often based on knowledge. Some examples are ironworking and other crafts, ritual knowledge, rainmaking, warfare, circumcision, the knowledge of leadership itself, and perhaps the knowledge of history and chiefly or kingly successions. Knowledge specialists were often uniquely positioned to move across social boundaries, offering their ritual services or providing leaders with technology or information. Guyer (1995) and Guyer and Belinga (1995) have made the point that wealth and power can just as aptly be measured as wealth in people and their knowledge. Multiethnic mosaics and their relationships to the territorial states emphasized by Vansina (1966) are important areas of research in Iron Age Africa (Stahl 2005).

One method through which mosaics of relationships can consolidate into hierarchies is in the formation of segmentary states. Segmentary states, including the Atyak state (Southall 1999), the Central African state of Kuba, the Suku polity (Kopytoff 1965), and the Amhara (Weissleder 1967), have been very common in sub-Saharan Africa. Segmentation was the means through which groups expanded their territories and through which individuals expanded their power. In these societies, the chief's sphere of ritual power is often much larger than his area of political control. Partially overlapping chiefdoms with political centers within wider ritual zones are related to one another pyramidally at several levels (Southall 1999). As these units expanded among the Alur, for example, other populations were peacefully incorporated as allies through gifts of food, rain, drink, and entertainment. The ritual leader could make rain and bring fertility but did not have political power. The relationships between segments were usually weak and were maintained in many cases by occasional trips to collect tribute. The quest for power was a stimulus for accumulation and eventually for migration as populations expanded and as individuals, failing to find room at the top, especially in large polygynous lineages with many sons, went elsewhere, taking notions of leadership with them and establishing ritual authority through rainmaking and gift giving, as in the case of the Atyak (Southall 1999). In expanding and setting up new leadership, these leaders also diffused the idea of leadership.

Jan Vansina's study of the Lunda Kingdom in Central Africa (1993) shows how more centralized systems can grow out of kin- or knowledge-based social relationships. In Lunda, leaders had little authority over many parts of the area from which they exacted only tribute, enough to support a capital of ten thousand people in 1875. A successor king inherited the deceased's personal status, including his name and kinship relationships. Thus, successive kings inherited relationships between the king and his various subjects. This flexible system could insinuate power into a variety of conquered areas, regardless of their kinship systems. Some in the area were matrilineal, and some patrilineal. The Lunda Kingdom could take over other areas with little resistance, even when the areas already had segmentary lineage systems. The Lunda put their own chiefs adjacent to local "owners of the land" and lineage heads. Many Central African chiefdoms had similar characteristics: the ruler was at the apex of the political structure and personally guided the kingdom. A kind of "indirect rule" was practiced in the peripheries, allowing only weak control of these areas. The ruled often felt that little was given for their tribute, and they often defected to other areas. Many of these kingdoms collapsed as a result of the slave trade (Vansina 1993:120).

In many areas, leaders surrounded the development of trade networks. Although trade may have received too much attention as a route to power in Africa, it was a significant opportunity by which to become a leader. The Shaba-Kasai trade network (Reefe 1993:122) spanned 1,000 kilometers north–south and connected the peoples of Central Africa. It involved a variety of luxury and essential goods and was one of the largest trade networks in Africa to develop independently of the international ivory/slave trade. How this trade was organized is another interesting example of leadership. For a single trip, villagers organized themselves into ad hoc groups under a designated leader. After soliciting the protection of spirits, they traveled to near or distant regions to trade. These groups, which ranged in size from about five to twenty individuals, consisted of adult males accompanied by their clients and by women who carried and prepared food. At their destination, people might manufacture at least some of the products they needed, such as salt, and remit a portion to local earth-priests in return for the right of exploitation. However, the smelting of ore and even lake fishing required technology that visitors often did not possess or specialized materials they could not bring with them, in which case they had to trade with local producers for all the goods they sought. The development of state societies facilitated trade. Around trade issues, there were still societies, such as the Bambudye society in the Luba Empire, that provided cooperation and mutual support when members traveled. Luba kings exploited the trade by taking a tribute portion. The king of Baluba distributed baskets of tribute beads and other goods, especially iron and salt (Reefe 1993:122). States and kingdoms of Central Africa tended to develop near sources of copper, salt, gold, and iron (Reefe 1993:124). According to Wrigley, the rise of complexity from the eleventh century to the thirteenth century was a result of copper deposits being exploited in the Congo-Zambezi and the copper-trading princes investing their profits in cattle (Wrigley 1993:111). Excavations at Bigo (circa AD 1350 to 1500) in Uganda by the British Institute in Eastern Africa have revealed extensive earthworks around central hills and rivers and a ditch system of almost 7 miles, including 15-foot ditches cut into solid rock. A central enclosure at the site has been defined as a possible royal enclosure. These earthworks may provide evidence for centralized authority over labor (Robertshaw 2001, 2003).

David and Sterner (1999) also emphasize the diversity of forms and institutions of power and authority by comparing three West African societies in which different chiefly officers held various dimensions of chiefly power, including the political, economic, social, and ideological (Mann 1993). In Cameroon, Kopytoff (1999) finds a continuum, from acephalous collections of lineage heads to chiefdoms dominated by a single lineage but with kinship ties with immigrant subjects. In many areas, such as the East African Great Lakes region, the ritual king held sway over contact with the ancestors and dispute resolution. This office was certainly a locus of achieved authority and power, although the sphere was limited.

## SOCIAL CORPORATE GROUPS AND POWER/AUTHORITY

Another concept fruitful in the African context is nonhierarchical kinds of social complexity. One means of organizing this knowledge was the age set, which was crucial for turning people into fully acculturated adults and possessors of knowledge and for integrating and mobilizing people behind power and leadership across ethnicities, genders, and clans (see also Wiessner, chapter 9, this volume). Ritual kings, age sets, age grades, secret societies, title societies, specialized clans and lineages, and guilds are corporate groups with long histories in African societies (Evans-Pritchard 1956; Legesse 1973:50). These social groups show that numerous pathways to personal power can undercut the centralization of power in a society. Similarly, power is often shared between a religious king and others, such as a council of elders or title holders. Indeed, the typology of decision-making institutions and political systems in Africa is tremendously varied.

Rarely is a scholar working in Europe asked to represent his entire "world area" in one paper. By contrast, Africanists are often asked to provide the "African chapter" for a survey volume such as this one. Realizing that we have no hope of adequately representing the variety of "African leadership" in one coherent essay and that such a task will homogenize tremendous variation, we have decided to give three case studies of very different forms of political organization from three societies in East Africa to show but a segment of the ethnographic evidence of variation in forms and processes of social power. These case studies provide comparative and contrasting examples to case studies discussed in this book (especially by Bird and Bliege Bird, Stanish, Arnold, Vaughn, Wiessner, and Kantner).

The three examples are from an egalitarian society without hereditary forms of status or leadership, the Bukusu; from a hierarchical society with hereditary elites, the Swahili; and from a society with a well-developed indigenous tradition of elected representative government, the Oromo. All of these ethnographic cases illustrate the complex tapestry of kingdoms and chiefdoms, acephalous societies, settled communities, and nomadic bands that made up African societies before colonialism. Understanding the interaction of this mosaic of societies has taken African archaeologists away from a typological and evolutionary framework and toward a concern with process and interaction among the shifting boundaries of these diverse societies (Stahl 2005).

## CASE STUDY IN "ACEPHALOUS" SOCIETIES: THE BUKUSU OF WESTERN KENYA AND EASTERN UGANDA

The eighteenth and nineteenth centuries in sub-Saharan Africa were periods of rapid social and political change as areas were drawn into webs of international commerce in people and in goods such as ivory. In many areas, notions of leadership changed radically as long-distance trade presented new opportunities and as societies were destabilized or destroyed by the slave trade. In the Pare region, chiefdoms fragmented as local merchant chiefs and entrepreneurs bartered ivory, food, and slaves to coast-bound caravans (Hakansson 1998; Wimmelbucker 2002). In Lake Baringo, farmers intensified crop production to barter with caravan traders, and among the Kamba, skilled hunters amassed wealth from ivory trade (Steinhart 2001). Around Lake Victoria and the East African Great Lakes, complex societies developed around local economies in salt and cattle, but long-distance trade opportunities were particularly important to the wealth bases of kingdoms such as Bunyoro and Ankole (Beattie 1960, 1970). In the hinterlands of these complex societies, ripple effects of flows of wealth and the competition they engendered created systems of intensive agriculture and warfare with intent to capture cattle and people (Hakansson 1994, 1998).

Against this backdrop of slave trade, warfare, and competition, many acephalous societies, in which decision making was governed by councils of elders, received a challenge to power from entrepreneurs and outsiders. Furthermore, positions of power related specifically to trade and warfare came to exist alongside the traditional lineage head. The Bukusu, today of western Kenya, were a society previously ruled through consensus decision making by councils of patrilineal elders. By the 1940s, councils of elders could include any married male (Wagner 1949, 1970), and there was broad recognition of the achieved leadership position of the *omukasa*, a man who "talks gently and wisely and who can make the people listen and return to reason when they want to quarrel or fight" (Wagner 1970). However, more than one of these could exist at any particular time.

Sometime after the sixteenth century, Bukusu people migrated onto the slopes of Mount Elgon from a variety of origin places, including Malaba and Karamoja in Uganda (Makila 1978; Osogo 1966). Even today Bukusu clans maintain several origin stories. Bukusu adapted to a multiethnic mosaic west of Lake Victoria that included other ethnic groups, such as the Nandi, Masai, Sabaot, and Elgon Masai. Warfare and raiding were endemic, and Bukusu, who held considerably more cattle than most farmers, adapted by surrounding their habitation sites, living in defensive, walled, and moated villages called *chingoba* (singular *lukoba*), which were up to 150 meters in diameter. Similar structural ruins still exist in western Kenya (Scully 1969, 1974). Wagner (1947) described them as having circular mud walls about 10 feet high and 1 to 2 feet thick, with several entrances that could be closed with heavy logs. Around the wall ran a moat that was 3 to 4 feet deep.

Ethnohistorical and archaeological evidence indicates that increasing regionwide insecurity was associated with these fortified settlements in many parts of East Africa and even the rest of the continent (Fadiman 1982; Kusimba 2004; Wagner 1949:40). Large-scale fortification of settlements and migration to hillside locations began in the sixteenth century in East Africa. Moated, fortified settlements were widespread in East Africa during the latter part of the eighteenth and nineteenth centuries (Fadiman 1982; Forsbrooke 1960; Gillman 1944; Perham 1979; Scully 1969, 1974; Spear 1978; Wagner 1949). These fortifications correspond to three kinds identified by Keeley (1996:57–58): fortified settlements, refuges, and maroon settlements. Fortifications are a regionwide phenomenon. Mount Kasigau, a prominent inselberg and a stop along the foot caravan route to Mombasa, contains ironworking sites and eight fortified rock shelters that can also be linked to regional insecurity (Kusimba 2004). In western Kenya, fortified settlements include earth and stone enclosures called *ohingini* or *gunda*, the largest of which is Thimlich Ohinga (Onjala 2003; Wandibba 1986).

Ethnographic fieldwork was conducted among Bantu-speaking Bukusu and Samia people of western Kenya in 2006 and 2007. Our fieldwork discovered more than twenty sites with ruined earthworks of walled villages in the Samia region (Kusimba and Kusimba 2007). Scully's surveys (1969, 1974) discovered more than seventy sites on the southern slopes of Mount Elgon. Most were up to 3 kilometers in diameter and accommodated as many as five homesteads, probably from one clan. When two or more clans made up a walled village, the village was generally larger, and each clan had a separate entrance or gate. The different gates provided the social distance so important to the exogamous Bukusu and Samia (figure 10.1).

The problem of walled villages gives us an opportunity to study

**FIGURE 10.1**

*Chetambe Fortress, circa 1895, Webuye, Kenya. Illustration by Moses Chetambe. Courtesy the Field Museum.*

another example of power and authority in a precolonial African society. How were the walled villages organized? What was the relationship between chiefs and other offices of power and authority? Village and supravillage war leaders shared power in complex ways with traditional leaders of kin groups and religious practices. Specific positions of authority, held by clans but also partly achieved, existed around political and religious functions such as rainmaking, consoling the bereaved, and communicating with ancestral spirits. These positions were inherited through clan membership and signaled through supernatural experiences or callings (Kusimba and Kusimba 2007). The positions of rainmaking and divining the future were probably most important.

According to the sage Manguliechi (figure 10.2), the leaders of the walled villages were called *bekamuchebe*. The senior leader was called *wepokote* and wore an ivory armlet; he was usually the leader of several villages that often joined forces in warfare. Lesser leaders of single villages were called *enjapasi* (plural *wenjapasi*) and wore wristlets, also of ivory. These leaders' authority was partly inherited; they made decisions together with a council of elder males.

Each village included families from several clans. Each clan had its own gate or entrance into the village in the outside wall. The word for these gates, *silibwa*, also means "lineage." The separate gates served to maintain

**Figure 10.2**

*Mzee Manguliechi, a revered Bukusu sage and ritual leader, 2006. Photograph by Sibel B. Kusimba.*

the social differences among these patrilineal clans, who were strictly exogamous. Each lineage had an elected authority to the village's councils of elders. The leader of this council was known as Omwene Lukova. Together with the council leaders, the *bakaasa* (singular *omukaasa*), the wepokote had the ability to mobilize and coordinate people from several villages in case of attack.

The powers of the council, its leaders, and the war leader were also balanced by the authority of several ritual specialists who incorporated important abilities to apprehend and harness the power of the supernatural. Inherited abilities were unique to particular clans and lineages. Individuals experienced a supernatural sign or "calling," after which their abilities would be manifest. These specialists included rainmakers, diviners, circumcisers, sacrificers, oracle readers, dream seers, and witches/sorcerers. All these specialists had a connection to the supernatural or occult. Some accepted tribute in the form of grain, iron hoes, or beads as payment for their services (Makila 1978).

The diviners were the highest-ranking of the people of authority surrounding the chiefs of the walled villages and served as special advisers to political and war leaders. In warfare, their prognostications about defeat or victory were key to strategy. Diviners, seers, and sacrificers were all involved in the politics of village formation, fission, and alliance building. Rainmakers were some of the wealthiest men and often accepted generous tributes. They were also involved in demographic shifts and issues of timing concerning agricultural and military events.

The authority of the ritual specialist was associated with particular clans and was considered a quasi-essential talent passed through the generations and made manifest by a vision, a sense of calling, or some other spiritual experience (Kusimba and Kusimba 2007). The presence of so many ritual specialists served the important function of distributing supernatural power across clans. Clans consequently needed one another for the purposes of alliance, intermarriage, and the sharing of ritual specialties. The distribution of power into the hands of many political, warfare, and supernatural leaders prevented consolidation by single offices of leadership in the fortified villages of western Kenya. The case of the Late Iron Age of western Kenya shows that the contexts of ivory and slave trade in the nineteenth century created opportunities for new forms of leadership that could either challenge or reinforce the authority of traditional leaders.

## REPRESENTATIVE DEMOCRACY: THE GADAA SYSTEM OF THE OROMO OF KENYA AND ETHIOPIA

The Oromo people who live in Ethiopia and Kenya developed a complex democratic system of leadership beginning in the sixteenth century (Hassen 1990). The name *Gadaa* is traced from the word *gaddisa*, a shelter or shade that protects one from the heat of the sun. The Gadaa system was a political umbrella, and its function was to maintain internal peace and cohesion and to protect the Oromo against external enemies. It was essentially a republican system of elected leaders who formed representative councils on national, regional, and local levels. Each Gadaa class remained in power during a term of eight years, which began and ended with a formal power transfer ceremony (Baissa 1994:48).

The Gadaa Council was the executive organ; it had collective leadership responsibilities, and each councillor had duties as minister of the government. Eric Knutsson (1967:166) summed up the functions of the Gadaa system thus: "Abba Gadaa and the other top Gadaa officials must make decisions about war expeditions and peace negotiations and other matters involving contact with neighboring peoples. They are also responsible for settling disputes and delivering judgments in conflict within the tribe."

The council negotiated with foreign leaders on boundary disputes and all other matters of interest. The council had to have approval of the people before making major decisions. Local chiefs were prohibited from making decisions on war and peace. The councillors resided in the same area during their eight years in office, and their residence became the seat of government. The council also regularly traveled through the entire country to oversee development, settle disputes, and ensure that laws and policies passed by the general assembly were implemented (Haberland 1963:784; table 10.2; figure 10.3).

## THE ELECTORAL PROCEDURE IN OROMO SOCIETY

Office bearers were elected to the council following a three-month campaign. An electoral commission (EC) consisting of six men elected by the Kora, or general meeting, oversaw the elections. The EC's term was eight years (Legesse 1973:206). Candidates peacefully campaigned all over the state. Eric Knutsson (1967:164) witnessed one campaign in the 1960s and commented, "The procedure is not unlike the pre-election campaign with which we are familiar in Western political systems."

The Oromo viewed the following as virtues of leadership: (1) oratory skills, (2) knowledge of history and tradition of the society, (3) past military achievements, and (4) recognizable potential for future leadership (Hassen 1990:48). Elections were held to fill seats left vacant by members of the Gadaa Council before a term ended. Death while in office—on the battleground or by natural causes—or impeachment because of misconduct were reasons to hold bi-elections.

After power was formally transferred, the age grade from which the

**TABLE 10.2**

*Gadaa Power Structure and Functions*

| Title | Translation | Functions | Reference |
|---|---|---|---|
| Abba Gadaa (1) | President of the confederacy | Spokesman of the council, symbol of political authority, commander in chief of the army; presides over council meetings | Knutsson 1967:167 |
| Abba Gadaa Kontoma (2) | First and second vice presidents | Recruited from different regions to represent each subgroup of Oromo regions | Legesse 1973:63 |
| Abba Chaffee (3) | Three leaders of the popular assembly | Chairmen of the assembly | Legesse 1973:94 |
| Abba Dubbi | Speaker | Presents new proposals from the class presidium to the assembly | Knutsson 1967:173 |
| Abba Sera is | Attorney general | Expert on traditional law law whose duty is to memorize the results of the assembly's deliberations | |
| Abba Duula | Minister of defense | Military leader of the ruling class, orator and tactician versed in the military exploits of the past generation; marches at the head of the army and recites war poems, motivating the army to fight; has dictatorial powers when the nation is at war | |
| Abba Alanga | Chief whip | Functions as a judge; has the responsibility to execute decisions passed in the assembly | |
| Abba Sa'aa | Minister of economy and finance | Oversees the wealth of the people | Lewis 1965:28 |

outgoing leadership was drawn underwent partial retirement. The new council assumed status and made decisions in complete independence from the former. At the handing-over-power ceremony, the outgoing Abba Gadaa (president of the council) handed over the *bokku* (scepter) to the new Abba Gadaa, signaling the beginning of the new leadership. The bokku was a wooden or iron scepter kept by Abba Gadaa in his belt during all assembly meetings. It was an emblem of authority and a symbol of unity, common law, and government.

**FIGURE 10.3**
*Oromo elected leaders, Addis Ababa, Ethiopia, 1927. Photograph by Alfred M. Bailey (digital identifier CSZ56342). Courtesy the Field Museum.*

## LEADERSHIP IN URBAN SOCIETIES

A third example shows yet another kind of leadership: hereditary rule by a noble class among the Swahili city-states of the East African coast. Archaeologists and historians have accumulated enormous data on the development of urbanism among the Swahili beginning in the late first millennium (Abungu 1998; Fleisher 2003; Horton 1996; Juma 2004; Kusimba 1999a; LaViolette and Fleisher 2005). Cities emerged along the coast, from Somalia to Mozambique, around AD 500. The residents included farmers, fishers, traders, scribes, rulers, and enslaved persons. Wealth from Indian Ocean trade was the main catalyst for the rapid development of urbanization. Equally important in its emergence was the commercial and cultural dialogue maintained between the coast and hinterland African peoples (tables 10.3 and 10.4). The residents of the cities and city-states were initially drawn from different language groups, but in time, one language—Kiswahili—became dominant. Introduced around AD 800, Islam gradually expanded to become the primary religion and means of elite cultural expression by the time of European contact in early AD 1500 (Horton 1996; Horton and Middleton 2000; Middleton 2004; Pouwells 1987, 2000).

Economic and social interaction among diverse groups that made their living from hunting, herding, farming, and ironworking laid the

**TABLE 10.3**
*Periodization and Nature of Relationships between the Coast, the Hinterland,
and the Indian Ocean*

| Period | Time | Archaeological Finds in Cities | Hinterland Trade | International Trade |
|---|---|---|---|---|
| V | AD 1750–1950 | Indo-Pacific beads, glass bangles, Chinese blue on white, Japanese Karatzu ware, European floral ware, Islamic monochrome pottery, iron | Regular coastal, regional, and interregional | |
| IV | AD 1500–1750 | Stylistically diverse pottery, Indian pottery, European peasant floral ware | Regular coastal, regional, and interregional | Regular regional and international |
| IIIb | AD 1250–1500 | Stylistically diverse pottery, spindle whorls, coins, chlorite schist, Islamic monochromes, Chinese Longquan and Tongan ware, Indonesian Sawankholok jars, Indo-Pacific beads, Egyptian glass | Regular coastal, regional, and interregional | Regular regional and international with China, Southeast Asia, India, Persian Gulf |
| IIIa | AD 1000–1250 | Stylistically diverse pottery, rock crystal, spindle whorls, copper and silver coins, Islamic sgraffito, Chinese Qing Bai, Cizhou ware, bronze mirrors, Indo-Pacific beads | Regular coastal, regional, and interregional | Regular regional and international with Persian Gulf, Egypt, India, and possibly China |
| IIb | AD 600–1000 | Zanjian pottery: red burnished and hag-shaped cooking pots, graphite finish and trellis patterns; Partho-Sassanian Islamic, white glazed, Chinese Dusun Yueh, Guangdon coastal green, Egyptian glass, carnelian beads, iron | Regular coastal, regional, and interregional | Egypt, Persian Gulf, Indian subcontinent |
| IIa | AD 300–600 | Azanian pottery: triangular oblique and double zigzag patterns predominant; Sassanian Islamic, glass, carnelian beads, Roman amphora | Regular coastal and regional | Some |
| I | 100 BC–AD 300 | Local Early Iron Age pottery, iron, iron slag | Local and person-to-person | No evidence |

TABLE 10.4

*Trade Items Exchanged during Periods IV and V on the Coast*

| Time | Hinterland–Coast | Coast–Hinterland | Coast–Overseas | Overseas–Coast |
|---|---|---|---|---|
| 1750–1900 | Raw ivory, slaves, rhino horn, animal skins, gum arabic, rock crystal | Grains, iron tools, guns for hunting, imported cloth | Cut and raw ivory, slaves, rhino horn, animal skins, gum arabic, rock crystal | Prestige goods (ceramics, crafts), iron and steel tools, guns, cloth for direct use, grains, cereals, cattle |
| 1650–1750 | Raw ivory, animal skins, rhino horn, slaves, gum arabic, rock crystal | Grains, iron tools, dried fish, imported cloth, beads and beadwork, marine products | Cut ivory, animal skins, timber, gold, slaves, rock crystal, gum arabic | Prestige goods (ceramics, crafts), iron and steel tools, cloth for direct use, grains, cereals, cattle |
| 1550–1650 | Raw ivory, iron bloom, animal skins, rhino horn, slaves, gum arabic, rock crystal | Grains, iron tools, dried fish, local and imported cloth, beads and beadwork, marine products | Cut and worked ivory, animal skins, timber, gold, slaves, rock crystal, gum arabic | Prestige goods (ceramics, crafts), iron and steel tools, monochrome and colored cloth for reweaving, grains, cereals |
| pre-1550 | Iron bloom, animal skins, rhino horn, cut and raw ivory, slaves, gum arabic, rock crystal | Grains, iron tools, dried fish, local cloth, beads and beadwork, marine products | Iron bloom, wootz steel, cut and worked ivory, processed animal skins, cut timber, gold, slaves, rock crystal, gum arabic | Prestige goods (ceramics, crafts), iron and steel tools, monochrome and colored cloth for reweaving, grains, cereals |

foundation on which international trade systems interlocked (Kusimba and Kusimba 2005; Mutoro 1998). By the end of the first millennium AD, the coast had become a regular partner in the millennia-old long-distance exchanges that reached as far as the Arabian Peninsula, India, Sri Lanka, and China (Allen 1993; Mitchell 2005; Pearson 1998). By the thirteenth century, there had emerged an African urban elite that financed, managed, and controlled local, regional, and interregional trade and communications along the East African seaboard (Chami 1998; Kusimba 1999a, 1999b). In the late fifteenth century, however, the coast became embroiled in long-standing conflict between Christendom and Islam, represented by the Portuguese and Omani Arab mercantile interests. The Portuguese and Muslim rivalry for control of Indian Ocean commerce was economically crippling for East Africa (Alpers 1975; Kusimba 2004).

## PATHWAYS TO COMPLEXITY ON THE SWAHILI COAST

The independent city-states of the Swahili Coast are a case of cultural evolution in the direction of centralized ranked systems of leadership. In the period before AD 1000, itinerant traders and ritual and technical experts dominated local and some regional trade. Leaders were individuals who held sway over certain spheres of knowledge useful for the general welfare of the wider community. They included ritual experts, healers and herbalists, rainmakers, iron smelters and smiths, well diggers, big game hunters, pearl divers, canoe and boat makers, and itinerant hawkers and traders. These spheres of knowledge were often restricted to few people and, because of their usefulness, became rather jealously protected, maintained in small family or extended family networks. Moreover, because of their skills, the experts became highly desirable in every village or community. For example, rainmakers, well diggers, healers, and ironsmiths were highly desirable neighbors, and people would travel long distances to secure their services. It suffices to say that leadership was in place but was not sufficiently integrated. It was from these ranks that leaders and rulers would emerge around AD 1000.

Autonomous polities had emerged by at least AD 1200. Demand for African products increased, leading to the intensification of regional and Indian Ocean trade. The economic boom enabled people to engage in trade on a full-time basis rather that as vocational experts. For example, because of the increased demand for ivory, hunters became more specialized, demanding better weapons and poisons for killing elephants. They experimented and developed more potent poisons to efficiently procure their prey. As more people migrated to trading centers for longer periods, the need for lodges, houses, and wells increased. These developments required management and planning. The local leadership, consisting of ritual and technical experts, was likely to emerge as the managerial elite because of its knowledge.

The Portuguese appearance in Africa and Asia challenged the interregional elite hegemony, based upon networks of interaction, that extended from Mozambique through Mombasa, Cairo, Aden, Surat, Bombay, Siraf, and their outlying hinterlands. Portuguese and later Dutch, English, and French merchants challenged Afrasian elite power and the economy of these polities, states, and empires (Kusimba 1999a; Pearson 1998). By the eighteenth century if not earlier, the gradual establishment of European economic and political control in the Indian Ocean, along with climatic and disease factors, had precipitated the decline and collapse of states and polities, including those on the coast (Kusimba 1999a).

## THE EMERGENCE OF LEADERSHIP ON THE SWAHILI COAST

The emergence of leadership on the coast cannot be fully understood without knowledge of how the region's resources were exploited. Subsistence resources included water, arable land, grazing land, and fishing areas. Export resources included mangrove poles, ivory, rhinoceros horn, leopard skins, sharks, shells, pearls, ambergris, iron, and gold. As with the Oromo and other African societies, leadership on the coast was drawn from a council of elders that oversaw the distribution and use of land and sea resources, managed town affairs, and managed relations with other towns (Middleton 1992:89).

By what means did leadership on the coast emerge? Although every lineage was represented on the council, our archaeological data, supported by ethnographic research with local ethnohistorians, suggest that power after AD 1000 became increasingly dominated by a few lineages. Resources with high economic potential became monopolized (Kusimba 1999b). The council of elders manipulated rules of collective clan ownership of land in favor of ownership by specific families—those who had power at the council. As the towns prospered and more people migrated into the cities, the council promulgated rules prohibiting recent immigrants from electing their own lineage heads to the council. In doing so, the council disenfranchised new residents, ensuring that only "original" residents owned the land, with newcomers having only use rights. The rule was simple: ownership of land was held communally among patrilineally related kin descended from the first ancestor who had cleared a patch of virgin land and enclosed it with a wall. Kin who were not patrilineally related could rent land from *wenyeji asili*, the original owners or their descendants, by paying a fee called *moshi*, consisting of a share of the crop, which acknowledged the ownership rights of those credited with transforming the land from wilderness into a domesticated landscape.

The new system of land tenure established a landowning elite among the "original settlers" and their descendants, enabling them to control vast tracts of land, labor, and goods through the political offices of the council of elders. Newcomers from other coastal towns, the hinterland, and abroad were welcomed and in many cases encouraged to stay and exploit the resources. But they rented the land. The landowning gentry maintained tight control of basic resources through a complex system of patronage and clientship. They forged mutually beneficial alliances and friendships with the hinterland and other coastal communities, guaranteeing a peaceful environment, a supply of human labor power for the purpose of

**FIGURE 10.4**

*The siwa (side-blown horn), usually made of ivory, was a symbol of royalty and leadership
among the Swahili. The one shown here is presently exhibited at the Lamu Museum. It is still
used to commemorate the Muslim new year. Photograph by Chapurukha M. Kusimba.*

exploiting resources (such as fishing, mangrove cutting, hunting, and
portage), and commercial interdependence (Nicholls 1971:65; Willis 1993).

Through the council, the landowning gentry influenced the creation
of more restrictions: Commoners could not trade directly or forge relationships with hinterland or foreign merchants. Those relationships
became the domain of the chief and his council. The wenyeji asili, who now
called themselves *waungwana* (patricians), also appropriated certain material and structural elements as symbols of their power and legitimacy (see also
Eerkens, chapter 4, this volume). Membership into the *uungwana* (patrician
class) could be claimed through length of residence and wealth, as well as
patrilineal descent. These traits could be demonstrated through ownership
of stone houses, fertile land, fishing areas, cattle, and exotic trade items
including jewelry, imported ceramics, and clothing (Prins 1961). Patrician
privileges included (1) the right to religious scholarship; (2) the right to
property such as fertile farmland, stretches of beach, mangrove forests,
and fishing areas; (3) the right to own cattle; (4) the right to build and live
in stone houses in one's own *mtaa* (town ward); (5) the right to receive,
entertain, and trade with foreign merchants; (6) the right to elect town and
mosque officials; (7) the right to blow the great *siwa* (horn), at weddings
(figure 10.4); (8) the right to hold the hereditary offices of Mkuu wa Jela

(prison warden), Mweka Hazina (keeper of the town treasury), Mkuu wa Pwani (warden of the sea), and Khatib (Friday preacher); and (9) the right to slaughter the expiatory ox after the cleansing ritual of *kuzinga mui*, purifying the town (Pouwels 2000; Prins 1961:103).

## LEADERSHIP: POWER AND AUTHORITY

The urban elite built stone houses at great expense, not only as places to live in but also as status symbols to manipulate the existing sociopolitical and economic order. The stone house was one of the main material and social symbols of uungwana (Donley-Reid 1990). It symbolized permanence, creditworthiness, trustworthiness, and economic power (see also chapters 5, 6, and 7 by Stanish, Vaughn, and Pauketat, respectively, this volume).

The Swahili stone house's permanence became a symbol of originality. At the same time, the architecture of the stone house contained Islamic stylistic elements such as niches and arches. These foreign elements gave the elite access to rare cultural and social economic knowledge.

Areas set aside for the exclusive burial of patrician clans served to maintain, identify, and legitimate power. Tombs were tangible manifestations of ancestry that reinforced prestige, validated family and authority, and strengthened kin group hold on social, religious, and political power. Tombs were symbols of hereditary succession and supernatural authority, the foundations upon which leadership rested. Tombs were also places where individual families would display wealth by decorating them with exotic ceramics, offering sacrifices to ancestors in a public display of generosity. Cemeteries at many Swahili sites show distinct levels of wealth indicated by size, decorative motifs, and forms.

The patricians also appropriated formal Islamic religious regalia for their exclusive use during Friday prayers. Model dress included a long white robe (the *kanzu*), a sword and dagger, a turban, and sandals made of hide. Handles of swords and daggers were often made of ebony and inlaid with ivory (Nurse and Spear 1985:83). This public display of exotica and of devotion to one God, Allah, linked the patricians to a wider pan-Islamic identity. Literacy became a powerful symbol of knowledge power that legitimized political and economic power. Literacy enabled patricians to read and write in Arabic; some even claimed direct ancestry from the centers of such knowledge and power and to the Prophet himself. Commoners and other nonpatricians were prohibited from literacy. The association of exotic and powerful knowledge with the wealthy symbolized and encapsulated the elites' divinity and legitimacy (Nurse and Spear 1985).

Nonlocal trade items and other exotica from Europe and from southwestern, southern, and eastern Asia became status symbols. These included expensive clothing, jewelry, beadwork, glass, and bronze mirrors. They were displayed in special niches called *zidaka* in the inner sections of houses (Donley-Reid 1990:121) for the consumption of inner-core family members and for display during weddings and funerals (Ahmed Sheikh Nabhany, personal communication, March 1996). Through cunning manipulation of technical and social power, the patricians successfully legitimized their position as leaders of the coast, monopolizing all the means of production after AD 1200.

This account shows that the rise of urbanism on the coast of East Africa is closely allied to the distributor role that local leaders played in international trade. According to the archaeological evidence, considerable craft production on Swahili sites indicates that coastal cities originally arose as manufacturing centers rather than trade entrepôts. Since the early first millennium AD, inland trade had been more important than coast–international trade. Thus, coastal urban polities served both as cores in relation to the peripheries of the hinterland and as peripheries in the circum–Indian Ocean interaction sphere.

## CONCLUSIONS

The wealth of African ethnographic and historical evidence reveals a spectrum of political forms that belies any simple characterization. The Bukusu system shows a variety of offices of power spread among ritual specialists and political and war leaders but organized around patrilineal clans, each with appointed leaders and with presumed innate spheres of knowledge. The Oromo Gadaa system is a prime example of leadership by elected representatives, demonstrating the kind of diffuse power that has developed in Africa and has much in common with other systems through which power is shared by several offices, title holders, corporate groups, and other heterarchical organizations. The case of the Swahili Coast is a much more hierarchical development, with elites emerging through their access to external trade goods. The lack of such an external stimulus may explain the Oromo emphasis on power sharing among elected officials. The link that takes us from the acephalous Bukusu to the hierarchical Swahili is the concept of clan leadership and especially the innate knowledge specialties purportedly held by each clan. These knowledge spheres formed the basis of inherited prestige and authority and forced the essential nature of clan cooperation and accommodation. Around these cooperating clans and councils of elders, hereditary leaders arose on the coast in the context of tremendous trade wealth.

# 11

## Identifying the Pathways to Permanent Leadership

### John Kantner

It used to be much easier to become a chief. In the late 1980s and 1990s, archaeological models for the evolution of sociopolitical differentiation tended to emphasize an inherently competitive nature for humanity, describing processes of self-aggrandizement and political factionalism as rampant in small-scale societies and inexorably pushing them to greater levels of social and political differentiation (for example, Boone 1992; Clark and Blake 1994; Diehl 2000; Flanagan 1989; Hayden 1995; Hayden and Gargett 1990; Kantner 1996; Maschner and Patton 1996; Spencer 1994). These viewpoints were in large part a reaction against the unmitigated adaptationism of the 1970s and early 1980s, which regarded the emergence of leadership positions as necessary sociocultural adjustments to environmental or demographic crisis (for example, Dean et al. 1985; Flannery 1972; Johnson 1978; Lightfoot 1983; Peebles and Kus 1977). According to both perspectives, leaders were regarded as emerging rather routinely, to fulfill their self-interest or to sustain group interests.

New research, in contrast, is identifying an apparently powerful human desire to maintain sociopolitical equity. Despite abstract models in decision theory that predict competitive behavior and a drive toward inequity, experiments in the lab and field are revealing again and again that people cooperate—or at least favor equity—much more readily than abstract mathematical models of rationality would otherwise suggest (Caporael et al. 1989; Dawes et al. 2007; Fehr and Rockenbach 2003; Hauert et al. 2007; Ostrom 1998). As a result, several researchers are attempting to identify modifications of agent-based models of rational self-interest that can accommodate the higher levels of egalitarianism and cooperation that seem to characterize human social interactions (for example, Bowles and Gintis 2003a; Henrich et al. 2006; Hruschka and Henrich 2006; Jensen, Call, and Tomasello 2007; Millinski, Semmann, and Krambeck 2002; Nowak and Sigmund 2005; Stanish, chapter 5). Other scholars are developing evolutionary scenarios that propose the existence of evolved moralistic propensities and innate prosocial behaviors beyond kin selection (for example, Boehm 1999, 2000; Bowles 2006; Fehr and Fischbacher 2003; Fehr and Gächter 2002; Fehr, Bernhard, and Rockenbach 2008; Haidt 2007; Herrmann et al. 2007; Wood et al. 2007).

All of this work leaves us with the question of how and why incipient levels of inequity and decision-making differentiation could ever develop, a topic tackled by all the chapters in this book. In the face of so many ways to enforce cooperation, how could centralized and institutionalized leadership emerge? This chapter considers this issue by starting at the most basic level: by first defining *leadership* and *leader* in abstract terms. It then considers the factors that determine how, when, why, and in what contexts leaders emerge. Next, the chapter explores mechanisms by which more permanent forms of leadership become established and the archaeological signatures of this process. The chapter ends with a case study from the US Southwest that illustrates the process by which decision-making inequities emerge in an otherwise egalitarian society.

## DEFINING LEADERSHIP

Leadership can be described in many ways, and different disciplines variably emphasize the political, economic, psychological, social, and cultural aspects of the concept. The most essential definition of leadership, however, is that it is decision making in which decisions are made, or at least heavily guided, by one individual or a small number of individuals—the leader(s)—on behalf of other people who are likely to be affected by the outcomes of those decisions—the followers. Such decisions are typically about the allocation of resources and power, broadly conceived to include not only material goods essential for somatic and reproductive success but also intangible resources such as knowledge and materialized ideology. Insofar as leaders do not exist without followers, a critical element of leadership is the faith of followers that the leader can provide the decision-making benefits that the followers desire, especially in situations that are not routine (Bailey 2001:37). Because routine decision making is largely culturally prescribed and predictable, a population is less likely to value leadership in those situations. Instead, the value of a leader to potential followers is his or her ability to dispel the uncertainty and indecision that unusual circumstances create and that therefore are especially problematic when collective action is needed.

Most leaders enjoy some combination of authority and power, as articulated by Weber (1958) and many others (for example, McIntosh 1999a; O'Donovan 2002; Roscoe 2000a; Wolf 1999). At one end of this classic continuum is authority, a quality based on charisma or tradition that endows a leader with the ability to influence—but not overtly and directly to control —group decision making. At the other end is power, the ability to coerce people into adhering to the leader's decisions through the threat of physical or supernatural sanction. An important point of departure for the arguments presented in this chapter, however, is that complete physical domination of followers will not lead to sustainable leadership, especially because many forms of resistance to despotic rule are possible. Leaders must maintain some degree of legitimacy through which followers consent to be led. Even the most despicable leaders in human history—including those who met unpleasant ends—had a contingent of supportive followers. The tyrant–powerless relationship builds upon the leader–follower dynamic; no individual has ever developed despotic rule without the followers needed to establish and maintain that rule, and the growth of power usually consists of the construction of legitimizing ideologies that enhance political authority and sustain the support of followers even while coercive measures are employed (Brown 2006; Kopytoff 1999; Smith 2003:105–109; Vansina 1999). For the purposes of this chapter, therefore, the initial construction of decision-making authority and the creation of positions of leadership are emphasized, and issues of coercive and hegemonic or structural power are discussed only as relevant for understanding the emergence of institutionalized political positions. As in other chapters of this book, of particular interest is how the former contributes to the latter.

### Skills and Abilities of Leaders

Discussions of leadership often focus on the necessary qualities of authoritative leaders. Clearly, leadership requires some combination of essential skills and abilities (for example, Boehm 1999:70–72, 106–108; Kusimba and Kusimba, chapter 10), but less clear is the relative importance of any particular quality. Charisma is one of the most often invoked leadership traits. Defined as the capacity to inspire devotion and enthusiasm and thereby build faith in the leader's capabilities among followers, charisma can be created in two ways (Bailey 2001:56–57; see also Weber 1968). One strategy is to come across as "godlike"—not necessarily by *actually* demonstrating qualities and abilities that are beyond those typical of humans, but by generating the *belief* that the charismatic leader possesses such superhuman characteristics. As Pauketat describes in chapter 8, such charisma is often constructed through the creation of narratives that establish the legitimacy of leaders. The second strategy for building charisma is for the aspiring leader to present him- or herself as everyone's "friend," "sister," or "brother," generating fraternal identification. Both strategies likely are components of displays of exceptional generosity, such as those described by Bird and Bliege Bird (chapter 2), in which one's renown is demonstrated through self-effacing magnanimity. For all forms of charisma, the outcome is the creation of what Bailey (2001:132–133) calls direct or unanimous consensus, in which the consent of followers is provided to the leader simply because people believe that it is the "right thing to do." The result is the authority that allows the leader to make decisions on behalf of followers.

Diplomacy is another quality identified as promoting successful leadership. The aspiring leader needs to appear to be advice-seeking while still coming across as resolute and decisive. Such diplomacy reassures followers that the leader is well informed and not despotic. This creates what Bailey (2001:133) calls brokered or pluralistic consensus, in which consent for leadership decisions is given because each follower has been led to believe that he or she will benefit. For this process to work, the leader must have some mastery of, and perhaps control over, information about what people want and the potential outcomes of alternative decisions. Open confrontation that might rend consensus needs to be avoided by a diplomatic leader. And the effective application of delayed and discounted reciprocity often must be employed to diplomatically build brokered consensus (Boehm 1999:184–185). Bowser and Patton (chapter 3), as well as Wiessner (chapter 9), identify a potential gendered component to diplomacy (see also Passes 2004). Bowser and Patton detail the role of women in sustaining diplomatic relations across factional boundaries. Women with large households and less strongly defined kinship with particular factions emerge as especially influential political brokers, even as the husbands of these women tend to have the strongest alliances within particular factions. For the people in Conambo at least, this "division of labor" provides a route to political status for both wife and husband, with the benefit of greater access to cooperative labor and garden resources, at least for the women.

Although charisma and diplomacy promote different forms of consensus among followers, effective and sustainable leadership requires both qualities. To be able to generate and balance both direct and brokered consensus, therefore, effective leaders need a third quality—intelligence—which in turn can be broken down into "sociopolitical acumen" and "actuarial problem-solving" (Boehm 1999:182–185), as well as access to and control of knowledge that make both effective. On the one hand, successful leaders are intimately aware of the normative social and political arenas in which they operate, including the ability to anticipate the unintended and unforeseen results of their actions on the sociopolitical landscape. On the other hand, successful leaders are also effective at rational decision making, or what Bailey (2001:10) defines as "the considered allocation of scarce resources to given ends." This form of intelligence is an especially important quality from the perspective of followers; an aspiring leader who acts irrationally is not one who dispels uncertainty and indecision in the face of abnormal circumstances that require collective action, as the morality tale of Nero "fiddling" while Rome burned evokes.

Sociopolitical and problem-solving intelligences relate to the fourth, oft-maligned leadership quality: manipulative skills. To generate charisma and diplomacy, a leader can manipulate contextual circumstances and unusual opportunities to his or her advantage to build direct and brokered forms of consensus (see Arnold, chapter 6). For example, an intelligent and manipulative leader can appeal to emotions surrounding particular events to shape both the goals of collective action and the calculi that people use to evaluate decision making. This process can result in the construction of brokered consensus around perceived rather than actual values, costs, and benefits, further promoting the leader's authority (for example, Roscoe 2000b; Wiessner 2001). The resulting collective action can serve the ends of the group, as well as the desires of the leader, by mobilizing labor and creating economies of scale that benefit everyone but might especially benefit the leader, as detailed in chapter 5 by Stanish and Chapter 6 by Arnold (see also Adams 2004). Of course, after institutionalized leadership is established, such unexpected events are just as likely to jeopardize authority, unless context and circumstances can be turned to advantage by quick-thinking leaders.

Manipulation has its limits, however. Bailey (2001) usefully distinguishes between the normative, strategic, and pragmatic rules of behavior that guide the efforts of leaders to create authority. Normative rules are the culturally prescribed, proper forms of interaction; they define the acceptable limits of leadership behavior. Strategic "rules" describe what needs to be done to come out ahead, even if it means violating normative prescriptions. Leaders who act purely strategically, with no acknowledgement of normative rules or in clear violation of them, are very unlikely to be able to build consensus. Pragmatic rules describe how to manipulate the normative setting to achieve strategic goals. They fulfill strategic goals without openly defying normative rules, even if they subtly violate the spirit of normative prescriptions. The trick for an aspiring leader is to master pragmatic rules most effectively through the creation of what Bailey calls a normative facade, in which the normative characteristics of pragmatic leadership activities are touted.

Despite the role of manipulation in the establishment and maintenance of leadership, all consensus building is based on some level of trust (Ostrom 1998; Ruttan 2006). Charisma and diplomacy enhance the trustworthiness of the leader, whereas manipulation generates and sustains a veneer of trustworthiness. Followers are not dupes, however, and they engage in "tit-for-tat" evaluations of leadership behavior (Axelrod 1984, 1997); if the leader cannot come through at least some of the time and build and sustain a positive reputation, his or her charisma, diplomatic abilities, and manipulative prowess eventually fail, followers become suspicious, and the leader's authority is compromised. Such checks on leadership and on the desire for autonomy that drives them may inhibit the coordination needed to maintain cooperative labor and economies of scale (Stanish, chapter 5).

## Related Socioeconomic Qualities

Leadership, as defined above, emphasizes authoritative decision making by the few on behalf of the many. In much of the archaeological literature on leaders, however, the characteristics of leadership are conflated with socioeconomic qualities such as status and wealth (Renfrew 1982; Roscoe 2000b:105–107). Althuogh any holistic consideration of leadership should acknowledge the interrelated nature of all these characteristics—particularly in their respective roles in influencing charisma and diplomacy and reflecting intelligence—an analytical separation is important for understanding what leadership is and how it forms.

Wealth is often correlated with leadership. In small-scale societies, however, wealth often has no relationship with decision-making authority, or if it does, it frequently possesses an inverse relationship in which a leader's wealth decreases as his or her authority increases (for example, Bird and Bliege Bird, chapter 2), at least until the point at which it is institutionalized. The possible reasons for this are discussed later, but suffice it to say that the definitions of wealth are as nuanced as those for leadership. Wealth can be measured in a variety of culturally contextualized ways, including by physical accumulation of critical resources, influence over others and their labor, and, as detailed in Vaughn's chapter 7, control of esoteric material culture (Ames 1995; Earle 1991; Graves and Spielmann 2000; Hayden 1995:67–69; Potter and Perry 2000). Specialized knowledge, or what Arnold (chapter 6) generalizes as "intellectual property," provides a related form of wealth that often is the only differentially distributed resource, as in the case of the Martu "ritual gerontocracy" (Bird and Bliege Bird, chapter 2). In all cases, as described in chapters 4, 6, and 9 by Eerkens, Arnold, and Wiessner, respectively, as well as by Fried (1967), Sahlins (1972), and Earle (1991), wealth and its political utility are contingent on privatization and heritability—one cannot practice magnanimity, fund centralized authority, or ensure intergenerational continuity without the ability to control resources.

Similarly, status and prestige suffer an imprecise relationship with leadership. Both terms refer to social relationships between people, with *status* emphasizing group-level social divisions that may be ascribed through kinship (Carneiro 1998) and *prestige* referring to an individually achieved quality (Redmond 1998b:4). Certainly, the ability for an aspiring leader to establish decision-making consensus for collective action is situated within the social settings of status relationships and prestige building (Spikins 2008). Charisma, for example, can be founded upon status differences between a leader and followers that promote a sense of trust or idolization of the authority figure. As in the case with wealth, however, an analytical separation of status, prestige, and leadership is of value for determining any meaningful causal relationships between these qualities. Rather than focus on ascribed decision-making status, discussions in this chapter, as well as in the book as a whole, emphasize the creation and maintenance of individual prestige as it contributes to authority.

## SCALES OF LEADERSHIP

Leadership exists at multiple social and temporal scales. From the nuclear family to empires, the need for decision making for effective collective action occurs at all social scales and can be hierarchically nested even in small-scale societies (for example, Frangipane 2007; Redmond 1998b). Decision making accordingly is situated both among and between social groups (for example, Kusimba and Kusimba, chapter 10), and factionalism will develop when, for any particular scale, multiple leaders strive for authority over the same decision-making realms and therefore compete for followers from the same social group. Alternatively, heterarchical political relationships in which decision making is normatively shared or distributed at one particular scale and consensus building typically precedes any action theoretically can develop (Crumley 1987, 2001).

Leadership also varies along a temporal scale, as variously identified in all chapters in this book. Transitory leaders enjoy a realm of decision-making authority that is generally limited to specific temporally and culturally constrained contexts, such as a healer who makes decisions on behalf of others regarding individual or community ailments but who enjoys no authority on a hunting excursion or in intergroup diplomacy. Transitory leaders achieve their authority by building charisma and trust within a particular limited arena of expertise. Permanent leaders in contrast extend their authority beyond specific contexts and practice decision making at larger social and temporal scales such that decision making is increasingly centralized among fewer leaders. The roles of institutionalized leaders, in contrast, are normatively defined such that the leadership position exists no matter the quality or permanence of any individual who might fill that role. This situation contrasts with hereditary leadership, which is based on the lineal passage of authority and is not necessarily limited to a particular realm or sensitive to the qualities of the individual. A king, as an obvious example, enjoys expansive and permanent authority, even if he has no aptitude for effective decision making. Like social scale, the temporal and contextual scales of decision making are relevant for understanding the evolution of leadership.

## ROUTES TO LEADERSHIP

Leaders do not simply spring forth in every social setting. Instead, the route to leadership requires complex and costly negotiations between aspiring leaders and potential followers. So why would anyone want to become a leader? Two fundamental perspectives on human nature provide potential answers to this question. Although often presented as opposing viewpoints, elements of both explanations are compatible and arguably contribute to a third possible answer that, although more nuanced, is more difficult to evaluate.

The first explanation is that aspiring leaders are martyrs who recognize a societal need for effective collective action through centralized decision making in the face of unusual circumstances. A key assumption behind this explanation is that leadership is a costly and thankless job that only the most socially responsible members of society would ever take. The presumed costs of leadership take many forms, from the investments needed to build charisma and engage in diplomacy to the costs of competing with other aspiring leaders (for example, Redmond 1998a; Stanish, chapter 5; Vaughn, chapter 7; Wiessner, chapter 9). Costs include material expenditures for activities such as political gifting and feasting (see contributions in Dietler and Hayden 2001) and the social costs of activities such as calling in favors and becoming indebted to others, especially to the kin whose labor so often supports these activities (Strathern 1969, 1982a). Leadership is also risky, for if a leader's decisions lead to bad collective outcomes, particularly on a consistent basis, the consequences can be punitive actions taken against the leader (for example, Poyer 1991). The premise of this perspective is that all of these costs outweigh any potential socioeconomic benefits for leaders.

The second explanation for why people strive to become leaders is that they are "Machiavellian princes" looking out for their own self-interest and that centralized decision-making authority provides substantial benefits that outweigh the costs (Hayden 1996). At least some leaders receive direct material benefits in the form of tribute or gifts of food and other needed or valuable resources. Leaders often receive other indirect material benefits also, such as the ability to mobilize labor on their behalf, as described in Bowser and Patton (chapter 3) for Conambo women with high political status and in Arnold (1996b, chapter 6) for the Chumash. Finally, there are also indirect social and reproductive rewards for leadership, such as preferential access to potential mates, the ability to funnel benefits to relatives and descendants, and opportunities to exact proactive and punitive revenge on potential competitors—all of which enhance one's direct and indirect fitness.

A third explanation says that people strive for positions of leadership not because of responsibilities they feel to society as a whole or because leadership provides them with an avenue toward unadulterated self-interest through the extraction of benefits. Instead, leaders understand that collective action will benefit both themselves and others, and they perhaps believe, even if erroneously, that they have the skills and qualities for effective decision making. The aspiring leader is not Machiavellian in the sense that he or she is going to use a position of authority to aggressively extract resources to the detriment of others. Instead, aspiring leaders enhance collective action in such a way that the resource base grows or is maintained for everyone—including themselves (Arnold 1995a, 2000a; Feinman 1995). They might recognize, for example, that a particular public goods problem requires centralized leadership to avert a "tragedy of the commons" (Hardin 1968; Ostrom 1998)—which in fact may be a proportionally greater threat to the aspiring leader than to the followers. As discussed in chapters 5 and 6 by Stanish and Arnold, respectively, leaders can mobilize the collective labor needed to achieve mutually beneficial economic and sociopolitical goals (Adams 2004; Arnold 1996b, 2000b; Dietler and Herbich 2001; Saitta 1997; Stanish 2004) such that everyone is receiving benefits of leadership—even if a leader is disproportionately benefiting from his or her decision-making role.

### Limitations on Leaders

Assuming that leadership does provide benefits to those in decision-making positions, why do so few leaders actually exist in any given social setting? Several answers are possible. First, to successfully attain a decision-making position, no matter what the motivation for doing so, someone needs a set of essential skills and abilities, and presumably not everyone has these. Through enlightened self-awareness or painful trial and error, most people have some idea as to whether they can effectively lead (for example, Boehm 1999:55). And for those who know they lack the talent, the best strategy for achieving their interests is to support someone who has the skills to be an effective leader and whom they trust to support their personal interests. Similarly, some people may fear the destabilizing consequences of leadership competition and prefer to promote their interests by following an aspiring leader of their choice rather than contribute to sociopolitical instability. Of course, plenty of individuals do not have the requisite skills, recognition of their abilities, and understanding of the potential costs of political factionalism, leading to situations in which they try and fail, often miserably, to achieve and maintain positions of leadership.

Although self-selection might limit the number of aspiring leaders, the most significant check against unbridled leadership is what Boehm (1993, 1999) refers to as a reverse dominance hierarchy, in which leveling mechanisms are employed by a population to ensure that the actions of a leader are conducted with the consensus of those who will be impacted by those actions (Bowles and Gintis 2003a). Although people recognize that leadership is needed to guide effective collective action (Ostrom 1998) and that not everyone can be a leader, they do not want to be completely disenfranchised from decision making. As described by Bird and Bliege Bird (chapter 2) and Wiessner (chapter 9), the ultimate purpose of leveling mechanisms is not to stamp out leadership completely but to sustain some measure of individual autonomy and maintain individual self-interest (Boehm 1999:67–69, 87–88; Friesen 2007). Leaders are evaluated according to a socioculturally mediated code that defines the contexts of appropriate leadership and limits centralized decision-making behavior to what Bailey (2001) refers to as dutiful action—the normative expectations of leadership. Ridicule, gossip, disobedience, banishment, and even assassination are oft-cited leveling mechanisms employed to punish individuals in positions of leadership who appear to be pushing the limits of such "dutiful action" (Boehm 1999:74–84; Roscoe 2000b:91; Spikins 2008: 177–179).

Reverse dominance hierarchies often create a society that appears "acephalous"; the limitations on leadership make it seem as if the society has no leaders at all. Leadership is restricted to particular contexts and temporal boundaries to ensure that the authority of a leader is limited to unusual circumstances of crisis and novelty in which centralized decision making benefits everyone. During normal conditions, established cultural mechanisms guide decision making, and leaders are not needed, so they effectively "disappear." Bailey (2001:48) describes the classic example of Nuer society, which is traditionally strongly egalitarian with severe leveling mechanisms that maintain an egalitarian ethos. Leaders are rare when circumstances are predictable and normal. However, in times of crisis, influential Nuer "prophets" emerge to guide collective action. Their authority, though temporary, is sustained by a powerful divinity that can even be inherited by their sons, providing the seeds for ascribed leadership (see also Wiessner, chapter 9). In the absence of crisis, Nuer prophets lose their larger decision-making responsibilities, and the society again appears acephalous and comparatively egalitarian (see also Redmond 2002).

### Establishing Permanent Leaders

If small-scale societies can contend with crisis and novelty through transitory leadership positions and if reverse dominance hierarchies successfully restrict leaders from overstepping the limits of their authority, how do lasting forms of leadership and inequities in decision making ever develop? Assuming that aspiring leaders—as well as their followers—do have the potential of benefiting from positions of authority, they must overcome three limiting factors to establish themselves as permanent leaders with broad decision-making authority. First, they must demonstrate the appropriate skills and abilities for effective leadership, as described earlier. Second, they need to win competitions against other aspiring decision makers, by directly vanquishing opponents, allying with them in political coalitions, or some combination of defeating and allying with competitors (Beck 2006; Boehm 1999:25, 155–162). Third, and most importantly, aspiring leaders who seek greater permanence and benefits from their authority must overcome the powerful leveling mechanisms designed to maintain an egalitarian ethos.

To overcome all three challenges to the establishment of permanent leaders, the solution is in principle quite simple: the aspiring leader demonstrates to people that at the very least they will not suffer from his or her leadership and more likely will benefit. If this point can be established, the egalitarian ethos is relaxed, the behaviors that constitute "dutiful action" are expanded, and authority is not as closely monitored. However, the solution to overcoming limited authority is simple in principle but in practice much more complex because there are relatively few opportunities for someone to break the limits on centralized leadership without exacting some cost on other individuals, evoking reverse dominance sanctions. Although not exactly a zero-sum game, in which a benefit to one is an equal and direct cost to another, the struggle between aspiring leaders and wary followers often approximates this kind of tension (Feinman 2001). Accordingly, the following arguments treat the development of increasingly inequitable leadership as a cost-benefit contest between aspiring leaders and self-interested followers (Boehm 1999:169; Stanish 2004).

Egalitarian societies with transitory leaders and strong reverse dominance hierarchies are the starting point from which increasingly permanent leaders with inequitable decision-making authority emerge. For this to happen, the context has to change in such a way that cost-benefit calculations are modified and new opportunities emerge for aspiring leaders. Three interrelated contextual situations are likely important: demographic change, environmental change, and sociocultural opportunity. Changes in these contexts can occur in such a way that aspiring leaders can overcome leveling mechanisms and build inequities in decision making—and potentially build wealth, status, and even power (for example, Friesen 2007).

Population growth provides the first and in some ways the most important contextual change for promoting inequity. Smaller numbers of people make leveling mechanisms most effective because violations of egalitarian ethos are easier to monitor in small groups of regularly interacting individuals and appropriate leveling mechanisms can be enacted at the slightest sign of inappropriate behavior (Bowles and Gintis 2008; Gächter, Renner, and Sefton 2008). This is more difficult to do in larger groups, in which individual behavior is harder to monitor. From another demographic perspective, leveling mechanisms require investment in collective action, which sets up a situation referred to as a second-order collective action problem—the groups or individuals who are depended upon to support the enacting of leveling mechanisms, themselves, have to be monitored to ensure their contribution to and support of the reverse dominance actions (Ostrom 1998). As populations grow, therefore, not only does monitoring the behavior of aspiring leaders become more challenging, but so does the monitoring of the monitors (but see Bowles and Gintis 2003a; Hauert et al. 2007; Panchanathan and Boyd 2004).

One possible solution to population growth, at least in the abstract, is to establish scaled or nested social groupings such that *groups* of individuals effectively *act as* individuals in a reverse dominance hierarchy (see Frangipane 2007). For example, as opposed to having one hundred people trying to monitor one another's behavior, ten groups of ten people can emerge. Each group internally monitors its members, and the group as a whole monitors the other groups, creating a scaled reverse dominance hierarchy (for example, Kusimba and Kusimba, chapter 10). The problem of course is that the establishment of such scaled demographics is a collective-action problem itself; insofar as the structuring element of such scaling is likely to be kinship, this introduces complicating factors such as inclusive fitness and the influence of kin-based identity. In fact, the ethnographic record suggests that the formation of scaled social groupings is more likely to lead to greater rather than lesser levels of competition for centralized leadership. For example, kinship groups often become ranked based on perceived, culturally constructed, or real ancestral claims to place, resources, and ceremony (for example, Kusimba and Kusimba, chapter 10), often situated within the authority of "founding families" (for example, Frangipane 2007; Gezon 1999; Kopytoff 1999; Kunen 2006). Demographic change therefore provides many openings for aspiring leaders to centralize authority.

The physical environment is the second context in which a change can alter the cost-benefit assessments of leadership activities and the leveling mechanisms that keep them in check. Note that this perspective is not advocating a deterministic relationship between environmental conditions and decision-making structure (a criticism well summarized in Boehm 1999:35–38 and illustrated in Eerkens's chapter 4 example from Owens Valley). Rather, environmental conditions provide one of many sets of factors that humans consider when evaluating individual behavior in group contexts. The structure of the environment at any given moment in time is significant (Boone 1992; Frangipane 2007; Pauketat 1996; Smith and Choi 2007). Researchers observe, for example, that physical settings in which needed resources are equitably and homogeneously distributed contribute to equity in wealth and authority because no one can gain economic advantage over anyone else. Contexts in which resources are patchy and heterogeneously distributed in time and space provide the seeds for inequity due to "despotic distributions" whereby some individuals are always ahead of others in producing food and other basic resources. Even in these situations, leveling mechanisms keep excessive economic and political competition in check, but despotic distributions tend to promote incipient inequities in social obligations and debt formation as those individuals in prime settings consistently produce more food—and give away more through sharing, gifting, and feasting (for example, Adams 2004:72–73; Boehm 1999:46, 138–139)—which in turn promotes the centralization of authority in fewer and permanent leaders.

In considerations of the physical environment, especially important are *unusual* changes. As an example, imagine a climate marked by interannual instability in rainfall; some years there is plenty of rain, but in others not enough falls, and the good and bad years do not follow a predictable pattern. People are going to expect that the good times will not last, and normative expectations of appropriate sociopolitical behavior will be structured accordingly. If the rain keeps coming year after year, however, those same normative rules no longer apply, memories of the potential for bad years fade, and the calculi by which people set goals and evaluate their strategies and the behaviors of others change. Aspiring leaders in these situations can benefit. Whereas before, their behaviors were evaluated in reference to the riskiness of the environment, now everyone is doing comparatively well, and strong measures enforcing equity may be relaxed as people discount the potential costs of risky competitive behavior and the loss of their decision-making autonomy. If a leader can tie the positive contextual changes to his or her own past leadership decisions—such as might be the case for a leader with religious authority who can claim influence over the climate (for example, Fowles 2002; Lucero 2006)—the reverse dominance hierarchy can begin to fall apart. Thus, environmental change can provide opportunities for leaders to cement their authority (for example, chapters 4, 6, and 7, by Eerkens, Arnold, and Vaughn, respectively).

Sociocultural opportunity is the third context that can contribute to increasingly permanent leadership. Inequities in decision making do not emerge in a social and cultural vacuum, and clearly some sociocultural contexts in which aspiring leaders can leverage demographic and environmental changes to their advantage exist. An obvious situation would be the chronic threat of warfare, in which leaders can establish some permanence to their positions because followers need the centralized decision-making authority to contend with the external threat (for example, Boehm 1999:94; Carneiro 1998; Redmond 2002). Of course, an aspiring leader might also exaggerate the threat and build emotions in such a way that the *perceived* benefits of his or her authority—as well as the perceived costs of not having a leader—are inflated (Roscoe 2000b).

Religion and ceremony represent another arena of sociocultural behavior in which an aspiring leader can overcome restrictions on authority, particularly if his or her role is engaged with or legitimized by religion. Bailey (2001:150) notes that ceremony creates "spectacles" and promotes what he calls diseducation, through which a religious leader can appear "bigger than life" and therefore more godlike and charismatic, important qualities for building permanent consensus around decision-making authority. Religion and ceremony also provide contexts in which an aspiring leader can claim some level of responsibility for positive demographic and environmental changes (for example, Fowles 2002). And religious leaders may have the ability to invoke supernatural powers against potential competitors and enemies (for example, Boehm 1999:83; Redmond 2002) or control access to essential ceremonies and ritual objects (for example, Bird and Bliege Bird, chapter 2; Vaughn, chapter 7). This sociocultural context also gives aspiring leaders some level of influence or control over esoteric ritual knowledge—Arnold's "intellectual property" (chapter 6)—based in the society's ideological system (for example, Brown 2006; Hollimon 2004).

Religious specialists are often in the best position to build consensus and guide collective action through their special associations with supernatural forces (Aldenderfer 1993; Redmond 1998a). Because such specialists are the spokespeople for or conduits of power, rather than the holders of power, they receive special exemptions from the criteria that guide reverse dominance hierarchies. At the same time, recent experimental and cross-cultural studies demonstrate how religiosity within a social group reduces the individual self-interest that might lead to reverse dominance behavior (Norenzayan and Shariff 2008). Religious leaders enjoy an intimate knowledge of—and potential control over—the normative rules of leadership and the ideological legitimation of those rules (for example, McAnany 2001, 2004; Roscoe 2000b; Smith 2000). This is not to say that a religious leader "makes up religion" to enhance his or her decision-making authority, but rather that the leader, even as a believer, is responsible for ideological interpretation and religious dogma and can manipulate these to achieve his or her individual goals. (See, for example, Bailey's description [2001:82] of how Gandhi manipulated religion.) Religion also provides the rubric for simple messages that can help a leader unify culturally and socially diverse groups, thereby increasing the number of followers who support his or her decision making (Bailey 2001:91; Smith 2000).

Pauketat (chapter 8) and Kusimba and Kusimba (chapter 10) further identify how the construction of historical narratives, often based on religious understandings and shaped by religious leaders, is critical for institutionalizing leadership and its sustaining practices.

When combined with inequitable resource productivity, religion and ceremony provide an aspiring leader with unparalleled opportunities to change how people evaluate the leader's behavior and their own self-interest (Bowles and Gintis 2008), particularly when combined with other contextual changes that present unusual situations and undermine existing normative rules. It is perhaps for this reason that Feinman and Neitzel (1984) identify ceremonial responsibilities as the most ubiquitous function of leaders in western North American native societies. And, as described by Bird and Bliege Bird (chapter 2), this is also possibly why aspiring Martu leaders sacrifice much as young hunters, thereby building charisma and trust so that later they can join the ritual leadership, where real authority lies.

The results of these contextual circumstances—demographic change, environmental change, and sociocultural opportunity—allow aspiring leaders to avoid leveling mechanisms, subvert reverse dominance hierarchies, and build greater permanence to their positions of authority. Such changing contingencies and their effects are difficult to build into predictive models for the evolution of leadership, but clearly they are important factors in any explanation for why increasingly inequitable forms of leadership develop (Pauketat 2004b). The essence of the problem is that reverse dominance hierarchies and the leveling mechanisms they so effectively employ have to be subverted before aspiring leaders can establish institutionalized and hereditary positions. Clearly, there are structural problems shared in all contexts that must be overcome, but equally clear is the importance of contingency in creating the right opportunity for leadership to evolve beyond its egalitarian foundations. After this threshold is crossed, greater institutionalization of leadership and hereditary positions of power are much more easily attained (Redmond 1998a). It is perhaps for this reason that so-called middle-range societies feature such intense gifting and feasting, coalition behavior, and ceremonialism.

## ARCHAEOLOGICAL IDENTIFICATION OF LEADERSHIP

Research on the identification of leaders in the archaeological record almost universally focuses on societies in which leadership is institutionalized and hereditary. Archaeologists are quite good at identifying chiefs and kings, using measures such as investment in mortuary treatment, monumental architecture, and differences in domestic settings (for example,

Peebles and Kus 1977; Spencer 1998:106–108; Wason 1994). Until very recently, comparatively fewer scholars considered the identification of transitory leaders in egalitarian societies or incipient leaders moving toward greater institutionalized roles and hereditary ascription (but see Feinman and Neitzel 1984; Hayden 1995, 2001). By their very nature, such leaders are nearly invisible sociopolitically—and certainly archaeologically—for they lead through authority and face leveling mechanisms that prevent the formalization of their leadership in individualizing material culture (Spikins 2008:179–181). How can archaeologists investigate this important transition in human history if it is not readily accessible in the archaeological record? Although challenging, three interrelated strategies might provide us with insight into this process: First, we can identify the changing contexts in which leadership likely was valued by other group members. Second, we can identify transitions in leadership rather than try to find the remains of individual leaders in the archaeological record. Third, we can identify the contextual changes that would have provided aspiring leaders with the opportunity to expand and centralize permanent authority.

In what contexts would leadership be valuable or at least appreciated? As discussed earlier, centralized decision making and the collective action it facilitates are most valued by followers in those circumstances that are uncommon and therefore not anticipated and remedied by existing cultural institutions. Through guidance and consensus building, leaders dispel the uncertainty and indecision that unusual circumstances create and that confound collective action at a time it is most needed. If this premise is accepted, then archaeologists can look for material evidence of these unusual circumstances, which might include abnormal environmental changes such as extended drought, excessive flooding, and new crop or livestock diseases (Arnold 1992, 2001b), all identifiable archaeologically. Other uncommon events might be social, such as rampant internal factionalism and the appearance of new groups, both of which are frequently recorded as changes in material culture (for example, Bowser 2000; Kantner 1996). Ideological crises, in addition to those potentially created by environmental change—such as unexplainable human disease and worrisome astronomical events—might also call for the guidance of a leader.

For archaeologists, identifying whether leadership would have been valuable in a particular context requires an assessment of whether the circumstances were typical from a historical perspective. Paleoclimatic records beginning well before the period of interest can be assessed, for example, to look for unusual changes in the amount, type, and seasonality of rainfall that might have caused socioeconomic stresses requiring new forms of concerted collective action. The osteological record similarly might reveal the appearance of new human pathogens—such as those introduced by new populations—that could have created uncertainty and confusion and necessitated centralized guidance. No simple formula for predicting the need for leadership exists, but archaeologists can build compelling circumstantial arguments identifying when an otherwise egalitarian society might see the need for sustained decision-making authority.

Of course, simply identifying that a context would have benefited from centralized leadership does not mean that the latter existed. In the absence of institutionalized leaders with a comparatively clear archaeological signature, archaeologists might instead attempt to identify evidence of the practice of centralized leadership. How do transitory leaders establish some authority and avoid leveling mechanisms? They must build their charisma, guide effective group decisions, and manipulate circumstances to their advantage. Archaeologists accordingly should look for evidence for these behaviors or at least for the contexts in which these would have occurred. Feasting, as described by several authors in this book, provides an ideal opportunity for aspiring leaders to accomplish many of these goals, for feasts hosted by them and their supporters demonstrate their generosity and their organizational capabilities (Adams 2004; Clark and Blake 1994; Godelier 1986; Godelier and Strathern 1991; Kirch 2001; Rosenswig 2007). Fortunately, feasting leaves substantial material signatures that archaeologists have become skilled at identifying and assessing (for example, Adams 2004; Dietler and Hayden 2001; Potter 2000a; Twiss 2008).

Religious and ideological contexts provide additional avenues for an aspiring leader to build authority, as described earlier, for they possess what Pauketat (chapter 8) calls a "materiality and spatiality" that can be assessed archaeologically. For example, ceremony occurs in particular places that are archaeologically identifiable, including special infrastructure. Religious leaders often are involved in the production, gifting, and possession of valuable items that represent materialized ideology, such as staffs, masks, lithic "eccentrics," and vessels imbued with material wealth, historical resonance, and special supernatural qualities (for example, Inomata 2007; Vaughn 2006, chapter 7). And insofar as ceremonial contexts include feasting and gift-giving events, religious specialists enjoy special opportunities for ideological manipulation, providing additional payoffs for such "spectacles" (Dietler 2001; Wiessner 2001), which often are the centers of the political economy (for example, Vaughn, chapter 7; Wiessner, chapter 9). Archaeologists can assess the contexts of both feasting and religious ceremony for evidence of the practice of leadership and related efforts to build authority (for example, Kirch 2001; McAnany 2001). An important caution is that religious practitioners may not achieve positions of leadership with widespread influence but instead are often "attached" to aspiring leaders who are more secular and whose separation from supernatural power protects them from its imagined dangers and potential political burden (see also Hollimon 2004; Kelekna 1998).

Evidence for other behaviors also can provide insight into the changing practices of leadership. Bowser and Patton (2004, chapter 3) describe how changes in the size of and access to public spaces in household settings provide insight into less formal arenas of gendered political decision making. Low-intensity warfare and raiding also need not indicate centralized decision making, but as the scale of violence increases, the organizational needs of both offensive actions and defensive preparations call for centralized leadership. Ritualized warfare such as Wiessner (chapter 9) describes also provides opportunities for the rise of leaders whose authority can be quite extensive. Irrigation or similar infrastructural projects requiring coordinated labor are also often identified as evidence of centralized decision making, although again the scale of such efforts needs to be considered to determine whether they reflect the guidance of authoritative leadership (for example, Fash and Davis-Salazar 2006; Nichols et al. 2006; Scarborough 2003).

The final archaeological problem to address is the identification of the contextual changes that would have provided the opportunity for leaders to centralize and extend their authority. This was discussed previously, but the important question is whether archaeologists can identify the contextual changes that allow aspiring leaders to build inequities without invoking leveling mechanisms (Boehm 1999:215). An evaluation of demography and the social structure is needed to identify changes in the potential effectiveness of reverse dominance hierarchies (Smith and Boyd 1990). Assessments of productive potential for the area in question are important for identifying the presence of a despotic resource distribution, which in turn necessitates reconstruction of the subsistence base (Boone 1992). An understanding of the impact of paleoclimatic change on subsistence distributions across a population also is needed, as is identification of new technologies or cultigens that might alter productive capacity and relations, as Wiessner (chapter 9) describes for the Enga with the introduction of the sweet potato. Finally, and perhaps even more challenging, is the identification of changes to the sociocultural context. Have new religious movements been introduced? Have climatic changes stimulated migration and the new sociopolitical contexts it creates, with new immigrants joining existing populations? To what degree are resources becoming privatized and thus eligible for accumulation and use in a political economy (for example, Eerkens 2004, chapter 4)? Although often challenging, all these factors can be identified archaeologically and assessed for their impact on leaders and leadership.

## CASE STUDY: THE CHACOANS OF THE PUEBLOAN SOUTHWEST

Having outlined a detailed model for how leadership emerges and becomes more permanent, I now take the perspective on leadership developed in this chapter and apply it to a well-known case from the Puebloan Southwest, the Chacoan tradition of the tenth through early eleventh centuries AD. Emerging out of a sociocultural context characterized by ephemeral and likely transitory positions of authority, the Chacoan tradition is probably the first in the Puebloan Southwest to see the emergence of permanent, and perhaps even institutionalized, leadership.

Chaco Canyon in northwestern New Mexico has long been the subject of intense archaeological interest (for example, Fagan 2005; Kantner 2004; Lekson 2005, 2006; Reed 2004). Situated in the center of the desolate San Juan Basin (figure 11.1), the broad and shallow canyon with its intermittent wash, low rainfall, and short growing season does not appear to be a prime location for establishing farming villages. Yet, this did happen around the AD 700s, when Puebloan people who had long used Chaco Canyon on a seasonal basis began to live in more permanent villages at points where side canyons enter the main drainage (Windes 2001). Except for the challenging location, these early Chacoan communities were not appreciably different from the multitude of contemporaneous Puebloan villages found across the northern American Southwest.

By the late AD 800s, however, clearly something new was developing in Chaco Canyon (figure 11.2), most obviously characterized by the appearance of an architectural form—the so-called great house—that differed from the typical Puebloan domestic structures (Lekson 1984; Windes 2007; Windes and Ford 1996). In the AD 1000s, great houses grew to remarkable sizes, eventually reaching several stories and containing hundreds of rooms, all in an environment devoid of trees large enough to roof these buildings. The corresponding explosion of religious and economic activity, including the construction of ceremonial causeways and the import of copper bells and even live macaws from Mesoamerica, accompanies compelling evidence for centralized and perhaps even hereditary leaders (Lekson 1999, 2006). One burial room in the famous great house of Pueblo Bonito contains around four times as much turquoise as has ever

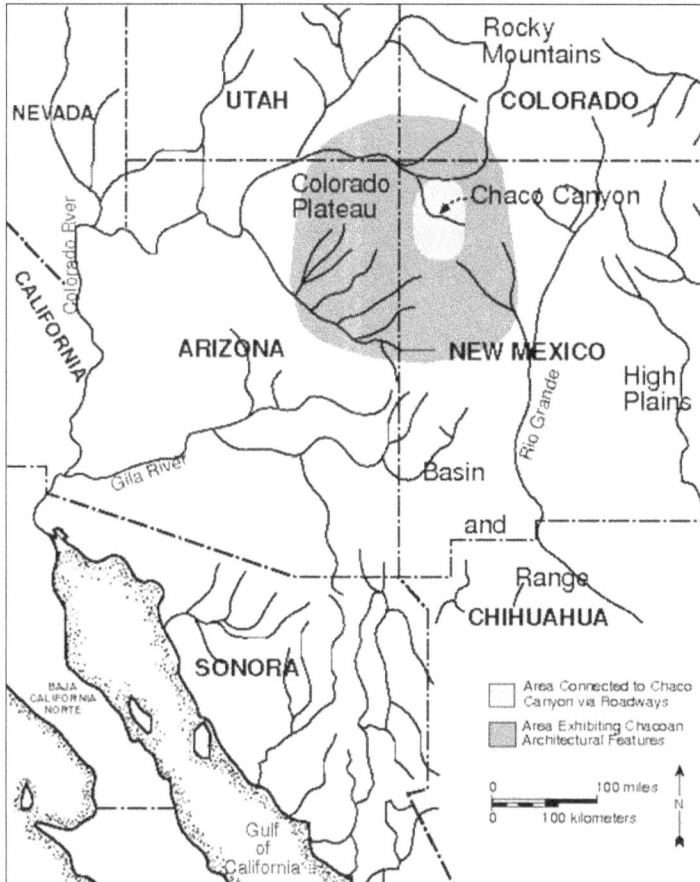

**FIGURE 11.1**

*Location of Chaco Canyon in the American Southwest, including the surrounding San Juan Basin and the larger area influenced by the Chacoan tradition. Map by John Kantner.*

been recovered from all prehistoric contexts in the Southwest (Snow 1973). Although the height of the Chacoan "phenomenon" did not exceed two or three generations, its impact on the trajectory of Puebloan history is unquestionable (Kantner 2004).

### Evidence for Pre-Chacoan Leadership

How can these developments be explained, particularly regarding the evolution of Chacoan leadership? To answer this question, we need to return to the small farming villages of the eighth century, which emerged during an extended climatic downturn in rainfall beginning in the mid–AD

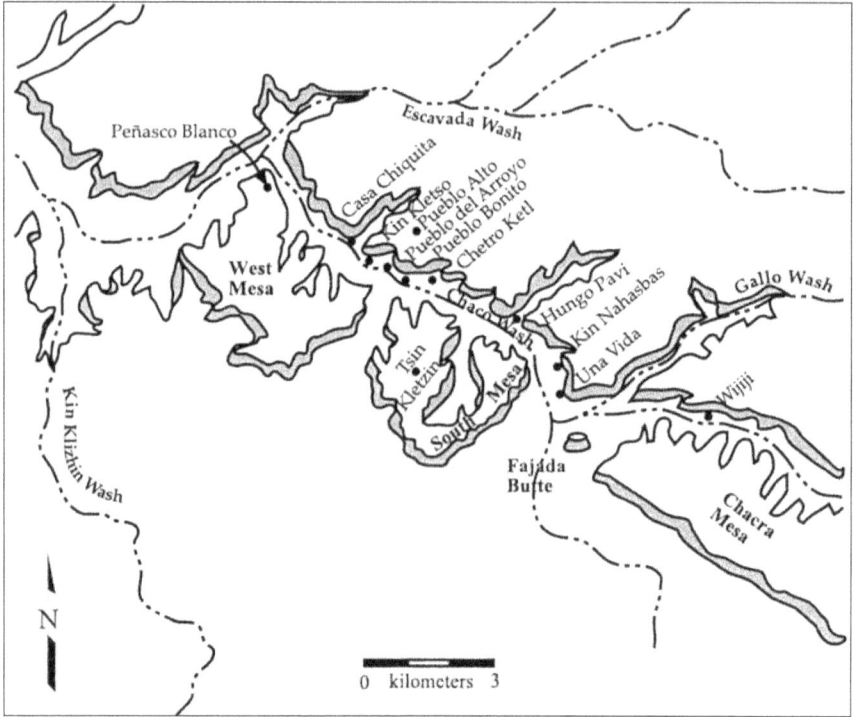

**FIGURE 11.2**

*Location of great houses within Chaco Canyon in the first decades of the AD 1100s. Peñasco
Blanco, Pueblo Bonito, and Una Vida were the earliest great houses to be built in the ninth century.
Most of the others were not constructed until more than a century later. Map by John Kantner.*

700s (Force et al. 2002; Grissino-Mayer 1996; Gumerman 1988). Although
the archaeological record in Chaco Canyon unfortunately is dominated by
the later developments of the AD 1000s, existing evidence from the earliest
villages in Chaco can be fleshed out with evidence from contemporaneous
Puebloan settlements elsewhere in the northern Southwest.

In Chaco Canyon (see figure 11.2), early villages such as the one around
Fajada Butte were loosely aggregated clusters of extended-family households that exhibit very few material differences (Mathien 2005; McKenna
and Truell 1986). Each household likely produced its own food through
*akchin* farming, which takes advantage of rainfall runoff, and perhaps with
small-scale water-control features (Vivian et al. 2006). Archaeologists agree
that early Puebloan villages were geared toward overproduction to contend
with climatic instability, storing and sharing surpluses through delayed reciprocal exchanges with neighbors (Hegmon 1991, 1996; Kohler, Van Pelt,

and Yap 2000). Although limited authority may have helped to moderate sharing networks, no evidence of extensive irrigation works, sizable ceremonial infrastructure, or endemic warfare exists to suggest the need for—or presence of—centralized decision making.

In other areas of the Puebloan world during the eighth and ninth centuries, large subterranean structures spatially associated with particular households presage the ceremonial great kivas of later Chaco-era villages (Van Dyke 2007; Wilshusen and Van Dyke 2006). In the Mesa Verde region to the north, early protokivas notably are associated with evidence of feasting (Blinman 1989). Similar oversized pit structures are identified in early villages in and around Chaco Canyon, but the remains of feasts have not yet been identified (Lekson, Windes, and McKenna 2006; McKenna and Truell 1986; Roberts 1929). This evidence of ceremony and feasting is suggestive of the presence of religious authority (Potter and Perry 2000), but attempts to identify differences in individual or family wealth and status have come up empty (for example, Lightfoot and Feinman 1982; Schachner 2001). What this reveals is a sociopolitical setting in which reverse dominance hierarchies maintained equity, likely employing leveling mechanisms to keep aspiring leaders from engaging in self-aggrandizement and asserting too much decision-making authority. Transitory leaders almost certainly did exist in a variety of sociocultural contexts, not the least of which would have been part-time religious authorities, whose existence is attested to by the ceremonial kivas associated with some households in these villages.

### Ninth-Century Changes in Chaco Canyon

The late AD 800s mark the emergence of great house architecture (Lekson, Windes, and McKenna 2006; Windes 2003, 2007; Windes and Ford 1996; Windes and McKenna 2001). Scholars still do not agree on the function of these structures, an issue complicated by later additions and remodeling that obscure their earliest uses. However, early great houses such as Pueblo Bonito (figure 11.3) are associated with important material patterns: they exhibit ceremonial features that include sizable kivas (for example, Van Dyke 2003); many unusual artifacts with apparent religious significance have been recovered from great houses (for example, Durand 2003); and they reveal some evidence for feasting and related communal events (for example, Toll 2001; Wills 2001), suggesting that they were centers of community activity and arenas for leadership activities (Kantner 1996; Lekson 1999; Sebastian 1992). Whether or not they had residential or purely ceremonial functions, the thick walls, oversized rooms, multiple

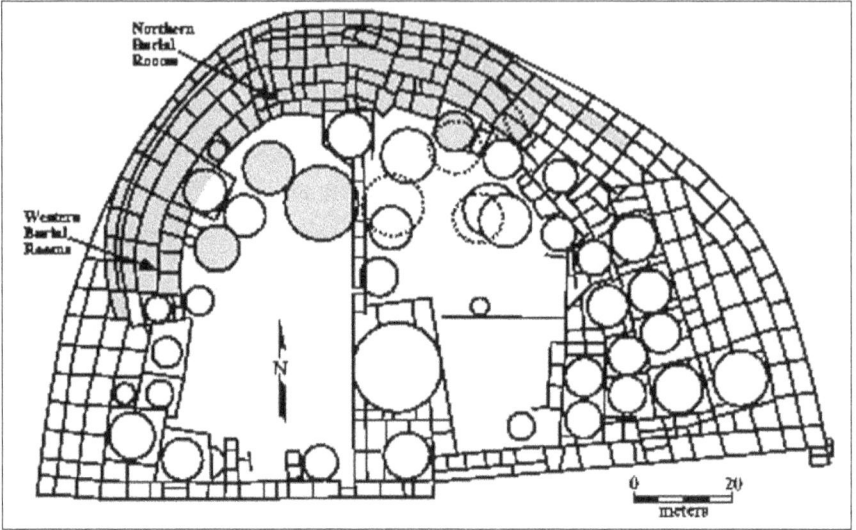

**FIGURE 11.3**

*Pueblo Bonito, showing construction sequence and burial rooms. Shaded areas were completed by*
*AD 1040. Expansion and reorientation of the great house from southeast to south occurred in the*
*AD 1080s. Drawing by John Kantner.*

stories, and imported timber that characterize great houses required collective action to construct, so some degree of guidance and consensus
building by leaders would be expected.

What contextual changes in the AD 800s might have stimulated the
appearance of these new forms of authoritative decision making? The
archaeological and paleoclimatic reconstructions suggest two possibilities:
first, the climate becomes wetter in the Chaco region (figure 11.4), and,
second, substantial numbers of new immigrants may have arrived in Chaco
Canyon from the Mesa Verde region north of the San Juan River. These
two developments likely are related. After an extended drought through
the mid–AD 700s, rainfall was increasing by the early AD 800s, especially in
Chaco Canyon and areas to the south, making the ninth century especially
beneficial for farming in this region (Force et al. 2002; Grissino-Mayer
1996). This improvement, however, was not seen everywhere in the
Puebloan Southwest. To the north, the latter half of the AD 800s was characterized by an extended drought that was further exacerbated by a cold
period in the final two decades of the ninth century, truncating an already
short growing season (Petersen 1987, 1994). Wilshusen and Van Dyke (2006)
note the correlation between the depopulation of the Mesa Verde region

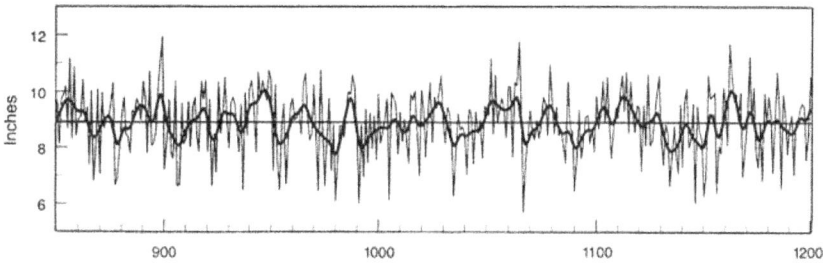

**FIGURE 11.4**

*Paleoclimatic reconstruction of August-through-July precipitation for the Chaco Canyon region (from Force et al. 2002:fig. 3.5b). Courtesy Arizona State Museum, University of Arizona.*

and the apparent growth of population in the Chaco area, and they identify architectural similarities between Mesa Verde and Chaco that they believe reflect immigration into the canyon.

In accordance with the model outlined in this chapter, the result of these two developments was, first, to introduce stress and uncertainty and, second, to positively impact farming productivity. Villages in Chaco Canyon had to decide how to contend with arriving immigrants: should they accept them, and if so, in what capacity? Should they drive them away, or was their labor useful? Should they be accepted but relegated to less desirable areas for living and farming? The need for consensus building and guided decision making on these issues provided opportunities for preexisting yet transitory authority figures to enhance their roles. Meanwhile, the greater farming productivity would have led to greater stores of food, particularly in a society long geared toward overproduction. Although the largely homogeneous resource structure of Chaco Canyon is not conducive to a despotic distribution—soil quality is uniform throughout the canyon (Mytton and Schneider 1987)—subtle differences in productivity may have benefited aspiring leaders and their supporters. For example, some parts of the canyon are ideal for capturing rainfall runoff from the sandstone cliffs, and gaps in the south wall of the canyon funnel rainstorms into particular areas (Force et al. 2002; Vivian et al. 2006).

Sebastian (1992) suggests that with the climatic conditions during the late ninth century, aspiring leaders could have invested their growing surpluses in feasting and debt-building activities that benefited them in the long run. Continuing instability could have been leveraged for building debts, especially with newcomers who had no stored supplies and who were probably relegated to marginal farmlands. The combination of new immigrants to be dealt with—and taken advantage of—and the improving climate likely endowed aspiring leaders with both additional decision-making authority and the material surpluses for cautiously self-aggrandizing activities. In this light, the early great house form might have served as the locus for feasting, ceremonial activities, and consensus building among the increasingly disparate social groups in Chaco Canyon, as well as the perfect arena for building narratives that sustained the changing socio-political situation. The expansion of the earliest great houses was, of aspiring leaders, a comparatively safe means of investing accrued social debt in indirect self-aggrandizement, particularly of those with existing ceremonial responsibilities (Brandt 1994; Kantner 1996, 2004).

Who were these "aspiring leaders"? We might expect them to have been charismatic and diplomatic kin leaders. They probably possessed ceremonial responsibilities, because Puebloan society historically does not separate the secular from the sacred. Yet, because authority was couched in communal ceremony, leaders are not individually visible in the archaeological record (Hegmon 2005:218). Scholars have tended to avoid the issue of gender—or have assumed that early Puebloan leaders were men—but changes in domestic spaces during this time provided many gendered yet public spaces in which political activity very likely occurred (for example, Hegmon, Ortman, and Mobley-Tanaka 2000; Mobley-Tanaka 1997). Furthermore, several studies from later periods of Puebloan history have identified evidence of female leadership (for example, Howell 1996; Neitzel 2000), suggesting that antecedents to this pattern could have existed during the Chaco era. Ultimately, we are not able to identify leaders in ninth-century Chaco Canyon, but we do see compelling evidence for the practice of leadership.

After the initial great house construction in the late AD 800s and early decades of the AD 900s, more than one hundred years pass before any significant new developments in Chaco Canyon (figure 11.5). In the intervening four or five generations, little additional construction occurred at the early great houses (Lekson 1984; Windes and Ford 1996). Neither did any of the other famous Chacoan features—such as roadways, solar and lunar observatories, and Mesoamerican imports—definitively emerge during this period (for example, Kantner 1997b; Nelson 2006; Windes 1991). This situation seems consistent with the lack of new opportunities for leadership to develop any further. In essence, the changes characterizing the late AD 800s and early AD 900s became integrated into the Chacoan cultural milieu, and the emerging differentiation in leadership stabilized. Environmental conditions also became more challenging during the tenth

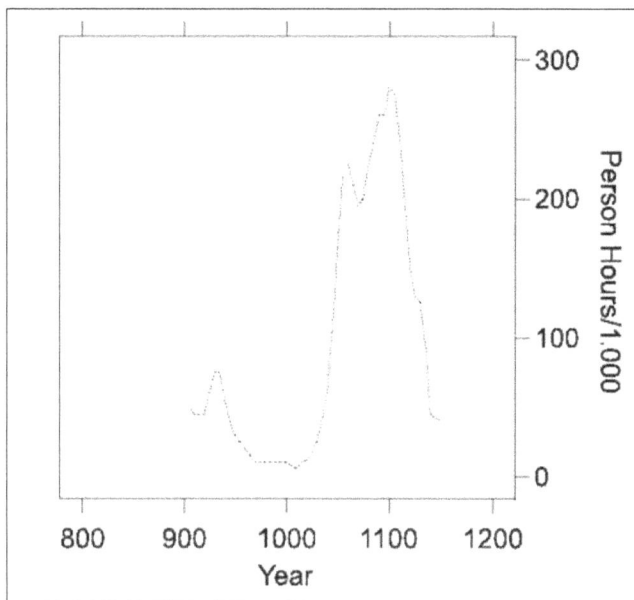

**FIGURE 11.5**

*Intensity of construction events in Chaco Canyon. The dotted line shows Chaco Canyon great house construction labor estimates (Lekson 1984:263, values estimated from figure 5.2).*

century (Force et al. 2002:28), with greater temporal instability in rainfall that would have heightened the sensitivity of the canyon's population to costly aggrandizing activities. A shallow lake at the west end of Chaco Canyon also disappeared when the natural dune dam that created it was breached by flooding, leading to a gradual but significant degradation of farming soils (Force et al. 2002).

### Institutionalizing Leadership in the Eleventh Century

A new contextual situation emerged in the AD 990s. After a few years of good rainfall, the ensuing twenty years were characterized by consistently below-normal rainfall (see figure 11.4). Decent conditions prevailed again between approximately AD 1015 and 1030, but this interlude was followed by a terrible drought that lasted twenty-five years (Force et al. 2002:28). Facing a substantial collective-action challenge, the population of Chaco Canyon seems to have been mobilized; the broken natural dam at the end of the canyon, for example, was repaired with a masonry wall, and the canyon's soils again began to aggregate. However, perhaps surprisingly, the greatest investment of collective action was in great house construction, especially during the extended drought. Pueblo Bonito was modestly expanded, and initial construction at the nearby great houses of Chetro Ketl and Pueblo Alto occurred in the first few years of the AD 1040s (see figure 11.5), a period with very low precipitation (Windes and McKenna 2001).

What was happening during this period? One notable factor is that the climatic instability in the first half of the AD 1000s differs from the instability of the AD 900s (see figure 11.4). In the tenth century, temporal variability in rainfall was more predictable, especially when considering only the bad years; droughts never lasted longer than a couple years. In their predictability, poor climatic conditions would have evoked less stress and uncertainty among the population, providing aspiring leaders with little opportunity to leverage their decision-making prowess into any kind of lasting authority. The nature of instability in the early AD 1000s, however, is almost the opposite, with extended yet inconsistent droughts interspersed with wet periods of equally uncertain longevity. This situation would have created considerable indecisiveness about farming and storage strategies, promoting the need for the consensus-building and decision-making strengths of leadership. Interestingly, the strategy adopted in the late AD 1030s and 1040s was to expand the great houses. The ceremonial nature of this new strategy—and thus the religious nature of leadership—is apparent from the cardinal orientations and landscape alignments of the new great houses (Doxtater 2002; Sofaer 1997, 2007). Considering what happens next in Chaco Canyon, this ceremonial emphasis likely was a very fortuitous decision for priestly leaders.

In the early AD 1050s, two important events occurred. First, in the space of only a couple years, annual precipitation increased to levels not seen since the ninth century (see figure 11.4). This wet period would last almost two decades (Force et al. 2002). Second, in April or May of AD 1054, the Crab Nebula supernova appeared in the daytime sky, and it continued to be visible for at least two years. This event, and the appearance of Halley's Comet ten years later, arguably was recorded in canyon rock art (Malville 1994; Malville and Putnam 1993). The ideological and religious importance of these events, especially for emerging priestly leaders in Chaco Canyon, would have been extremely significant in the evolution of Chacoan leadership (Reyman 1987). Most of the major construction in Chaco Canyon and the expansion of its influence occurred in the second half of the eleventh century (see figure 11.5). Great houses were rapidly expanded and new ones built (Lekson 1984; Windes 2003; Windes and Ford 1996; Windes and McKenna 2001); the famous road "system"—almost certainly ceremonial causeways—was established (Kantner 1997a, 1997b;

Vivian 1997a, 1997b; Windes and Ford 1996; Windes and McKenna 2001); and great volumes of materials were imported into the canyon from as far away as Mesoamerica (Nelson 2006), albeit probably indirectly through down-the-line trade and as pilgrimage offerings. Casa Rinconada, the huge great kiva located across the canyon from Pueblo Bonito, may have been constructed in AD 1054, the year of the supernova. A brief dry period around AD 1060 seems only to have intensified activity in Chaco Canyon, with the absolute height of construction occurring between AD 1075 and 1085—representing an estimated 23,428 person-hours per year just at Pueblo Bonito (Metcalf 2003).

Directly identifying the shift in leadership in the latter half of the AD 1050s from transitory authority to something more permanent has proven challenging. Tantalizing clues abound, especially in the so-called burial rooms of Pueblo Bonito (see figure 11.3) (Akins 1986, 2001, 2003; Palkovich 1984; Schillaci 2003). Known details of both burial clusters are comprehensively described in Akins (2001, 2003). The four rooms of the North Burial Cluster are in the oldest section of the great house and contain the remains of twenty-four to twenty-eight individuals, mostly males but also several children. Unfortunately, because the burials were excavated in the late 1890s (Pepper 1920), associations between the human remains and the material culture are difficult to reconstruct, and the burials had been disturbed at some point in the distant past. But what is clear is that a tremendous wealth of imported material and ceremonial paraphernalia was found in these rooms, particularly accompanying two males placed in elaborately prepared burials. Reconstructions of the original stratigraphy of the rooms suggest that most individuals were interred over a number of years rather than all at once.

Like the North Burial Cluster, the West Burial Cluster consists of four adjacent rooms, in one of the older areas of Pueblo Bonito's western wing (see figure 11.3). A total of ninety-five individuals, including twenty-nine children and a small majority of adult females, was interred here (Akins 2003). Again, because the excavations occurred approximately eighty years ago, interpretation of the West Burial Cluster archaeological record is difficult. Although not exhibiting as much wealth as the burials in the North Burial Cluster, investment in the mortuary treatments still was substantial. The evidence shows that these burials also were added to the rooms over many years.

Several osteological studies indicate that the individuals interred in the two Pueblo Bonito burial clusters were generally healthier than individuals recovered elsewhere in Chaco Canyon. Comparisons of femur lengths rank

the members of the North Burial Cluster as the tallest in the canyon, followed closely by the individuals in the West Burial Cluster; individuals
recovered from non–great house burials were significantly shorter (Akins
1986). Other indicators of nutritional health and infectious disease further
reveal that the individuals from the Pueblo Bonito burial rooms enjoyed
access to superior nutrition and worked less than other Chaco Canyon residents (Akins 2003; Nelson, Kohler, and Kintigh 1994; Palkovich 1984).
Recent isotope analyses of skeletal materials suggest that individuals interred
in Pueblo Bonito enjoyed greater access to meat and less reliance on maize
than their contemporaries outside the canyon (Coltrain 2007).

Even more interesting is recent research demonstrating biological kinship among the people buried in the Pueblo Bonito burial rooms.
Statistical analyses of osteometric data conducted by Akins (1986) and
more recently by Schillaci (2003; Schillaci, Ozolins, and Windes 1998,
2001; Schillaci and Stojanowski 2003) indicate that the individuals from
each of the two burial clusters—especially the males—are more closely
related to one another than they are to the members of the other cluster.
Each burial cluster also shares some relationship with other non–great
house populations in Chaco Canyon. Whether each mortuary cluster represented the burials from a single residential group is unknown—the interments may have come from outside Pueblo Bonito and the rooms used as
mortuary chambers—but the osteological evidence indicates that the burials were of biological kin and especially of related males. The exceptional
nature of the burial rooms suggests the presence of incipient levels of
ascribed status and wealth in Chaco Canyon.

When were the interments in the North and West burial clusters made?
Researchers agree that the burial rooms were established at some point
after the rooms had served other functions, and they also agree that some
of the early pottery associated with the burials could have been "heirloom"
pieces. Clues for dating the rich mortuary rooms include the eastern orientation of the interments, a consistently later pattern throughout Chaco
Canyon (Akins 2001, 2003). The presence of many imports from Mesoamerica, including copper bells, also reflects a later date; Nelson (2006)
proposes that such imports into the canyon occurred after AD 1040.
Although far from definitive, the chronological placement of these burials
is consistent with the argument that the mid-eleventh-century climato-
logical and astronomical events contributed to the establishment of permanent, perhaps even institutionalized, religious leaders with hereditary
decision-making roles.

### The Demise of Chacoan Leadership

Perhaps because it was founded on priestly authority rather than physical control over people and resources, permanent leadership in Chaco Canyon did not last. The wealthier of the two Pueblo Bonito cemeteries, the North Burial Cluster, was centered on the interments of two adult men between twenty-five and thirty-five years of age who were buried with items such as ceremonial staffs and a shell trumpet. If we consider the establishment of permanent and hereditary leadership to have occurred after the AD 1050s and the demise of Chaco to have started with two decades of sustained drought in the AD 1080s and 1090s (see figure 11.4), then these two men may represent the temporal extent of this form of leadership. It is noteworthy that one of these two men exhibited several chop marks on his cranial bones, as well as his left thigh, indicating a violent and presumably involuntary demise (Akins 2003). Apparently, the extent of his authority could not prevent the (re)emergence of a reverse dominance hierarchy or factional competition in the face of environmental crisis. By the early AD 1100s, despite a rebound in precipitation, construction in Chaco Canyon had slowed down substantially (see figure 11.5), with new "McElmo-style" great houses requiring a fraction of the labor seen in the preceding century (Lekson 1984).

A ten-year drought beginning in AD 1130 and another beginning in AD 1145 ended the ambitions of Chaco's leaders once and for all (see figure 11.4), and although the canyon saw sporadic use for several more generations, its glory days were over. Why should its end have been so precipitous? After all, the late-eleventh-century and mid-twelfth-century droughts were not that terrible. But after the apparent excesses of the latter half of the AD 1000s, with the tremendous demands on regional labor, growing inequities in wealth, and beginnings of hereditary decision-making status, religious leaders were especially vulnerable to the reemergence of a reverse dominance hierarchy. After all, they had no control over resources or coercive power; they enjoyed religious authority promoted only by a series of unique circumstances. When deteriorating conditions challenged this authority, Chacoan leadership could not be sustained and the entire "phenomenon" collapsed like a house of cards. Particularly telling is the pattern of collapse, starting first in Chaco Canyon and then expanding into nearby communities that apparently were most directly engaged with Chaco (Kantner and Kintigh 2006). More distant communities with less direct connections to the central canyon in contrast continued to exist, almost unfazed by Chaco's ending (Kintigh 1996). Nevertheless, the struggle between aspiring leaders and cautious followers in Chaco Canyon set the foundation for the future of Puebloan leadership, and still today oral histories recount the events of the eleventh century (for example, Hegmon 2005; Kantner 2004).

## CONCLUDING THOUGHTS

As in the case study from Chaco Canyon, the emphasis of this chapter, like the others in this volume, has been on the most incipient levels of emerging differentiation in decision making. With the collective force of reverse dominance hierarchies and the leveling mechanisms that enforce them, the challenge is to explain how individuals with transitory decision-making authority could ever extend the scale and temporality of leadership. The chapters in this book have tackled the theoretically challenging and archaeologically elusive point at which this significant reversal in human relationships occurs. When the egalitarian ethos is compromised and reverse dominance hierarchies broken, the development of increasingly permanent forms of leadership—and the inequities in wealth and status that often accompany them—is not a surprising outcome, for structural power and hegemonic relationships develop much more easily when leaders can shape the ideologies that determine appropriate sociopolitical behavior. This is not to invoke neo-evolutionary explanations and suggest that leadership develops in progressive stages. In the case of the Puebloan Southwest, the Chacoan sequence did not inexorably lead to chiefs and kings, and egalitarian reactions and the likely reemergence of reverse dominance hierarchies followed the events of the eleventh century (Kantner 2006; Kintigh 1994).

The chapters in this book mostly avoid classificatory schemes, although Kusimba and Kusimba (chapter 10) do invoke the popular dual-processual theory in which two modes by which differentiation emerges—network and corporate strategies—are outlined (Blanton et al. 1996; Feinman, Lightfoot, and Upham 2000). Many criticisms of dual-processual theory have been published (for example, Adler 2002; Heitman and Plog 2005:81–84; King 2006:77–78; Yoffee 2006:400), expressing concerns that applications of the corporate and network models tend to classify societies at one extreme or the other or to see a society as changing from corporate to network strategies over time, without explaining why this should be the case. Elements of dual-processual theory are useful for answering certain questions about the past, but the chapters in this book emphasize the individual dynamics of human behavior in group settings at the archaeological moment when sociopolitical checks on authority were transcended, exactly the point at which we might be able to understand why sociopolitical competition eventually takes on the characteristics of network or corporate strategy.

This book emphasizes the role of individual decision making in the evolution of leadership. Accordingly, the focus is on the causes of increasingly centralized and permanent leadership from an emic perspective rather than on the evolutionary reasons why particular forms of leadership might persevere (for example, Roscoe 2000a) or be selected, in a sense advocated by selectionism. The majority of contributors to this volume regard agentive behavior in the face of social and structural forces as the explanatory foundation for reconstructing the development of leadership, with several of us explicitly or implicitly assuming an evolved human capacity for making calculated self-interested decisions in social settings. The fact of the matter is that we live today in a sociopolitical world characterized by great differences in decision-making power and by leadership dynamics that appear very similar everywhere. Equally true is that this situation did not emerge in one place and diffuse across the world. Instead, evolutionary trajectories guided by individual cost-benefit assessments within sociocultural contexts appear quite similar everywhere. But because individual cognition is shaped as much by cultural forces as by evolutionary history, a central theme in this book is that emic evaluations of one's place in the sociopolitical world reflect ideological concerns as much as they do evolved propensities (Kantner 2003). Only by reconciling the two positions can we fully understand how, after a million years of successfully sustained reverse dominance checks on decision-making inequity, hierarchical sociopolitical systems emerged and persevered.

# References

**Abungu, George H. O.**

1998     City States of the East African Coast and Their Maritime Contacts. *In* Transformations in Africa: Essays on Africa's Later Past. Graham Connah, ed. Pp. 204–218. Leicester, UK: Leicester University Press.

**Adams, Robert McC.**

1966     The Evolution of Urban Society. Chicago: Aldine.

**Adams, Ron L.**

2004     An Ethnoarchaeological Study of Feasting in Sulawesi, Indonesia. Journal of Anthropological Archaeology 23:56–78.

**Adler, Michael A.**

2002     Building Consensus: Tribes, Architecture, and Typology in the American Southwest. *In* The Archaeology of Tribal Societies. William A. Parkinson, ed. Pp. 155–172. Archaeological Series, 15. Ann Arbor, MI: International Monographs in Prehistory.

**Akins, Nancy J.**

1986     A Biocultural Approach to Human Burials from Chaco Canyon, New Mexico. Reports of the Chaco Center, 9. Santa Fe, NM: US Department of the Interior, National Park Service, Branch of Cultural Research.

2001     Chaco Canyon Mortuary Practices: Archaeological Correlates of Complexity. *In* Ancient Burial Practices in the American Southwest: Archaeology, Physical Anthropology, and Native American Perspectives. Douglas R. Mitchell and Judy L. Brunson-Hadley, eds. Pp. 167–190. Albuquerque: University of New Mexico Press.

2003     The Burials of Pueblo Bonito. *In* Pueblo Bonito: Center of the Chacoan World. Jill E. Neitzel, ed. Pp. 94–106. Washington, DC: Smithsonian Books.

## References

**Aldenderfer, Mark**

1991    Continuity and Change in Ceremonial Structures at Late Preceramic Asana, Southern Peru. Latin American Antiquity 2:227–258.

1993    Ritual, Hierarchy, and Change in Foraging Societies. Journal of Anthropological Archaeology 12:1–40.

2005    Preludes to Power in the Highland Late Preceramic Period. *In* The Foundations of Power in the Prehispanic Andes. K. J. Vaughn, D. E. Ogburn, and C. A. Conlee, eds. Pp. 13–35. Archeological Papers, 14. Washington, DC: American Anthropological Association.

**Allen, James de Vere**

1993    Swahili Origins: Swahili Culture and the Shungwaya Phenomenon. London: James Currey.

**Alpers, Edward A.**

1975    Ivory and Slaves in East and Central Africa. London: Heinemann.

**Alt, Susan M.**

2002    Identities, Traditions, and Diversity in Cahokia's Uplands. Midcontinental Journal of Archaeology 27:217–236.

2008    Unwilling Immigrants: Culture, Change, and the "Other" in Mississippian Societies. *In* Invisible Citizens: Slavery in Ancient Pre-State Societies. C. M. Cameron, ed. Pp. 205–222. Salt Lake City: University of Utah Press.

**Alt, Susan M., and Timothy R. Pauketat**

2007    Sex and the Southern Cult. *In* The Southeastern Ceremonial Complex. Adam King, ed. Pp. 232–250. Tuscaloosa: University of Alabama Press.

**Altman, Jon C.**

1987    Hunter-Gatherers Today: An Aboriginal Economy in North Australia. Canberra: Australian Aboriginal Studies Press.

**Ames, Kenneth M.**

1981    The Evolution of Social Ranking on the Northwest Coast of North America. American Antiquity 46:789–805.

1995    Chiefly Power and Household Production on the Northwest Coast. *In* Foundations of Social Inequality. T. Douglas Price and Gary M. Feinman, eds. Pp. 155–188. New York: Plenum.

2001    Slaves, Chiefs, and Labor on the Northern Northwest Coast. World Archaeology 33:1–17.

**Anderson, Benedict**

1983    Imagined Communities: Reflections on the Origins and Spread of Nationalism. London: Verso.

**Anderson, David G.**

1994    The Savannah River Chiefdoms: Political Change in the Late Prehistoric Southeast. Tuscaloosa: University of Alabama Press.

**Arnold, Jeanne E.**

1987     Craft Specialization in the Prehistoric Channel Islands, California. Berkeley: University of California Press.

1992     Complex Hunter-Gatherer-Fishers of Prehistoric California: Chiefs, Specialists, and Maritime Adaptations of the Channel Islands. American Antiquity 57:60–84.

1993     Labor and the Rise of Complex Hunter-Gatherers. Journal of Anthropological Archaeology 12:75–119.

1995a    Social Inequality, Marginalization, and Economic Process. *In* Foundations of Social Inequality. T. D. Price and G. M. Feinman, eds. Pp. 87–103. New York: Plenum.

1995b    Transportation Innovation and Social Complexity among Maritime Hunter-Gatherer Societies. American Anthropologist 97:733–747.

1996a    The Archaeology of Complex Hunter-Gatherers. Journal of Archaeological Method and Theory 3:77–126.

1996b    Organizational Transformations: Power and Labor among Complex Hunter-Gatherers and Other Intermediate Societies. *In* Emergent Complexity: The Evolution of Intermediate Societies. Jeanne E. Arnold, ed. Pp. 59–73. Archaeological Series, 9. Ann Arbor, MI: International Monographs in Prehistory.

2000a    The Origins of Hierarchy and the Nature of Hierarchical Structures in Prehistoric California. *In* Hierarchies in Action: Cui Bono? Michael W. Diehl, ed. Pp. 221–240. Occasional Paper, 27. Carbondale: Center for Archaeological Investigations, Southern Illinois University.

2000b    Revisiting Power, Labor Rights, and Kinship: Archaeology and Social Theory. *In* Social Theory in Archaeology. Michael B. Schiffer, ed. Pp. 14–30. Salt Lake City: University of Utah Press.

2001a    The Channel Islands Project: History, Objectives, and Methods. *In* The Origins of a Pacific Coast Chiefdom: The Chumash of the Channel Islands. Jeanne E. Arnold, ed. Pp. 21–52. Salt Lake City: University of Utah Press.

2001b    The Chumash in World and Regional Perspectives. *In* The Origins of a Pacific Coast Chiefdom: The Chumash of the Channel Islands. Jeanne E. Arnold, ed. Pp. 1–19. Salt Lake City: University of Utah Press.

2001c    Social Evolution and the Political Economy in the Northern Channel Islands. *In* The Origins of a Pacific Coast Chiefdom: The Chumash of the Channel Islands. Jeanne E. Arnold, ed. Pp. 287–296. Salt Lake City: University of Utah Press.

2007     Credit Where Credit Is Due: The History of the Chumash Oceangoing Plank Canoe. American Antiquity 72:196–209.

**Arnold, Jeanne E., ed.**

2004     Foundations of Chumash Complexity. Los Angeles: Cotsen Institute of Archaeology, University of California.

# References

**Arnold, Jeanne E., and Julienne Bernard**
2005    Negotiating the Coasts: Status and the Evolution of Boat Technology in California. World Archaeology 37:109–131.

**Arnold, Jeanne E., and Anthony P. Graesch**
2001    The Evolution of Specialized Shellworking among the Island Chumash. *In* The Origins of a Pacific Coast Chiefdom: The Chumash of the Channel Islands. Jeanne E. Arnold, ed. Pp. 71–112. Salt Lake City: University of Utah Press.

**Arnold, Jeanne E., and Terisa M. Green**
2002    Mortuary Ambiguity: The Ventureño Chumash Case. American Antiquity 67:760–771.

**Arnold, Jeanne E., and Ann Munns**
1994    Independent or Attached Specialization: The Organization of Shell Bead Production in California. Journal of Field Archaeology 21:473–489.

**Arnold, Jeanne E., Aimee M. Preziosi, and Paul Shattuck**
2001    Flaked Stone Craft Production and Exchange in Island Chumash Territory. *In* The Origins of a Pacific Coast Chiefdom: The Chumash of the Channel Islands. Jeanne E. Arnold, ed. Pp. 113–131. Salt Lake City: University of Utah Press.

**Ashmore, Wendy**
2004    Social Archaeologies of Landscape. *In* A Companion to Social Archaeology. Lynn M. Meskell and Robert W. Preucel, eds. Pp. 255–271. Oxford: Blackwell.

**Ashmore, Wendy, and Richard Wilk**
1988    House and Household in the Mesoamerican Past. *In* Household and Community in the Mesoamerican Past. R. Wilk and W. Ashmore, eds. Pp. 1–28. Albuquerque: University of New Mexico Press.

**Asombang, Raymond N.**
1999    Sacred Centers and Urbanization in West Central Africa. *In* Beyond Chiefdoms: Pathways to Complexity in Africa. S. K. McIntosh, ed. Pp. 80–87. Cambridge: Cambridge University Press.

**Axelrod, Robert**
1984    The Evolution of Cooperation. New York: Basic Books.
1997    The Complexity of Cooperation: Agent-Based Models of Competition and Cooperation. Princeton Studies in Complexity. Princeton, NJ: Princeton University Press.

**Bailey, F. G.**
2001    Treasons, Stratagems, and Spoils. Boulder, CO: Westview.

**Bailey, Garrick A.**
1995    The Osage and the Invisible World: From the Works of Francis La Flesche. Norman: University of Oklahoma Press.

**Baissa, Lemmu**

1994    Gada Values: The Building Blocks of a Democratic Policy. Journal of Oromo Studies 1:47–52.

**Ballard, Chris**

1995    The Death of a Great Land: Ritual History and Subsistence Revolution in the Southern Highlands of Papua New Guinea. Ph.D. dissertation, Australian National University.

**Barth, Fredrik**

1959    Political Leadership among Swat Pathans. London School of Economics Monographs on Social Anthropology, 19. London: Athlone Press/University of London.

1990    The Guru and the Conjurer: Transactions in Knowledge and the Shaping of Culture in Southeast Asia and Melanesia. Man, n.s., 25:640–653.

**Basgall, Mark E.**

1989    Obsidian Acquisition and Use in Prehistoric Central Eastern California: A Preliminary Assessment. *In* Current Directions in California Obsidian Studies. R. E. Hughes, ed. Pp. 111–126. Contributions of the Archaeological Research Facility, 48. Berkeley: University of California.

1999    Comments on "Environmental Imperatives Reconsidered: Demographic Crises in Western North America during the Medieval Climatic Anomaly." Current Anthropology 40:157–158.

**Basgall, Mark E., and Kelly R. McGuire**

1988    The Archaeology of CA-INY-30: Prehistoric Culture Change in the Southern Owens Valley, California. Sacramento: California Department of Transportation.

**Bawden, Garth**

2004    The Art of Moche Politics. *In* Andean Archaeology. H. Silverman, ed. Pp. 116–129. Malden, MA: Blackwell.

**Beaman, C. Philip**

2002    Why Are We Good at Detecting Cheaters? A Reply to Fodor. Cognition 83:215–220.

**Beattie, John H. M.**

1960    Bunyoro: An African Kingdom. New York: Holt, Rinehart, and Winston.

1970    The Nyoro State. Oxford: Clarendon.

**Beck, Robin A., Jr.**

2003    Consolidation and Hierarchy: Chiefdom Variability in the Mississippian Southeast. American Antiquity 68:641–661.

2006    Persuasive Politics and Domination at Cahokia and Moundville. *In* Leadership and Polity in Mississippian Society. Brian M. Butler and Paul D. Welch, eds. Pp. 19–42. Occasional Paper, 33. Carbondale: Center for Archaeological Investigations, Southern Illinois University.

# References

**Beckerman, Stephen, and Paul Valentine**

1996    On Native American Conservation and the Tragedy of the Commons. Current Anthropology 37:659–661.

**Bern, John**

1979    Ideological Domination. Oceania 50:118–132.

**Bettinger, Robert L.**

1975    The Surface Archaeology of Owens Valley, Eastern California: Prehistoric Man-land Relationships in the Great Basin. Ph.D. dissertation, University of California, Riverside.

1982    Aboriginal Exchange and Territoriality in Owens Valley, California. *In* Contexts for Prehistoric Exchange. J. E. Ericson and T. K. Earle, eds. Pp. 103–128. New York: Academic Press.

1983    Aboriginal Sociopolitical Organization in Owens Valley: Beyond the Family Band. *In* Development of Political Organization in Native North America. E. Tooker and H. M. Fried, eds. Pp. 45–58. Washington, DC: American Ethnological Society.

1989    The Archaeology of Pinyon House, Two Eagles, and Crater Midden: Three Residential Sites in Owens Valley, Inyo County, California. Anthropological Papers of the American Museum of Natural History, 67. New York: American Museum of Natural History.

1999    What Happened in the Medithermal. *In* Models for the Millennium. C. Beck, ed. Pp. 62–74. Salt Lake City: University of Utah Press.

**Bettinger, Robert L., and Martin A. Baumhoff**

1982    The Numic Spread: Great Basin Cultures in Competition. American Antiquity 47:485–503.

**Bettinger, Robert L., and Thomas F. King**

1971    Interaction and Political Organization: A Theoretical Framework for Archaeology in Owens Valley, California. Annual Reports of the University of California Archaeological Survey 13:139–150.

**Bettinger, Robert L., and R. E. Taylor**

1974    Suggested Revisions in Archaeological Sequences of the Great Basin in Interior Southern California. Nevada Archaeological Survey Research Papers 5:1–26.

**Betzig, Laura L.**

1986    Despotism and Differential Reproduction: A Darwinian View of History. New York: Aldine.

**Bird, Douglas W., and Rebecca Bliege Bird**

2004    Evolutionary and Ecological Understandings of the Economics of Desert Societies. *In* Desert Peoples: Archaeological Perspectives. P. M. Veth, M. Smith, and P. Hiscock, eds. Pp. 81–99. London: Blackwell Scientific.

2005    Martu Children's Hunting Strategies in the Western Desert, Australia. *In* Hunter-Gatherer Childhoods: Evolutionary, Developmental and Cultural

Perspectives. B. S. Hewlett and M. E. Lamb, eds. Pp. 129–146. New Brunswick, NJ: Aldine Transaction.

**Bird, Douglas W., Rebecca Bliege Bird, and Brian F. Codding**
2009    In Pursuit of Mobile Prey: Martu Hunting Strategies and Archaeofaunal Interpretation. American Antiquity 74:3–30.

**Bird, Douglas W., Rebecca Bliege Bird, and Christopher H. Parker**
2004    Women Who Hunt with Fire. Australian Aboriginal Studies 1:90–96.
2005    Aboriginal Burning Regimes and Hunting Strategies in Australia's Western Desert. Human Ecology 33:443–464.

**Black Hawk**
1994[1916]   Life of Black Hawk. Milo M. Quaife, ed. New York: Dover Publications.

**Blackburn, Thomas C., ed.**
1975    December's Child: A Book of Chumash Oral Narratives. Berkeley: University of California Press.

**Blanton, Richard**
1998    Beyond Centralization: Steps Toward a Theory of Egalitarian Behavior in Archaic States. *In* Archaic States. G. M. Feinman and J. M. Marcus, eds. Pp. 135–172. Santa Fe, NM: School of American Research Press.

**Blanton, Richard E., Gary M. Feinman, Stephen A. Kowalewski, and Peter N. Peregrine**
1996    A Dual-Processual Theory for the Evolution of Mesoamerican Civilization. Current Anthropology 37:1–14.

**Blaut, James**
1994    The Colonizers Model of the World. New York: Guilford.

**Bliege Bird, Rebecca, and Douglas W. Bird**
2005    Human Hunting Seasonality. *In* Primate Seasonality: Studies of Living and Extinct Human and Nonhuman Primates. D. Brockman and C. van Shaik, eds. Pp. 243–266. Cambridge: Cambridge University Press.
2008    Why Women Hunt: Risk and Contemporary Foraging in a Remote Aboriginal Community. Current Anthropology 49:655–693.

**Bliege Bird, Rebecca, Douglas W. Bird, Brian F. Codding, C. H. Parker, and J. Holland Jones**
2008    The "Fire Stick Farming" Hypothesis: Australian Aboriginal Foraging Strategies, Biodiversity and Anthropogenic Fire Mosaics. Proceedings of the National Academy of Science, USA 105:14796–14801.

**Bliege Bird, Rebecca, Brian F. Codding, and Douglas W. Bird**
2009    What Explains Differences in Men's and Women's Production? Determinants of Gendered Foraging Inequalities among Martu. Human Nature 20:105–129.

**Bliege Bird, Rebecca, and Eric Alden Smith**
2005    Signaling Theory, Strategic Interaction, and Symbolic Capital. Current Anthropology 46:221–248.

## REFERENCES

**Bliege Bird, Rebecca, Eric Alden Smith, and Douglas W. Bird**
2001    The Hunting Handicap: Costly Signaling in Male Foraging Strategies. Behavioral Ecology and Sociobiology 50:9–19.

**Blinman, Eric**
1989    Potluck in the Protokiva: Ceramics and Ceremonialism in Pueblo I Villages. *In* The Architecture of Social Integration in Prehistoric Pueblos. William D. Lipe and Michelle Hegmon, eds. Pp. 113–124. Occasional Paper, 1. Cortez, CO: Crow Canyon Archaeological Center.

**Blurton Jones, Nicholas G.**
1984    A Selfish Origin for Food Sharing: Tolerated Theft. Ethology and Sociobiology 5:1–3.
1987    Tolerated Theft: Suggestions about the Ecology and Evolution of Sharing, Hoarding and Scrounging. Social Science Information 26:31–54.

**Boas, Franz**
1921    Ethnology of the Kwakiutl, Based on Data Collected by George Hunt. Washington, DC: Smithsonian Institution.

**Boehm, Christopher**
1993    Egalitarian Behavior and Reverse Dominance Hierarchy. Current Anthropology 34:227–254.
1999    Hierarchy in the Forest: The Evolution of Egalitarian Behavior. Cambridge, MA: Harvard University Press.
2000    Forager Hierarchies, Innate Dispositions, and the Behavioral Reconstruction of Prehistory. *In* Hierarchies in Action: Cui Bono? Michael W. Diehl, ed. Pp. 31–58. Occasional Paper, 27. Carbondale: Center for Archaeological Investigations, Southern Illinois University.

**Boone, James L.**
1992    Competition, Conflict, and the Development of Social Hierarchies. *In* Evolutionary Ecology and Human Behavior. Eric Alden Smith and Bruce Winterhalder, eds. Pp. 301–337. New York: Aldine de Gruyter.

**Borgerhoff Mulder, Monique**
1995    Bridewealth and Its Correlates. Current Anthropology 36:573–603.

**Boster, James**
1984    Classification, Cultivation, and Selection of Aguaruna Cultivars of *Manihot esculenta (Euphorbiaceae)*. Advances in Economic Botany 1:34–47.

**Bourdieu, Pierre**
1977    Outline of a Theory of Practice. Cambridge: Cambridge University Press.

**Bowles, Samuel**
2006    Group Competition, Reproductive Leveling, and the Evolution of Human Altruism. Science 314:1569–1572.

**Bowles, Samuel, Robert Boyd, Ernst Fehr, and Herbert Gintis**
1997    Homo Reciprocans: A Research Initiative on the Origins, Dimensions, and

Policy Implications of Reciprocal Fairness. Electronic document, http://www.umass.edu/preferen/gintis/homo.pdf, accessed June 12, 2009.

**Bowles, Samuel, and Herbert Gintis**

2002 Homo Reciprocans. Nature 415:125–128.

2003a The Evolution of Cooperation in Heterogeneous Populations. Santa Fe, NM: Santa Fe Institute.

2003b Origins of Human Cooperation. *In* Genetic and Cultural Evolution of Cooperation. P. Hammerstein, ed. Pp. 429–443. Boston: MIT Press.

2008 Cooperation. *In* The New Palgrave Dictionary of Economics. 2nd edition Stephen Durlauf and Lawrence Blume, eds. Pp. 228–234. New York: Palgrave Macmillan.

**Bowser, Brenda J.**

2000 From Pottery to Politics: An Ethnoarchaeological Case Study of Political Factionalism, Ethnicity, and Domestic Pottery Style in the Ecuadorian Amazon. Journal of Archaeological Method and Theory 7:219–248.

2002 The Perceptive Potter: An Ethnoarchaeological Study of Pottery, Ethnicity, and Political Action in Amazonia. Ph.D. dissertation, University of California, Santa Barbara.

2004 The Amazonian House: A Place of Women's Pottery, Politics, and Prestige. Special issue, "Ritual Places," Expedition 46:18–23.

**Bowser, Brenda J. and John Q. Patton**

2004 Domestic Spaces as Public Places: An Ethnoarchaeological Case Study of Houses, Gender, and Politics in the Ecuadorian Amazon. Journal of Archaeological Method and Theory 11:157–181.

2008 Learning and Transmission of Pottery Style: Women's Life Histories and Communities of Practice in the Ecuadorian Amazon. *In* Cultural Transmission and Material Culture: Breaking Down Boundaries. Miriam T. Stark, Brenda J. Bowser, and Lee Horne, eds. Pp. 105–129. Tucson: University of Arizona Press.

**Boyd, Robert N., Herbert Gintis, Samuel Bowles, and Peter J. Richerson**

2003 The Evolution of Altruistic Punishment. Proceedings of the National Academy of Sciences 100:3531–3535.

**Brand-Miller, Janette, Patricia M. A. Maggiore, and Keith W. James**

1993 Tables of Composition of Australian Aboriginal Foods. Canberra: Aboriginal Studies Press.

**Brandt, Elizabeth A.**

1994 Egalitarianism, Hierarchy, and Centralization in the Pueblos. *In* The Ancient Southwestern Community. W. H. Wills and Robert D. Leonard, eds. Pp. 9–24. Albuquerque: University of New Mexico Press.

**Brennan, Paul**

1982 Communication. *In* Enga: Foundations for Development, Enga Yaaka Lasemana, 3. B. Carrad, D. Lea, and K. Talyaga, eds. Pp. 198–216. Armidale, Australia: University of New England.

## REFERENCES

**Brown, Donald E.**
1976    Principles of Social Structure. London: Duckworth.
1991    Human Universals. New York: McGraw-Hill.

**Brown, James A.**
1996    The Spiro Ceremonial Center: The Archaeology of Arkansas Valley Caddoan Culture in Eastern Oklahoma. Memoirs, 29. Ann Arbor: University of Michigan, Museum of Anthropology.
2003    The Cahokia Mound 72-Sub 1 Burials as Collective Representation. Wisconsin Archaeologist 84:83–99.
2004    The Cahokian Expression: Creating Court and Cult. *In* Hero, Hawk, and Open Hand: American Indian Art of the Ancient Midwest and South. R. F. Townsend, ed. Pp. 105–123. New Haven, CT: Art Institute of Chicago/Yale University Press.
2006    Where's the Power in Mound Building? An Eastern Woodlands Perspective. *In* Leadership and Polity in Mississippian Society. B. M. Butler and P. D. Welch, eds. Pp. 197–213. Occasional Paper, 33. Carbondale: Center for Archaeological Investigations, Southern Illinois University.

**Brown, Joseph Epes**
1989[1953]   The Sacred Pipe: Black Elk's Account of the Seven Rites of the Oglala Sioux. Norman: University of Oklahoma Press.

**Browne, David, Helaine Silverman, and Rubén García**
1993    A Cache of 48 Nasca Trophy Heads from Cerro Larapo, Peru. Latin American Antiquity 4:274–294.

**Brumfiel, Elizabeth**
1992    Distinguished Lecture in Archeology: Breaking and Entering the Ecosystem—Gender, Class, and Faction Steal the Show. American Anthropologist 94:551–567.

**Brumfiel, Elizabeth M., and Timothy K. Earle**
1987    Specialization, Exchange, and Complex Societies: An Introduction. *In* Specialization, Exchange, and Complex Societies. Elizabeth M. Brumfiel and Timothy K. Earle, eds. Pp. 1–9. Cambridge: Cambridge University Press.

**Burger, Richard L.**
1992    Chavín and the Origins of Andean Civilization. New York: Thames and Hudson.

**Butler, Brian M., and Paul D. Welch, eds.**
2006    Leadership and Polity in Mississippian Society. Occasional Paper, 33. Carbondale: Center for Archaeological Investigations, Southern Illinois University.

**Byrd, Brian F.**
2005    Reassessing the Emergence of Village Life in the Near East. Journal of Archaeological Research 13:231–290.

**Cameron, Catherine M.**

2008    Captives in Prehistory as Agents of Social Change. *In* Invisible Citizens: Captives and Their Consequences. C. M. Cameron, eds. Pp. 1–24. Salt Lake City: University of Utah Press.

**Caporael, Linnda R., Robyn M. Dawes, John M. Orbell,**
**and Alphons J. C. van de Kragt**

1989    Selfishness Examined: Cooperation in the Absence of Egoistic Incentives. Behavioral and Brain Sciences 12:683–739.

**Carlyle, Thomas**

1888    On Heroes, Hero-Worship and the Heroic in History. New York: Fredrick A. Stokes and Brother.

**Carmichael, Patrick H.**

1988    Nasca Mortuary Customs: Death and Ancient Society on the South Coast of Peru. Ph.D. dissertation, University of Calgary.

1992    Interpreting Nasca Iconography. *In* Ancient Images, Ancient Thought: The Archaeology of Ideology. Proceedings of the 23rd Annual Chacmool Conference. A. S. Goldsmith, S. Garvie, D. Selin, and J. Smit, eds. Pp. 187–197. Calgary: Department of Archaeology, University of Calgary.

1994    The Life from Death Continuum in Nasca Imagery. Andean Past 4:81–90.

1998    Nasca Ceramics: Production and Social Context. *In* Andean Ceramics: Technology, Organization, and Approaches. I. Shimada, ed. Pp. 213–231. Philadelphia: University of Pennsylvania Museum of Archaeology and Anthropology.

**Carneiro, Robert L.**

1967    On the Relationship between Size of Population and Complexity of Social Organization. Southwestern Journal of Anthropology 23:234–243.

1970    A Theory of the Origin of the State. Science 169:733–738.

1998    What Happened at the Flashpoint? Conjectures on Chiefdom Formation at the Very Moment of Conception. *In* Chiefdoms and Chieftaincy in the Americas. Elsa M. Redmond, ed. Pp. 18–42. Gainesville: University Press of Florida.

**Carr, Christopher, and D. Troy Case, eds.**

2005    Gathering Hopewell: Society, Ritual, and Ritual Interaction. New York: Kluwer Academic/Plenum.

**Carruthers, Bruce G., and Laura Ariovich**

2004    The Sociology of Property Rights. Annual Review of Sociology 30:23–46.

**Cashdan, Elizabeth A.**

1985    Coping with Risk: Reciprocity among the Basarwa of Northern Botswana. Man 20:454–474.

**Chagnon, Napoleon A.**

1990    Reproductive and Somatic Conflicts of Interest in the Genesis of Violence and Warfare among Tribesmen. *In* The Anthropology of War. Jonathan Haas, ed. Pp. 77–104. Cambridge: Cambridge University Press.

# REFERENCES

**Chalfant, Walter A.**

1933      The Story of Inyo. 2nd edition. Bishop, CA: Pinyon Bookstore.

**Chami, Felix A.**

1998      A Review of Swahili Archaeology. African Archaeological Review 15:199–218.

**Chapman, John**

2000      Fragmentation in Archaeology: People, Places and Broken Objects in the Prehistory of South-Eastern Europe. London: Routledge.

**Chávez, Sergio, and Karen L. Mohr-Chávez**

1975      A Carved Stela from Taraco, Puno, Peru and the Definition of an Early Style of Stone Sculpture from the Altiplano of Peru and Bolivia. Ñawpa Pacha 13:45–83.

**Childe, V. Gordon**

1936      Man Makes Himself. London: Watts and Co.

1942      What Happened in History. Hammondsworth, UK: Penguin.

1946      What Happened in History. New York: Penguin Books.

1951      Man Makes Himself. New York: Mentor Books.

**Clark, John E.**

1997      The Arts of Government in Early Mesoamerica. Annual Review of Anthropology 26:211–234.

2004      The Birth of Mesoamerican Metaphysics: Sedentism, Engagement, and Moral Superiority. In Rethinking Materiality: The Engagement of Mind with the Material World. E. DeMarrais, C. Gosden, and C. Renfrew, eds. Pp. 205–224. Cambridge: McDonald Institute for Archaeological Research, University of Cambridge.

**Clark, John E., and Michael Blake**

1994      The Power of Prestige: Competitive Generosity and the Emergence of Rank Societies in Lowland Mesoamerica. In Factional Competition and Political Development in the New World. E. M. Brumfiel and J. W. Fox, eds. Pp. 17–30. Cambridge: Cambridge University Press.

**Cobb, Charles R.**

1996      Specialization, Exchange, and Power in Small-Scale Societies and Chiefdoms. Research in Economic Anthropology 17:251–294.

**Coltrain, Joan Brenner**

2007      The Stable- and Radio-Isotope Chemistry of Western Basketmaker Burials: Implications for Early Puebloan Diets and Origins. American Antiquity 72:301–321.

**Conkey, Margaret, and Janet D. Spector**

1984      Archaeology and the Study of Gender. In Advances in Archaeological Method and Theory. Michael B. Schiffer, ed. Pp. 1–38. New York: Academic Press.

**Conlee, Christina A.**

2007      Decapitation and Rebirth: A Headless Burial from Nasca, Peru. Current Anthropology 48:438–445.

**Connah, Graham**

1987    African Civilizations: Precolonial Cities and States in Tropical Africa. Cambridge: Cambridge University Press.

**Cook, Anita**

1999    Asentamientos Paracas en el Valle Bajo de Ica, Perú. Gaceta Arqueológica Andina 25:61–90.

**Corbett, Ray**

2004    Chumash Bone Whistles: The Development of Ceremonial Integration in Chumash Society. *In* Foundations of Chumash Complexity. Jeanne E. Arnold, ed. Pp. 65–73. Los Angeles: Cotsen Institute of Archaeology, University of California.

**Cosmides, Leda**

1989    The Logic of Social Exchange: Has Natural Selection Shaped How Humans Reason? Studies with the Wason Selection Task. Cognition 31:187–276.

**Coupland, Gary**

2006    A Chief's House Speaks: Communicating Power on the Northern Northwest Coast. *In* Household Archaeology on the Northwest Coast. Elizabeth A. Sobel, D. Ann Trieu Gahr, and Kenneth M. Ames, eds. Pp. 80–96. Ann Arbor, MI: International Monographs in Prehistory.

**Cowgill, George L.**

2004    Origins and Development of Urbanism: Archaeological Perspectives. Annual Review of Anthropology 33:525–549.

**Crumley, Carole L.**

1987    A Dialectical Critique of Hierarchy. *In* Power Relations and State Formation. Thomas C. Patterson and C. W. Gailey, eds. Pp. 155–169. Washington, DC: American Anthropological Association.

1995    Heterarchy and the Analysis of Complex Societies. *In* Heterarchy and the Analysis of Complex Societies. R. M. Ehrenreich, C. L. Crumley, and J. E. Levy, eds. Pp. 1–5. Archeological Papers, 6. Washington, DC: American Anthropological Association.

2001    Communication, Holism, and the Evolution of Sociopolitical Complexity. *In* From Leaders to Rulers. Jonathan Haas, ed. Pp. 19–36. New York: Kluwer Academic/Plenum.

**D'Altroy, Terence N., and Timothy Earle**

1985    Staple Finance, Wealth Finance, and Storage in the Inka Political Economy. Current Anthropology 26:187–206.

**Davenport, Sue, Peter Johnson, and Yuwali**

2005    Cleared Out: First Contact in the Western Desert. Canberra: Aboriginal Studies Press.

**David, Nicholas, and Judy Sterner**

1999    Wonderful Society: The Burgess Shale Creatures, Mandara Polities, and the Nature of Prehistory. *In* Beyond Chiefdoms: Pathways to Complexity in Africa. Susan Keech McIntosh, ed. Pp. 1–30. Cambridge: Cambridge University Press.

# REFERENCES

**Dawes, Christopher T., James H. Fowler, Tim Johnson, Richard McElreath, and Oleg Smirnov**
2007      Egalitarian Motives in Humans. Nature 446:794–796.

**Dean, Jeffrey S., Robert C. Euler, George J. Gumerman, Fred Plog, R. H. Hevly, and T. N. V. Karlstrom**
1985      Human Behavior, Demography, and Paleoenvironment on the Colorado Plateaus. American Antiquity 50:537–554.

**DeLeonardis, Lisa**
1997      Paracas Settlement in Callango, Lower Ica Valley, First Millennium B.C., Peru. Ph.D. dissertation, Catholic University of America.
2000      The Body Context: Interpreting Early Nasca Decapitated Burials. Latin American Antiquity 11:363–386.

**DeMaret, Pierre**
1985a    The Smith's Myth and the Origin of Leadership in Central Africa. *In* African Ironworking: Ancient and Traditional. Randi Haaland and Peter Shinnie, eds. Pp. 73–87. Bergen, Norway: Bergen University Press.
1985b    Urban Origins in Central Africa: The Case of Kongo. *In* Comparative Study of Thirty City-State Cultures. Mogens Herman Hansen, ed. Pp. 461–482. Copenhagen: CA Reizels Forlog.

**DeMarrais, Elizabeth, Luis J. Castillo, and Timothy K. Earle**
1996      Ideology, Materialization, and Power Strategies. Current Anthropology 37:15–31.

**Diehl, Michael W.**
2000      Thoughts on the Study of Hierarchy. *In* Hierarchies in Action: Cui Bono? Michael W. Diehl, ed. Pp. 11–30. Occasional Paper, 27. Carbondale: Center for Archaeological Investigations, Southern Illinois University.

**Dietler, Michael**
1996      Feasts and Commensal Politics in the Political Economy: Food, Power, and Status in Prehistoric Europe. *In* Food and the Status Quest. P. Wiessner and W. Schiefenhovel, eds. Pp. 87–126. Providence, RI: Berghahn Books.
2001      Theorizing the Feast: Rituals of Consumption, Commensal Politics, and Power in African Contexts. *In* Feasts: Archaeological and Ethnographic Perspectives on Food, Politics, and Power. M. Dietler and B. Hayden, eds. Pp. 65–114. Washington, DC: Smithsonian Institution Press.

**Dietler, Michael, and Brian Hayden**
2001      Digesting the Feast: Good to Eat, Good to Drink, Good to Think. *In* Feasts: Archaeological and Ethnographic Perspectives on Food, Politics, and Power. M. Dietler and B. Hayden, eds. Pp. 1–20. Washington, DC: Smithsonian Institution Press.

**Dietler, Michael, and Brian Hayden, eds.**
2001      Feasts: Archaeological and Ethnographic Perspectives on Food, Politics, and Power. Washington, DC: Smithsonian Institution Press.

**Dietler, Michael, and Ingrid Herbich**
2001    Feasts and Labor Mobilization: Dissecting a Fundamental Economic Practice. *In* Feasts: Archaeological and Ethnographic Perspectives on Food, Politics, and Power. M. Dietler and B. Hayden, eds. Pp. 240–266. Washington, DC: Smithsonian Institution Press.

**Dixon, David**
2005    Never Come to Peace Again: Pontiac's Uprising and the Fate of the British Empire in North America. Norman: University of Oklahoma Press.

**Dobres, Marcia-Anne, and Christopher R. Hoffman**
1994    Social Agency and the Dynamics of Prehistoric Technology. Journal of Archaeological Method and Theory 1:211–258.

**Donley-Reid, Linda**
1990    A Structuring Structure: The Swahili House. *In* Domestic Architecture and the Use of Space: An Interdisciplinary Cross-Cultural Study. S. Kent, ed. Pp. 114–126. Cambridge: Cambridge University Press.

**Dorsey, George A.**
1997    The Pawnee Mythology. Norman: University of Oklahoma Press.

**Doxtater, Dennis**
2002    A Hypothetical Layout of Chaco Canyon Structures via Large-Scale Alignments between Significant Natural Features. Kiva 68:23–47.

**Drennan, Robert D.**
1991    Pre-Hispanic Chiefdom Trajectories in Mesoamerica, Central America and Northern South America. *In* Chiefdoms: Power, Economy, and Ideology. Timothy K. Earle, ed. Pp. 263–287. Cambridge: Cambridge University Press.

**Durand, Kathy Roler**
2003    Function of Chaco-Era Great Houses. Kiva 69:141–170.

**Dyson-Hudson, Rada, and Eric Alden Smith**
1978    Human Territoriality: An Ecological Reassessment. American Anthropologist 80:21–41.

**Earle, Timothy K.**
1978    Economic and Social Organization of a Complex Chiefdom: The Halelea District Kaua'i, Hawaii. Museum of Anthropology, University of Michigan, Anthropological Papers, 63. Ann Arbor, MI: University of Michigan.
1987    Chiefdoms in an Archaeological and Ethnohistorical Perspective. Annual Review of Anthropology 16:279–308.
1991    The Evolution of Chiefdoms. *In* Chiefdoms: Power, Economy, and Ideology. Timothy K. Earle, ed. Pp. 1–15. Cambridge: Cambridge University Press.
1997    How Chiefs Come to Power: The Political Economy in Prehistory. Stanford, CA: Stanford University Press.
2000    Archaeology, Property, and Prehistory. Annual Review of Anthropology 29:39–60.

REFERENCES

**Earle, Timothy K., ed.**
1991    Chiefdoms: Power, Economy, and Ideology. Cambridge: Cambridge University Press.

**Edmunds, R. David**
1983    The Shawnee Prophet. Norman: University of Oklahoma Press.

**Eerkens, Jelmer W.**
1999    Common Pool Resources, Buffer Zones, and Jointly Owned Territories: Hunter-Gatherer Land and Resource Tenure in Fort Irwin, Southeastern California. Human Ecology 27:297–318.

2003a    Towards a Chronology of Brownware Pottery in the Western Great Basin: A Case Study from Owens Valley. North American Archaeologist 24:1–27.

2003b    Sedentism, Storage, and the Intensification of Small Seeds: Prehistoric Developments in Owens Valley, California. North American Archaeologist 24:281–309.

2004    Privatization, Small-Seed Intensification, and the Origins of Pottery in the Western Great Basin. American Antiquity 69:653–670.

**Eerkens, Jelmer W., G. S. Herbert, J. S. Rosenthal, and H. J. Spero**
2005    Provenance Analysis of *Olivella biplicata* Shell Beads from the California and Oregon Coast by Stable Isotope Fingerprinting. Journal of Archaeological Science 32:1501–1514.

**Eerkens, Jelmer W., J. King, and E. Wohlgemuth**
2004    The Prehistoric Development of Intensive Green-Cone Piñon Processing in Eastern California. Journal of Field Archaeology 29:17–27.

**Eerkens, Jelmer W., and A. M. Spurling**
2008    Obsidian Acquisition and Exchange Networks: A Diachronic Perspective on Households in the Owens Valley. Journal of California and Great Basin Anthropology 28:111–126.

**Eerkens, Jelmer W., A. M. Spurling, and M. A. Gras**
2008    Measuring Prehistoric Mobility Strategies Based on Obsidian Geochemical and Technological Signatures in the Owens Valley, California. Journal of Archaeological Science 35:668–680.

**Ehrenreich, Robert M., Carole L. Crumley, and Janet E. Levy, eds.**
1995    Heterarchy and the Analysis of Complex Societies. Washington, DC: American Anthropological Association.

**Eibl-Eibesfeldt, Irenäus**
1989    Human Ethology. Chicago: Aldine.

**Eitel, B., S. Hecht, B. Mächtle, G. Schukraft, A. Kadereit, G. A. Wagner, B. Kromer, I. Unkel, and M. Reindel**
2005    Geoarchaeological Evidence from Desert Loess in the Nazca-Palpa Region, Southern Peru: Paleoenvironmental Changes and Their Impact on Pre-Columbian Cultures. Archaeometry 47:137–158.

**Emerson, Thomas E.**
1997    Cahokia and the Archaeology of Power. Tuscaloosa: University of Alabama Press.
2003    Materializing Cahokia Shamans. Southeastern Archaeology 22:135–154.

**Emerson, Thomas E., Randall E. Hughes, Mary R. Hynes, and Sarah U. Wisseman**
2002    Implications of Sourcing Cahokia-Style Flintclay Figures in the American Bottom and the Upper Mississippi River Valley. Midcontinental Journal of Archaeology 27:309–338.
2003    The Sourcing and Interpretation of Cahokia-Style Figurines in the Trans-Mississippi South and Southeast. American Antiquity 68:287–313.

**Emerson, Thomas E., and Timothy R. Pauketat**
2002    Embodying Power and Resistance at Cahokia. *In* The Dynamics of Power. M. O'Donovan, ed. Pp. 105–125. Occasional Paper, 30. Carbondale: Center for Archaeological Investigations, Southern Illinois University.
2008    Historical-processual Archaeology and Culture Making: Unpacking the Southern Cult and Mississippian Religion. *In* Belief in the Past: Theorizing an Archaeology of Religion. D. S. Whitley and K. Hays-Gilpin, eds. Pp. 167–188. Walnut Creek, CA: Left Coast Press.

**Engels, Frederick**
1972[1884]   The Origin of the Family, Private Property, and the State. New York: International Publishers.

**Evans-Pritchard, E. E.**
1956    The Nuer: A Description of the Modes of Livelihood and Political Institutions of Nilotic People. Oxford: Oxford University Press.

**Fadiman, Jeffrey**
1982    An Oral History of Tribal Warfare: The Meru of Mt. Kenya. Athens: Ohio University Press.

**Fagan, Brian**
2005    Chaco Canyon: Archaeologists Explore the Lives of an Ancient Society. New York: Oxford University Press.

**Fash, Barbara W., and Karla L. Davis-Salazar**
2006    Copan Water Ritual and Management: Imagery and Sacred Place. *In* Precolumbian Water Management: Ideology, Ritual, and Power. Lisa J. Lucero and Barbara W. Fash, eds. Pp. 129–152. Tucson: University of Arizona Press.

**Fattovich, Rodolfo**
1997    The Near East and Eastern Africa: Their Interaction. *In* Encyclopedia of Precolonial Africa. J. O. Vogel, ed. Pp. 479–484. Walnut Creek, CA: AltaMira.

**Fehr, Ernst, Helen Bernhard, and Bettina Rockenbach**
2008    Egalitarianism in Young Children. Nature 454:1079–1083.

**Fehr, Ernst, and Urs Fischbacher**
2003    The Nature of Human Altruism. Nature 425:785–791.

## REFERENCES

**Fehr, Ernst, and Simon Gächter**
2002    Altruistic Punishment in Humans. Nature 415:137–140.

**Fehr, Ernst, and Bettina Rockenbach**
2003    Detrimental Effects of Sanctions on Human Altruism. Nature 422:137–140.

**Fehr, Ernst, and K. Schmidt**
1999    A Theory of Fairness, Competition, and Cooperation. Quarterly Journal of Economics 114:817–868.

**Feil, Daryl K.**
1984    Ways of Exchange: The Enga Tee of Papua New Guinea. St. Lucia, Australia: University of Queensland Press.
1987    The Evolution of Highland Papua New Guinea Societies. Cambridge: Cambridge University Press.

**Feinman, Gary M.**
1995    The Emergence of Inequality: A Focus on Strategies and Processes. *In* Foundations of Social Inequality. T. D. Price and G. M. Feinman, eds. Pp. 255–280. New York: Plenum.
2001    Mesoamerican Political Complexity: The Corporate-Network Dimension. *In* From Leaders to Rulers. J. Haas, ed. Pp. 151–176. New York: Plenum.
2005    The Institutionalization of Leadership and Inequality: Integrating Process and History. *In* A Catalyst for Ideas: Anthropological Archaeology and the Legacy of Douglas W. Schwartz. Vernon L. Scarborough, ed. Pp. 101–120. Santa Fe, NM: School of American Research Press.

**Feinman, Gary M., Kent G. Lightfoot, and Steadman Upham**
2000    Political Hierarchies and Organizational Strategies in the Puebloan Southwest. American Antiquity 65:449–470.

**Feinman, Gary M., and Jill Neitzel**
1984    Too Many Types: An Overview of Sedentary Prestate Societies in the Americas. *In* Advances in Archaeological Method and Theory. Michael B. Schiffer, ed. New York: Academic Press.

**Firth, Raymond**
1936    We the Tikopia: A Sociological Study of Kinship in Primitive Polynesia. Boston: Beacon.
1959    Economics of the New Zealand Maori. Wellington, New Zealand: Government Printer.
1967    Tikopia Religion and Belief. Boston: Beacon.
1975    Primitive Polynesian Economy. New York: Norton.

**Fitzhugh, Ben**
2003    The Evolution of Complex Hunter-Gatherers: Archaeological Evidence from the North Pacific. New York: Plenum.

**Flanagan, James G.**
1989    Hierarchy in Simple "Egalitarian" Societies. Annual Review of Anthropology 18:245–266.

**Flannery, Kent V.**

1972    The Cultural Evolution of Civilizations. The Annual Review of Ecology and Systematics 3:399–426.

1976    Evolution of Complex Settlement Systems. *In* The Early Mesoamerican Village. Kent V. Flannery, ed. Pp. 162–173. New York: Academic Press.

**Flannery, Kent V., and M. C. Winter**

1976    Analyzing Household Activities. *In* The Early Mesoamerican Village. K. V. Flannery, ed. Pp. 34–47. New York: Academic Press.

**Fleisher, Jeffrey B.**

2003    Viewing Stonetowns from the Countryside: An Archaeological Approach to Swahili Regions, A.D. 800–1500. Ph.D. dissertation, University of Virginia.

**Fletcher, Alice C., and Francis La Flesche**

1992    The Omaha Tribe. Vols. 1–2. Lincoln: University of Nebraska Press.

**Folds, Ralph**

2001    Crossed Purposes: The Pintupi and Australia's Indigenous Policy. Sydney: University of New South Wales Press.

**Force, Eric R., R. Gwinn Vivian, Thomas C. Windes, and Jeffrey S. Dean**

2002    Relation of "Bonito" Paleo-Channels and Base-Level Variations to Anasazi Occupation, Chaco Canyon, New Mexico. Archaeological Series, 94. Tucson: Arizona State Museum, University of Arizona.

**Forgey, Kathleen**

2006    Investigating the Origins and Function of Nasca Trophy Heads Using Osteological and Ancient DNA Analyses. Ann Arbor, MI: University Microfilms.

**Forsbrooke, H. A.**

1960    The "Masai Walls" of Moa: Walled Towns of the Segeju. Tanganyika Notes and Records 41:30–37.

**Fortes, Mayer, and E. E. Evans-Pritchard, eds.**

1958    African Political Systems. Oxford: Oxford University Press.

**Fowler, Chris**

2004    The Archaeology of Personhood: An Anthropological Approach. London: Routledge.

**Fowler, Melvin L., Jerome Rose, Barbara Vander Leest, and Steven A. Ahler**

1999    The Mound 72 Area: Dedicated and Sacred Space in Early Cahokia. Reports of Investigations, 54. Springfield: Illinois State Museum.

**Fowles, Severin M.**

2002    Inequality and Egalitarian Rebellion, a Tribal Dialectic in Tonga History. *In* The Archaeology of Tribal Societies. William A. Parkinson, ed. Pp. 74–96. Archaeological Series, 15. Ann Arbor, MI: International Monographs in Prehistory.

**Fox, John Gerald**

1996    Playing with Power: Ballcourts and Political Ritual in Southern Mesoamerica. Current Anthropology 37:483–509.

## REFERENCES

**Frame, Mary**

2003–2004   What the Women Were Wearing: A Deposit of Early Nasca Dresses and Shawls from Cahuachi, Peru. Textile Museum Journal 42–43:13–53.

**Frangipane, Marcella**

2007   Different Types of Egalitarian Societies and the Development of Inequality in Early Mesopotamia. World Archaeology 39:151–176.

**Fried, Morton**

1967   The Evolution of Political Society: An Essay in Political Economy. New York: Random House.

**Friesen, T. Max**

2007   Hearth Rows, Hierarchies, and Arctic Hunter-Gatherers: The Construction of Equality in the Late Dorset Period. World Archaeology 39:194–214.

**Gächter, Simon, Elke Renner, and Martin Sefton**

2008   The Long-Run Benefits of Punishment. Science 322:1510.

**Gell, Alfred**

1998   Art and Agency: An Anthropological Theory. Oxford: Clarendon.

**Gezon, Lisa L.**

1999   From Adversary to Son: Political and Ecological Process in Northern Madagascar. Journal of Anthropological Research 55:71–97.

**Gibson, Jon L., and Phillip J. Carr**

2004   Signs of Power: The Rise of Cultural Complexity in the Southeast. Tuscaloosa: University of Alabama Press.

**Giddens, Anthony**

1979   Central Problems in Social Theory: Action, Structure and Contradiction in Social Analysis. Berkeley: University of California Press.

**Gillespie, Susan D.**

2001   Personhood, Agency, and Mortuary Ritual: A Case Study from the Ancient Maya. Journal of Anthropological Archaeology 20:73–112.

**Gillman, Clement**

1944   An Annotated List of Ancient and Modern Indigenous Structures in Eastern Africa. Tanganyika Notes and Records 17:44–55.

**Gilreath, A. J., and K. L. Holanda**

2000   By the Lake by the Mountains: Archaeological Investigations at CA-INY-4554 and CA-INY-1428. Davis, CA: Far Western Anthropological Research Group.

**Gintis, Herbert**

2000   Game Theory Evolving. Princeton, NJ: Princeton University Press.

**Gintis, Herbert, Samuel Bowles, Robert Boyd, and Ernst Fehr**

2003   Explaining Altruistic Behavior in Humans. Evolution and Human Behavior 24:153–172.

**Gitlow, Abraham**

1947    Economics of the Mt. Hagen Tribes, New Guinea. Seattle: University of Washington Press.

**Godelier, Maurice**

1986    The Making of Great Men: Male Dominance and Power among the New Guinea Baruya. Cambridge: Cambridge University Press.

**Godelier, Maurice, and Marilyn Strathern, eds.**

1991    Big Men and Great Men: Personifications of Power in Melanesia. Cambridge: Cambridge University Press.

**Goldstein, Paul S.**

2000    Exotic Goods and Everyday Chiefs: Long-Distance Exchange and Indigenous Sociopolitical Development in the South-Central Andes. Latin American Antiquity 11:335–361.

**Gordon, Robert, and Mervyn Meggitt**

1985    Law and Order in the New Guinea Highlands. Hanover, NH: University Press of New England.

**Gosden, Chris**

2005    What Do Objects Want? Journal of Archaeological Method and Theory 12:193–211.

**Gould, Richard**

1967    Notes on Hunting, Butchering, and Sharing of Game among the Ngatatjara and Their Neighbors in the West Australian Desert. Kroeber Anthropological Society Papers 36:41–66.

1981    Comparative Ecology of Food-Sharing in Australia and Northwest California. *In* Omnivorous Primates: Gathering and Hunting in Human Evolution. R. S. O. Harding and G. Teleki, eds. Pp. 422–454. New York: Columbia University Press.

1982    To Have and Have Not: The Ecology of Sharing among Hunter-Gatherers. *In* Resource Managers: North American and Australian Hunter-Gatherers. N. M. Williams and E. S. Hunn, eds. Pp. 69–91. Selected Symposium, 67. Washington, DC: AAAS.

**Graesch, Anthony P.**

2004    Specialized Bead Making among Island Chumash Households: Community Labor Organization during the Historic Period. *In* Foundations of Chumash Complexity. Jeanne E. Arnold, ed. Pp. 133–171. Los Angeles: Cotsen Institute of Archaeology, University of California.

**Gramsci, Antonio**

1971    Selections from the Prison Notebooks of Antonio Gramsci. Q. Hoare and G. Nowell-Smith, eds. and trans. New York: International Publishers.

**Graves, William M., and Katherine A. Spielmann**

2000    Leadership, Long-Distance Exchange, and Feasting in the Protohistoric Rio Grande. *In* Alternative Leadership Strategies in the Prehispanic Southwest. Barbara J. Mills, ed. Pp. 45–59. Tucson: University of Arizona Press.

# References

**Griffin, Arthur, and Charles Stanish**

2007    An Agent-Based Model of Prehistoric Settlement Patterns and Political Consolidation in the Lake Titicaca Basin of Peru and Bolivia. Structure and Dynamics: eJournal of Anthropological and Related Sciences 2(2), article 2. Electronic document, http://repositories.cdlib.org/imbs/socdyn/sdeas/vol2/iss2/art2/, accessed June 12, 2009.

**Grinnell, George B.**

1961    Pawnee Hero Stories and Folk-Tales. Lincoln: University of Nebraska Press.

**Grissino-Mayer, Henri D.**

1996    A 2129-Year Reconstruction of Precipitation for Northwestern New Mexico, USA. *In* Tree Rings, Environment, and Humanity. Radiocarbon 1996. J. S. Dean, D. M. Meko, and T. W. Swetnam, eds. Pp. 191–204. Tucson: Department of Geosciences, University of Arizona.

**Gumerman, George J., ed.**

1988    The Anasazi in a Changing Environment. Cambridge: Cambridge University Press.

**Guyer, Jane I.**

1995    Wealth in People, Wealth in Things—Introduction. Journal of African History 36:83–90.

**Guyer, Jane I., and S. E. Belinga**

1995    Wealth in People, as Wealth in Knowledge: Accumulation and Composition in Equatorial Africa. Journal of African History 36:91–120.

**Haas, Jonathan**

1982    The Evolution of the Prehistoric State. New York: Columbia University Press.

1990    Foreword. *In* The Evolution of Political Systems: Sociopolitics in Small-Scale Sedentary Societies. Steadman Upham, ed. Pp. xv–xvii. Cambridge: Cambridge University Press.

**Haas, Jonathan, and Winifred Creamer**

2006    Crucible of Andean Civilization: The Peruvian Coast from 3000 to 1800 B.C. Current Anthropology 47:745–775.

**Haberland, Eike**

1963    Völker Süd Äthiopiens, 2: Galla Süd Äthiopiens. Stuttgart: Kohlhamer.

**Hagan, William T.**

1993    Quanah Parker, Comanche Chief. Norman: University of Oklahoma Press.

**Haidt, Jonathan**

2007    The New Synthesis in Moral Psychology. Science 316:998–1002.

**Hakansson, N. Thomas**

1994    Grain, Cattle, and Power: Social Processes of Intensive Cultivation and Exchange in Precolonial Western Kenya. Journal of Anthropological Research 50:249–276.

1998        Rulers and Rainmakers in Precolonial South Pare, Tanzania: Exchange and
            Ritual Experts in Political Centralization. Ethnology 37:263–283.

**Hall, Martin**

1991        Farmers, Kings and Traders: The Peoples of Southern Africa, 200–1860.
            Chicago: University of Chicago Press.

**Hall, Robert L.**

1997        An Archaeology of the Soul: North American Indian Belief and Ritual. Urbana:
            University of Illinois Press.

2000        Sacrificed Foursomes and Green Corn Ceremonialism. *In* Mounds, Modoc, and
            Mesoamerica: Papers in Honor of Melvin L. Fowler. S. R. Ahler, ed. Pp.
            245–253. Scientific Papers, 28. Springfield: Illinois State Museum.

**Hardin, Garrett**

1968        The Tragedy of the Commons. Science 162:1243–1248.

**Harris, Marvin**

1985        Culture, People, Nature: An Introduction to General Anthropology. New York:
            Harper and Row.

**Harrison, Simon**

1990        Stealing People's Names: History and Politics in a Sepik River Cosmology.
            Cambridge: Cambridge University Press.

**Hassen, Mohammed**

1990        The Oromo of Ethiopia: A History of 1570–1860. Cambridge: Cambridge
            University Press.

**Hastorf, Christine**

2001        Studying Ritual in the Past. Kroeber Anthropological Society Papers 85:1–15.

2003        Community with the Ancestors: Ceremonies and Social Memory in the Middle
            Formative at Chiripa, Bolivia. Journal of Anthropological Archaeology
            22:305–332.

**Hastorf, Christine, ed.**

1999        Early Settlement at Chiripa, Bolivia: Research of the Taraco Archaeological
            Project. Contributions of the University of California Archaeological Research
            Facility, 57. Berkeley: University of California.

**Hauert, Christoph, Arne Traulsen, Hannelore Brandt, Martin A. Nowak,
and Karl Sigmund**

2007        Via Freedom to Coercion: The Emergence of Costly Punishment. Science
            316:1905–1907.

**Hawkes, Kristen**

1992        Sharing and Collective Action. *In* Evolutionary Ecology and Human Behavior.
            Eric Alden Smith and Bruce Winterhalder, eds. Pp. 269–300. New York: Aldine
            de Gruyter.

1993        Why Hunter-Gatherers Work: An Ancient Version of the Problem of Public
            Goods. Current Anthropology 34:341–361.

2000    Big Game Hunting and the Evolution of Egalitarian Societies: Lessons from
        the Hadza. *In* Hierarchies in Action: Cui Bono? M. Diehl, ed. Pp. 59–83.
        Occasional Paper, 27. Carbondale: Center for Archaeological Investigations,
        Southern Illinois University Press.

**Hawkes, Kristin, and Rebecca Bliege Bird**

2002    Showing Off, Handicap Signaling, and the Evolution of Men's Work.
        Evolutionary Anthropology 11:58–67.

**Hayden, Brian**

1995    Pathways to Power: Principles for Creating Socioeconomic Inequalities. *In*
        Foundations of Social Inequality. T. Douglas Price and Gary M. Feinman, eds.
        Pp. 15–86. New York: Plenum.

1996    Thresholds of Power in Emergent Complex Societies. *In* Emergent
        Complexity: The Evolution of Intermediate Societies. Jeanne E. Arnold, ed.
        Pp. 50–58. Archaeological Series, 6. Ann Arbor, MI: International Monographs
        in Prehistory.

1997    The Pithouses of Keatley Creek. Fort Worth, TX: Harcourt Brace.

2001    Richman, Poorman, Beggarman, Chief: The Dynamics of Social Inequality.
        *In* Archaeology at the Millennium: A Sourcebook. G. M. Feinman and
        T. D. Price, eds. Pp. 231–272. New York: Kluwer Academic.

**Hayden, Brian, and Rob Gargett**

1990    Big Man, Big Heart? A Mesoamerican View of the Emergence of Complex
        Society. Ancient Mesoamerica 1:3–20.

**Heckenberger, Michael J.**

2005    The Ecology of Power: Culture, Place, and Personhood in the Southern
        Amazon, A.D. 1000–2000. New York: Routledge.

**Hegmon, Michelle**

1991    The Risks of Sharing and Sharing as Risk Reduction: Interhousehold Food
        Sharing in Egalitarian Societies. *In* Between Bands and States. Susan A. Gregg,
        ed. Pp. 309–329. Occasional Paper, 9. Carbondale: Center for Archaeological
        Investigations, Southern Illinois University.

1996    Variability in Food Production, Strategies of Storage and Sharing, and the
        Pithouse-to-Pueblo Transition in the Northern Southwest. *In* Evolving
        Complexity and Environmental Risk in the Prehistoric Southwest. Vol. 24.
        Joseph A. Tainter and Bonnie Bagley Tainter, eds. Pp. 223–250. Reading, MA:
        Addison-Wesley.

2005    Beyond the Mold: Questions of Inequality in Southwest Villages. *In* North
        American Archaeology. Timothy R. Pauketat and Diana DiPaolo Loren, eds.
        Pp. 212–234. Malden, MA: Blackwell.

**Hegmon, Michelle, Scott G. Ortman, and Jeannette L. Mobley-Tanaka**

2000    Women, Men, and the Organization of Space. *In* Women and Men in the

Prehispanic Southwest: Labor, Power, and Prestige. Patricia L. Crown, ed. Pp. 43–90. Santa Fe, NM: School of American Research Press.

**Heitman, Carolyn, and Stephen Plog**
2005    Kinship and the Dynamics of the House: Rediscovering Dualism in the Pueblo Past. *In* A Catalyst for Ideas: Anthropological Archaeology and the Legacy of Douglas W. Schwartz. Vernon L. Scarborough, ed. Pp. 69–100. Santa Fe, NM: School of American Research Press.

**Henrich, J., R. Boyd, S. Bowles, C. Camerer, E. Fehr, H. Gintis, J. Ensminger, N. S. Henrich, K. Hill, F. Gil-White, M. Gurven, F. Marlowe, J. Patton, and D. Tracer**
2005    "Economic Man" in Cross-Cultural Perspective: Behavioral Experiments in 15 Small-Scale Societies. Behavioral and Brain Sciences 28:795–855.

**Henrich, Joseph, Richard McElreath, Abigail Barr, Jean Ensminger, Clark Barrett, Alexander Bolyanatz, Juan Camilo Cardenas, Michael Gurven, Edwins Gwako, Natalie Henrich, Carolyn Lesorogol, Frank Marlowe, David Tracer, and John Ziker**
2006    Costly Punishment across Human Societies. Science 312:1767–1770.

**Herring, Joseph B.**
1988    Kenekuk, the Kickapoo Prophet. Lawrence: University Press of Kansas.

**Herrmann, Esther, Josep Call, María Victoria Hernández-Lloreda, Brian Hare, and Michael Tomasello**
2007    Humans Have Evolved Specialized Skills of Social Cognition: The Cultural Intelligence Hypothesis. Science 317:1360–1366.

**Herskovitz, Melville J.**
1940    Economic Anthropology: The Economic Life of Primitive Peoples. New York: W. W. Norton.

**Hiatt, Lester R.**
1996    Arguments about Aborigines: Australia and the Evolution of Social Anthropology. Cambridge: Cambridge University Press.

**Hildebrandt, William R., and Kelly R. McGuire**
2002    The Ascendance of Hunting during the California Middle Archaic: An Evolutionary Perspective. American Antiquity 67:231–255.

**Hill, Kim**
1982    Hunting and Human Evolution. Journal of Human Evolution 11:521–544.

**Hobart, Mark**
1975    Orators and Patrons: Two Types of Political Leader in Balinese Village Society. *In* Political Language and Oratory in Traditional Society. Maurice Bloch, ed. Pp. 65–92. London: Academic Press.

**Hold, B.**
1976    Attention Structure and Rank Specific Behavior in Pre-school Children. *In* The Social Structure of Attention. M. Chance and R. Larsen, eds. Pp. 177–201. London: Wiley.

REFERENCES

**Hollimon, Sandra E.**
2004    The Role of Ritual Specialization in the Evolution of Prehistoric Chumash Complexity. *In* Foundations of Chumash Complexity. Jeanne E. Arnold, ed. Pp. 53–63. Perspectives in California Archaeology, 7. Los Angeles: Cotsen Institute of Archaeology, University of California.

**Horton, Mark**
1996    Shanga: The Archaeology of a Muslim Trading Community on the Coast of East Africa. Memoirs of the British Institute in Eastern Africa, 14. London: British Institute in Eastern Africa.

**Horton, Mark, and John Middleton**
2000    The Swahili: The Social Landscape of a Mercantile Society. Oxford: Blackwell.

**Howard, Harold P.**
1971    Sacajewea. Norman: University of Oklahoma Press.

**Howell, Todd L.**
1996    Identifying Leaders at Hawikku. Kiva 62:61–82.

**Hoxie, Frederick E., ed.**
1996    Encyclopedia of North American Indians. Boston: Houghton Mifflin.

**Hruschka, Daniel J., and Joseph Henrich**
2006    Friendship, Cliquishness, and the Emergence of Cooperation. Journal of Theoretical Biology 239:1–15.

**Hudson, Travis, Thomas Blackburn, Rosario Curletti, and Janice Timbrook, eds.**
1977    The Eye of the Flute: Chumash Traditional History and Ritual as Told by Fernando Librado Kitsepawit to John P. Harrington. Santa Barbara, CA: Santa Barbara Museum of Natural History.
1981    The Eye of the Flute: Chumash Traditional History and Ritual as Told by Fernando Librado Kitsepawit to John P. Harrington. 2nd edition. Banning and Santa Barbara, CA: Malki Museum Press/Santa Barbara Museum of Natural History.

**Hudson, Travis, Janice Timbrook, and Melissa Rempe, eds.**
1978    Tomol: Chumash Watercraft as Described in the Ethnographic Notes of John P. Harrington. Anthropological Papers, 9. Socorro, NM: Ballena Press/Santa Barbara Museum of Natural History.

**Hudson, Travis, and Ernest Underhay**
1978    Crystals in the Sky: An Intellectual Odyssey Involving Chumash Astronomy, Cosmology and Rock Art. Anthropological Papers, 10. Santa Barbara, CA: Ballena Press/Santa Barbara Museum of Natural History.

**Huffman, Thomas**
1996    Snakes and Crocodiles: Power and Symbolism in Ancient Zimbabwe. Johannesburg: Witwatersrand University Press.

**Hyde, George E.**
1974    The Pawnee Indians. Norman: University of Oklahoma Press.

**Inomata, Takeshi**
2003    Comment on "The Politics of Ritual, Lisa J. Lucero." Current Anthropology 44:546–547.
2006    Plazas, Performers, and Spectators: Political Theaters of the Classic Maya. Current Anthropology 47:805–842.
2007    Knowledge and Belief in Artistic Production in Classic Maya Elites. *In* Rethinking Craft Specialization in Complex Societies: Archaeological Analyses of the Social Meaning of Production. Zachary X. Hruby and Rowan K. Flad, eds. Pp. 129–142. Archaeological Papers, 17. Washington, DC: American Anthropological Association.

**Irwin, Lee**
1994    The Dream Seekers: Native American Visionary Traditions of the Great Plains. Norman: University of Oklahoma Press.

**Isaac, Glynn**
1978    The Food Sharing Behavior of Proto-human Hominids. Scientific American 238:90–108.

**Isbell, William H.**
2000    What We Should Be Studying: The "Imagined Community" and the "Natural Community." *In* The Archaeology of Communities: A New World Perspective. M. A. Canuto and J. Yaeger, eds. Pp. 243–266. London: Routledge.

**Isla Cuadrado, Johny**
1990    La Esmeralda: Una Ocupación del Período Arcáico en Cahuachi, Nasca. Gaceta Arqueológica Andina 20:67–80.

**Isla Cuadrado, Johny, and Markus Reindel**
2006    Burial Patterns and Sociopolitical Organization in Nasca 5 Society. *In* Andean Archaeology III: North and South. W. H. Isbell and H. Silverman, eds. Pp. 374–400. New York: Kluwer.

**Jackson, Jason Baird**
2003    Yuchi Ceremonial Life: Performance, Meaning, and Tradition in a Contemporary American Indian Community. Lincoln: University of Nebraska Press.

**Jackson, Kennell**
1971    An Ethnographic Study of the Oral Traditions of the Akamba. Department of Anthropology, University of Michigan. Ann Arbor: University Microfilms.

**Janusek, John**
2004    Tiwanaku and Its Precursors: Recent Research and Emerging Perspectives. Journal of Archaeological Research 12:121–183.

**Jensen, Keith, Josep Call, and Michael Tomasello**
2007    Chimpanzees Are Rational Maximizers in an Ultimatum Game. Science 318:107–109.

**Johnson, Allen, and Timothy K. Earle**
1987    The Evolution of Human Societies. Stanford, CA: Stanford University Press.

**Johnson, Gregory A.**
1978    Information Sources and the Development of Decision-Making Organizations. *In* Social Archaeology: Beyond Subsistence and Dating. C. L. Redman, M. J. Berman, E. V. Curtin, W. T. Langhorne Jr., N. M. Versaggi, and J. C. Wanser, eds. Pp. 87–112. New York: Academic Press.

**Johnson, John R.**
2001    Ethnohistoric Reflections of Cruzeño Chumash Society. *In* The Origins of a Pacific Coast Chiefdom: The Chumash of the Channel Islands. Jeanne E. Arnold, ed. Pp. 53–70. Salt Lake City: University of Utah Press.
2007    Ethnohistoric Descriptions of Chumash Warfare. *In* North American Indigenous Warfare and Ritual Violence. Richard Chacon and Ruben Mendoza, eds. Pp. 74–113. Tucson: University of Arizona Press.

**Johnson, John R., and Sally McLendon**
1999    The Nature of Chumash Social-Political Groups. *In* Cultural Affiliation and Lineal Descent of Chumash Peoples in the Channel Islands and Santa Monica Mountains. Sally McLendon and John R. Johnson, eds. Pp. 29–39. Washington, DC: National Park Service.

**Jones, Doug**
2003    The Generative Psychology of Kinship, Part 1: Cognitive Universals. Evolution and Human Behavior 24:303–319.

**Joyce, Rosemary, and Jeanne Lopiparo**
2005    Postscript: Doing Agency in Archaeology. Journal of Archaeological Method and Theory 12:365–374.

**Juma, Abdulrahman**
2004    Unguja Ukuu on Zanzibar: An Archaeological Study of Early Urbanism. Uppsala, Sweden: Department of Archaeology and Ancient History, University of Uppsala.

**Junker, Laura L.**
2001    The Evolution of Ritual Feasting Systems in Prehispanic Philippine Chiefdoms. *In* Feasts: Archaeological and Ethnographic Perspectives on Food, Politics, and Power. M. Dietler and B. Hayden, eds. Pp. 267–310. Washington, DC: Smithsonian Institution Press.

**Kaestle, Frederika A., and D. G. Smith**
1992    Ancient Native American DNA from Western Nevada: Implications for the Numic Expansion Hypothesis. American Journal of Physical Anthropology 115:1–12.

**Kan, Sergei**
1989    Symbolic Immortality: The Tlingit Potlatch of the Nineteenth Century. Washington, DC: Smithsonian Institution Press.

**Kantner, John**
1996    Political Competition among the Chaco Anasazi of the American Southwest. Journal of Anthropological Archaeology 51:41–105.

1997a     Ancient Roads, Modern Mapping: Evaluating Prehistoric Chaco Anasazi Roadways Using GIS Technology. Expedition Magazine 39:49–62.

1997b    What We Know about Chaco Anasazi Roads. Paper presented at the Chaco Virtual Conference, University of Colorado, February 9.

2002      Complexity. *In* Darwin and Archaeology: A Handbook of Key Concepts. John P. Hart and John Edward Terrell, eds. Pp. 89–106. Westport, CT: Bergin and Garvey.

2003      Biological Evolutionary Theory and Individual Decision-Making. *In* Essential Tensions in Archaeological Method and Theory. Todd L. VanPool and Christine S. VanPool, eds. Pp. 67–87. Salt Lake City: University of Utah Press.

2004      Ancient Puebloan Southwest. Cambridge: Cambridge University Press.

2006      Religious Behavior in the Post-Chaco Years. *In* Religion in the Prehispanic Southwest. Christine S. VanPool, Todd L. VanPool, and David A. Phillips Jr., eds. Pp. 31–52. Lanham, MD: AltaMira.

**Kantner, John, and Keith Kintigh**

2006      The Chaco World. *In* The Archaeology of Chaco Canyon. Stephen H. Lekson, ed. Pp. 153–188. Santa Fe, NM: School of American Research Press.

**Kaplan, Hillard, and Kim Hill**

1985      Food Sharing among Ache Foragers: Tests of Explanatory Hypotheses. Current Anthropology 26:223–245.

**Kaplan, Hillard, Kim Hill, Jane Lancaster, and A. M. Hurtado**

2000      The Evolution of Intelligence and the Human Life History. Evolutionary Anthropology 9:156–184.

**Kasfir, Sydney L.**

1992      Ivory from Zariba Country to the Land of Zinj. *In* Elephant: The Animal and Its Ivory in African Culture. D. D. Ross, ed. Pp. 309–327. Los Angeles: Fowler Museum of Cultural History.

**Keeley, Lawrence H.**

1988      Hunter-Gatherer Economic Complexity and "Population Pressure": A Cross-Cultural Analysis. Journal of Anthropological Archaeology 7:373–411.

1996      War before Civilization. New York: Oxford University Press.

**Keen, Ian**

2004      Aboriginal Economy and Society: Australia at the Threshold of Colonisation. Melbourne: Oxford University Press.

2006      Constraints on the Development of Enduring Inequalities in Late Holocene Australia. Current Anthropology 47:7–38.

**Kehoe, Alice Beck**

2002      Theaters of Power. *In* The Dynamics of Power. M. O'Donovan, ed. Pp. 259–272. Occasional Paper, 30. Carbondale: Center for Archaeological Investigations, Southern Illinois University.

2006      The Ghost Dance: Ethnohistory and Revitalization. 2nd edition. Long Grove, IL: Waveland.

**Kelekna, Pita**

1998     War and Theocracy. *In* Chiefdoms and Chieftaincy in the Americas.
         Elsa M. Redmond, ed. Pp. 164–188. Gainesville: University Press of Florida.

**Kellner, Corina A.**

2002     Coping with Environmental and Social Challenges in Prehistoric Peru:
         Bioarchaeological Analyses of Nasca Populations. Ann Arbor, MI: University
         Microfilms.

**Kelly, John E.**

1994     The Archaeology of the East St. Louis Mound Center: Past and Present.
         Illinois Archaeology 6:1–57.

2006     The Ritualization of Cahokia: The Structure and Organization of Early
         Cahokia Crafts. *In* Leadership and Polity in Mississippian Society. B. M. Butler
         and P. D. Welch, eds. Pp. 236–263. Occasional Paper, 33. Carbondale: Center
         for Archaeological Investigations, Southern Illinois University.

**Kelly, Raymond**

1993     Constructing Inequality: The Fabrication of a Hierarchy of Virtue among the
         Etoro. Ann Arbor: University of Michigan Press.

**Kelly, Robert L.**

1995     The Foraging Spectrum. Washington, DC: Smithsonian Institution Press.

**King, Adam**

2003     Etowah: The Political History of a Chiefdom Capital. Tuscaloosa: University of
         Alabama Press.

2004     Power and the Sacred: Mound C and the Etowah Chiefdom. *In* Hero, Hawk,
         and Open Hand: American Indian Art of the Ancient Midwest and South.
         R. F. Townsend, ed. Pp. 151–166. New Haven, CT: Art Institute of Chicago/
         Yale University Press.

2006     Leadership Strategies and the Nature of Mississippian Chiefdoms in Northern
         Georgia. *In* Leadership and Polity in Mississippian Society. Brian M. Butler and
         Paul D. Welch, eds. Pp. 73–90. Occasional Paper, 33. Carbondale: Center for
         Archaeological Investigations, Southern Illinois University.

**Kintigh, Keith W.**

1994     Chaco, Communal Architecture, and Cibolan Aggregation. *In* The Ancient
         Southwestern Community. W. H. Wills and Robert D. Leonard, eds. Pp.
         131–140. Albuquerque: University of New Mexico Press.

1996     The Cibola Region in the Post-Chacoan Era. *In* The Prehistoric Pueblo World,
         A.D. 1150–1350. Michael A. Adler, ed. Pp. 131–144. Tucson: University of
         Arizona Press.

**Kirch, Patrick V.**

2001     Polynesian Feasting in Ethnohistoric, Ethnographic, and Archaeological
         Contexts: A Comparison of Three Societies. *In* Feasts: Archaeological and
         Ethnographic Perspectives on Food, Politics, and Power. Michael Dietler and

Brian Hayden, eds. Pp. 168–184. Washington, DC: Smithsonian Institution Press.

**Klarich, Elizabeth**

2005    From the Monumental to the Mundane: Defining Early Leadership Strategies at Lat Formative Pukara, Peru. Ph.D. dissertation, University of California, Santa Barbara.

**Knappett, Carl, and Lambros Malafouris**

2008    Material and Nonhuman Agency: An Introduction. *In* Material Agency: Towards a Non-anthropocentric Approach. Carl Knappett and Lambros Malafouris, eds. Pp. ix–xix. New York: Springer.

**Knauft, Bruce**

1991    Violence and Sociality in Human Evolution. Current Anthropology 32:391–428.

**Knutsson, Karl Eric**

1967    Authority and Change: A Study of the Kallu Institution among the Macha Galla of Ethiopia. Göteborg: Ethnografiska Museet.

**Kohler, Timothy A., Matthew W. Van Pelt, and Lorene Y. L. Yap**

2000    Reciprocity and Its Limits: Considerations for a Study of the Prehispanic Pueblo World. *In* Alternative Leadership Strategies in the Prehispanic Southwest. Barbara J. Mills, ed. Pp. 180–206. Tucson: University of Arizona Press.

**Kopytoff, Igor**

1965    The Suku of Southern Congo. *In* Peoples of Africa. J. Gibbs, ed. Pp. 441–447. New York: Holt, Rinehart, and Winston.

1999    Permutations in Patrimonialism and Populism: The Aghem Chiefdoms of Western Cameroon. *In* Beyond Chiefdoms: Pathways to Complexity in Africa. S. K. McIntosh, ed. Pp. 88–96. Cambridge: Cambridge University Press.

**Kristiansen, Kristian**

1991    Chiefdoms, States, and Systems of Social Evolution. *In* Chiefdoms: Power, Economy, and Ideology. T. K. Earle, ed. Pp. 16–43. Cambridge: Cambridge University Press.

**Kuijt, Ian, and Nigel Goring-Morris**

2002    Foraging, Farming, and Social Complexity in the Pre-pottery Neolithic of the Southern Levant: A Review and Synthesis. Journal of World Prehistory 16:361–439.

**Kunen, Julie L.**

2006    Water Management, Ritual, and Community in Tropical Complex Societies. *In* Precolumbian Water Management: Ideology, Ritual, and Power. Lisa J. Lucero and Barbara W. Fash, eds. Pp. 100–115. Tucson: University of Arizona Press.

**Kusimba, Chapurukha M.**

1996    The Social Context of Iron-Forging on the Kenya Coast. Africa 66:386–410.

1999a    The Rise and Fall of Swahili States. Walnut Creek, CA: AltaMira.

1999b    The Rise of Elites among the Precolonial Swahili of the East African Coast. *In* Material Symbols in Prehistory. John Robb, ed. Pp. 318–341. Carbondale: Southern Illinois University Press.

2004    Archaeology of Slavery in East Africa. African Archaeological Review 21:59–88.

**Kusimba, Chapurukha M., and Sibel B. Kusimba**

1999    Regional Trends Towards Social Complexity in Eastern and Southern Africa. Paper presented at the Sixty-Fourth Society for American Archaeology Annual Meeting, Chicago, March 25.

2005    Mosaics and Interactions: East Africa, 2000 B.P. to the Present. *In* African Archaeology. A. B. Stahl, ed. Pp. 392–419. Oxford: Blackwell.

**Kusimba, Sibel B., and Chapurukha M. Kusimba**

2007    17th–19th Century Walled Villages among Luyia-Speaking Communities of Western Kenya: Architectural Features of Leadership. Paper presented at the Annual Meeting of the African Studies Association, New York City, October 19.

**Kyakas, Alome, and Polly Wiessner**

1992    From Inside the Women's House: Enga Women's Lives and Traditions. Brisbane, Australia: Robert Brown.

**Lacey, Roderic**

1975    Oral Traditions as History: An Exploration of Oral Sources among the Enga of the New Guinea Highlands. Ph.D. thesis, University of Wisconsin.

1979    Holders of the Way: A Study of Precolonial Socio-economic History in Papua New Guinea. Journal of the Polynesian Society 88:277–325.

**Lambers, Karsten**

2006    The Geoglyphs of Palpa, Peru: Documentation, Analysis, and Interpretation. Bonn, Germany: Forschungen zur Archäologie AuBereuropáischer Kulturen.

**Latour, Bruno**

1999    Pandora's Hope: Essays on the Reality of Science Studies. Cambridge, MA: Harvard University Press.

2005    Reassembling the Social: An Introduction to Actor-Network Theory. Oxford: Oxford University Press.

**LaViolette, Adria, and Jeffrey B. Fleisher**

2005    The Archaeology of Sub-Saharan Urbanism: Cities and Their Countryside. *In* African Archaeology. Ann B. Stahl, ed. Pp. 327–352. Oxford: Blackwell.

**Lawton, Harry W., Philip J. Wilke, Mary DeDecker, and William M. Mason**

1976    Agriculture among the Paiute of Owens Valley. Journal of California Anthropology 3:13–50.

**LeCount, Lisa J.**

2001    Like Water for Chocolate: Feasting and Political Ritual among the Late Classic Maya at Xunantunich, Belize. American Anthropologist 103:935–953.

**Lederman, Rena**

1986    What Gifts Engender. Social Relations and Politics in Mendi, Highlands Papua New Guinea. Cambridge: Cambridge University Press.

1990    Big Men Large and Small? Towards a Comparative Perspective. Ethnology
        29:3–15.

**Lee, Richard B.**
1993    The Dobe Ju/'hoansi. New York: Harcourt Brace.

**Legesse, Asmarom**
1973    Gada: The Study of African Society. New York: Free Press.

**Lekson, Stephen H.**
1984    Great Pueblo Architecture of Chaco Canyon. Publications in Archaeology, 18B.
        Albuquerque, NM: National Park Service.
1999    The Chaco Meridian: Centers of Political Power in the Ancient Southwest.
        Walnut Creek, CA: AltaMira.
2005    Chaco and Paquimé: Complexity, History, Landscape. *In* North American
        Archaeology. Timothy R. Pauketat and Diana DiPaolo Loren, eds. Pp. 235–272.
        Malden, MA: Blackwell.
2006    The Archaeology of Chaco Canyon: An Eleventh-Century Pueblo Regional
        Center. Santa Fe, NM: School of American Research Press.

**Lekson, Stephen H., Thomas C. Windes, and Peter J. McKenna**
2006    Architecture. *In* The Archaeology of Chaco Canyon: An Eleventh-Century
        Pueblo Regional Center. Stephen H. Lekson, ed. Pp. 67–116. Santa Fe, NM:
        School of American Research Press.

**Lewis, Herbert S.**
1965    The Origins of the Galla and Somali. Journal of African History 7:27–46.

**Li, H. C., J. L. Bischoff, T. L. Ku, S. P. Lund, and L. D. Stott**
2000    Climate Variability in East-Central California during the Past 1000 Years
        Reflected by High-Resolution Geochemical and Isotopic Records from Owens
        Lake Sediments. Quaternary Research 54:189–197.

**Lightfoot, Kent G.**
1983    Resource Uncertainty and Buffering Strategies in an Arid, Marginal
        Environment. *In* Ecological Models in Economic Prehistory. Gordon Bronitsky,
        ed. Pp. 189–218. Anthropological Research Papers, 29. Phoenix: Arizona State
        University.

**Lightfoot, Kent G., and Gary M. Feinman**
1982    Social Differentiation and Leadership Development in Early Pithouse Villages
        in the Mogollon Region of the American Southwest. American Antiquity
        47:64–86.

**Linderman, Frank B.**
2002[1930]   Plenty-Coups: Chief of the Crow. Lincoln: University of Nebraska Press.

**Lovejoy, Owen**
1981    The Origin of Man. Science 211:341–350.

**Low, Bobbi S.**
1992    Sex, Coalitions, and Politics in Preindustrial Societies. Politics and the Life
        Sciences 11:63–80.

## REFERENCES

**Lucero, Lisa**

2003    The Politics of Ritual: The Emergence of Classic Maya Rulers. Current
        Anthropology 44:523–558.

2006    The Political and Sacred Power of Water in Classic Maya Society. *In*
        Precolumbian Water Management: Ideology, Ritual, and Power. Lisa J. Lucero
        and Barbara W. Fash, eds. Pp. 116–128. Tucson: University of Arizona Press.

**Mair, Lucy**

1961    Primitive Government. Baltimore: Penguin Books.

**Makila, F. E.**

1978    An Outline History of the Babukusu of Western Kenya. Nairobi: Kenya
        Literature Bureau.

**Malinowski, Bronislaw**

1961[1922]   Argonauts of the Western Pacific. New York: E. P. Dutton.

1984[1922]   Argonauts of the Western Pacific. Prospect Heights, IL: Waveland.

**Malville, J. McKim**

1994    Astronomy and Social Integration among the Anasazi. *In* Proceedings of the
        Anasazi Symposium 1991. Art Hutchinson and Jack E. Smith, eds. Pp. 149–164.
        Cortez, CO: Mesa Verde Museum Association.

**Malville, J. McKim, and Claudia Putnam**

1993    Prehistoric Astronomy in the Southwest. 2nd edition. Boulder, CO: Johnson
        Printing Company.

**Mann, Michael**

1993    The Sources of Social Power: A History of Power from the Beginning to A.D.
        1760. Cambridge: Cambridge University Press.

**Marquardt, William H.**

1988    Politics and Production among the Calusa of South Florida. *In* Hunters and
        Gatherers I: History, Evolution, and Social Change. Tim Ingold, David Riches,
        and James Woodburn, eds. Pp. 161–188. Oxford: Berg.

**Martin, M. Kay, and Barbara Voorhies**

1975    Female of the Species. New York: Columbia University Press.

**Martindale, Andrew**

2006    Tsimshian Houses through the Contact Period. *In* Household Archaeology
        on the Northwest Coast. Elizabeth A. Sobel, D. Ann Trieu Gahr, and
        Kenneth M. Ames, eds. Pp. 140–158. Ann Arbor, MI: International
        Monographs in Prehistory.

**Maschner, Herbert D. G., and John Q. Patton**

1996    Kin Selection and the Origins of Hereditary Social Inequality: A Case Study
        from the Northern Northwest Coast. *In* Darwinian Archaeologies.
        Herbert D. G. Maschner, ed. Pp. 89–108. New York: Plenum.

**Mathien, Frances Joan**

2005    Culture and Ecology of Chaco Canyon and the San Juan Basin. Publications in

Archeology, Chaco Canyon Studies, 18H. Santa Fe, NM: US Department of the Interior, National Park Service.

**Mauss, Marcel**
1924    The Gift: Forms and Functions of Exchange in Archaic Societies. London: Cohen and West.

**Mawe, Theodore**
1985    Mendi Culture and Tradition: A Recent Survey. National Museum Record no. 10. Port Moresby, Papua New Guinea: PNG.

**McAnany, Patricia A.**
2001    Cosmology and the Institutionalization of Hierarchy in the Maya Region. *In* From Leaders to Rulers. Jonathan Haas, ed. Pp. 125–150. New York: Kluwer Academic/Plenum.

2004    Appropriative Economies: Labor Obligations and Luxury Goods in Ancient Maya Societies. *In* Archaeological Perspectives on Political Economies. Gary M. Feinman and Linda M. Nicholas, eds. Pp. 145–166. Salt Lake City: University of Utah Press.

**McCleary, Timothy P.**
1997    The Stars We Know: Crow Indian Astronomy and Lifeways. Prospect Heights, IL: Waveland.

**McGee, W. J.**
1897    The Siouan Indians: A Preliminary Sketch. *In* Fifteenth Annual Report of the Bureau of American Ethnology. Pp. 153–204. Washington, DC: Government Printing Office.

**McGuire, Kelly, and William Hildebrandt**
2005    Re-thinking Great Basin Foragers: Prestige Hunting and Costly Signaling during the Middle Archaic Period. American Antiquity 70:695–712.

**McIntosh, Roderick**
1998    The Peoples of the Middle Niger. Oxford: Blackwell.

**McIntosh, Susan Keech**
1999a   Pathways to Complexity: An African Perspective. *In* Beyond Chiefdoms: Pathways to Complexity in Africa. Susan Keech McIntosh, ed. Pp. 1–30. Cambridge: Cambridge University Press.

**McIntosh, Susan Keech, ed.**
1999b   Beyond Chiefdoms: Pathways to Complexity in Africa. Cambridge: Cambridge University Press.

**McKenna, Peter J., and Marcia L. Truell**
1986    Small Site Architecture of Chaco Canyon, New Mexico. Publications in Archeology, Chaco Canyon Studies, 18D. Santa Fe, NM: US Department of the Interior, National Park Service.

**McNaughton, Patrick**
1988    The Mande Blacksmiths: Knowledge, Power and Art in West Africa. Bloomington: Indiana University Press.

# REFERENCES

**Meggitt, Mervyn**

1962    Desert People: A Study of the Walbiri Aborigines of Central Australia. Chicago: University of Chicago Press.

1965    The Lineage System of the Mae-Enga of New Guinea. New York: Barnes and Noble.

1972    System and Sub-system: The "Te" Exchange Cycle among the Mae Enga. Human Ecology 1:111–123.

1977    Blood Is Their Argument. Palo Alto, CA: Mayfield.

**Menzel, Dorothy, John H. Rowe, and Lawrence E. Dawson**

1964    The Paracas Pottery of Ica: A Study of Style and Time. University of California Publications in American Archaeology and Ethnology, 50. Berkeley: University of California Press.

**Meskell, Lynn**

2004    Object Worlds in Ancient Egypt: Material Biographies Past and Present. Oxford: Berg.

**Metcalf, Mary P.**

2003    Construction Labor at Pueblo Bonito. *In* Pueblo Bonito: Center of the Chacoan World. Jill E. Neitzel, ed. Pp. 72–79. Washington, DC: Smithsonian Books.

**Middleton, John**

1992    The World of the Swahili: An African Mercantile Civilization. New Haven, CT: Yale University Press.

2004    African Merchants of the Indian Ocean: Swahili of the East African Coast. Long Grove, IL: Waveland.

**Millinski, Manfred, Dirk Semmann, and Hans-Jürgen Krambeck**

2002    Reputation Helps Solve the "Tragedy of the Commons." Nature 415:424–426.

**Mills, Barbara J.**

2000    Alternative Models, Alternative Strategies: Leadership in the Prehispanic Southwest. *In* Alternative Leadership Strategies in the Prehispanic Southwest. Barbara J. Mills, ed. Pp. 3–18. Tucson: University of Arizona Press.

2007    Performing the Feast: Visual Display and Suprahousehold Commensalism in the Puebloan Southwest. American Antiquity 72:210–239.

**Milner, George R.**

2005    The Moundbuilders: Ancient Peoples of Eastern North America. Oxford: Thames and Hudson.

**Mitchell, Peter**

2005    African Connections: Archaeological Perspectives on Africa and the Wider World. Walnut Creek, CA: AltaMira.

**Mobley-Tanaka, Jeannette L.**

1997    Gender and Ritual Space during the Pithouse to Pueblo Transition: Subterranean Mealing Rooms in the North American Southwest. American Antiquity 62:437–448.

**Mooney, James**
1896       The Ghost-Dance Religion and the Sioux Outbreak of 1890. *In* Fourteenth
           Annual Report of the Bureau of American Ethnology, part 2. Washington, DC:
           Bureau of American Ethnology.
1973       The Ghost-Dance Religion and Wounded Knee. New York: Dover Publications.

**Muller, Jon**
1997       Mississippian Political Economy. New York: Plenum.

**Mutoro, Henry W.**
1998       Precolonial Trading Systems of the East African Interior. *In* Transformations in
           Africa: Essays on Africa's Later Past. G. Connah ed. Pp. 186–203. Leicester, UK:
           Leicester University Press.

**Myers, Fred R.**
1986       Pintupi Country, Pintupi Self. Canberra: Australian Institute of Aboriginal
           Studies; Washington, DC: Smithsonian Institution Press.
1988       Burning the Truck and Holding the Country: Property, Time and the
           Negotiation of Identity among Pintupi Aborigines. *In* Hunters and Gatherers,
           vol. 2: Property, Power and Ideology. T. Ingold, D. Riches, and J. Woodburn,
           eds. Pp. 52–74. New York: Berg.

**Mytton, James W., and Gary B. Schneider**
1987       Interpretive Geology of the Chaco Area, Northwestern New Mexico.
           Miscellaneous Investigation Series. Washington, DC: US Geological Survey.

**Neitzel, Jill E.**
2000       Gender Hierarchies: A Comparative Analysis of Mortuary Data. *In* Women and
           Men in the Prehispanic Southwest: Labor, Power, and Prestige. Patricia L.
           Crown, ed. Pp. 137–168. Santa Fe, NM: School of American Research Press.

**Nelson, Ben A.**
2006       Mesoamerican Objects and Symbols in Chaco Canyon Contexts. *In* The Archae-
           ology of Chaco Canyon: An Eleventh-Century Pueblo Regional Center. Stephen
           H. Lekson, ed. Pp. 339–371. Santa Fe, NM: School of American Research Press.

**Nelson, Ben A., Timothy A. Kohler, and Keith W. Kintigh**
1994       Demographic Alternatives: Consequences for Current Models of Southwestern
           Prehistory. *In* Understanding Complexity in the Prehistoric Southwest. George
           J. Gumerman and Murray Gell-Mann, eds. Pp. 113–146. Santa Fe Institute
           Studies in the Sciences of Complexity Proceedings, 16. Reading, MA: Addison-
           Wesley.

**Nelson, Sarah Milledge**
2004       Gender in Archaeology: Analyzing Power and Prestige. 2nd edition. Walnut
           Creek, CA: AltaMira.

**Nicholls, Christine S.**
1971       Swahili Coast: Politics, Diplomacy and Trade on the African Littoral
           (1798–1856). London: George Allen and Unwin Limited.

Nichols, Deborah L., Charles D. Frederick, Luis Morett Alatorre,
and Fernando Sánchez Martínez
2006    Water Management and Political Economy in Formative Period Central
Mexico. *In* Precolumbian Water Management: Ideology, Ritual, and Power.
Lisa J. Lucero and Barbara W. Fash, eds. Pp. 51–66. Tucson: University of
Arizona Press.

Noah, Anna C.
2005    Household Economies: The Role of Animals in a Historic Period Chiefdom on
the California Coast. Ph.D. dissertation, University of California, Los Angeles.

Norenzayan, Ara, and Azim F. Shariff
2008    The Origin and Evolution of Prosociality. Science 322:62–66.

North, Douglass C.
1990    Institutions, Institutional Change, and Economic Performance. Cambridge:
Cambridge University Press.

Nowak, Martin A., K. Page, and Karl Sigmund
2000    Fairness versus Reason in the Ultimatum Game. Science 289:1773–1775.

Nowak, Martin A., and Karl Sigmund
2005    Evolution of Indirect Reciprocity. Nature 437:1291–1298.

Nurse, Derek, and Thomas Spear
1985    The Swahili: Reconstructing the History and Language of an African Society.
Philadelphia: University of Pennsylvania Press.

O'Connell, James F., and Brendan Marshall
1989    Analysis of Kangaroo Body Part Transport among the Alyawara of Central
Australia. Journal of Archaeological Science 16:393–405.

O'Donovan, Maria, ed.
2002    The Dynamics of Power. Occasional Paper, 30. Carbondale: Center for
Archaeological Investigations, Southern Illinois University.

Oka, Rahul, and Chapurukha Kusimba
2008    The Archaeology of Trading Systems, Part 1: Towards a New Trade Synthesis.
Journal of Archaeological Research 16:339–395.

Oliver, Douglas
1949    Studies in the Anthropology of Bougainville, Solomon Islands. Papers of the
Peabody Museum of American Archaeology and Ethnology, vol. 29, nos. 1–4.
Cambridge, MA: Harvard University.

Onjala, Isaiah
2003    Spatial Distribution and Settlement System of the Stone Structures of South-
Western Kenya. Azania 38:99–120.

Orefici, Giuseppe
1988    Una Expresión de Arquitectura Monumental Paracas-Nasca: El Templo de
Escalonado de Cahuachi. *In* Atti Convegno Internazionale: Archeologia,

Scienza y Societa nell'America Precolombina. Pp. 191–201. Brescia, Italy: Centro Italiano Studi e Richerche Archeologiche Precolombiane.

1993     Nasca: Arte e Societa del Popolo Dei Geoglifi. Milan: Jaca.

**Orefici, Giuseppe, and Andrea Drusini**

2003     Nasca, Hipótesis y Evidencias de su Desarrollo Cultural. Documentos e Investigaciones 2. Lima, Peru: Centro Italiano Studi e Ricerche Archeologiche Precolombiane.

**Ortner, Sherry**

1984     Theory in Anthropology since the Sixties. Comparative Studies in Society and History 26:126–166.

**Osogo, John**

1966     A History of the Baluyia. London: Oxford University Press.

**Ostrom, Elinor**

1998     A Behavioral Approach to the Rational Choice Theory of Collective Action: Presidential Address, American Political Science Association, 1997. American Political Science Review 92:1–23.

**Palkovich, Ann M.**

1984     Disease and Mortality Patterns in the Burial Rooms of Pueblo Bonito: Preliminary Considerations. *In* Recent Research on Chaco Prehistory. W. James Judge and John D. Schelberg, eds. Pp. 103–113. Reports of the Chaco Center, 8. Albuquerque, NM: National Park Service, Division of Cultural Research.

**Panchanathan, Karthik, and Robert Boyd**

2004     Indirect Reciprocity Can Stabilize Cooperation without the Second-Order Free Rider Problem. Nature 432:499–502.

**Passes, Alan**

2004     The Place of Politics: Powerful Speech and Women Speakers in Everyday Pa'ikwené (Palikur) Life. Journal of the Royal Anthropological Institute 10:1–18.

**Patton, John Q.**

1996     Thoughtful Warriors: Status, Warriorship, and Alliance in the Ecuadorian Amazon. Ph.D. dissertation, University of California, Santa Barbara.

2000     Reciprocal Altruism and Warfare: A Case from the Ecuadorian Amazon. *In* Human Behavior and Adaptation: An Anthropological Perspective. Napoleon L. Chagnon, Lee Cronk, and William Irons, eds. Pp. 417–436. New York: Aldine de Gruyter.

2004     Coalitional Effects on Reciprocal Fairness in the Ultimatum Game: A Case from the Ecuadorian Amazon. *In* Foundation of Human Sociality: Economic Experiments and Ethnographic Evidence from Fifteen Small-Scale Societies. Joseph Henrich, Robert Boyd, Samuel Bowles, Herbert Gintis, Colin Camerer, and Ernst Fehr, eds. Pp. 96–124. Oxford: Oxford University Press.

## REFERENCES

2005     Meat Sharing for Coalitional Support. Evolution and Human Behavior 26:137–157.

**Pauketat, Timothy R.**

1994     The Ascent of Chiefs: Cahokia and Mississippian Politics in Native North America. Tuscaloosa: University of Alabama Press.

1996     The Foundations of Inequality within a Simulated Shan Community. Journal of Anthropological Archaeology 15:219–236.

1998     Refiguring the Archaeology of Greater Cahokia. Journal of Archaeological Research 6:45–89.

2000a    Politicization and Community in the Pre-Columbian Mississippi Valley. *In* The Archaeology of Communities: A New World Perspective. M. A. Canuto and J. Yaeger, eds. Pp. 16–43. London: Routledge.

2000b    The Tragedy of the Commoners. *In* Agency in Archaeology. M.-A. Dobres and J. Robb, eds. Pp. 113–129. London: Routledge.

2001a    A New Tradition in Archaeology. *In* The Archaeology of Traditions: Agency and History Before and After Columbus. T. Pauketat, ed. Pp. 1–16. Gainesville: University Press of Florida.

2001b    Practice and History in Archaeology: An Emerging Paradigm. Anthropological Theory 1:73–98.

2004a    Ancient Cahokia and the Mississippians. Cambridge: Cambridge University Press.

2004b    The Economy of the Moment: Cultural Practices and Mississippian Chiefdoms. *In* Archaeological Perspectives on Political Economies. Gary M. Feinman and Linda M. Nicholas, eds. Pp. 25–40. Salt Lake City: University of Utah Press.

2005     The Forgotten History of the Mississippians. *In* North American Archaeology. Timothy R. Pauketat and Diana D. Loren, eds. Pp. 187–212. Oxford: Blackwell.

2006     Missing Persons: Ridge-Top Mound Spectacle and the Agency of Audiences. Paper presented at the 63rd Southeastern Archaeological Conference, Little Rock, AR, November 8–12.

2007     Chiefdoms and Other Archaeological Delusions. Walnut Creek, CA: AltaMira.

2008a    Founders' Cults and the Archaeology of *Wa-kan-da*. *In* Memory Work: Archaeologies of Material Practice. Barbara Mills and William Walker, eds. Pp. 61–80. Santa Fe, NM: School for Advanced Research Press.

2008b    The Grounds for Agency in Southwestern Archaeology. *In* The Social Construction of Communities: Agency, Structure, and Identity in the Prehispanic Southwest. Mark D. Varien and James M. Potter, eds. Pp. 233–250. Walnut Creek, CA: AltaMira.

**Pauketat, Timothy R., and Susan M. Alt**

2003     Mounds, Memory, and Contested Mississippian History. *In* Archaeologies of Memory. Ruth Van Dyke and Susan Alcock, eds. Pp. 149–179. Oxford: Blackwell.

2005     Agency in a Postmold? Physicality and the Archaeology of Culture-Making. Journal of Archaeological Method and Theory 12:213–236.

**Pauketat, Timothy, and T. Emerson**

1999    The Representation of Hegemony as Community at Cahokia. *In* Material Symbols: Culture and Economy in Prehistory. John E. Robb, ed. Pp. 302–317. Occasional Paper, 26. Carbondale: Center for Archaeological Investigations, Southern Illinois University.

**Pauketat, Timothy R., and Thomas E. Emerson, eds.**

1997    Cahokia: Ideology and Domination in the Mississippian World. Lincoln: University of Nebraska Press.

**Paul, Anne**

1990    Paracas Ritual Attire: Symbols of Authority in Ancient Peru. Norman: University of Oklahoma Press.

**Paynter, Robert**

1989    The Archaeology of Equality and Inequality. Annual Review of Anthropology 18:369–399.

**Pearson, Michael N.**

1998    Port Cities and Intruders: The Swahili Coast, India, and Portugal in the Early Modern Era. Baltimore: Johns Hopkins University Press.

**Peebles, Christopher S., and Susan M. Kus**

1977    Some Archaeological Correlates of Ranked Societies. American Antiquity 42:421–447.

**Penney, David W.**

2004    The Archaeology of Aesthetics. *In* Hero, Hawk, and Open Hand: American Indian Art of the Ancient Midwest and South. Richard F. Townsend, ed. Pp. 43–55. New Haven, CT: Chicago Art Institute/Yale University Press.

**Pepper, George H.**

1920    Pueblo Bonito. Anthropological Papers, 27. New York: American Museum of Natural History.

**Peregrine, Peter**

1991    Some Political Aspects of Craft Specialization. World Archaeology 23:1–11.

**Perham, Margery**

1979    East African Journey: Kenya and Tanganyika 1929–30. London: Faber and Faber.

**Perodie, James R.**

2001    Feasting for Prosperity: A Study of Southern Northwest Coast Feasting. *In* Feasts: Archaeological and Ethnographic Perspectives on Food, Politics, and Power. M. Dietler and B. Hayden, eds. Pp. 185–214. Washington, DC: Smithsonian Institution Press.

**Petersen, Kenneth Lee**

1987    Reconstruction of Droughts for the Dolores Project Area Using Tree-Ring Studies. *In* Dolores Archaeological Program: Supporting Studies: Settlement and Environment. Kenneth Lee Petersen and Janet D. Orcutt, eds. Pp. 91–104. Denver: US Department of the Interior Bureau of Reclamation Engineering and Research Center.

1994 A Warm and Wet Little Climatic Optimum and a Cold and Dry Little Ice Age in the Southern Rocky Mountains, USA. Climatic Change 26:243–269.

**Peterson, Nicolas**

1969 Secular and Ritual Links: Two Basic and Opposed Principles of Australian Social Organization as Illustrated by Walbiri Ethnography. Mankind 7:27–35.

1993 Demand Sharing: Reciprocity and the Pressure for Generosity among Foragers. American Anthropologist 95:860–874.

**Peterson, Nicolas, and Jeremy Long**

1986 Australian Territorial Organization: A Band Perspective. Sydney: University of Sydney Press.

**Plourde, Aimee**

2006 Prestige Goods and Their Role in the Evolution of Social Ranking: A Costly Signaling Model with Data from the Formative Period of the Northern Lake Titicaca Basin, Peru. Ph.D. dissertation, University of California, Los Angeles.

**Porubcan, Paula J.**

2000 Human and Nonhuman Surplus Display at Mound 72. *In* Mounds, Modoc, and Mesoamerica: Papers in Honor of Melvin L. Fowler. S. R. Ahler, ed. Pp. 207–225. Scientific Papers, 28. Springfield: Illinois State Museum.

**Potter, James M.**

2000a Pots, Parties, and Politics: Communal Feasting in the American Southwest. American Antiquity 65:471–492.

2000b Ritual, Power, and Social Differentiation in Small-Scale Societies. *In* Hierarchies in Action: Cui Bono? M. W. Diehl, ed. Pp. 295–316. Occasional Paper, 27. Carbondale: Center for Archaeological Investigations, Southern Illinois University.

**Potter, James M., and Elizabeth M. Perry**

2000 Ritual as a Power Resource in the American Southwest. *In* Alternative Leadership Strategies in the Prehispanic Southwest. Barbara J. Mills, ed. Pp. 60–78. Tucson: University of Arizona Press.

**Pouwels, Randall L.**

1987 The Horn and the Crescent: Cultural Change and Traditional Islam on the East African Coast, 800–1900. Cambridge: Cambridge University Press.

2000 The East African Coast, c. 780–1900 C.E. *In* The History of Islam in Africa. N. Levitzioni and R. L. Pouwels, eds. Pp. 251–272. Athens: Ohio University Press.

**Povinelli, Elizabeth**

1992 Where We Gana Go Now: Foraging Practices and Their Meanings among the Belyuen Australian Aborigines. Human Ecology 20:169–202.

**Powers, William K.**

1977 Oglala Religion. Lincoln: University of Nebraska Press.

**Poyer, Lin**

1991   Maintaining Egalitarianism: Social Equality on a Micronesian Atoll. *In* Between Bands and States. Susan A. Gregg, ed. Pp. 359–375. Occasional Paper, 9. Carbondale: Center for Archaeological Investigations, Southern Illinois University.

**Prentiss, William C., and Ian Kuijt, eds.**

2004   Complex Hunter-Gatherers: Evolution and Organization of Prehistoric Communities on the Plateau of Northwestern North America. Salt Lake City: University of Utah Press.

**Price, T. Douglas, and Gary M. Feinman, eds.**

1995   Foundations of Social Inequality. New York: Plenum.

**Prins, Adrian H. J.**

1961   The Swahili-Speaking Peoples of Zanzibar and the East African Coast. London: International African Institute.

**Proulx, Donald A.**

1971   Headhunting in Ancient Peru. Archaeology 24:16–21.

2006   A Sourcebook of Nasca Ceramic Iconography. Iowa City: University of Iowa Press.

**Pwiti, Gilbert**

1997   Snakes and Crocodiles: Power and Symbolism in Ancient Zimbabwe. South African Archaeological Bulletin 52:137–138.

**Radin, Paul**

1948   Winnebago Hero Cycles: A Study in Aboriginal Literature. Baltimore: Waverly.

1963[1920]   The Autobiography of a Winnebago Indian: Life, Ways, Acculturation, and the Peyote Cult. New York: Dover Publications.

1990   The Winnebago Tribe. Lincoln: University of Nebraska Press.

**Rathje, William L.**

1971   The Origin and Development of Lowland Classic Maya Civilization. American Antiquity 36:275–285.

**Redmond, Elsa M.**

1998a   In War and Peace: Alternative Paths to Centralized Leadership. *In* Chiefdoms and Chieftaincy in the Americas. Elsa M. Redmond, ed. Pp. 68–103. Gainesville: University Press of Florida.

1998b   Introduction: The Dynamics of Chieftaincy and the Development of Chiefdoms. *In* Chiefdoms and Chieftaincy in the Americas. Elsa M. Redmond, ed. Pp. 1–17. Gainesville: University Press of Florida.

2002   The Long and the Short of a War Leader's Arena. *In* The Archaeology of Tribal Societies. William A. Parkinson, ed. Pp. 53–73. Archaeological Series, 15. Ann Arbor, MI: International Monographs in Prehistory.

**Reed, Paul F.**

2004   The Puebloan Society of Chaco Canyon. Westport, CT: Greenwood.

**Reefe, Thomas**

1993    The Luba-Lunda Empire. *In* Problems in African History: The Precolonial Centuries. R. O. Collins, ed. Pp. 121–126. Princeton, NJ: Marcus Wiener.

**Reinhard, Johann**

1988    The Nazca Lines, Water and Mountains: An Ethnoarchaeological Study. *In* Recent Studies in Pre-Columbian Archaeology. N. J. Saunders and O. de Montmollin, eds. Pp. 363–502. BAR International Series, 421. Oxford: BAR.

**Renfrew, Colin M.**

1974    Beyond a Subsistence Economy: The Evolution of Social Organization in Prehistoric Europe. *In* Reconstructing Complex Societies: An Archaeological Colloquium. C. B. Moore, ed. Pp. 69–95. Supplement, vol. 20. Ann Arbor, MI: American Schools of Oriental Research.

1982    Socio-economic Change in Ranked Societies. *In* Ranking, Resource and Exchange: Aspects of the Archaeology of Early European Society. Colin Renfrew and Stephen Shennan, eds. Pp. 1–8. Cambridge: Cambridge University Press.

**Reyman, Jonathan E.**

1987    Priests, Power, and Politics: Some Implications of Socioceremonial Control. *In* Astronomy and Ceremony in the Prehistoric Southwest. John B. Carlson and W. James Judge, eds. Pp. 121–148. Papers of the Maxwell Museum of Anthropology, 2. Albuquerque, NM: Maxwell Museum of Anthropology.

**Richerson, Peter, and Richard Boyd**

2000    Institutional Evolution in the Holocene: The Rise of Complex Societies. Electronic document, http://www.des.ucdavis.edu/faculty/Richerson/evolu-tioninstitutions.pdf, accessed June 12, 2009.

**Richerson, Peter J., Robert Boyd, and Robert L. Bettinger**

2001    Was Agriculture Impossible during the Pleistocene but Mandatory during the Holocene? A Climate Change Hypothesis. American Antiquity 66: 387–411.

**Rick, John W.**

2005    The Evolution of Authority at Chavín de Huántar. *In* The Foundations of Power in the Prehispanic Andes. K. J. Vaughn, D. E. Ogburn, and C. A. Conlee, eds. Pp. 71–89. Archaeological Papers, 14. Washington, DC: American Anthropological Association.

**Ringrose, David**

2001    Expansion and Global Interaction, 1200–1700. New York: Longman.

**Robb, John**

1999    Secret Agents: Culture, Economy and Social Reproduction. *In* Material Symbols: Culture and Economy in Prehistory. J. Robb, ed. Pp. 3–15. Carbondale: Center for Archaeological Investigations, Southern Illinois University.

**Robbins, Joel**

1994    Equality as Value: Ideology in Dumont, Melanesia and the West. Social Analysis 36:21–70.

**Roberts, Frank H. H., Jr.**

1929    Shabik'eshchee Village: A Late Basket Maker Site in the Chaco Canyon, New Mexico. Bureau of American Ethnology Bulletin, 92. Washington, DC: Smithsonian Institution.

**Robertshaw, Peter**

2001    The Swahili: The Social Landscape of a Mercantile Society. South African Archaeological Bulletin 56:104–105.

2003    Examining the Origins of the State in East Africa. *In* East African Archaeology: Foragers, Potters, Smiths and Traders. C. M. Kusimba and S. B. Kusimba, eds. Pp. 149–166. Philadelphia: University of Pennsylvania Press.

**Rodney, Walter**

1969    Upper Guinea and the Significance of the Origins of Africans Enslaved in the New World. The Journal of Negro History 54:327–345.

**Rollings, Willard H.**

1992    The Osage: An Ethnohistorical Study of Hegemony on the Prairie-Plains. Columbia: University of Missouri Press.

**Roscoe, Paul**

1993    Practice and Political Centralisation: A New Approach to Political Evolution. Current Anthropology 34:111–140.

2000a   Costs, Benefits, Typologies, and Power: The Evolution of Political Hierarchy. *In* Hierarchies in Action: Cui Bono? Michael W. Diehl, ed. Pp. 113–133. Occasional Paper, 27. Carbondale: Center for Archaeological Investigations, Southern Illinois University.

2000b   New Guinea Leadership as Ethnographic Analogy: A Critical Review. Journal of Archaeological Method and Theory 7:79–126.

**Rosenswig, Robert M.**

2007    Beyond Identifying Elites: Feasting as a Means to Understand Early Middle Formative Society on the Pacific Coast of Mexico. Journal of Anthropological Archaeology 26:1–27.

**Ross, A.**

2006    Comment on I. Keen, Constraints on the Development of Enduring Inequalities in Late Holocene Australia. Current Anthropology 47:24–25.

**Ross, Marc H.**

1983    Political Decision Making and Conflict: Additional Cross-Cultural Codes and Scales. Ethnology 22:169–192.

1986    Female Political Participation: A Cross-Cultural Explanation. American Anthropologist 88:843–858.

## References

**Ross, William**
1936    Ethnological Notes on Mt. Hagen Tribes (Mandated Territory of New Guinea). Anthropos 31:341–363.

**Rountree, Helen C.**
1989    The Powhatan Indians of Virginia: Their Traditional Culture. Norman: University of Oklahoma Press.

**Ruttan, Lore M.**
2006    Sociocultural Heterogeneity and the Commons. Current Anthropology 47:843–853.

**Sackett, Lee**
1979    The Pursuit of Prominence: Hunting in an Australian Aboriginal Community. Anthropologica, n.s., 21:223–246.

**Sahlins, Marshall**
1963    Poor Man, Rich Man, Big-Man, Chief: Political Types in Melanesia and Polynesia. Comparative Studies in Society and History 5:285–303.
1972    Stone Age Economics. Chicago: Aldine.

**Sahlins, Marshall D., and Elman Service**
1960    Evolution and Culture. Ann Arbor: University of Michigan Press.

**Saitta, Dean J.**
1997    Power, Labor, and the Dynamics of Change in Chacoan Political Economy. American Antiquity 62:7–26.
1999    Prestige, Agency and Change in Middle-Range Societies. *In* Material Symbols: Culture and Economy in Prehistory. J. Robb, ed. Pp. 135–152. Carbondale: Center for Archaeological Investigations, Southern Illinois University.

**Saitta, Dean J., and Arthur S. Keene**
1990    Politics and Surplus Flow in Prehistoric Communal Societies. *In* The Evolution of Political Systems: Sociopolitics in Small-Scale Sedentary Societies. Steadman Upham, ed. Pp. 203–224. Cambridge: Cambridge University Press.
1994    Agency, Class, and Archaeological Interpretation. Journal of Anthropological Archaeology 13:201–227.

**Salzer, Robert J., and Grace Rajnovich**
2000    The Gottschall Rockshelter: An Archaeological Mystery. St. Paul, MN: Prairie Smoke Press.

**Sanday, Peggy R.**
1972    Toward a Theory on the Status of Women. American Anthropologist 75:1682–1700.

**Sassaman, Kenneth**
2004    Complex Hunter-Gatherers in Evolution and History: A North American Perspective. Journal of Archaeological Research 12:227–280.
2005    Poverty Point as Structure, Event, Process. Journal of Archaeological Method and Theory 12:335–364.

**Sawyer, Alan R.**

1961    Paracas and Nazca Iconography. *In* Essays in Pre-Columbian Art and Archaeology. S. K. Lothrop, ed. Pp. 269–298. Cambridge, MA: Harvard University Press.

1968    Mastercraftsmen of Ancient Peru. New York: Solomon Guggenheim Foundation.

1997    Early Nasca Needlework. London: Laurence King Publishing.

**Scarborough, Vernon L.**

2003    The Flow of Power: Ancient Water Systems and Landscapes. Santa Fe, NM: School of American Research Press.

**Scelza, Brooke, and Rebecca Bliege Bird**

2008    Group Structure and Female Cooperative Networks in Australia's Western Desert. Human Nature 19:231–248.

**Schachner, Gregson**

2001    Ritual Control and Transformation in Middle-Range Societies: An Example from the American Southwest. Journal of Anthropological Archaeology 20:168–194.

**Schillaci, Michael A.**

2003    The Development of Population Diversity at Chaco Canyon. Kiva 68:221–245.

**Schillaci, Michael A., Erik G. Ozolins, and Thomas C. Windes**

1998    A Multivariate Analysis of Craniometric Variation among Ten Prehistoric Pueblo Indian Populations. Paper presented at the Annual Pecos Conference, Pecos, NM, August 14.

2001    A Multivariate Assessment of Biological Relationships among Prehistoric Southwest Amerindian Populations. *In* Collected Papers in Honor of Phyllis S. Davis. Regge N. Wiseman, Cornelia T. Snow, and Thomas O. Laughlin, eds. Papers of the Archaeological Society of New Mexico, 27. Albuquerque: Archaeological Society of New Mexico.

**Schillaci, Michael A., and Christopher M. Stojanowski**

2003    Postmarital Residence and Biological Variation at Pueblo Bonito. American Journal of Physical Anthropology 120:1–15.

**Schortman, Edward M., and Patricia A. Urban**

1992    Resources, Power, and Interregional Interaction. New York: Plenum.

2004    Modeling the Roles of Craft Production in Ancient Political Economies. Journal of Archaeological Research 12:185–226.

**Schreiber, Katharina**

1998    Afterword. *In* The Archaeology and Pottery of Nazca, Peru: Alfred L. Kroeber's 1926 Expedition. P. H. Carmichael, ed. Pp. 261–270. Walnut Creek, CA: AltaMira.

1999    Regional Approaches to the Study of Prehistoric Empires: Examples from Ayacucho and Nasca, Peru. *In* Fifty Years Since Virú. B. Billman and G. Feinman, eds. Pp. 160–171. Washington, DC: Smithsonian Institution Press.

## REFERENCES

**Schreiber, Katharina J., and Josue Lancho Rojas**
2003    Irrigation and Society in the Peruvian Desert: The Puquios of Nasca. Lanham, MD: Lexington Books.

**Scully, R. T.**
1969    Fort Sites of East Bukusu, Kenya. Azania 4:105–114.
1974    Two Accounts of the Chetambe War of 1895. The International Journal of African Historical Studies 7:480–492.

**Sebastian, Lynne**
1992    The Chaco Anasazi: Sociopolitical Evolution in the Prehistoric Southwest. Cambridge: Cambridge University Press.

**Seeman, Mark F.**
2004    Hopewell Art in Hopewell Places. *In* Hero, Hawk, and Open Hand: American Indian Art of the Ancient Midwest and South. Richard F. Townsend, ed. Pp. 57–71. New Haven, CT: Chicago Art Institute/Yale University Press.

**Service, Elman R.**
1962    Primitive Social Organization: An Evolutionary Perspective. New York: Random House.
1975    Origins of the State and Civilization. New York: W. W. Norton.

**Shady Solís, Ruth**
2004    Caral: La Ciudad del Fuego Sagrado. M. Dalton, trans. Lima, Peru: Interbank.

**Shennan, Stephen J.**
2002    Genes, Memes, and Human History: Darwinian Archaeology and Cultural Evolution. New York: Thames and Hudson.

**Silverman, Helaine**
1993    Cahuachi in the Ancient Nasca World. Iowa City: University of Iowa Press.
1996    The Formative Period on the South Coast of Peru: A Critical Review. Journal of World Prehistory 10:95–147.
1997    The First Field Season of Excavations at the Alto del Molino Site, Pisco Valley, Peru. Journal of Field Archaeology 24:441–458.

**Silverman, Helaine, and Donald A. Proulx**
2002    The Nasca. Malden, MA: Blackwell.

**Sinopoli, Carla M.**
2003    The Political Economy of Craft Production: Crafting Empire in South India, c. 1350–1650. Cambridge: Cambridge University Press.

**Smith, Adam**
1937[1776]   The Wealth of Nations. New York: Random House.

**Smith, Adam T.**
2000    Rendering the Political Aesthetic: Political Legitimacy in Urartian Representations of the Built Environment. Journal of Anthropological Archaeology 19:131–163.

2003    The Political Landscape: Constellations of Authority in Early Complex Polities. Berkeley: University of California Press.

**Smith, Eric Alden**

2004    Why Do Good Hunters Have Higher Reproductive Success? Human Nature 15:342–363.

**Smith, Eric Alden, Rebecca Bliege Bird, and Douglas W. Bird**

2003    The Benefits of Costly Signaling: Meriam Turtle-Hunters and Spearfishers. Behavioral Ecology 14:116–126.

**Smith, Eric Alden, and Robert Boyd**

1990    Risk and Reciprocity: Hunter-Gatherer Socioecology and the Problem of Collective Action. *In* Risk and Uncertainty in Tribal and Peasant Economies. Elizabeth Cashdan, ed. Pp. 167–191. Boulder, CO: Westview.

**Smith, Eric Alden, and Jung-Kyoo Choi**

2007    The Emergence of Inequality in Small-Scale Societies: Simple Scenarios and Agent-Based Simulations. *In* The Model-Based Archaeology of Socionatural Systems. Timothy A. Kohler and Sander E. van der Leeuw, eds. Pp. 105–119. Santa Fe, NM: School for Advanced Research Press.

**Smith, Michael E.**

1993    New World Complex Societies: Recent Economic, Social, and Political Studies. Journal of Archaeological Research 1:5–41.

**Snow, David H.**

1973    Prehistoric Southwestern Turquoise Industry. El Palacio 79:33–51.

**Sobel, Elizabeth A., D. Ann Trieu Gahr, and Kenneth M. Ames, eds.**

2006    Household Archaeology on the Northwest Coast. Ann Arbor, MI: International Monographs in Prehistory.

**Sofaer, Anna**

1997    The Primary Architecture of the Chacoan Culture: A Cosmological Expression. *In* Anasazi Architecture and American Design. Baker H. Morrow and V. B. Price, eds. Pp. 88–132. Albuquerque: University of New Mexico Press.

2007    The Primary Architecture of the Chacoan Culture: A Cosmological Expression. *In* The Architecture of Chaco Canyon, New Mexico. Stephen H. Lekson, ed. Pp. 225–254. Salt Lake City: University of Utah Press.

**Southall, Aidan**

1999    The Segmentary State and the Ritual Phase in Political Economy. *In* Beyond Chiefdoms: Pathways to Complexity in Africa. S. K. McIntosh, ed. Pp. 31–38. Cambridge: Cambridge University Press.

**Spear, Thomas**

1978    The Kaya Complex: A History of the Mijikenda Peoples of the Kenya Coast to 1900. Nairobi: Kenya Literature Bureau.

## REFERENCES

**Spencer, Charles S.**

1993    Human Agency, Biased Transmission, and the Cultural Evolution of Chiefly Authority. Journal of Anthropological Archaeology 12:41–74.

1994    Factional Ascendance, Dimensions of Leadership, and the Development of Centralized Authority. *In* Factional Competition and Political Development in the New World. Elizabeth M. Brumfiel and John W. Fox, eds. Pp. 31–43. Cambridge: Cambridge University Press.

1998    Investigating the Development of Venezuelan Chiefdoms. *In* Chiefdoms and Chieftaincy in the Americas. Elsa M. Redmond, ed. Pp. 104–137. Gainesville: University Press of Florida.

**Spielmann, Katherine**

2002    Feasting, Craft Specialization, and the Ritual Mode of Production in Small-Scale Societies. American Anthropologist 104:195–207.

**Spikins, Penny**

2008    "The Bashful and the Boastful": Prestigious Leaders and Social Change in Mesolithic Societies. Journal of World Prehistory 21:173–193.

**Stahl, Ann**

2005    Political Economic Mosaics: Archaeology of the Last Two Millennia in Tropical Sub-Saharan Africa. Annual Review of Anthropology 33:145–172.

**Stanford, C. B., and H. T. Bunn**

2001    Meat-Eating and Human Evolution. Oxford: Oxford University Press.

**Stanish, Charles**

2003    Ancient Titicaca: The Evolution of Complex Society in Southern Peru and Northern Bolivia. Berkeley: University of California Press.

2004    The Evolution of Chiefdoms: An Economic Anthropological Model. *In* Archaeological Perspectives of Political Economies. G. M. Feinman, ed. Pp. 7–24. Salt Lake City: University of Utah Press.

2008    Explanation in Archaeology, Overview. *In* Encyclopedia of Archaeology. D. Pearsall, ed. Pp. 1358–1364. New York: Academic Press.

**Stein, Gil J.**

1998    Heterogeneity, Power, and Political Economy: Some Current Research Issues in the Archaeology of Old World Complex Societies. Journal of Archaeological Research 6:1–44.

**Steinhart, Edward I.**

2001    Elephant Hunting in 19th-Century Kenya: Kamba Society and Ecology in Transformation. International Journal of African Historical Studies 33:335–349.

**Steward, Julian H.**

1930    Irrigation without Agriculture. Papers of the Michigan Academy of Science, Arts, and Letters 12:149–156.

1933    Ethnography of the Owens Valley Paiute. University of California Publications in American Archaeology and Ethnography 33:233–350.

1934    Two Paiute Autobiographies. University of California Publications in American Archaeology and Ethnology 33:423–438.

1936    Myths of the Owens Valley Paiute. University of California Publications in American Archaeology and Ethnology 34:355–440.

1938    Basin-Plateau Aboriginal Sociopolitical Groups. Washington, DC: US Government Printing Office.

**Stewart, Omer C.**

1987    Peyote Religion: A History. Norman: University of Oklahoma Press.

**Stigand, Chaucy**

1913    The Land of Zinj: Being an Account of the British East Africa, Its Ancient History and Present Inhabitants. London: Constable.

**Stine, Scott**

2000    On the Medieval Climatic Anomaly. Current Anthropology 41:627–628.

**Strathern, Andrew**

1969    Finance and Production: Two Strategies in New Guinea Highlands Exchange Systems. Oceania 15:42–67.

1982a   Two Waves of African Models in the New Guinea Highlands. *In* Inequality in New Guinea Highlands Societies. Andrew Strathern, ed. Pp. 35–49. Cambridge: Cambridge University Press.

**Strathern, Andrew, ed.**

1982b   Inequality in New Guinea Highlands Societies. Cambridge: Cambridge University Press.

**Strathern, Marilyn**

1972    Women in Between. London: Seminar Press.

1988    The Gender of the Gift: Problems with Women and Problems with Society in Melanesia. Berkeley: University of California Press.

**Strehlow, Theodor**

1970    Geography and the Totemic Landscape in Central Australia: A Functional Study. *In* Australian Aboriginal Anthropology. R. Berndt, ed. Pp. 92–140. Nedlands: University of Western Australia Press.

**Strong, William D.**

1957    Paracas, Nazca, and Tiahuanacoid Cultural Relationships in South Coastal Peru. Memoirs of the Society for American Archaeology 13, Salt Lake City, UT: Society for American Archaeology.

**Sugden, John**

1997    Tecumseh: A Life. New York: Henry Holt.

**Swanton, John R.**

1942    Source Material on the History and Ethnology of the Caddo Indians. Bureau of American Ethnology, bulletin 132. Washington, DC: Smithsonian Institution.

1985    The Indians of the Southeastern United States. Washington, DC: Smithsonian Institution.

# References

2001     Source Material for the Social and Ceremonial Life of the Choctaw Indians. Tuscaloosa: University of Alabama Press.

**Talyaga, Kundapen**

1982     The Enga Yesterday and Today: A Personal Account. *In* Enga: Foundations for Development. B. Carrad, D. Lea, and K. Talyaga, eds. Pp. 59–75. Armidale, Australia: Department of Geography, University of New England.

**Terrell, John**

1986     Prehistory in the Pacific Islands. A Study of Variation in Language, Customs, and Human Biology. Cambridge: Cambridge University Press.

**Terrell, John, and Robert Welsch**

1997     Material Culture, Social Fields, and Social Boundaries. *In* The Archaeology of Social Boundaries. Miriam Stark, ed. Pp. 50–77. Washington, DC: Smithsonian Institution Press.

**Thomas, David H.**

1981     Complexity among Great Basin Shoshoneans: The World's Least Affluent Hunter-Gatherers? *In* Affluent Foragers: Pacific Coasts East and West. S. Koyama and D. H. Thomas, eds. Pp. 19–52. Senri Ethnological Studies, 9. Osaka: National Museum of Ethnology.

**Thompson, L. G., E. Mosley-Thompson, J. F. Bolzan, and B. R. Koci**

1985     A 1500-Year Record of Tropical Precipitation in Ice Cores from the Quelccaya Ice Cap, Peru. Science 229:971–973.

**Thorbahn, Frederick**

1979     The Precolonial Trade of East Africa: Reconstruction of a Human-Elephant Ecosystem. Ph.D. dissertation, University of Massachusetts.

**Tiger, Lionel**

1969     Men in Groups. London: Nelson.

**Toll, H. Wolcott**

2001     Making and Breaking Pots in the Chaco World. American Antiquity 66:56–78.

**Tonkinson, Robert**

1974     The Jigalong Mob: Aboriginal Victors of the Desert Crusade. Menlo Park, CA: Cummings.

1978     Semen vs. Spirit Child in a Western Desert Culture. *In* Australian Aboriginal Concepts. L. R. Hiatt, ed. Pp. 81–92. Canberra, Australia: Aboriginal Studies Press.

1988a     Egalitarianism and Inequality in a Western Desert Culture. Anthropological Forum 5:545–558.

1988b     Ideology and Dominations in Aboriginal Australia: A Western Desert Test Case. *In* Hunters and Gatherers 2: Property, Power and Ideology. T. Ingold, D. Riches, and J. Woodburn, eds. Pp. 150–164. Oxford: Berg.

1990     The Changing Status of Aboriginal Women: "Free Agent" at Jigalong. *In* Going

It Alone? Prospects for Aboriginal Autonomy. R. Tonkinson and M. Howard, eds. Pp. 125–144. Canberra, Australia: Aboriginal Studies Press.

1991    The Mardu Aborigines: Living the Dream in Australia's Desert. 2nd edition. New York: Holt, Rinehart and Winston.

2000    Gender Role Transformation among Australian Aborigines. *In* Hunters and Gatherers in the Modern World: Conflict, Resistance, and Self-Determination. P. P. Schweitzer, M. Biesele, and R. K. Hitchcock, eds. Pp. 343–360. New York: Berghahn Books.

2007a   Aboriginal "Difference" and "Autonomy" Then and Now: Four Decades of Change in a Western Desert Society. Anthropological Forum 17:41–60.

2007b   The Mardu Aborigines: On the Road to Somewhere. *In* Globalization and Change in Fifteen Cultures: Born in One World, Living in Another. G. Spindler and J. E. Stockard, eds. Pp. 225–255. Belmont, CA: Wadsworth/Thomson Learning.

**Tooby, John, and Leda Cosmides**

1992    The Psychological Foundations of Culture. *In* The Adapted Mind: Evolutionary Psychology and the Generation of Culture. J. H. Barkow, L. Cosmides, and J. Tooby, eds. Pp. 19–136. New York: Oxford University Press.

**Townsend, Richard F.**

1985    Deciphering the Nazca World: Ceramic Images from Ancient Peru. Art Institute of Chicago Museum Studies 11:117–139.

**Townsend, Richard F., ed.**

2004    Hero, Hawk, and Open Hand: American Indian Art of the Ancient Midwest and South. New Haven, CT: Art Institute of Chicago/Yale University Press.

**Trivers, Robert L.**

1971    The Evolution of Reciprocal Altruism. Quarterly Review of Biology 46:35–57.

**Tuzin, Donald F.**

2001    Social Complexity in the Making: A Case Study among the Arapesh of New Guinea. New York: Routledge.

**Twiss, Katheryn C.**

2008    Transformations in an Early Agricultural Society: Feasting in the Southern Levantine Pre-pottery Neolithic. Journal of Anthropological Archaeology 27:418–442.

**Upham, Steadman**

1990    Analog or Digital? Towards a Generic Framework for Explaining the Development of Emergent Political Systems. *In* The Evolution of Political Systems. Steadman Upham, ed. Pp. 87–118. Cambridge: Cambridge University Press.

**Valdez Cardenas, Lidio**

1994    Cahuachi: New Evidence for an Early Nasca Ceremonial Role. Current Anthropology 35:675–679.

1998    The Nasca and the Valley of Acarí: Cultural Interaction on the Peruvian South Coast. Ph.D. dissertation, University of Calgary.

**Van Dyke, Ruth M.**

2003    Memory and the Construction of Chacoan Society. *In* Archaeologies of Memory. Ruth M. Van Dyke and Susan E. Alcock, eds. Pp. 180–200. Malden, MA: Blackwell.

2007    Great Kivas in Time, Space, and Society. *In* The Architecture of Chaco Canyon, New Mexico. Stephen H. Lekson, ed. Pp. 93–126. Salt Lake City: University of Utah Press.

**Van Gijseghem, Hendrik**

2004    Migration, Agency, and Social Change on a Prehistoric Frontier: The Paracas–Nasca Transition in the Southern Nasca Drainage, Peru. Ph.D. dissertation, University of California, Santa Barbara.

2006    A Frontier Perspective on Paracas Society and Nasca Ethnogenesis. Latin American Antiquity 17:419–444.

**Vansina, Jan**

1966    Kingdoms of the Savanna. Madison: University of Wisconsin Press.

1993    Kingdoms of the Savannah. *In* Problems in African History: The Precolonial Centuries. R. O. Collins, ed. Pp. 115–120. Princeton, NJ: Marcus Wiener.

1999    Pathways to Political Development in Equatorial Africa and Neo-evolutionary Theory. *In* Beyond Chiefdoms: Pathways to Complexity in Africa. Susan Keech McIntosh, ed. Pp. 166–172. Cambridge: Cambridge University Press.

**Vaughn, Kevin J.**

2004    Households, Crafts, and Feasting in the Ancient Andes: The Village Context of Early Nasca Craft Consumption. Latin American Antiquity 15:61–88.

2005    Crafts and the Materialization of Chiefly Power in Nasca. *In* The Foundations of Power in the Prehispanic Andes. K. J. Vaughn, D. E. Ogburn, and C. A. Conlee, eds. Pp. 113–130. Archeological Papers, 14. Washington, DC: American Anthropological Association.

2006    Craft Production, Exchange, and Political Power in the Pre-Incaic Andes. Journal of Archaeological Research 14:313–344.

**Vaughn, Kevin J., Christina A. Conlee, Hector Neff, and Katharina Schreiber**

2005    A Compositional Analysis of Nasca Polychrome Pigments: Implications for Craft Production on the Prehispanic South Coast of Peru. *In* Laser Ablation ICP-MS: A New Frontier in Archaeological Characterization Studies. R. J. Speakman and H. Neff, eds. Pp. 138–154. Albuquerque: University of New Mexico Press.

2006    Ceramic Production in Ancient Nasca: Provenance Analysis of Pottery from the Early Nasca and Tiza Cultures through INAA. Journal of Archaeological Science 33:681–689.

**Vaughn, Kevin J., and M. Linares Grados**

2006    Three Thousand Years of Occupation in Upper Valley Nasca: Excavations at Upanca. Latin American Antiquity 17:595–612.

**Vaughn, Kevin J., and Hector Neff**

2000    Moving Beyond Iconography: Neutron Activation Analysis of Ceramics from Marcaya, Peru, an Early Nasca Domestic Site. Journal of Field Archaeology 27:75–90.

2004    Tracing the Clay Source of Nasca Polychrome Pottery: Results from a Preliminary Raw Material Survey. Journal of Archaeological Science 31:1577–1586.

**Vaughn, Kevin J., and Hendrik Van Gijseghem**

2007    A Compositional Perspective on the Origins of the Nasca Cult. Journal of Archaeological Science 34:814–822.

**Veth, Peter**

1987    Martujarra Prehistory: Variation in Arid Zone Adaptations. Australian Archaeology 25:102–111.

1989    Islands in the Interior: A Model for the Colonization of the Australian Arid Zone. Archaeology in Oceania 24:81–92.

1995    Aridity and Settlement in NW Australia. Antiquity 69:733–746.

2000    Origins of the Western Desert Language: Convergence in Linguistic and Archaeological Space and Time Models. Archaeology in Oceania 35:11–19.

**Veth, Peter, and Fiona Walsh**

1988    The Concept of "Staple" Plant Foods in the Western Desert of Western Australia. Australian Aboriginal Studies 2:19–25.

**Vicedom, Georg, and Herbert Tischner**

1943–  Die Mbowamb. 3 vols. Hamburg: Gram, de Gruyter.
 1948

**Vivian, R. Gwinn**

1997a    Chacoan Roads: Function. Kiva 63:35–68.

1997b    Chacoan Roads: Morphology. Kiva 63:7–34.

**Vivian, R. Gwinn, Carla R. Van West, Jeffrey S. Dean, Nancy J. Akins, Mollie S. Toll, and Thomas C. Windes**

2006    Ecology and Economy. In The Archaeology of Chaco Canyon: An Eleventh-Century Pueblo Regional Center. Stephen H. Lekson, ed. Pp. 45–65. Santa Fe, NM: School of American Research Press.

**Waddell, Eric**

1972    The Mound Builders: Agricultural Practices, Environment, and Society in the Central Highlands of New Guinea. Seattle: University of Washington Press.

**Wagner, Gunter**

1947    The Bantu of Western Kenya. Oxford: Oxford University Press.

1949    The Bantu of North Kavirondo. Oxford: Oxford University Press.

1970    The Bantu of North Kavirondo, vol. 2. Oxford: Oxford University Press.

**Wagner, Henry R.**

1929    Spanish Voyages to the Northwest Coast of America in the Sixteenth Century. California Historical Society Special Publications, 4. San Francisco: California Historical Society.

# REFERENCES

**Wagner, Roy**

1991    The Fractal Person. *In* Big Men and Great Men: Personifications of Power in Melanesia. Maurice Godelier and Marilyn Strathern, eds. Pp. 159–173. Cambridge: Cambridge University Press.

**Wakefield, Thomas**

1870    Routes of Native Caravans from the Coast to the Interior of East Africa. Journal of the Royal Geographical Society 40:303–338.

**Walker, William H., and Lisa J. Lucero**

2000    The Depositional History of Ritual and Power. *In* Agency in Archaeology. M.-A. Dobres and J. Robb, eds. Pp. 130–147. London: Routledge.

**Walsh, Fiona**

1990    An Ecological Study of Traditional Aboriginal Use of "Country": Martu in the Great and Little Sandy Deserts, Western Australia. Proceedings of the Ecological Society of Australia 16:23–37.

**Wandibba, Simiyu**

1986    Thimlich "Ohingini." Azania 21:134.

**Washburn, Sherwood L., and Irven DeVore**

1961    The Social Life of Baboons. San Francisco: Freeman.

**Washburn, Sherwood L., and Chet S. Lancaster**

1968    The Evolution of Hunting. *In* Man the Hunter. R. B. Lee and I. DeVore, eds. Pp. 293–303. Chicago: Aldine.

**Wason, Paul K.**

1994    The Archaeology of Rank. Cambridge: Cambridge University Press.

**Watson, James B.**

1965a    From Hunting to Horticulture in the New Guinea Highlands. Ethnology 4:295–309.

1965b    The Significance of Recent Ecological Change in the Central Highlands of New Guinea. Journal of the Polynesian Society 74:438–450.

1977    Pigs, Fodder, and the Jones Effect in Post-Ipomoean New Guinea. Ethnology 6:57–70.

**Weber, Max**

1958    The Three Types of Legitimate Rule. Berkeley Publications in Society and Institutions 4:1–11.

1968[1921]   Max Weber on Law in Economy and Society. Max Rheinstein, ed. Edward Shils and Max Rheinstein, trans. New York: Simon and Schuster.

1968    Max Weber on Charisma and Institution Building. Chicago: University of Chicago Press.

**Weissleder, Wolfgang**

1967    The Political Economy of Amhara Domination. Ph.D. dissertation, University of Chicago.

**Welck, Karin, and R. Konig**

1990    Manner Bande, Manner Bunde: Zur Rolle des Mannes in Kulturvergleich. Cologne: Rautenstrauch-Joest-Museum.

**Wenke, Robert J.**

1981    Explaining the Evolution of Cultural Complexity: A Review. *In* Advances in Archaeological Method and Theory, vol. 4. Michael B. Schiffer, ed. Pp. 79–127. New York: Academic Press.

**Whyte, Martin K.**

1979    The Status of Women in Preindustrial Societies. Princeton, NJ: Princeton University Press.

**Wiener, Annette B.**

1992    Inalienable Possessions: The Paradox of Keeping-While-Giving. Berkeley: University of California Press.

**Wiessner, Polly**

1982    Beyond Willow Smoke and Dogs' Tails: A Comment on Binford's Analysis of Hunter-Gatherer Settlement Systems. American Antiquity 47:171–178.

2001    Of Feasting and Value: Enga Feasts in a Historical Perspective (Papua New Guinea). *In* Feasts: Archaeological and Ethnographic Perspectives on Food, Politics, and Power. Michael Dietler and Brian Hayden, eds. Pp. 115–143. Washington, DC: Smithsonian Institution Press.

2002    The Vines of Complexity: Egalitarian Structures and the Institutionalization of Inequality among the Enga. Current Anthropology 43:233–269.

2004    Of Human and Spirit Women: From the Seductress to Second Wife. *In* Women as Unseen Characters in Male Ritual in Papua New Guinea. Pascale Bonnemere, ed. Pp. 154–178. Philadelphia: University of Pennsylvania Press.

2005    Norm Enforcement among the Ju./'hoansi Bushmen: A Case of Strong Reciprocity? Human Nature 16:115–145.

2006    From Spears to M-16s: Testing the Imbalance of Power Hypothesis among the Enga. Journal of Anthropological Research 62:165–191.

**Wiessner, Polly, and Wulf Schiefenhövel**

1996    Food and the Status Quest. Oxford: Berghahn Books.

**Wiessner, Polly, and Akii Tumu**

1998    Historical Vines: Enga Networks of Exchange, Ritual, and Warfare in Papua New Guinea. Washington, DC: Smithsonian Institution Press.

1999    A Collage of Cults. Canberra Anthropology 22:34–65.

**Williams, Sloan R., Kathleen Forgey, and Elizabeth Klarich**

2001    An Osteological Study of Nasca Trophy Heads Collected by A. L. Kroeber during the Marshall Field Expeditions to Peru. Fieldiana: Anthropology 33:1–132.

**Willis, Justin**

1993    Mombasa, the Swahili, and the Making of the Mijikenda. Oxford: Clarendon.

# REFERENCES

**Wills, W. H.**

2000      Political Leadership and the Construction of Chacoan Great Houses, A.D. 1020–1140. *In* Alternative Leadership Strategies in the Prehispanic Southwest. Barbara J. Mills, ed. Pp. 19–44. Tucson: University of Arizona Press.

2001      Ritual and Mound Formation During the Bonito Phase in Chaco Canyon. American Antiquity 66:433–451.

**Wilmsen, Edwin**

1989      Land Filled with Flies. Chicago: University of Chicago Press.

**Wilshusen, Richard H., and Ruth M. Van Dyke**

2006      Chaco's Beginnings. *In* The Archaeology of Chaco Canyon: An Eleventh-Century Pueblo Regional Center. Stephen H. Lekson, ed. Pp. 211–259. Santa Fe, NM: School of American Research Press.

**Wimmelbucker, Ludger**

2002      Kilimanjaro: A Regional History, vol. 1: Production and Living Conditions c. 1800–1920. Hamburg: Lit Verlag Munster.

**Windes, Thomas C.**

1991      The Prehistoric Road Network at Pueblo Alto, Chaco Canyon, New Mexico. *In* Ancient Road Networks and Settlement Hierarchies in the New World. Charles D. Trombold, ed. Pp. 111–131. Cambridge: Cambridge University Press.

2001      House Location Patterns in the Chaco Canyon Area: A Short Description. *In* Chaco Society and Polity: Papers from the 1999 Conference. Linda S. Cordell, W. James Judge, and June-el Piper, eds. Pp. 31–46. Special Publication, 4. Albuquerque: New Mexico Archeological Council.

2003      This Old House: Construction and Abandonment at Pueblo Bonito. *In* Pueblo Bonito: Center of the Chacoan World. Jill E. Neitzel, ed. Pp. 14–32. Washington, DC: Smithsonian Books.

2007      Gearing Up and Piling On: Early Great Houses in the Interior San Juan Basin. *In* The Architecture of Chaco Canyon, New Mexico. Stephen H. Lekson, ed. Pp. 45–92. Salt Lake City: University of Utah Press.

**Windes, Thomas C., and Dabney Ford**

1996      The Chaco Wood Project: The Chronometric Reappraisal of Pueblo Bonito. American Antiquity 61:295–310.

**Windes, Thomas C., and Peter J. McKenna**

2001      Going against the Grain: Wood Production in Chacoan Society. American Antiquity 66:119–140.

**Winterhalder, Bruce**

1986      Diet Choice, Risk, and Food Sharing in a Stochastic Environment. Journal of Anthropological Archaeology 5:369–392.

2001      The Behavioral Ecology of Hunter-Gatherers. *In* Hunter-Gatherers: An Interdisciplinary Perspective. C. Panter-Brick, R. Layton, and P. Rowley-Conwy, eds. Pp. 12–38. Cambridge: Cambridge University Press.

**Wirz, Paul**

1952a    Die Enga. Ein Beitrag zue Ethnographie eines Stammes im Nordoestlischen Neuguinea. Zeitschrift fur Ethnologie 77:7–56.

1952b    Quelques Notes sur la Ceremonie du Moka Chez les Tribus do Mount Hagen et du Wabaga Sub-district, Nouvelle-Guinee du nordest. Bulletin de la Societe Royal Belge d'Anthropologie et de Prehistoire 63:65–71.

**Wissler, Clark**

1974[1934]    North American Indians of the Plains. New York: Burt Franklin Reprints.

**Wittfogel, Karl**

1957    Oriental Despotism: A Comparative Study of Total Power. New Haven, CT: Yale University Press.

**Wobst, Martin**

1978    The Archaeo-ethnology of Hunter-Gatherers and the Tyranny of the Ethnographic Record in Archaeology. American Antiquity 43:303–307.

**Wohlt, Paul**

1978    Ecology, Agriculture, and Social Organization: The Dynamics of Group Composition in the Highlands of New Guinea. Ann Arbor, MI: University Microfilms.

**Wolf, Eric**

1982    Europe and the People without History. Berkeley: University of California Press.

1990    Distinguished Lecture: Facing Power—Old Insights, New Questions. American Anthropologist 92:586–596.

1999    Envisioning Power: Ideologies of Dominance and Crisis. Berkeley: University of California Press.

2001    Pathways of Power: Building an Anthropology of the Modern World. Berkeley: University of California Press.

**Wood, Justin N., David D. Glynn, Brenda C. Phillips, and Marc D. Hauser**

2007    The Perception of Rational, Goal-Directed Action in Nonhuman Primates. Science 317:1402–1405.

**Woodburn, James**

1982    Egalitarian Societies. Man 17:431–451.

**Woodward, Grace Steele**

1963    The Cherokees. Norman: University of Oklahoma Press.

**Wright, Henry T., and Gregory A. Johnson**

1975    Population, Exchange and Early State Formation in Southwestern Iran. American Anthropologist 77:267–289.

**Wrigley, Christopher C.**

1993    State Formation in Uganda. In Problems in African History: The Precolonial Centuries. R. O. Collins, ed. Pp. 109–114. Princeton, NJ: Marcus Wiener.

## REFERENCES

**Yanca, Catherine, and Bobbi Low**

2004    Female Allies and Female Power: A Cross-Cultural Analysis. Evolution and Human Behavior 25:9–23.

**Yoffee, Norman**

2006    Afterword: Lenses on Mississippian Leadership. *In* Leadership and Polity in Mississippian Society. Brian M. Butler and Paul D. Welch, eds. Pp. 398–401. Occasional Paper, 33. Carbondale: Center for Archaeological Investigations, Southern Illinois University.

**Yohe, Robert M., II**

1998    The Introduction of the Bow and Arrow and Lithic Resource Use at Rose Spring (CA-INY-372). Journal of California and Great Basin Anthropology 20:26–52.

# Index

# School for Advanced Research Advanced Seminar Series

Participants in the School for Advanced Research advanced seminar "The Emergence of Leadership: Transitions in Decision Making from Small-Scale to Middle Range Societies," Santa Fe, New Mexico, December 3–7, 2006. Left to right: Kevin J. Vaughn, Jeanne E. Arnold, Chapurukha M. Kusimba, Polly Wiessner, Jelmer W. Eerkens, Brenda J. Bowser, Timothy R. Pauketat, Charles Stanish, Douglas W. Bird, and John Kantner.